Bread, Justice, and Liberty

Critical Human Rights

Steve J. Stern and Scott Straus
Series Editors

Books in the series Critical Human Rights emphasize research that opens new ways to think about and understand human rights. The series values in particular empirically grounded and intellectually open research that eschews simplified accounts of human rights events and processes.

This vividly written book brings to life two Chilean shantytowns whose searing histories of violence, and reputation for resilience and combativeness, raised human rights awareness that helped bring down the 1973–90 dictatorship of General Augusto Pinochet. Alison J. Bruey's extraordinary research shows that struggles for human rights in the shantytowns emerged not simply from the life-and-death emergencies under military rule but also from a longer history of mobilization for community rights that saw socioeconomic justice and civil-political liberty as equally important and mutually dependent. Bruey also reveals a once untold story within the story: the role of grassroots Catholic activists and lay communities whose emancipating religious vision nourished conversation and collaboration with the Left, including Marxists. The dialogues of religious, political, and civil society activists in the face of violent repression and socioeconomic dispossession advanced values and demands more sweeping than the narrow reforms available in a democratic transition constrained by neoliberal economics. This book tells what "human rights" meant to shantytown communities that took religious faith seriously and rattled a dictatorship, and why moral and political disillusion soon troubled the culture of democratic transition.

Bread, Justice, and Liberty

*Grassroots Activism and
Human Rights in Pinochet's Chile*

Alison J. Bruey

The University of Wisconsin Press

The University of Wisconsin Press
728 State Street, Suite 443
Madison, Wisconsin 53706
uwpress.wisc.edu

Gray's Inn House, 127 Clerkenwell Road
London EC1R 5DB, United Kingdom
eurospanbookstore.com

Printed in the United States of America

This book may be available in a digital edition.

Library of Congress Cataloging-in-Publication Data

Names: Bruey, Alison J., author.
Title: Bread, justice, and liberty : grassroots activism and human rights in
    Pinochet's Chile / Alison J. Bruey.
Other titles: Critical human rights.
Description: Madison, Wisconsin : The University of Wisconsin Press, [2018] |
    Series: Critical human rights | Includes bibliographical references and index.
Identifiers: LCCN 2017044986 | ISBN 9780299316105 (cloth : alk. paper)
Subjects: LCSH: Protest movements—Chile—Santiago. | Political activists—
    Chile—Santiago. | Human rights workers—Chile—Santiago. | Government,
    Resistance to—Chile—Santiago. | Poor—Chile—Santiago. | Chile—
    History—1973–1988.
Classification: LCC F3100 .B77 2018 | DDC 983.06/5—dc23
LC record available at https://lccn.loc.gov/2017044986

ISBN 9780299316143 (pbk. : alk. paper)

For my family

Contents

Illustrations

Acknowledgments

Historians spend much time working alone, but historians' projects are collaborative ventures. I am pleased to thank all who have provided support, advice, and encouragement along the way.

Several institutions provided funding, a formal or informal institutional home, or an affiliation as I researched and wrote. I thank the Yale University Graduate School of Arts and Sciences; the Yale Center for International and Area Studies; the Yale University Department of History; the Yale Council on Latin American and Iberian Studies; Fulbright-Hays; the Mellon Foundation; ECO-Educación y Comunicaciones; the Pontificia Universidad Católica de Chile and its Instituto de Estudios Urbanos y Territoriales; the Universidad de Santiago de Chile; the University of Florida Center for Latin American Studies; the University of North Florida Department of History; and the University of North Florida's Faculty Scholarship Development Grant program and College of Arts and Sciences Research Enhancement Award program.

I have received valuable feedback from colleagues at conferences, workshops, and meetings of the Yale University Mellon Conference on Latin American History; the Yale Council on Latin American and Iberian Studies; the American Historical Association; the Latin American Studies Association; the Conference on Latin American History; the Tepoztlán Institute for the Transnational History of the Americas; the Urban History Association; the University of Florida Center for Latin American Studies; the Feminism, Transnationalism, and Nationalism Seminar, Religion and Empire Seminar, and Latin American and Caribbean Studies Institute of the University of Georgia; and the women scholars' writing group and Neoliberalism Working Group at the University of North Florida. Thank you to all who have commented on drafts and ideas.

I have been fortunate to have crossed paths with many generous intellectuals and teachers. Hernán Vidal introduced me to sociohistorical theory and the study of Cold War–era ideological conflict. Steve Stern, Florencia Mallon, and Ksenija Bilbija provided opportunities to research legacies of authoritarianism in Latin America. Elizabeth Q. Hutchinson first introduced me to the Chilean national archives and offered kind encouragement. Gil Joseph's staunch support was critical as I contended with the challenges of researching the history of everyday people's lives under a notoriously repressive dictatorship. Michael Denning broadened my field of vision, always asking how Chile fit into the larger picture. Stuart Schwartz's down-to-earth advice made a daunting research agenda more manageable. Peter Winn's generosity, advice, and moral support made what at times seemed impossible, possible. Mario Garcés went above and beyond the call of collegiality, teaching me Chilean oral history methodology, lending books, discussing ideas, providing contacts, and sharing research materials. My colleagues in the Department of History at the University of North Florida have been a constant source of intellectual engagement and good cheer.

Although they might not have known it at the time, Elizabeth Lira, Nara Milanich, Bethany Moreton, Edward Murphy, Anne Perotin-Dumont, the late Patricia Pessar, Margaret Power, Tony Rosenthal, Heidi Tinsman, Teresa Valdés, Pamela Voekel, Steve Volk, and Alexander Wilde offered valuable advice at important junctures. My colleagues in the Colectivo Memoria Histórica of the Corporación José Domingo Cañas in Santiago, and the Graduate Employees and Students Organization and Federation of Hospital and University Employees in New Haven, Connecticut, set examples of socially engaged research and dedicated activism. The late Florence Thomas of the Yale University Department of History and the inimitable Marianne Roberts of the University of North Florida Department of History cut through miles of red tape, helped navigate institutional bureaucracies, and provided crucial administrative support.

Archivists and librarians hold the keys to historical treasures. I thank César Rodríguez of Yale University's Latin American Studies Collection, the librarians and archivists of the University of Florida's Latin American and Caribbean Collection, and especially the archivists, librarians, and staff who facilitated access to collections in Santiago. I also thank Barbara Tuck, Lauren Newton, Alisa Craddock, and Rachel Dobbs of the University of North Florida's Thomas G. Carpenter Library, who answered bibliographic queries and fulfilled unusual interlibrary loan requests. My research assistants, Cecilia Riveros, Sandie A. Stratton, and Anthony Rossodivito, did excellent work transcribing and digitalizing interview recordings, and organizing and annotating documents. I thank Andra Chastain for sending archival map images from Santiago.

Over the years, many people have provided advice, contacts, encouragement, feedback, intriguing conversation, a warm meal, lodging, or all of the above. My gratitude goes to Rolando Álvarez, María Luz Araya, Paulina Barberán, Claudio Barrientos, Denise Bossy, Catherine Boumkwo Baneni, Fernando Camacho, Juan Carrera, José Celso Castro Alves, Lorena Chaves, Rachel Chrastil, Charles Closmann, Lisa Edwards, Brenda Elsey, Raphael Folsom, J. J. Fueser, Catherine Griebel Bowman, Sue Gronewold, Boris Hau, Nicolás Hau, Jenny Herbst, Sandra Herrera, David Home, Michael Jo, Noemí Lima, Sam Martland, Carolyn McCarthy, Eden Medina, Edward Melillo, Karla Miranda, Francisco Morales, Luis Morales, Jenne Nolan, Elvis Parraguez, Laura Passmore, Theo Prousis, Kate Reed Hauenstein, Gabriela Raposo, Andrew Sackett, Alicia Salomone, David Sanders, Anita Seth, Kristie Starr, Jessica Stites Mor, Stephen Vella (rest in peace, dear friend), Louise Walker, and Kirsten Weld. I thank the Hau Espinosa, Herrera Herrera, Morales Aguilera, Silva Jara, and Videla Sotomayor families, Mario Garcés and Susana Costamagna, and the sisters of the Compañía del Divino Maestro-Villa Francia, especially the late María Dolores Cruzat, for their warmth and hospitality in Chile.

Special thanks go to J.T. Way for his commentary, sense of humor, and careful reading of many chapters. Claudia Videla taught me to make *cazuela* and shared hours of conversation and camaraderie. Pamela Zeiser provided a wealth of levelheaded advice and applied her laserlike editing pen to the text. Jennifer Adair offered important feedback during critical stages of the writing process. Claire Goldstene provided sound counsel in the darkest days of writing. Linda Howell taught me that to write is to play and gave me Luna, whose single-minded feline pursuits often lend perspective. Suzanne Simon sent encouragement, humor, and wisdom from near and far. Marian Schlotterbeck's comments and questions challenged me to imagine and reimagine ideas from various angles. Chau Johnsen Kelly has been a stalwart reader, critic, and friend whose generosity and breadth of knowledge never cease to inspire.

Thank you to Steve J. Stern and Scott Straus, series editors, for bringing the book into the Critical Human Rights series. Gwen Walker and Sheila McMahon at the University of Wisconsin Press shepherded this book through the publication process with care and utmost professionalism. I thank the peer reviewers for their helpful comments, the editorial staff for their work on this project, and Mary Sutherland for her thoughtful copyediting. Michael Boyles at the University of North Florida's Center for Instruction and Research Technology brought his design expertise to bear on the maps, with a discerning eye and attention to detail.

The most profound debts of gratitude are the most difficult to express. Gil Joseph, Peter Winn, Mario Garcés, and Steve Stern: thank you. Your encouragement, generosity, intellectual engagement, and thoughtful guidance have been fundamental.

I owe a most special debt of gratitude to all who invited me into their neighborhoods, homes, and offices to talk about their experiences, especially the residents of La Legua and Villa Francia who shared their thoughts and histories with me. You taught me more than books ever could.

My infinite gratitude goes to my family: To the memory of my grandparents, Helen, Dorothy, and Arthur, and my niece, Oleander. To Doug, for his calm and constant presence. To Tom, who has always understood. To Gwen, for her wit and imagination. To Veronica, for what we share. To Amy, for her spark and energy. To Derek, for his dedication and care. To Hawthorne and Maxwell, for the joy they bring each day. To Paul Carelli, who has endured years of "the book" with good humor, for his laughter, sagacity, and love. And most especially to my parents, Nancy and David, for everything.

Abbreviations

ACE   Actas del Consejo de Estado (Proceedings of the Council of State)

AD   Alianza Democrática (Democratic Alliance)

ADJ   Actas de las Sesiones de la Honorable Junta de Gobierno (Proceedings of the Sessions of the Honorable Governing Junta)

AFDD   Agrupación de Familiares de Detenidos-Desaparecidos (Association of Family Members of Disappeared Detainees)

AIR   Agencia Informativa de la Resistencia (Information Agency of the Resistance)

ANEF   Asociación Nacional de Empleados Fiscales (National Association of Public Employees)

ANH   Archivo Nacional Histórico (National Historical Archive)

ARNAD   Archivo Nacional de la Administración (National Administrative Archive)

ARNAD/FOS   ARNAD/Fondo Organizaciones Sociales (Social Organizations Collection)

BCNSC   Biblioteca del Congreso Nacional-Sede Compañía (Library of the National Congress-Compañía Branch)

BMINVU	Biblioteca del Ministerio de Vivienda y Urbanismo (Library of the Ministry of Housing and Urbanism)
BSI	Biblioteca San Ignacio (San Ignacio Library)
CAP	Comité de Abastecimiento Popular (Popular Supply Committee)
CCP	Comunidad Cristiana Popular (Popular Christian Community)
CEB	Comunidad Eclesial de Base (Ecclesial Base Community)
CECH	Conferencia Episcopal de Chile (Episcopal Conference of Chile)
CEDOC-CODEPU	Centro de Documentación-Corporación de Promoción y Defensa de los Derechos del Pueblo (Documentation Center-Corporation for the Promotion and Defense of the Rights of the People)
CEDOC-ECO	Centro de Documentación-Educación y Comunicaciones (Documentation Center-Education and Communications)
CEME/AC	Centro de Estudios Miguel Enríquez/Archivo Chile (Study Center Miguel Enríquez/Chile Archive)
Church	Catholic Church
CIA	US Central Intelligence Agency
CIDU	Centro Interdisciplinario de Desarrollo Urbano y Regional (Interdisciplinary Center of Urban and Regional Development)
CNI	Central Nacional de Informaciones (National Information Center)
CNS	Coordinadora Nacional Sindical (National Trade-Union Coordinator)
CNT	Comando Nacional de Trabajadores (National Workers' Command)

COAPO	Coordinadora de Agrupaciones Poblacionales (Coordinator of Poblador Associations)
CODELCO	Corporación Nacional del Cobre (National Copper Corporation)
CODEPU	Corporación de Promoción y Defensa de los Derechos del Pueblo (Corporation for the Promotion and Defense of the Rights of the People)
COFFLA	Common Front for Latin America
CONAR	Comité Nacional de Ayuda a los Refugiados (National Committee for Refugee Assistance)
COPACHI	Comité de Cooperación para la Paz en Chile (Comité Pro Paz) (Committee of Cooperation for Peace in Chile) (Pro Peace Committee)
CORMU	Corporación de Mejoramiento Urbano (Urban Improvement Corporation)
CPS	Cristianos por el Socialismo (Christians for Socialism)
CTC	Confederación de Trabajadores del Cobre (Confederation of Copper Workers)
CUT	Central Única de Trabajadores (Unified Workers' Center)
DDRS	Declassified Documents Reference System
DESAL	Centro Para el Desarrollo Económico y Social de América Latina (Center for Latin American Economic and Social Development)
DINA	Dirección de Inteligencia Nacional (National Intelligence Directorate)
DINAC	Dirección Nacional de Abastecimiento y Comercialización (National Supply and Commercialization Directorate)
DIRINCO	Dirección Nacional de Industria y Comercio (National Industry and Commerce Directorate)

DWAICD	"Los Archivos Secretos de la Dictadura" (The Secret Archives of the Dictatorship)
ECO	Educación y Comunicaciones (Education and Communications)
ELN	Ejército de Liberación Nacional (National Liberation Army)
EMO	Equipo Misión Obrera (Worker Mission Team)
FAO	Food and Agriculture Organization of the United Nations
FASIC	Fundación de Ayuda Social de las Iglesias Cristianas (Social Assistance Foundation of the Christian Churches)
FAVS	Fundación Documentación y Archivo de la Vicaría de la Solidaridad (Foundation Documentation and Archive of the Vicariate of Solidarity)
FER	Frente de Estudiantes Revolucionarios (Revolutionary Students Front)
FLACSO	Facultad Latinoamericana de Ciencias Sociales-Chile (Latin American School of Social Sciences-Chile)
FLACSO/FERT	FLACSO/Fondo Eugenio Ruiz-Tagle (Eugenio Ruiz-Tagle Collection)
FOCH	Federación Obrera de Chile (Worker Federation of Chile)
FPMR/Frente	Frente Patriótico Manuel Rodríguez (Manuel Rodríguez Patriotic Front)
G	Group (e.g., G1, G3)
GAP	Grupo de Amigos Personales (Group of Personal Friends)
GI	Group Interview
GNP	Gross National Product

ICNPPT	*Informe de la Comisión Nacional sobre prisión política y tortura* (Report of the National Commission on Political Prison and Torture)
ICNRR	*Informe sobre calificación de víctimas de violaciones de derechos humanos y de violencia política* (Report on the Qualification of Victims of Human Rights Violations and Political Violence)
ICNVR	*Informe de la Comisión Nacional de Verdad y Reconciliación* (Report of the National Truth and Reconciliation Commission)
IM-IC	Vicaría de la Solidaridad "Informe Mensual-Informe Confidencial" (Vicariate of Solidarity "Monthly Report-Confidential Report")
INDH	Instituto Nacional de Derechos Humanos (National Human Rights Institute)
INE	Instituto Nacional de Estadísticas (National Institute of Statistics)
JAP	Junta de Abastecimiento y Precios (Supply and Price Committee)
JLAS	*Journal of Latin American Studies*
JOC	Juventud Obrera Católica (Catholic Worker Youth)
LACC-UF	Latin American and Caribbean Collection-University of Florida
LARR	*Latin American Research Review*
Lautaro	Movimiento Juvenil Lautaro (Lautaro Youth Movement)
MAPU	Movimiento de Acción Popular Unitaria (Unitary Popular Action Movement)
MDP	Movimiento Democrático Popular (Popular Democratic Movement)
METRO	Coordinadora Metropolitana de Pobladores (Metropolitan Coordinator of Pobladores)

MINVU	Ministerio Nacional de Vivienda y Urbanismo (National Ministry of Housing and Urbanism)
MIR	Movimiento de Izquierda Revolucionaria (Revolutionary Left Movement)
MOAC	Movimiento Obrero de Acción Católica (Catholic Action Workers' Movement)
NACLA	North American Congress on Latin America
NGO	Non-governmental organization
OECD	Organization for Economic Cooperation and Development
PAAJB	Personal Archive Alison J. Bruey
PAMG	Personal Archive Mario Garcés
PDC	Partido Demócrata Cristiano (Christian Democrat Party)
PEM	Programa de Empleo Mínimo (Minimum Employment Program)
POJH	Programa de Ocupación para Jefes de Hogar (Occupation Program for Heads of Household)
SENDET	Secretaría Ejecutiva Nacional de Detenidos (National Executive Secretariat of Detainees)
SEPADE	Servicio Evangélico para el Desarrollo (Evangelical Service for Development)
TVN	Televisión Nacional de Chile (National Television of Chile)
UNCTAD	United Nations Conference on Trade and Development
UP	Unidad Popular (Popular Unity)
Vicaría	Vicaría de la Solidaridad (Vicariate of Solidarity)
WCC	World Council of Churches
WHO	World Health Organization

Map 1. Chile

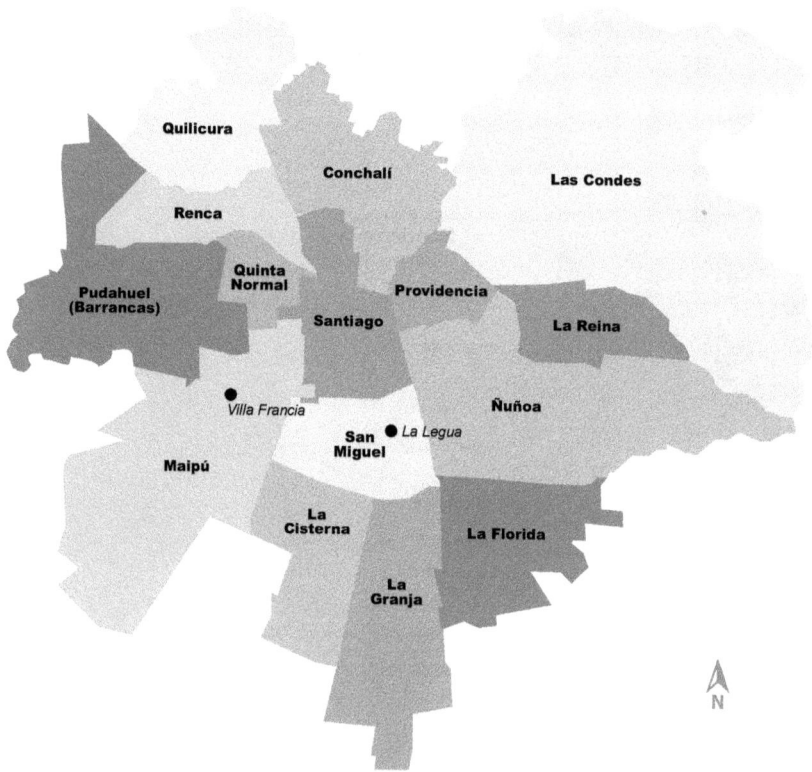

Map 2. Greater Santiago, 1973–1981, La Legua and Villa Francia

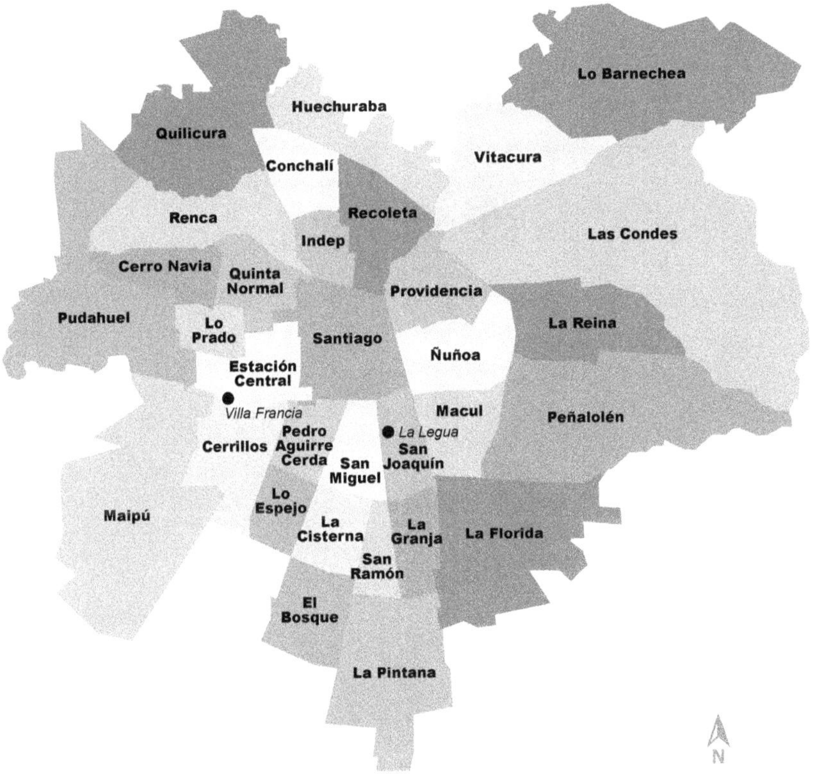

Map 3. Greater Santiago, 1981–1990, La Legua and Villa Francia

Bread, Justice, and Liberty

Introduction

Defying Dictatorship, Reclaiming Freedom

Demonstrators: Bread, justice, and liberty!
Police Official: Listen to how they yell against the Government!
Fr. Gustavo Ferraris: How so? Doesn't the government want bread, justice, and
   liberty?
>   Conversation at Don Bosco Church, La Cisterna, Santiago, May 1, 1978[1]

Human rights
Rights denied
Beautiful words
With springtime sunshine
Lies of centuries
Dreams truncated
Hopes flown
Bitterness in the soul
Of the man with callused hands . . .
>   Juan Ávalos, "Odas al pueblo humillado"[2]

Month of Kites

On the morning of Tuesday, September 11, 1973, Juan's school
principal sent the students home before class started, without explanation.
Juan went home to his neighborhood, La Legua Emergencia, changed into his
street clothes, and left the house. September was the traditional *mes de volan-
tines* (month of kites), and the roof of the nearby textile factory, Comandari,

was an ideal place to fly them. Despite the chilly weather, Juan climbed to the roof, where he and another boy spent the rest of the morning coaxing their kites through the air. From their perch on the rooftop, they saw two airplanes sweep low over downtown Santiago. As the planes raced away, the boys watched as a column of black smoke rose into the late-winter sky, above the bombed and burning presidential palace, La Moneda.[3]

Earlier that morning, the Chilean Armed Forces, with the support of the Chilean right, Christian Democrat Party, and the Nixon administration, perpetrated a coup d'état against the democratically elected Unidad Popular (UP, Popular Unity) government and socialist president Salvador Allende Gossens. The coup brought a violent end to the "Chilean Way to Socialism" less than three years into Allende's six-year presidential term. That day, as the Air Force bombed La Moneda, President Allende's residence, and pro-UP radio towers, soldiers and police (Carabineros) swept the city. Primary targets were factories, universities, and *poblaciones* (urban poor and working-class neighborhoods like Juan's) notable for their histories of collective action.[4] As Juan watched the warplanes bomb La Moneda, he was unaware that the coup meant the end of both the UP government and his education-based climb out of La Legua Emergencia, one of Santiago's most hardscrabble poblaciones. Thirty years later, Juan reflected, "I saw that [the UP] was something being created for our strata, starting with good education, food . . . not like now [2003], when education is pure commerce." After the coup he returned to school, but everything had changed: class sizes increased, the food deteriorated, and pedagogy suffered. The change was brutal and disconcerting. Juan's experience illustrates how, seemingly overnight, a new system was installed in Chile: "[During the UP] you experienced everything that was lovely, and then overnight—pah!—they drop the curtain. That's it for you; you can't get ahead if you don't have money, if you don't have connections. Allende said that education and health care were something the government had to provide its fellow citizens, and now, if you don't have money you don't study, if you don't have money you die."[5]

Juan's recollections highlight a theme prevalent in oral history conversations with residents of Santiago's poblaciones in the early twenty-first century: emphasis on continuity, rather than rupture, between the Pinochet dictatorship (1973–90) and the post-dictatorship Concertación governments (1990–2010).[6] In Juan's case, continuity referred to an economic regime—neoliberalism—and its systematic violation of social rights. In other cases the emphasis on continuity centers on repression and the violation of political rights. For yet others, the violation of social *and* political rights under dictatorship *and* democracy points to a mutually reinforcing relationship between human rights violations and neoliberalism. Interpretations of continuity vary across generations. In informal conversations, community activists old enough to have experienced the dictatorship as adults drew clear distinctions between the intensity and type of repression under the dictatorship and the Concertación, and opined that young radicals tend to overstate the periods' similarities. Nevertheless, while older activists preferred a more nuanced view, they consistently highlighted important continuities: torture, abuse of power, state-perpetrated killing, derogatory media portrayals of poblaciones, a culture of impunity for human rights violators, and the ravages of neoliberal policies in labor rights, education, health, and social security.[7] These grassroots interpretations marked a stark difference from the Concertación's human rights discourse that emphasized reconciliation and rejection of the dictatorship's political repression. The poet Juan Ávalos, from Villa Francia, offers a glimpse into alternative discourse in the post-dictatorship period in his 2008 poem "Ode to the Humiliated Pueblo." Citing, among other contemporary ills, "hunger wages," "vile laws," corrupt politicians, and gross social inequities, the poem asks, "And they call all this / justice democracy / human rights?"[8] After a decade of life in Chile's new democracy, it was clear to several generations of activists in poblaciones that the post-dictatorship political elite continued repressive practices and had no interest in significantly altering the dictatorship's neoliberal economic model.[9] One woman described the Concertación as a *dictablanda* rather than a *dictadura* (a "soft" dictatorship rather than a "hard" dictatorship). Another commented, "We paid the blood quota [in the struggle for democracy], but not for this."[10] What was this past that coexisted so uneasily with the concertacionista present in Santiago's poblaciones?[11] This book is about that past: the lived experience of dictatorship and activism against it from the perspective of anti-regime activists who participated in the struggle for democracy in poblaciones of Santiago, the city that was both the center of state power and epicenter of resistance to it.

Human Rights, Pobladores, and Democracy

Human rights, Micheline Ishay writes, are "the result of a cumulative historical process that takes on a life of its own, sui generis, beyond the speeches and writings of progressive thinkers, beyond the documents and main events that compose a particular epoch. . . . If the spirit of a time seems to meander whimsically and dangerously around the volcanic craters of social upheavals, it is transmitted consciously and unconsciously from one generation to another, carrying the scars of its tumultuous past."[12] Often lost amid grand language about human rights and history are the *people* who move historical processes, who create, express, preserve, and transmit ideas, and who pass on the "spirit of a time," together with its scars, to new generations who do with it what they will.[13] It is also people who enact, or fail to enact, the idea of rights, human or otherwise. Human rights are inventions of the human mind and do not exist in people's lived experiences without deliberate human action to enact them in concrete ways. "The idea of human rights conferred on us all by virtue of being human," write Steve Stern and Scott Straus, "is a convenient fiction." It is, though, a powerful fiction that people around the world have tried to make reality, with varying degrees of success.[14]

Chile is one of the foundational cases of the modern international human rights movement.[15] During the 1970s, the concept and language of human rights were relatively new to Chile, and people now recognized as human rights defenders had no ready guide or precedent for human rights discourse and advocacy as it is understood today. Human rights defenders—from the heights of the Catholic hierarchy to activists in poblaciones—had to create and adapt as conditions developed. Luis Van Isschot argues that "human rights are contingent norms and practices derived from lived experiences of authoritarianism, war, poverty, and exclusion," and this was certainly the case in Chile.[16] The *pobladores* at the heart of this study were on the receiving end of an onslaught of social and political violence that constituted human rights violations before "human rights talk" was firmly established in Chile and before "human rights" became a rallying cry for opposition to the dictatorship. Their struggle for social justice predated the coup and the widespread development of "human rights talk" in the mid-1970s, and the new language of human rights eventually provided a tool for furthering struggles for social justice and democracy, and seeking redress for abuse. During the dictatorship, pobladores and their allies created communities in pursuit of social justice and democracy. The struggle that these grassroots activists unleashed was a profoundly human endeavor in the most noble and base senses of the term. It was at once spectacular and mundane. It encompassed hope and horror, violence and pacifism, isolation and solidarity, utopian idealism and abject pragmatism, courage and terror. It laid bare vicissitudes and complexities of truth and deception, life and death, and love and hate.

Placing people and their communities at the center of the analysis allows for a closer look at the struggle for democracy and human rights on the ground, far from grand narratives, neat schematics, and clichés about the period. It also upsets widely accepted periodization and "common knowledge" about the lived experience of dictatorship in Chile.[17] In poblaciones, political repression and intimidation of workers and leftists began before September 11, 1973. There was no "economic miracle" in the late 1970s. The financial crash of 1981–83 marked a deepening, not the advent, of economic crisis. The first national protests of 1983 (*jornadas de protesta nacional*, so-called because of their national, multisectoral scope) represented an acceleration and expansion of mass protest, not its beginning. The national protests in poblaciones, which lasted from 1983 to 1987, were planned and organized; they were neither spontaneous nor irrational. The protests were explicitly against both the dictatorship and the neoliberal economic model that took its greatest toll in the poblaciones. The transition to democracy was not peaceful and was not won only, or even primarily, through the ballot box. This historical experience differs from mainstream discourse about the dictatorship and transition to democracy, and it clashes with Chile's dominant regimes of historicity and interpretations of human rights.

Chile's history of revolution, dictatorship, and democratization forms part of a broader legacy of political and social struggle in Latin America. Human rights became a watchword of the 1970s and 1980s as Cold War national security regimes across the Western Hemisphere made the mass, systematic commission of atrocity a cornerstone of state policy. Internationally, Chile was one of the most symbolic examples, given its history of institutional democracy, its strong popular sector organizations, and its national experiment in democratic socialism that ended on September 11, 1973. The resulting dictatorship repressed dissent and potential opposition with impunity as it implemented one of the world's first and most radical transitions to neoliberalism. It remained in power for seventeen years (1973–90) followed by an additional twelve during which the ex-dictator Augusto Pinochet and his supporters enjoyed substantial power within the new democracy. In this context, the post-dictatorship political elite narrowly confined the definition of human rights and redress for their violation to gross human rights violations committed during the dictatorship, specifically death, disappearance, political prison, and torture (this last not until 2005). Meanwhile, official, triumphalist return-to-democracy narratives highlighted the defeat of dictatorship through formal political process and Western liberal tradition—especially elections and negotiations between political elites. This was, to some extent, an accurate narrative, but it disinherited the mass popular sector protests that spurred the regime to negotiate with moderate opposition sectors and opened the way for transition. The political elite subsequently derided protest in poblaciones as violent, spontaneous explosions of rage-fueled irrationality and vandalism divorced from appropriate, modern political practices and undeserving of a place in the story of the return to democracy, much less in the new democracy itself.

This treatment of pobladores echoed influential currents of thought produced in Chile during the 1980s, when pobladores' participation in the national protests drew attention to pobladores' political potential.[18] Underlying this research was a sense of urgency regarding the social and political unrest of the mid-1980s, pobladores' role in that unrest, and what it could mean for the prospects for a return to democracy and the type of democracy that might ensue. Some thought that strong alliances with leftist political parties would offer the best prospects for a democratic transition (not only a transition to democracy), others viewed with alarm the apparent disconnect between poblador organizations and political parties in general, and still others considered the diminished influence of political parties in grassroots organizations an auspicious development for the construction of a participatory democracy based on nonparty-affiliated civil society organizations.

Attitudes toward pobladores' protagonism in the national protests ranged from trepidation to optimism. Overriding preoccupations included whether pobladores had built a social movement, and, if so, of what type. In Chile, sociologists affiliated with SUR Profesionales echoed paradigms of the 1960s, discussing pobladores' "integration" or "marginalization" relative to mainstream society, economic opportunity, and formal political institutions.[19] The most broadly influential current of thought to emerge from these studies held that pobladores did not constitute "social actors" and that their participation in the national protests was a manifestation of anomie and social disintegration.[20] One of the most prolific scholars in this vein, Eugenio Tironi, defined pobladores in the negative: "that mass that, lacking another identity, is called 'pobladores.'"[21] Pobladores' organizations were "defensive" and "reactive"; pobladores themselves were individualistic, ignorant, dependent, and adverse to politics. Pobladores were social disintegration incarnate, a "monster," a "ghost," that sowed "terror" in the hearts of the middle and upper classes. Pobladores constituted an "unarticulated, and because of that, uncontrollable protagonist," a potentially antidemocratic mass that harbored "latent violence" ripe for political manipulation.[22] As such, they were incompatible with the "construction of a democratic order according to the logic of pacts (*lógica concertacionista*)." Rather, they represented "a dangerous situation of masses 'available' to move from apathy to millenarian mobilization, and vice versa."[23]

According to this interpretation, pobladores were pathological elements requiring control and intervention rather than a place at the table in political decision-making processes. These analyses and others like them reinforced classist perceptions that viewed the poor majority with suspicion, as a threatening other from which the middle and upper classes must distance and defend themselves. Pobladores' position as powerful actors against the dictatorship disturbed and disrupted elites' ideas about how the politics of democratization should work, and the popular sectors' strength in the protests appeared to hold the potential to threaten elite hegemony in this political process. Although these sociological studies have since been strongly critiqued for epistemological and methodological shortcomings, at the time they were influential in scholarship and public policy.[24] Importantly, they found an audience in the Concertación and provided intellectual justification for continuing marginalization of pobladores in the post-1990 democracy.

Researchers in North America and Chile have challenged these theories, arguing that pobladores had formed a social movement and debating what type of social movement it was. One current of thought prioritized "old" sociopolitical actors such as the Communist Party and organized labor. This approach emphasized class-based identity formations, the weight of labor and the Left's historical presence in Chile's popular sectors, and their persistence during the dictatorship. Another current of thought, linked to "new social movement" theory, emphasized the rise of social organizations that formed around identity constructions beyond socioeconomic class (e.g., women and youth). These "new" identities and organizational processes generated hope among researchers who thought that they could lead to more inclusive forms of participatory democracy and give rise to new political subjects unencumbered by top-down party bureaucracies and ideological rigidity.[25]

Although politicians and some influential scholars depicted poblador protest as an anomic, spontaneous reaction *against* the dictatorship and the economic crash of the early 1980s, for many grassroots activists in the poblaciones, protest was a conscious struggle *for* democracy, *for* respect, *for* human rights broadly understood to include political and social rights, and, for some, renewed socialist revolution. Herein lies a primordial disconnect between the political elite and mainstream political and historical discourse of Chile's post-dictatorship democracy, and political culture and expectations forged in poblaciones during the 1970s and 1980s. The restricted understanding of rights undergirding the negotiated transition limited definitions of and redress for human rights violations, excluding especially social rights. In doing so, the new political system clashed with the pluralistic, participatory political culture, understandings of rights, and hopes for the future forged in oppositionist popular sector organizations during the 1970s and 1980s. This political culture, and memories of it, did not disappear with the return to civilian rule despite movement decline and attrition. The mass movement for "bread, justice, and liberty" of the 1970s and 1980s emerged during one of the darkest periods for democracy, human rights, and the Left in Cold War–era Latin America; it coincided with the rise of liberation theology across the hemisphere; and it was closely linked to Chile's transition to neoliberalism. It made possible Chile's return to democracy, although not with the results that many had hoped.

Jessica Stites Mor and others have argued that struggles for democracy and human rights in Latin America did not necessarily rely on activists "looking outward to universal notions of rights and models of democratic institutions in the North."[26] As Jeffrey N. Wasserstrom has noted regarding Asia, "there are real problems with presenting the United States (or the West in general) as a teacher of humanistic values whose Asian," or, in this case, Latin American, "students have been and continue to be slow to understand and accept the lessons being offered—a common theme in US discussions of human rights issues."[27] Indeed, conversations about human rights in Santiago's poblaciones emphasized the US's material and ideological contributions to the violation of human rights, not their promotion. Even so, grassroots opposition movements in Chile's poblaciones were not intellectually or materially divorced from Northern and/or Western-liberal proponents of rights and democracy. The US and Western European governments, along with Canada, the Soviet Union, and Latin American and Eastern Bloc countries, gave refuge to Chilean political exiles. International-solidarity activists from the Global North worked in Chile and abroad to assist anti-regime and pro–human rights efforts.[28] Grassroots activists in poblaciones were aware of the influence that the US and Western European governments could have on the situation in Chile. However, in their quest for inspiration and examples, poblador activists and their allies drew from a much broader range of historical experiences. They looked to the biblical Old and New Testaments, Chile's historical popular movements, the Sandinistas' overthrow of the Somoza dictatorship in Nicaragua, Archbishop Óscar Romero and the Farabundo Martí National Liberation Front in El Salvador, Gandhi and the anticolonial movement in India, Martin Luther King Jr. and the civil rights movement in the US, and the international labor movement. Grassroots activists looked to others who, from their own experiences of oppression, struggled against powerful entities that denied them freedom and rights. Rarely did these touchstones include the institutions so prevalent in many narratives about Cold War–era human rights: the United Nations, the US and Western European governments, Eastern European dissidents, and international nongovernmental organizations (NGOs) like Amnesty International.

Contrary to arguments that posit the centrality of Western-liberal and capitalist ideals to Cold War struggles for human rights and democracy, the most consistent and influential activism in favor of human rights and democracy in Chile came from politically progressive Catholics and the Marxist left.[29] Grassroots activists from these sectors built bridges with other ideological camps, in part, by using "rights talk" that intersected with Western-liberal understandings of human rights derived from the 1948 Universal Declaration of Human Rights (which itself owed a significant portion of its content to Latin American socialist and Catholic humanist principles).[30] As scholars disagree about the origins of human rights and the significance of the Universal Declaration's multicultural origins, and as policymakers and activists debate whether and how social rights should be included in the pantheon of human rights, what emerges is an image of human rights as a constantly changing, historically and contextually contingent set of ideas about how people should treat one another, especially in the context of relationships between states and those living within their jurisdictions.[31]

During the 1970s, international ideas about human rights and the mobilization of human rights discourse to challenge repressive Cold War national security regimes in Latin America were only just emerging, and "human rights talk" in Chile was just finding its feet. The Catholic Church brought human rights training into poblaciones during the mid-1970s, but not onto a blank slate. Pobladores had long experience with ideas of rights anchored in both liberal and socialist ideals of political freedom, democracy, and human entitlement to dignified living and work-ing conditions. Sociopolitical conflict and state-perpetrated violence were not new to Chile or to pobladores, but violence on the scale of the dictatorship's was unmatched in living memory. In poblaciones, the term "human rights" came to be used most consistently in relation to gross violations thereof, especially torture, political executions, and disappearance. This coincided with national and international attention to the urgency of these situations and the politics of solidarity. Yet activist pobladores also based claims to social rights on their status as human beings, not on their individual or collective need, merit, or social and political position.[32] In this sense, al-though the specific vocabulary of rights varies, often without clear delineation, the justification for pursuing and claiming them rested on the same powerful idea: these were rights inherent to all human beings.[33]

Histories of Continuity and Rupture

The broader implications of this study rest on several interlocking arguments. First, Catholic and leftist popular sector political traditions shaped the opposition movement that activists built in poblaciones during the 1970s and 1980s. This process of grassroots organization included activists of diverse generations and religious and political backgrounds. It involved the propagation and practice, within the post-coup context, of ideas about rights that drew on liberal, leftist, and Catholic traditions with long historical trajectories in popular sector political culture. Calling upon, teaching about, and claiming rights, in part through the practice of them despite their suppression by the authorities, forged a basis for common cause between seemingly disparate social actors. This led to alternative social imaginaries opposed to the regime's vision for a "new Chile"—a depoliticized, demobilized Chile organized around "natural" hierarchies redolent of nineteenth-century rural society, modernized for the twentieth century through the application of "scientific" neoliberal economic theory. The alternative imaginaries generated in the popular sectors included promotion of political and social rights as mutually necessary elements for democracy; positive valuation of the urban poor and working-class' labor and their place in national history; and democratic sociopolitical education. This not only contributed to the reconstruction of the social fabric; it also built a political culture that—while neither unitary nor uncontested from within opposition circles—contradicted the political, social, and economic norms that the regime sought to promote and consolidate.

Second, the activists and activism of the 1980s were directly related to those of the 1970s, and both were rooted in pre-coup organizing cultures and traditions.[34] Shifting focus from institutions and organizations to other arenas—cultural, personal, territorial—provides fresh insight into these collective struggles.[35] Leftists and politically progressive Catholics, in alliance with one another, formed the nexus around which oppositionist grassroots organization coalesced in the poblaciones during the 1970s. Extant literature treats Catholics and the secular Marxist left as separate, often antagonistic, entities and tends to rely on overly rigid organizational categories, such as "Catholic Church," "political parties," and "social organizations" (soup kitchens, homeless committees, human rights groups, cultural groups, etc.), as if these were the historical actors rather than the people who populated them. The distinctions between these categories break down at the local and individual level where grassroots organizing actually occurred. Individuals harbor multifaceted social and political identities and affiliations; in the poblaciones, these intersections were key to residents' ability to forge solidarity in a pervasive climate of fear, distrust, and economic misery.

During the 1970s, the split between Catholics and the secular left was less exaggerated than is generally assumed, and the relationship tended more toward cooperation than antagonism. In turn, the reemergence of national political parties in the 1980s relied on the neighborhood-based organizations and city-wide solidarity networks that Catholics and leftists built during the 1970s. This process of reemergence involved drawn-out and tensely negotiated accommodations and conflicts within local organizations, especially between non-Marxist Catholics, Marxist Catholics, and the atheist left, and between those who advocated "all forms of struggle" (meaning the acceptance of armed struggle as part of a broader repertoire of political practices) and those who did not. In the poblaciones, collaboration between the Left and the politically progressive Catholic Church had deep roots in local political cultures.

Third, the *trabajo de hormiga* (ant's work) of resistance that activists did in poblaciones during what are often referred to as the *años oscuros* (dark years) from 1973 to 1983 was key to the rise of mobilization and protest in the 1980s. The devastating 1980s debt crisis and crash of the radical neoliberal economic model was certainly a catalyst for protest. However, since the mid-1970s direct action and public protest were on the rise in poblaciones, well before the outbreak of national protest in 1983. During the años oscuros, activists of varied provenance engaged in grassroots organizing in poblaciones in the face of social atomization, economic crisis, and political repression. By 1978, activists had rebuilt social and political networks in poblaciones to the point that regime opponents could stage ever more frequent and sizeable demonstrations.

It was during this same period that young men and women who grew up within neighborhood organizations and Christian base communities (*comunidades cristianas*) populated by leftists and liberationist Catholics (who followed the tenets of liberation theology) came into their own as political actors. Bridling under the repression and fully aware that they were excluded from Chile's so-called economic miracle, youth gradually pushed community activism further into the streets and to the Left in their struggle for both democracy and revolution. Their increasing radicalization, and the decision some took to affiliate with political organizations that embraced "all forms of struggle," divided their elders and shaped the era of mass protest that would reach its peak in the national protests of the 1980s.

During the national protests, pobladores protested for an end to dictatorship and the neoliberal economic model and in favor of democracy and a more equitable economic system. The national protests were more intense and prolonged in poblaciones than in any other social sector. Protests in poblaciones were territorial in nature: they began early in the day and lasted long into the night, with the objective of expressing dissent and temporarily "liberating" neighborhoods from police and military incursions. At their high point in 1983 and 1984, protests in poblaciones extended beyond the official protest dates and beyond the control of national protest-coordinating bodies. Their tactical repertoire was broad, from absenteeism and boycott to marches, barricades, and—in the most extreme cases—political violence. The dominant stories of the national protests, then and now, have emphasized the role of organized labor and political elites and have treated "combative" poblaciones as the province of political extremists and enraged *lumpen* (a derogatory term that in popular parlance means criminal, societal detritus). Although labor leaders called the first protests, they were the public spokespeople for a movement whose strength lay in the poblaciones, not on the shop floors.

Researching Rebellion

This book takes consideration of popular sector organization and protest mobilization to the neighborhood and individual level, to explore how organizational processes worked and why people made the decisions they did. Poblaciones La Legua and Villa Francia were located in the most active national protest zones of the capital city and became well known for their robust protest cultures. La Legua dates to the 1920s, and the subsector known as Nueva La Legua originated in 1947, following one of the first successful, organized land takeovers (*tomas*) in Santiago, with strong Communist Party participation. Villa Francia was established in 1969 through a state housing program called Operación Sitio that was implemented by the Christian Democratic government of President Eduardo Frei Montalva (1964–70). As such, it does not occupy a place in the constellation of emblematic poblaciones that came into existence through tomas and whose residents are often assumed to have been more resistant to the dictatorship than those of neighborhoods that originated in public housing programs. Despite their differences, both La Legua and Villa Francia became known as politically combative poblaciones whose reputations survive into the present.

The research for this book included four years of fieldwork in Chile (in 2000 and 2001, 2003 through 2006, and in 2007, 2008, and 2013). Research on periods characterized by dictatorship, censorship, and clandestine activity presents challenges, among them the inaccessibility and destruction of documents, habits of political caution, and the scattered nature of archival material. In this case, seeking archival materials in many, and sometimes unpromising, places yielded positive results. Pobladores appear more often in the archival record during the dictatorship than I had expected.

Oral history is a necessary component of research into periods like these when the dangerous political environment prevented anti-regime activists from keeping written records. The oral history interviews at the heart of this book span the years 2000 to 2006. They include interviews that I conducted individually between 2003 and 2006 and others carried out in 2004 in collaboration with colleagues of the now-defunct Colectivo Memoria Histórica José Domingo Cañas. The historian Mario Garcés graciously shared a significant collection of oral history transcripts from the years 2000 to 2002, from his personal research archives. Overall, this study draws from ninety semi-structured oral history interviews, each with two to twenty participants, with activist pobladores and their allies, from Villa Francia, La Legua, and other poblaciones across the city, including Aníbal Pinto, La Pincoya, Angela Davis (officially "Héroes de la Concepción"), La Bandera, José María Caro, Santa Adriana, Madeco, San Ricardo (formerly Oscar Balboa), Nueva Lo Espejo, Nuevo Amanecer (formerly Nueva La Habana), Lo Hermida, La Faena, Población Pudahuel Sector 18 (aka Villa René Schneider), Yungay (formerly Santiago Pino), 14 de Enero, and Campamento Juan Francisco Frenso.

The interviews span three generational cohorts: the Chilean activist generations of 1948, 1968, and the 1980s. The generation of 1948 includes those who lived through the period of anti-Communist repression between 1948 and 1958, under the Law for the Permanent Defense of Democracy, or Ley Maldita ("Damned Law"). The 1968 generation came of political age during the 1960s—a time of global revolutionary upheaval and youth movements—and experienced the UP and coup as young adults. The generation of the 1980s includes the youth of the national protests, the children of the generations of 1948 and 1968 who took to Chile's streets to bring down the dictatorship.

The conversations included both men and women who were active in opposition networks in the poblaciones. They include priests, nuns, consecrated laypeople, social workers, and members of human rights organizations, Chilean NGOs, popular sector comunidades cristianas, and social organizations. Within the comunidades cristianas were Marxist and non-Marxist Catholics, agnostics and atheists, and people who withdrew from other public activity after the coup but rejoined grassroots organizations as opposition mobilization accelerated. They include pobladores and their allies who were members of dissident political collectives, including the Communist Party, Socialist Party, Movimiento de Izquierda Revolucionaria (MIR, Revolutionary Left Movement), Movimiento de Acción Popular Unitaria (MAPU, Unitary Popular Action Movement), Izquierda Cristiana (Christian Left), Frente Patriótico Manuel Rodríguez (FPMR/Frente, Manuel Rodríguez Patriotic Front) and the Movimiento Juvenil Lautaro (Lautaro, Lautaro Youth Movement). The historical conjuncture of the thirtieth anniversary of the coup, renewed poblador mobilization, and the further erosion of Pinochet's power provided the opportunity to conduct this combination of archival and oral history research.

Memorias Soterradas

Interpretations of continuity and rupture as they existed in the early twenty-first century were closely entangled with matters of *memoria histórica* (historical memory). The year 2003 was a watershed in its own right, as activities commemorating the thirtieth anniversary of the 1973 coup spurred public reflection on the UP and the coup itself. National television stations ran documentaries showcasing archival footage and interviews with participants. Anniversary activities included massive events in symbolic venues such as the Plaza de la Constitución, the Estadio Nacional, and the ex-UNCTAD (United Nations Conference on Trade and Development) building (now Centro Cultural Gabriela Mistral), attended by representatives of the Latin American left.[36] Events such as the reopening of the door at Morandé 80, through which Allende's mortal remains left La Moneda, were widely publicized. These and other activities contributed to a public rehabilitation of Allende's image, and they contributed to shifting the UP, the Left, and the coup from the realm of taboo topics into the light of public attention and discussion. An official truth commission investigation into political prison and torture under the dictatorship, the results of which were released in 2005, catalyzed awareness but also attracted criticism of its methodologies and omissions.[37] Meanwhile, some human rights circles expanded their traditional focus on repression and absence to emphasize the lives, social contributions, and political commitments of those lost, in the interest of reinvigorating contemporary struggles for democracy and justice.

With a few exceptions, pobladores' experiences were conspicuously absent from historical images and analyses that the media, scholars, and public officials projected into the public sphere during this period.[38] Nor did official truth commission reports shed much light on the matter. The military regime explicitly targeted pobladores as a social sector for the purposes of repression, public policy, and political propaganda, but truth commission reports do not systematically quantify or account for repression of pobladores as individuals or as a social sector. This reflects a certain level of disregard for pobladores' experiences as a group targeted for systematic political repression even as it underscores the difficulty of researching periods marked by repression, censorship, misinformation, and clandestine activity.

The intersections of past and present, trauma and resilience, and the challenges of research about this period were laid bare during an intense, but not anomalous, community oral history interview in which I participated in 2004. During this wide-ranging conversation, pobladores discussed the difficulty of revealing certain details of their experiences during the dictatorship. One woman explained that she and three others saw "them" (a common euphemism for state agents of repression) kill a man: "Through the kitchen window of my home . . . we saw how they dragged a man out of a vehicle . . . and they dragged him out in a very bad state, and they beat him and stopped; in other words, they killed him there." She warned that even today, "one can't give more details, you understand, today, it's terrible. . . . That person I saw through the window isn't on the list for the memorial [to victims of repression]; nobody reported it." She continued, "He paid for his family's safety with his life, you see, and today [his grandson] could still [have problems]. . . . It's terrible." Another participant concurred that "there are things that can't be told that are still secret and must not be spoken of." Another woman explained that "it's because of caution, of solidarity, because we know that people lived for so many years with that fear," a fear that she had experienced herself: "It occurred to me that they could arrive at any moment to take my son, you understand? And to know that somehow there are some people to whom this could still happen, it could happen to us, understand? It's putting oneself in someone else's place." Others disagreed. One woman, whose husband the regime had disappeared, intervened: "See, I was left with three children, and I always told them the truth. I told them 'this happened,' and I told them the truth."[39] It does not matter in this instance that participants did not want to share certain details. What matters is that decades after the fact, some still felt the need to keep secrets for fear that divulging them could lead to renewed repression. What truths could be told, and the risks associated with their telling, were matters of contention in poblaciones in the early twenty-first century. There had been no truth commission for pobladores. Their experiences of community-wide repression had never been officially solicited or investigated by the state, and the state, by many accounts, was still but a fair-weather friend.[40]

In poblaciones, narratives that emphasize continuity between the dictatorship and the Concertación are rooted, in part, in individual and collective trauma dating to the 1970s and 1980s, but they are also a product of the post-dictatorship period. Beginning in 2001, police occupied several poblaciones, including La Legua and parts of the Caro-Ochagavía sector of southern Santiago, in the name of anti-drug-trafficking measures and the politically malleable concept of *seguridad ciudadana* (citizen safety). In this context, pobladores drew parallels with mass repression during the dictatorship, when the police and military conducted mass *allanamientos* (search raids) in poblaciones. They suggested that contemporary occupations and raids did little to reduce trafficking even as they conjured intimidating specters of times supposedly past. Other poblaciones, like Villa Francia, endured incursions by anti-riot police and clashes between protestors and police on dates meaningful to the Left, such as September 11 and March 29.[41] The arrival of police with riot gear, weapons, and armored vehicles recalled police repression during the dictatorship. Meanwhile, the mainstream media depicted poblaciones as redoubts of violent extremists and criminals, echoing the pro-dictatorship media of the 1970s and 1980s. Television stations made a spectacle of drug problems in La Legua, peddling shows with sensationalistic, derogatory titles such as "La Legua: The

Ghetto of Death."[42] On traditional days of protest the airwaves filled with burning barricades, masked protesters, and vandalism. The mainstream media's focus on vandalism, violence, and drugs to the exclusion of peaceful protest and positive newsworthy events in poblaciones disgusted activists. They rightly worried that the negative imagery reinforced the deeply entrenched, classist discrimination that pobladores have long faced *afuera* (outside the población) and which has abated little in the new democracy.

It was in this context that, three decades after the coup, pobladores discussed mass repression and anti-regime struggle in their neighborhoods during the dictatorship. In some poblaciones, contentious debates brewed about regimes of historicity and the historical and contemporary legitimacy of direct action, including all forms of struggle.[43] These conflicts manifested themselves in diverse venues. In one neighborhood, young masked radicals appropriated the microphone during a community event and received a dressing-down from a nun who herself had opposed the dictatorship and who routinely levied strong critiques of the Concertación. In another instance, disagreement over the politics of a memorial to local victims of dictatorial repression resulted in the omission of some names. These disputes suggest political disagreements among activists, and between different generations of activists, regarding what constitutes appropriate political expression and who holds the legitimacy to interpret sociopolitical conditions and processes, past and present, for the benefit of younger generations. These local conflicts also highlight the gradual and continuous unfolding of "memory struggles" and the formation of collective *memorias soterradas* (underground memories) that occur below the radar of official discourse and media attention by virtue of their location and timing—which may place them out of sync with dominant politico-cultural trends—and the nature of their subject matter (e.g., the armed left, a relatively taboo topic under the Concertación and in mainstream society).[44] Nevertheless, despite persistent tensions, the national opening-up surrounding the thirtieth anniversary of the coup meant that some of the stigma and fear related to discussing the 1970–90 period or having been affiliated with the Left lifted, creating spaces for conversation and discussion about repression and activism in poblaciones during the dictatorship.

Bread, Justice, and Liberty

Although pobladores bore the brunt of economic crisis and repression during the dictatorship, they were far from passive victims unequipped to confront authoritarian, neoliberal "modernity," or to engage in reasoned sociopolitical negotiation and decision-making. They mobilized in defense of rights and their individual and collective interests under extremely adverse circumstances. Activist pobladores and their allies, regular people with workaday concerns, faced down unemployment, hunger, social atomization, repression, and, ultimately, a homicidal dictatorship that enjoyed the backing of the most powerful sectors of Chilean society and the US. From very early in the dictatorship, drawing on long traditions of liberal, leftist, and Catholic currents deeply rooted in popular sector political culture, pobladores organized around a wide range of rights. These included the right to physical integrity, political rights, and social rights (especially access to food, housing, education, and health care). They organized for rights violated by the dictatorship and its economic model, consciousness of which came early to pobladores, among those hit first and hardest by mass repression and neoliberal structural adjustment.

Activist pobladores built a political culture that incorporated understandings of rights tied to critiques of the military regime's political and economic systems. The pluralistic political culture cultivated in activist circles in poblaciones during the 1970s, and the ideas and values regarding human rights and expectations of democracy developed therein, laid the foundation for the broad political coalitions that emerged in the context of the protests and ultimately used the formal political system to usher in a return to civilian rule in the late 1980s. In Santiago, residents of the *comunas populares* (poor and working-class municipalities) carried the opposition to victory in the 1988 plebiscite that marked the formal beginning of the end of Pinochet's rule.[45] The plebiscite and subsequent 1989 presidential election victory of the Christian Democrat Patricio Aylwin marked a victory for oppositionists as a whole. However, the rise to power of the Concertación, a coalition anchored by renovated Socialists and Christian Democrats, the major opposition sectors with perhaps the least presence in poblaciones during the 1970s and 1980s, would have long-term consequences.

The restricted nature of Chile's new democracy, the continuance of the neoliberal model, and the narrow working definition of human rights that undergirded the negotiated transition clashed with understandings of rights and visions of society constructed in grassroots opposition circles in poblaciones during the 1970s and 1980s. With the transition to democracy, which changed the political administration but preserved the 1980 Constitution and the neoliberal economic model, activist pobladores who had struggled for a return to democracy and the defense of human rights experienced a jarring mixture of change and continuity that went unrecognized in elite-propagated political discourse and practice that tied the concept of democracy to neoliberal economics and sought to delegitimize protest against this arrangement.[46] One of the myths underlying the Chilean transition to democracy—that poblador protest was a spontaneous, convulsive, increasingly violent and unfortunate hiccup on the way to a properly managed political transition—is just that: a foundational myth elaborated to benefit the political and economic elite. The disconnect between understandings of human rights and democracy forged at the grassroots during the dictatorship and those advanced by the political elites of the post-dictatorial state has contributed to cycles of discontent and protest ever since.

1

La Legua, Villa Francia, and the Movimiento de Pobladores

I wanted to come [to our new housing site] right away. My husband said, "There's no water, there's nothing." [I told him], "It doesn't matter, I'm going. . . . Come if you want, if not, don't."

Carmen, Villa Francia[1]

When man landed on the moon, I landed on my site.

Anonymous, Villa Francia[2]

A Place on Earth

In 1972, Chilean musician and dramaturge Víctor Jara released the album *La Población*, whose playlist could serve as the score for a musical theater production about Santiago's *movimiento de pobladores* (pobladores movement). The first songs describe urban poverty and vulnerability: a homeless woman "without a place on earth" and only the work of her hands to sustain her ("Lo único que tengo"), the Mapocho River's destructive floods ("En el Río Mapocho"), and a cold, wet toddler named Luchín ("Luchín"). After setting the stage with depictions of the precarious lives of Santiago's urban poor, the album shifts tone with a song about the excitement and suffering of the *toma* (land takeover) of March 16, 1967, that gave rise to población Herminda de la Victoria. Rather than solitary, forlorn figures—a homeless woman, a toddler eating dirt and worms—the second half of the album highlights collective action, solidarity, and the *pueblo*'s knowledge and creativity.

Interviews with *pobladoras* (women pobladores) complement the songs, lending the album an air of documentary reportage: "And thanks to our triumph, now we're 'living like people,' as they say, we have our site and our house," says a pobladora from Herminda de la Victoria. The album ends with the "March of the Pobladores," a celebration of pobladores' collective potential as revolutionary subjects of the UP.[3] The pobladores movement peaked between 1967 and 1973, as a decades-long cycle of popular sector struggle for housing reached its height before grinding to a temporary halt following the 1973 coup.

Even before the pobladores movement took the national stage in the late 1960s, the urban poor had long been the subject of scholarly attention and policy debate. The nineteenth-century historian and intendent of Santiago Benjamín Vicuña Mackenna was preoccupied with the urban poor's presence in and around Santiago and the dangers that this "barbaric" city of the poor held for the "illustrated, opulent, and Christian" city of Santiago proper. At the city's southern periphery, he wrote to the municipality of Santiago and the National Congress in 1872, "the largest of our neighborhoods, situated windward of the city, is just an immense sewer of infection and vice, of crime and pestilence, a true 'pasture of death.'" In the northern sector called La Chimba, the report continues, the *conventillos* (tenements) were "a certain, active, and powerful cause of death" because of the living conditions they harbored and the disease epidemics these generated.[4] The living and working conditions and the social and political status of the urban poor—the "social question"—ignited animated debates through the mid-twentieth century and beyond, as Santiago's population grew, as mobilizations associated with pobladores and the Left increased, and as the urban housing crisis continued.

During the 1960s, as tomas multiplied and a discernable pobladores movement took shape, two major currents of thought developed regarding pobladores' place and potential in society. The first was the "theory of marginality" whose principal promotor in Chile was the Centro Para el Desarrollo Económico y Social de América Latina (DESAL, Center for Latin American Economic and Social Development, later the Centro Bellarmino) run by the Belgian Jesuit and sociologist Roger Vekemans.[5] The theory of marginality was an anti-Marxist sociopolitical theory that posited that the urban poor existed beyond the pale of society, outside economic and class structures. Pobladores, then, were not historical subjects or protagonists of social transformation. Rather, they were agents and victims of social disintegration who had failed to integrate into the capitalist system. President Eduardo Frei Montalva's administration (1964–70) adopted the theory of marginality and organized its social policy program, *Promoción Popular*, around the idea that the antidote to sociopolitical unrest and communist influence was to integrate the urban poor into the capitalist socioeconomic and political system. By legalizing *juntas de veci-nos* (neighborhood councils) and expanding public housing programs with the implementation of Operación Sitio, the Frei Montalva administration created official structures through which pobladores could pursue their interests. Theoretically, these would obviate the need for extralegal direct action by channeling pobladores' demands through official conduits. These conduits flowed in two directions: they provided pobladores with institutionalized access to the state, and they served as a means for the state to reach the vast electorate that pobladores represented.

Researchers associated with the Universidad Católica's Centro Interdisciplinario de Desarrollo Urbano y Regional (CIDU, Interdisciplinary Center of Urban and Regional Development) developed competing analyses anchored in Marxist social theory and dependency theory.[6] They rejected the idea of pobladores as paragons of social disintegration who existed outside of society, pointing out that poblaciones housed the working- and lower-middle classes, including laborers, industrial workers, schoolteachers, self-employed workers, and low-paid white-collar employees. Pobladores were not "marginalized" from class structures or society; their labor and the exploitation of it constituted society's economic foundation, yet they had no better alternative than to live in squatter camps and poblaciones because of the exploitation and superexploitation they endured in Chile's dependent, capitalist society. CIDU's theorists viewed pobladores' mobilizations for affordable housing as an endosystemic movement located within the "general framework of class struggle, urban grievances, and local government."[7] The political implication was that the pobladores movement held the revolutionary potential to upend capitalist property regimes and systems of governance. The theory of marginality and CIDU's competing approaches reflected contemporary political conflicts, and ongoing concern with the "social question" and pobladores' place in the city.

As these debates suggest, Santiago's urban property regimes, writes Edward Murphy, "did not lay the basis for a well-functioning city and polity, free of conflict and contradiction." Their "volatility" and "inequity" had long ignited political conflict and class anxieties as abysmal living conditions fueled an organized, popular sector struggle for dignified housing.[8] By the time of the coup, many thousands of Santiago families had taken collective action—from tomas to inscription in state housing programs—to *conquistar la casa propia* (conquer homeownership). Upon acquiring property, residents continued mobilizing collectively to build their houses, improve urban infrastructure, and form community organizations. These experiences of sociopolitical action shaped pobladores' responses to the coup and dictatorship. In post-coup poblador narratives, interpretations of neighborhood origin stories, the UP, the coup, the dictatorship, and the transition to democracy are often interlaced in a web of mutual meaning-making. In this sense they form part of broader "memory disputes" in Chile that, according to Mario Garcés and Sebastián Leiva, are linked not only to "truth and justice related to human rights violations, but also to social order and, even more precisely, to projects of social transformation." Garcés and Leiva found that pobladores in La Legua interpreted the coup and subsequent repression as "acts of social vengeance," "actions of conservative authoritarian discipline," "exercises in 'social cleansing,'" "social and political punishment," and "the armed forces' expression of fascistic, militant anti-communism," carried out in reaction to residents' historic pursuit of social change. As a result, write Garcés and Leiva, popular memory of the dictatorship "is not just the memory of the vanquished."[9] Rather, it forms part of broader memory struggles to define the meaning of past projects of social transformation and their contemporary relevance, including, in pobladores' case, the struggle for la casa propia.

Conquistar la Casa Propia

The struggle for dignified low-income housing began early in the twentieth century. Between 1885 and 1907 Santiago's population grew rapidly, from 189,332 to 332,724, as workers, mostly women, left the countryside and collapsing nitrate-mining regions to settle in Santiago.[10] They joined the ranks of Santiago's urban poor in shanties at the urban periphery (*rancherías* and *arrabales*) and tenements in the urban core (conventillos and *cités*). The living conditions in the peripheral neighborhoods and tenements became a perennial matter of debate among turn-of-the-century policymakers. Around this time, the word *pobladores* emerged as a synonym for *los pobres de la ciudad* (the urban poor). Later, and especially on the Left, the word acquired the additional, culturally positive, connotation of urban "settlers" and *constructores de ciudad* (city builders). Late nineteenth- and early twentieth-century government initiatives to *sanear* (sanitize, heal, and/or regulate) poor neighborhoods did little to resolve the public health problem and housing shortage. Rather, they reduced low-income housing stock in some areas of the city without creating replacement housing for evicted families, who found themselves crowding into yet another pestilent tenement or moving to shanties on the urban periphery.[11]

Turn-of-the-century reformers considered poor neighborhoods a biomedical and social "sanitation" crisis. Poor neighborhoods lacked the hygiene that clean water, sewage systems, and structurally sound shelter made possible. They were also places from which pobladores made their way into the streets, plazas, and public spaces of downtown Santiago, crossing into the erstwhile redoubt of the urban elite. Elites bridled at sharing public space with the poor in the "civilized" city as downtown Santiago became host to a diverse social demographic. In response to the housing crisis, workers and the Left organized mutual aid societies, cooperatives, and renters' leagues, and the labor movement incorporated housing into its struggle for workers' rights. The prospect of the "uncivilized" city expanding sans regulation alongside rising popular sector mobilization stoked elite fears of social upheaval and breakdown of the status quo.[12] During the first half of the twentieth century, policymakers took measures to regulate rental properties and expand low-income housing supply. In 1906 the Ley de Habitaciones Obreras marked one of the state's first attempts to promote construction of *vivienda social* (low-income housing). During the 1930s and 1940s, they created laws to further regulate urban property and facilitate loans for subdivided lots at the urban periphery. In 1935, as part of these programs, loans valued at 1,219,617.68 pesos (approximately US$63,400 in 1935) went to 328 people to purchase lots from landowners M. and J. Gandarillas in La Legua (Vieja).[13] These measures did little to stem Santiago's housing crisis.

Between 1940 and 1970 the state, the Left, and grassroots organizations entered a spiraling cycle of conflict and accommodation as pobladores sought their "place on earth" in the metropolis.[14] By the 1940s, low-income housing took several forms. Conventillos and cités, tenements in the urban core, were notorious for crowding, poor sanitation, unsound structures, and disease. Shantytowns called *callampas* (mushrooms), because they seemed to appear overnight, formed via disorganized agglomeration on marginal land along riverbanks, canals, and hillsides. Callampas' lack of infrastructure, flimsy construction, and the dangers of fire, flooding, and illegal tenancy left residents vulnerable to abuse, disease, and death. A minority had successfully acquired housing through worker-housing laws and state-backed loan programs, as in the case of La Legua (Vieja). Under these circumstances, pobladores—among them labor unionists, renters' league participants, and members of the Left— began organizing tomas in pursuit of solutions to their housing problems.

The *toma de Zañartu* that gave rise to Nueva La Legua in 1947 is one of the earliest examples of pobladores using a toma to exact concessions from the state and acquire legal property title. Its organizers included members of the Communist Party and people with experience in renters' leagues and labor unions. They remember this toma as "the national signal" that catalyzed more land takeovers.[15] Tomas like the one at Zañartu established *campamentos* (organized squatter settlements) from which pobladores pressured the state to arrange for property elsewhere or to legalize the campamento where it sat. State authorities arranged for the pobladores of the toma of Zañartu to move to land adjacent to La Legua (Vieja), where they built homes and eventually acquired property titles.

The most important difference between campamentos and poblaciones was property title—the key to *la casa propia*. In 1952 an estimated 60 percent of Santiago's urban poor lived without property title in conventillos, and 14 percent in callampas and campamentos. Only 26 percent lived in state-constructed, low-income housing.[16] Flooding and fires in the callampas often rendered families homeless. Between 1947 and 1957, fires destroyed an estimated six hundred shanties along the Zanjón de la Aguada canal near La Legua, generating recurring crises that pushed affected families and the state to seek solutions. In response, the state built emergency housing on land adjacent to the two Leguas (Vieja and Nueva), establishing a neighborhood called La Legua de Emergencia in 1951.

October 30, 1957, was a pivotal date in the history of the pobladores movement and in the rise of state attention to low-income housing. Throughout the 1950s, in response to the persistently abysmal conditions in Santiago's callampas and conventillos and the burgeoning number of homeless families living as *allegados* ("add-ons") in other families' homes, pobladores organized *comités sin casa* (committees of the homeless) with the support of the Communist Party to seek collective solutions.[17] During this period, tomas became an increasingly common tactic: between 1953 and 1963 there were thirty-two tomas in Santiago involving a total of 13,765 families.[18] In 1957, political unrest and state repression, fires in callampas along the Zanjón de la Aguada, and frustration born of years of fruitless negotiation with the state spurred two thousand families to carry out the *toma de La Victoria*.[19] This toma was notable for its size, the media attention it generated, the Communist Party's involvement, and pobladores' success in exacting concessions from the state. The pobladores remained on the site of the toma and established población La Victoria, building homes and acquiring property title on the land they had occupied. Their success set a precedent and catalyzed further mobilization.

In the context of ongoing housing crisis and related mobilization, President Jorge Alessandri's administration (1958–64) created the Programa Nacional de Vivienda (National Housing Program) to incentivize and regulate private construction and resettle families living in callampas. His administration created two massive poblaciones, San Gregorio and Cardenal José María Caro, to house eighty thousand people.[20] The Frei Montalva administration's popular Operación Sitio program also failed to satisfy demand, and by 1967 the government was unable to control the mass movement for housing or to channel demand through official conduits. With the successful toma of Herminda de la Victoria in 1967 (in which four thousand pobladores occupied the land in fifteen minutes and successfully resisted eviction), tomas became "generalized" as a way for pobladores to acquire residential property. Between 1967 and 1973, an estimated 256 tomas occurred in Santiago. During approximately the same period (1967–72), an estimated 54,710 families, or 10 percent of Santiago's population, acquired property in this way.[21] With the possible exception of a handful of MIR-organized tomas that created campamentos as experiments in revolutionary democracy, tomas were not necessarily antisystemic. Their ultimate goal, Murphy explains, was to acquire property titles, "a pillar of order within liberal forms of rule." A toma was an "exceptional . . . step" taken to achieve a "proper state of affairs." Through tomas, pobladores "asserted a right to popular sovereignty" in a "process of insurgent ownership" in which they transgressed the bounds of legality and political propriety in the interest of establishing legally sanctioned homes befitting citizens of the nation.[22] By the 1970s, Garcés argues, pobladores had become "the most dynamic social actor of the capital's urban society," "re-creating the city" and their place within it.[23]

By the 1970s, the city's population still grew through in-migration from other parts of the country, but only 13.2 percent of immigrants came from rural areas, which means that most probably migrated from secondary cities. New arrivals to Santiago tended not to rent conventillos or own property in poblaciones, which suggests that they lived as allegados in other families' homes.[24] It was families with accumulated experience in the capital city who acquired property through tomas and state housing programs. Achieving homeownership required knowledge of Santiago's sociopolitical terrain and property-acquisition tactics. Tomas required organizing or joining comités sin casa, selecting land, strategizing the toma, constructing shelter, defending the settlement from police, and negotiating with government authorities. Access to housing programs required navigating bureaucracy, completing applications, and saving down payments. The pobladores who organized comités sin casa and tomas were often activists in other areas of city life, in labor unions, political parties, and community organizations. They brought their political and organizational know-how to bear on the struggle for housing and, once they arrived at their new home sites, they often spearheaded local governance and campaigns for urban infrastructure.

Women were key figures in tomas and in the daily life of Santiago's poblaciones; they were not passive neophytes in the world of social struggle and direct action.[25] It was often women who initiated homeownership by registering for housing programs, saving down payments, and pressuring their husbands to move. Owning a home was an important social marker of maturity and autonomy for popular sector women, whom the sexual division of labor tasked with housekeeping, childcare, and domestic economy in addition to wage-earning work as necessary. The crowding and subordination to other women that occurred when families lived as allegados in other people's homes created such friction that some women joined tomas and moved to new home sites alone with their children or threatened to do so.[26]

Mobilization often continued when pobladores reached their new homes. Many poblaciones began as bare plots where pobladores dug pit toilets, lived in temporary shelters, drew water from communal standpipes, and built their own houses. Some poblaciones included a *caseta sanitaria* (stand-alone lava-tory) on each lot, while others included houses or apartments that pobladores dubbed *cajas de fósforos* (matchboxes) for their small size. So many Operación Sitio housing assignments consisted of only a marked-off plot that pobladores called the program Operación Tiza (Operation Chalk). Poblaciones' superior-ity in the hierarchy of low-income housing lay in legal property title and the relative security and social propriety it provided: the opportunity "to live like people," as the pobladora from Herminda de la Victoria explained on Jara's album *La Población*. Población origin stories are therefore of central impor-tance to many pobladores' life histories. The histories of La Legua and Villa Francia are no exception. Local history narratives from La Legua and Villa Francia emphasize residents' collective histories of community mobilization and solidarity, and these pre-coup experiences shaped the contours of post-coup survival and resistance in these neighborhoods.

Tres Leguas

As its residents point out, La Legua is actually *tres* Leguas (three Leguas), each with its own origins and characteristics. The first to emerge was the sector now known as La Legua Vieja, established during the 1920s and 1930s as working families migrated to Santiago from the nitrate-mining regions of northern Chile. The second was Nueva La Legua, a sector known for its leftist political culture and active civic life. Nueva La Legua dates to 1947, when one of Santiago's first organized tomas, the toma de Zañartu in the municipality of Ñuñoa, resulted in seven hundred families being resettled on land adjacent to La Legua Vieja.[27] The pobladores of the toma, with their organizational experience and Communist Party ties, shaped the new pobla-ción's political culture. La Legua de Emergencia dates to 1951, when the gov-ernment settled homeless families in what was supposed to be temporary emergency housing. The tiny wooden houses were never replaced and remained a defining feature of the neighborhood well into the twenty-first century.

La Legua Vieja originally sat among fields and pastures at the city's edge. Mago, whose family settled there in 1936, remembers playing in the fields and participating in the Communist Party's social events and the Catholic Church. The party organized theater contests and held chaperoned dances "where we drank non-alcoholic drinks, and when they were dancing, they'd

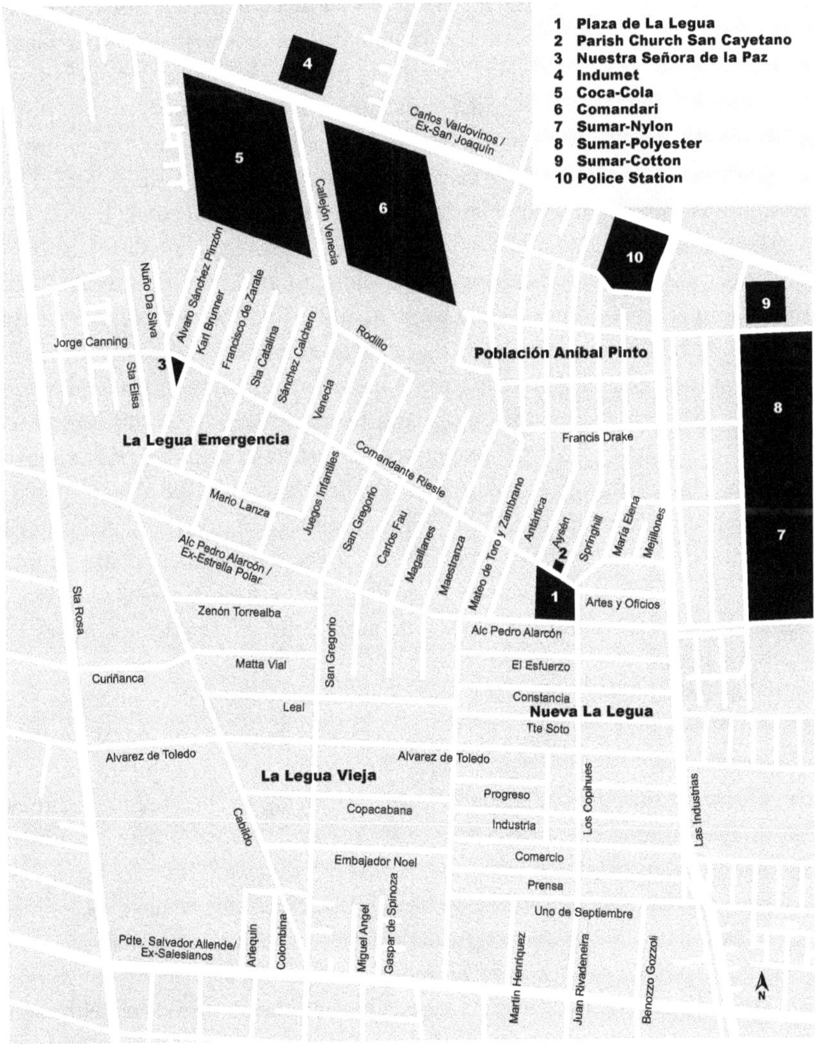

1 Plaza de La Legua
2 Parish Church San Cayetano
3 Nuestra Señora de la Paz
4 Indumet
5 Coca-Cola
6 Comandari
7 Sumar-Nylon
8 Sumar-Polyester
9 Sumar-Cotton
10 Police Station

Map 4. La Legua

say, 'with cakes,' and you had to buy a cake for the girl you were dancing with."[28] Until San Cayetano was established in Nueva La Legua, his family attended Santa Lucrecia, northwest of La Legua in Barrio Franklin. The Communist Party and the Catholic Church were two pillars of neighborhood life from La Legua's beginnings. This dynamic strengthened with the arrival of pobladores from the toma de Zañartu in 1947 and the founding of San Cayetano in 1948.

Nueva La Legua is known for its origins in the 1947 toma de Zañartu and its strong organizational culture. The event that precipitated the toma, its organizers explain, "was the eviction of renters from a tenement on Santa Elena Street, almost to Maule, about 200 people, more or less eighty families, most of them workers for the Municipality of Santiago. The eviction went like this," they recall: "they threw them into the street, sold the land, [and] an industry bought the tenement. You can't just throw 200 people into the street." The Communist Party's Dirección Comunal decided to "guide the toma; it occurred to some *viejo* that this could be the solution." The organizers surveyed the land they had chosen and marked individual plots, to avoid the disorderliness of the callampas, where "it was scary to go in and walk though there, absolutely disorganized," they explain; "with that negative experience, we said, 'no, *poh*, if this is a toma organized by the party it has to be thought out, planned; we're going to take ten meters of frontage and twenty of depth.'" They borrowed horse-drawn wagons from the mayor on the pretext of helping families move to rental plots. During the toma, the wagons led the way, piled with pobladores and their belongings. Others followed on foot. Participants had a week to permanently occupy their lots. The organizers remember telling people "'you have to come to fight alongside us; if you're not here in a week, we repossess the site.'"[29] The toma worked: state authorities relocated the families to land that became Nueva La Legua.

The pobladores of the toma were not initially allowed to purchase the land in Nueva La Legua, and the organizers kept working toward the goal of homeownership. "We always had faith," they recall, "and we communicated it to people, we told them that nobody was removing us, because at first they began by renting to us, in what they called *comodato precario*." The organizers encouraged their neighbors to build up their housing sites, "to strengthen our hold on the land, because once well-built, they couldn't remove us." This, along with legal maneuvers, eventually resulted in the state changing the pobladores' tenancy status from renters to buyers. Some residents, once this problem was resolved, "contented themselves with building a shack without a floor, without a ceiling, they conformed themselves to living in a place where the water didn't leak in, where it didn't rain on them, and there they resigned themselves to live." Others, though, "wanted to live better, they wanted a school, a clinic, to have cultural progress in the población and improve their quality of life, so, those moments served to continue struggling and keeping organization alive."[30] The names of the streets in Nueva La Legua reflect this history. For example, explains Niña, "*Esfuerzo* (Effort) meant to arrive at a place with nothing. *Constancia* (Constancy) meant to work hard to have your house. *Progreso* (Progress), that with electricity and water, people live better. *Industria* (Industry) means that as the years passed, many shoemakers' workshops appeared. *Prensa* (Press) symbolizes the Communist Party's newspaper, *El Siglo*. *Copihue* is in honor of our national flower."[31] As the neighborhood grew, pobladores joined mothers centers, sports clubs, and governance and urban improvement committees.

San Cayetano was established in Nueva La Legua in 1948, and in 1953 a chapel, Nuestra Señora de la Paz, opened a few blocks away in La Emergencia. The San Cayetano parish church became an important locus of community activity. Rafael Maroto, San Cayetano's first priest (1948–53), interceded on Communist pobladores' behalf when the Law for the Permanent Defense of Democracy outlawed the Communist Party and led to the blacklisting, disfranchisement, imprisonment, and exile of its members. Maroto also helped establish a local fire station and served as La Legua's second neighborhood president.[32] The Communists maintained cordial relations with Maroto although he had bested them in local elections, remembers one party member. "[It was] the only time we almost lost control of the neighborhood council," don Enrique recalls, "and not even that much, because we managed to get two or three compañeros on the council, and because the priest was better than if [the Communist candidate] had won, yes sir!" The priest led a public Assembly in Defense of Culture, he remembers, "to ask the government to allow Pablo Neruda to return from exile. A delegation of neighbors went to La Moneda to ask for Neruda's return in the name of La Legua. So with that kind of priest," he concludes, "[the Communist candidate] didn't need to be president."[33] Anita Gossens, a Catholic missionary, also lived and worked in La Legua for many years. A teacher by trade, she arrived in Chile in 1964 and worked in población Los Nogales and the impoverished area of Cerro Navia in western Santiago before settling in La Legua.[34] Gossens and Fr. Guido Peeters (1975–86) receive special mention in pobladores' narratives for their service to the community and protection of people's lives during the dictatorship.

Coexistence and cooperation between the Catholic Church and the Left began early in La Legua's history and continued through the UP and into the dictatorship. In the late 1960s and early 1970s, many youth in and around La Legua were active in political parties and Church-affiliated organizations, including the Socialist Party, Communist Youth, the MAPU, the Christian Left, and the Juventud Obrera Católica (JOC, Catholic Worker Youth). The political and religious organizations were not mutually exclusive. People participated in political parties and the Church with little sense of incongruence. Juan R. remembers that during the late 1960s and the UP, he participated in a Catholic youth organization that did social work in poblaciones La Legua, Aníbal Pinto, Germán Riesco, El Pinar, and Mussa. This movement of Catholic youth was part of a broader mobilization of young Catholics that "went hand in hand with the more macro social movement" he explains. "We never marginalized ourselves, we never stayed in the parish church, never. We participated in the youth centers of the MAPU, the Communist Youth, the Socialist Youth," he recalls. During the UP, the Catholic youth and the JOC from parishes San Cayetano, Santa Cristina, and Espíritu Santo formed an association with approximately eight hundred members that extended throughout the Decanato San Joaquín.[35]

The Communist Party, though, remained the principal organization in La Legua.[36] They organized social gatherings, block committees, community organizations, and campaigns to improve urban infrastructure. They cooperated with the Church and formed alliances with members of other political parties. Over the years pobladores also joined the Socialist Party, Christian Democrats, MIR, MAPU, Christian Left, and the right-wing National Party. La Legua's politics were at times contentious and represented a lively, pluralistic democracy. As parish youth joined left-wing parties in the 1960s and early 1970s, some left the Church to dedicate themselves to party work. "Those in the Communist Youth had always been in the Communist Youth," remembers Juan R., "no problem with that. Those in the Socialist Party, given the opportunity, formed their own youth centers. [As for] the MAPU, of course all the kids came through the parish, the Christian Left as well. We had double militancy in the party and in the parish."[37] This web of young leftists and Catholics organized summer camps, volunteer work, and sociopolitical education campaigns. It was "an entire educational campaign with young people from the poblaciones where we mobilized a more integral social and political formation."[38] He remembers too that local Catholic youth participated in the movement culture of the UP and in local politics.[39]

At the time of the coup, pobladores of La Legua were active in political parties, labor unions, the Church, and a wide range of community organizations. They participated in local, municipal, and national politics, and most supported Salvador Allende's UP government.[40] After the coup, Juan R. explains, "about a year and half afterward, the groups appear again, and those who formed the groups during the UP, from before, reincorporate themselves."[41]

Villa Francia

Villa Francia formed in 1969 through the Operación Sitio program. Many of the people who settled Villa Francia had previously organized themselves into comités sin casa in the areas of Santiago in which they lived as allegados. Villa Francia's residents included a mix of Socialists, Communists, Miristas (MIR members), Christian Democrats, rightists, and people without party affiliations. Many worked in construction, the textile and other manufacturing industries, the public health service, the state railway company, and

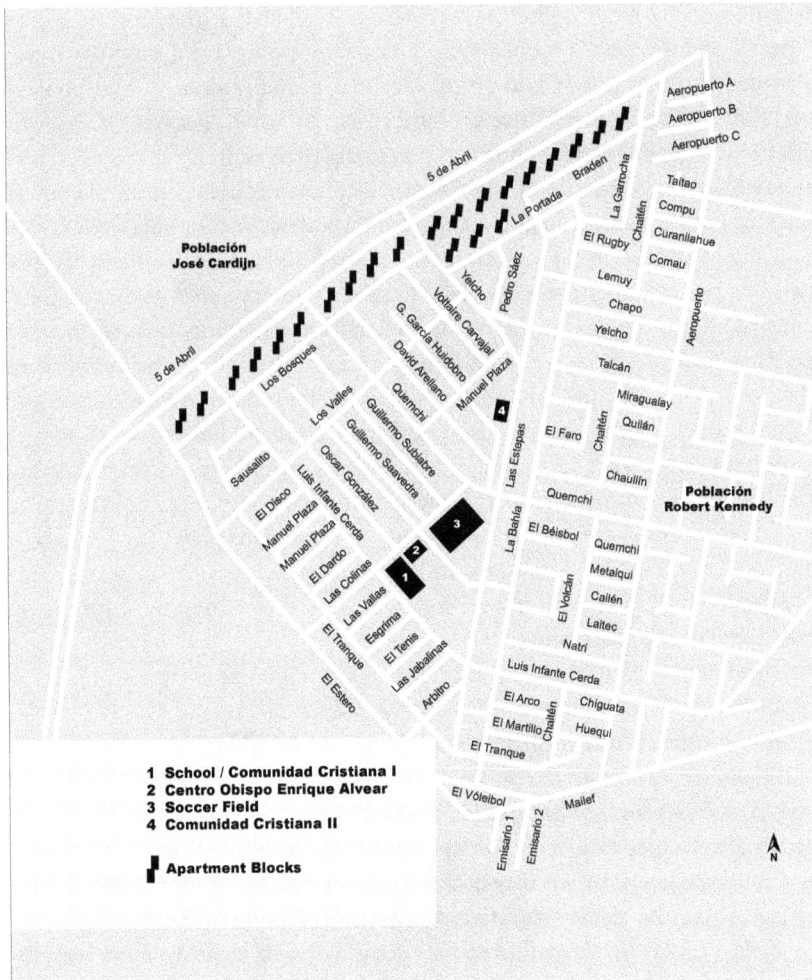

Población José Cardijn

Población Robert Kennedy

1 School / Comunidad Cristiana I
2 Centro Obispo Enrique Alvear
3 Soccer Field
4 Comunidad Cristiana II

Apartment Blocks

Map 5. Villa Francia

transportation. Villa Francia's residents settled a fast-developing, semirural area of the municipality of Maipú that had been a landed estate called San José de Chuchunco.[42] Población José Cardijn, across Av. Cinco de Abril, had already begun in 1963 as a housing cooperative that included many Christian Democrats, members of the Movimiento Obrero de Acción Católica (MOAC, Catholic Action Worker Movement), and neighborhood leaders who were "what today we would call socialist left or Christians for socialism," one resident explains.[43] Across the street from José Cardijn, where the poblaciones Villa Francia and Robert Kennedy would be, were fields dotted with peach trees and willows. "We arrived and it was countryside," remembers Luis, and "the only thing in Villa Francia were some small stakes [marking sites]. . . . There were no streets or numbers. . . . The people put up primitive huts, it was summer, [so] they improvised things with plastic and cardboard, to sleep in at night."[44] The pobladores arrived to find twelve hundred sites but no water or electricity. The first order of business was to dig latrines, install standpipes, and run wires to Av. Cinco de Abril to *colgarse* (siphon electricity) from the power lines. Some pobladores acquired two-room wooden shanties called *mediaguas* to live in while they built their houses.[45] In 1969 and 1970, Villa Francia's residents began building their houses through the state's *autoconstrucción* (self-construction) program but found the materials to be of poor quality. "So, the pobladores rejected them until a building materials 'factory' was installed in the población to supply solid materials," write pobladores in a local history.[46] Many residents were construction workers who knew how to build homes and urban infrastructure to their and their new neighbors' benefit.[47] During the UP, the government built 736 apartments along Av. Cinco de Abril. The apartment blocks—technically a separate población named Villa Canadá—are popularly considered part of Villa Francia. In 1971, comités sin casa including National Health Service workers, railway workers, and taxi drivers took over some of the apartments.[48]

Oral history narratives and local histories emphasize two pre-coup organizations in Villa Francia: a Comunidad Cristiana Popular (CCP, Popular Christian Community) called Cristo Liberador, and a Comité de Abastecimiento Popular (CAP, Popular Supply Committee). Local narratives about these organizations highlight pobladores' political pluralism and capacity for self-governance. These experiences were important to local political culture before and after the coup, which may account in part for the emphasis they receive in post-coup oral history narratives and local histories.

Cristo Liberador was affiliated with Jesús de Nazaret parish.[49] It was established in 1972 by the priests Mariano Puga, Pablo Richard, and three seminarians who moved to the neighborhood in May 1971. Comunidades Cristianas

Populares like Cristo Liberador were a type of *comunidad cristiana de base* (Christian base community). In the Chilean context, "comunidad cristiana de base" denotes organizational form, not theological or sociopolitical orientation. CCPs were a type of comunidad cristiana de base that adopted the tenets of liberation theology, combining religious practice with social action.[50] In Villa Francia, pobladores refer to Cristo Liberador simply as *la comunidad cristiana* (the Christian community) or *la comunidad* (the community).

Cristo Liberador's priests practiced liberation theology, and several were *curas-obreros* (worker-priests). Worker-priests and worker-nuns acquired working-class jobs and lived in poblaciones in solidarity with the people they wanted to serve and evangelize. They sought to build a new grassroots church closer in form and function to what they imagined the original Christian church to be, and they hoped to convince the Catholic hierarchy to support "base communities in which the worker feels at home."[51] Chilean worker-priests' decision to live in poblaciones and work alongside low-paid laborers set many on a path of religious and political radicalization that intensified during the UP. Still others had participated in the Catholic Action Movement during the 1950s and 1960s where they developed dedication to the poor and the issues affecting their lives.

In a departure from traditional practice, Villa Francia's priests held religious meetings in pobladores' homes and participated in local daily life. Fr. Puga worked in the housing materials factory, and Fr. Richards counseled a youth group.[52] By April 1972, Villa Francia's clergy and active lay Catholics had organized committees to prepare people for First Communion and tend to the sick. That October, as the Paro Patronal (Bosses' Strike) against the Allende administration unfolded, Cristo Liberador's laypeople decided to pursue "active Christian participation in the construction of the new society," endowing the comunidad with a decidedly liberationist and left-leaning orientation. In early 1973, Puga departed to northern Chile, where he, along with Fr. Rafael Maroto (who had been parish priest in La Legua), Fr. Roberto Bolton (who would move to Villa Francia after the coup), and others joined Fr. Juan Caminada's Calama Group, a project oriented toward building a church from and for the working classes. The experiment ended before the coup, and Puga returned to Villa Francia, where, in his absence, Cristo Liberador's laypeople had kept the comunidad alive.[53]

The CAP formed in response to consumer shortages, ineffective Juntas de Abastecimiento y Precios (JAP, government-affiliated supply and price-control organizations), and a MIR campaign to build local *poder popular* (popular power) as an experiment in grassroots self-governance and revolutionary democracy. By 1972, access to essential food and household products had become an arena of political conflict across Chile, and Villa Francia was no exception. To ameliorate shortages and combat the black market, the Allende administration formed JAPs to regulate prices and distribution at the neighborhood level. In Villa Francia, the JAPs were originally controlled by the Communist Party but were later taken over by the Christian Democrats. "It was chaos," remembers Irene, "because they created shortages; they didn't distribute the products, they created a black market" by distributing nonessential products like bullion, salt, and tomato sauce and withholding essential products like rice, cooking oil, and detergent.[54] Others criticize the JAPs for favoritism and corruption.[55] In Villa Francia, political conflicts over the JAPs mirrored political tensions at the national level, as the Christian Democrat Party mounted opposition to the UP.

While Villa Francia's Communists and Christian Democrats sparred over the JAPs, Miristas and Socialists organized the CAP. The CAP worked directly with the Dirección Nacional de Abastecimiento y Comercialización (DINAC, National Directorate of Distribution and Commerce) and with local farmers and factories to circumvent middlemen. The CAP became a politically pluralistic association that included an Asamblea de Vecinos (Neighbors Assembly).[56] The CAP, together with the Asamblea de Vecinos, eventually surpassed the government-affiliated JAPs and neighborhood council in participation, mobilization, and matters of local governance. The CAP, members of Cristo Liberador wrote in 1980, "brought together most of the Villa's pobladores. It was possible to clearly observe different modes of awareness and ideology among its members, but seeking and struggling in an organized way to acquire their daily food united everyone." The CAP was also important, they wrote, because it "brought together men and women with political motivations and Christians and the great majority," and it "forged new leaders, especially youth who weren't yet twenty years old, alongside mature pobladores." The CAP "was widely recognized and accepted in the población," they continued, "to the point that its assemblies drew nearly 1,000 people."[57]

The Asamblea de Vecinos planned one of the most oft-commented instances of collective direct action in Villa Francia during the UP: the highjacking of several city buses to force the state bus company to establish a route through Villa Francia.[58] Cecilia remembers that "people from Villa Francia took the buses and forced the drivers to turn down Av. Aeropuerto, and obliged them to go into [Villa Francia]. And there, with sticks, the *viejas* took over the buses, making them enter."[59] As in La Legua and other poblaciones across Santiago, community cooperation, political engagement, and direct action were central to poblaciones' social, political, and physical consolidation and development. By the time of the coup, Villa Francia's pobladores had established a short but intense local history of sociopolitical activism and collective action.

September 10, 1973

On eve of the coup, the pobladores of La Legua and Villa Francia had already conquered *la casa propia*, but organization and mobilization had not dissipated. On the contrary: during the UP, organization and mobilization expanded and accelerated. At the time of the coup, La Legua was a mature neighborhood with well-established sociopolitical networks, organizations, and a strong Communist Party presence. Villa Francia was a still a relatively new población with precarious construction and infrastructure. Sociopolitical dynamics within the neighborhood were vigorous, but local political networks and alliances were younger and less firmly entrenched. Both neighborhoods had histories of self-governance, collective action, political effervescence, and links to organizations outside the community, including labor unions, political parties, and the Catholic Church. The Left and the Catholic Church exercised significant influence in both poblaciones, and their members often provided leadership within their broader communities.

After the coup, local activists reoriented their energy toward survival, resistance, and a return to democracy, building upon relationships forged in the pre-coup period. The pobladores movement did not disappear with the coup, but it did bifurcate. During the 1970s and 1980s, a double-edged pobladores movement emerged, one part clearly identifiable as a reemergent, "traditional" pobladores movement for affordable housing that was enmeshed within a much broader movement for survival, resistance, and change rooted in popular sector social organizations, the liberationist Church, and the grassroots left. This book focuses on the latter. Despite their different ages and origins, both La Legua and Villa Francia came to be known as "combative" poblaciones during the dictatorship. In both poblaciones, leftists and Catholics with pre-coup activist experience organized the first initiatives to repair the torn social fabric of their neighborhoods and resist the dictatorship.

2

The Coup and the
Past That Is Present

The dictatorship, for so many years, tried to persuade people not to return to the past: "Listen, forget it. Stop living in the past; these things have passed and you mustn't return." But what happens? It turns out that that past, it's inside everyone. It's in each person and it harms you, and not sharing it with others is harmful.

Anonymous, Santa Adriana[1]

I don't like to ask names, and I never remember anything.

R.S., La Legua[2]

Event, Memory, and Narrative

"When they killed Allende, it started to rain, and a señora who's dead now came running to the house to tell me, 'Señora Margarita, Señora Margarita, they killed the President,'" Margarita recalls. "She was crying hard, and I really didn't know what to do, or say, or anything." Earlier that morning, Margarita's husband arrived home to Villa Francia from his shift at the Philips plant in the nearby Cerrillos-Maipú industrial corridor and told her not to send the children to school. When she turned on the radio, "the kids woke up. 'Mommy,' they said, 'aren't we going to school?' And I told them to just stay put." Her husband tried to reach his workplace but military and police presence forced him back. Upon returning home, in a ritual that soon became commonplace throughout Chile, he began destroying documents that could compromise his family's safety. Margarita stepped outside and surveyed the neighborhood from the street in front of their two-room, wooden house, noting that the corner-store owner was selling hoarded goods.

While she watched the "*desgraciado*" (lousy wretch) profiteer, a military jeep pulled up to her neighbor's house, where a mourning flag flew for President Allende, and soldiers began pounding on the door.[3]

Across town in La Legua, don Luis had risen early to begin his day's work. He was at home, balancing his books and listening to the radio, when "at about 6:30 in the morning, I heard that the Armed Forces had taken Valparaíso. Damn, I sat there thinking. Then I put everything away, I went outside, and all the compañeros were there." The assembled pobladores "started to shout that we had to prepare ourselves—that we had to defend ourselves," but "nobody came to give us any news, no news, damn, only afterward we started to see the smoke rising from La Moneda." They waited for instructions and weapons but nothing and nobody arrived, "so we were orphaned."[4] Meanwhile, on the northern edge of La Legua, Juan and his friend ended their kite-flying games on Comandari's roof as a flurry of movement spread through the building below. Gunshots rang out, and the boys overheard that President Allende had been overthrown. "The shit's going to hit the fan," Juan told his friend, and they climbed down to street level near Callejón Venecia, a long alley hemmed by factory walls. The sound of gunfire and engines echoed through the Callejón as dozens of armed civilians moved through the alley toward La Legua. "'Compañero,'" one of the strangers told Juan, "'go home, because they overthrew our president. There's going to be an armed struggle, and this is the stronghold of Santiago.'"[5]

Coup histories such as these are integral components of collective memories of the dictatorship in poblaciones. This chapter works on two levels: first, reconstructing the coup from the vantage points of La Legua and Villa Francia, and then analyzing narratives that pobladores constructed about the event in the early years of the twenty-first century (2000–2006).[6] At the time, mainstream culture did not regularly and openly address the coup and dictatorship, and critiques of neoliberalism had not reached the mainstream as later occurred during the 2006 and 2011 student protests. The early twenty-first century was, Steve Stern has argued, a time of "memory impasse" in Chile, when no one interpretation of the dictatorship's meaning and significance dominated collective historical memory. However, during those early years the impasse periodically loosened as human rights activists demanded truth and justice, and as scandals erupted over discoveries such as Pinochet's financial corruption. The impasse was not static; it was a "rolling impasse" in which gridlock "coexisted with [human rights advocates'] determination and eventual capacity to build cumulatively in the medium run."[7]

In poblaciones, the early twenty-first century saw heightened circulation of *memorias soterradas* (underground memories) that combined interpretations of the dictatorship with acid critiques of the Concertación's perpetuation of political and social injustice. After the 1973 coup, pobladores—unlike middle- and upper-class sectors of Chilean society that, as a whole, enjoyed relative economic stability until the early 1980s—experienced intense, simultaneous violations of political and social rights as the dictatorship, at the height of the political terror in the mid-1970s, instituted neoliberal structural adjustment measures that decimated poor and working-class Chileans' livelihoods. These violations contributed to the association of social with political rights in popular sector political culture, while the same association was not as marked (when present at all) among the middle class and elite. This changed as the 2006 and 2011 student protests brought critique of neoliberal education policy to public attention, and as police attacked reporters and student protesters, inciting opprobrium in the media and among concerned public. Unlike class- and territorially based critiques already circulating in poblaciones, this latter-day critique of "the model" centered on the relationship between the student subject, educational institutions, and the state, and it constructed a de-classed (or, if anything, middle-classed) student-subject who seemingly transcended socioeconomic and territorial boundaries. However, the underground memories and critiques of political and social violence that circulated among pobladores rarely found resonance outside poblaciones at that time. Mainstream media generally ignored them except for protest dates such as the September 11 coup anniversary and March 29, the Día del Joven Combatiente (Day of the Young Combatant). On these dates the mainstream media and the concertacionista government produced negative portrayals of protests in historically "combative" poblaciones. In doing so they attacked and criminalized popular sector protest, further contributing to collective trauma and the continued marginalization of memorias soterradas, whose decades-long roots feed current sociopolitical processes.

With few exceptions, what happened in poblaciones during and immediately after the coup has long been ignored in both scholarship and mainstream Chilean society.[8] As a result, such stories circulate most plentifully in personal recollection, urban myth, and popular legend. El Mercurio and La Tercera, the two mainstream newspapers allowed back into circulation shortly after the coup on September 13, 1973, displayed pictures of what happened in downtown Santiago on September 11, not what occurred in poblaciones. In 2003, in recognition of the thirtieth anniversary of the coup, Chilean television channels ran documentaries that did not address, to any significant extent, what happened in poblaciones during and after the coup. Published memoirs too tend to represent the experiences of people who did not live in poblaciones.[9] Events downtown received the most media coverage and international attention, although most of the city's population was not downtown that day, most did not live in middle- or upper-class neighborhoods, and many spent the day at home in the poblaciones.

La Legua and Villa Francia became known as "combative" poblaciones during the dictatorship, although the day of the coup unfolded very differently in each. On September 11, La Legua went down in history as one of the only places in the country where armed resistance to the coup occurred, garnering a legendary status of international proportions. Villa Francia, meanwhile, was relatively free of police and military presence. The coup and its immediate aftermath in each neighborhood defined, to a significant extent, the conditions under which later social and political organization would occur. It was those pobladores who were social and political activists before September 11 who mobilized to respond to the rapidly shifting situation on the day of the coup.

Much social-science literature artificially separates the categories of "poblador," "worker," and "party militant" to better suit theoretical paradigms, but such separation is simplistic. Pobladores often belonged to all these categories at once, and more (i.e., student, labor unionist, Catholic). Poblaciones were places of concentrated political and organizational experience and know-how, party-affiliated and otherwise. Some pobladores were apolitical and did not participate in party politics or neighborhood organizations. However, pobladores were no strangers to social and political struggle. They did not leave their accumulated knowledge at the door when they left the union hall or party headquarters or at the edge of the neighborhood when they left home. As a result, social and political alliances at the grassroots did not always align with official state or party policy or with activists' and scholars' theoretical assumptions. Alliances that defied expectations or official institutional positions appear repeatedly in pobladores' narratives about the coup and the dictatorship, as do examples of community relations that fractured for political or personal reasons.

In oral history conversations, the coup narratives that people construct refract through a prism of events spanning several decades: the experience of the UP, the coup itself, the dictatorship, and a transition to democracy that was generating increasing disillusionment at the time the conversations took place. In the case of the grassroots left, an overarching layer of disillusionment must be added to the prism: the 1973 coup, the FPMR's failed attempt on Pinochet's life in 1986, and the dissolution of the USSR as Chile transitioned to civilian rule. Narratives cannot always be disentangled from their contributing currents of experience and the internal worlds of their creators. However, remaining attuned to both dislocations and continuities within and between narratives offers intriguing windows into the lived experiences of these historical processes in popular sector Santiago as people simultaneously interpret the past through the present, and the present through the past. Until relatively recently, pobladores who resisted the dictatorship were reticent to talk about their experiences, and many still are. State-perpetrated repression was widespread in Santiago's poblaciones, and, as noted in the introduction, police repression is a continuing problem in some neighborhoods. One result is that in poblaciones, caution and secrecy were so important for so long that they have become a habit for some and remain a prudent self- and community-defense policy for others. Nevertheless, people remember and the memories hold power.

Discussion about secrecy often emerges during oral history conversations in poblaciones. Caution, especially where clandestine political activity and armed resistance are concerned, remains strong and deserves to be treated with delicacy and respect. Disagreements break along political and generational lines. For example, Renato Moreau, one of the militants from outside La Legua who fought there on September 11, states that members of La Legua's Communist Youth fought alongside the Socialists from outside the población and that pobladores took weapons from a police bus to continue fighting.[10] However, the older generation of political activists in La Legua is careful to protect the identities and details of locals' participation in the day's events. Don Ernesto, who lived on Toro y Zambrano where part of the firefight occurred, recounts that on September 11 a pickup truck with fifty machine guns stopped on the corner, and so many people wanted to fight that there were not enough weapons to go around. "All the youngsters wanted weapons and things to fight with," he explains. "They desired to fight; they wanted to fight with machine guns in hand."[11] He does not, however, specify who fought. Don Luis is even more careful to emphasize that those who fired on Carabineros that day were people from outside the población. Reticence to directly implicate individual legüinos, especially young people, in the day's most violent and controversial events is particularly strong in don Luis's 1948 generation of La Legua's Communists. By the twenty-first century they had endured one or more periods of clandestinity and persecution, including the torture and execution, disappearance, or exile of many of those who witnessed or participated in the events of September 11. Margarita D., of the generation of 1968, explains that what might initially seem an excess of caution is because "[don Luis] is an old-school Communist, and he says that nothing should be said because you never know what could happen later." She disagrees, commenting that "we have to go ahead and talk" because, should a coup happen again, "at least a testimony should remain."[12] While caution and secrecy present challenges, more important in this case than the question of *who* took up arms is *how* pobladores approach the issue and what this can tell us about local political culture and memorias soterradas.

A similar situation arises with discussions of solidarity, another theme that frequently emerges in conjunction with conversations about the coup and resistance. Narratives of the coup in La Legua include accounts of some pobladores acting in solidarity with anti-coup combatants from outside the neighborhood and some withholding solidarity from wounded policemen. Accounts of the weeks and years following the coup include stories of solidarity extended (sometimes openly, other times clandestinely), solidarity denied, and even betrayal perpetrated between and among neighbors. Establishing whether pobladores were solidary by nature is irrelevant: sometimes they were, and sometimes they were not. Individuals were selective in their practice of solidarity. More relevant is consideration of the practice of solidarity or lack thereof at specific junctures, and the coexistence of solidarity with betrayal in the same communities. These were potent undercurrents that influenced political culture and social relations in poblaciones during the 1970s and 1980s and continue to manifest themselves today, as pobladores lament the loss of or point to ongoing examples of solidarity in the post-1990 neoliberal democracy, as explicitly or implicitly situated against the backdrop of the dictatorial past. As the examples of armed resistance and solidarity suggest, rather than focusing on information or details that are not forthcoming, paying attention to the interplay between information that *is* shared and the silences, redirections, and indirect approaches that interlocutors employ to broach certain topics offers insight into the more subtle textures of political culture and historical narrative.

This chapter reconstructs the coup in La Legua and Villa Francia, decentering the analysis from its usual locus in downtown Santiago and the perspectives provided by middle- and upper-class vantage points. It then analyzes narratives about the coup produced in poblaciones, highlighting memorias soterradas that combine past and present. The most salient themes embedded in these coup narratives are violence and fear, resistance and solidarity, anger, justice, loss, and cross-generational experience. The stories matter, as Alessandro Portelli writes, because they "communicate what history means to human beings. . . . It may not be a true tale, but it was really told by a real person."[13]

All Those Days of the Eleventh

The experience of violence is a central feature of coup narratives in poblaciones, and pobladores often compress numerous violent events into a single running narrative with little regard for spacing over time. Nevertheless, it is possible to differentiate recurring reference points corresponding to the run-up to the coup, the coup itself, and the period immediately following it. In Villa Francia and La Legua, conversations incorporate more than just September 11. Discussions of "the coup" extend from several weeks before the event to about a week after the September 11 military onslaught. As one man from La Legua explains, "here on September 11 we held on, and we resisted until [September] 16, when all hope and everything was lost."[14] In La Legua, it was not until September 16—when the military conducted the first of several mass *allanamientos* (search raids) in the neighborhood—that the coup's irrevocability hit home. A woman from La Legua refers to "all those days of the eleventh," adjusting the common euphemism for the coup, "the eleventh" ("el once") to fit her experience of a coup that lasted longer than one day.[15]

In the popular sectors, a man from Villa Francia recalls, the coup "started selectively, beforehand. Afterward, it was declared."[16] Before September 11, the military raided the factory where he worked, a process repeated nationwide under the auspices of the Weapons Control Law, which allowed the military to search property with little civilian oversight. The raids disproportionately targeted the popular sector left and UP supporters. In a speech delivered two days before the coup, Carlos Altamirano, then senator and secretary general of the Chilean Socialist Party, reported that only three of seventy-five raids carried out between July 2 and September 6, 1973, targeted the Right.[17] Shortly before the coup, the Air Force raided factories in the vicinity of La Legua, including Mademsa and Madeco. On September 7 the Air Force attacked Sumar-Nylon, provoking consternation among pobladores, workers, and political leaders.[18] The raids extended to working-class residential areas, as in the cases of the Metropolitan Cemetery—located amid poblaciones in southern Santiago—and población Germán Riesco, near Sumar and La Legua.[19]

At home, pobladores sympathetic to the UP endured threats and rumors of violence during the weeks preceding the coup. Several rumors circulated in Villa Francia, including one that the Right would blow up a nearby gasometer, destroying the neighborhood along with it. Surveillance and threats created a climate of fear before September 11. At a school in población Dávila, an alumna recalls, surveillance of student leaders and pro-UP teachers began around the time of the June 1973 *tanquetazo* (a failed tank putsch). Residents of the apartment blocks at Villa Francia's edge noticed strange vehicles in the neighborhood before the coup. The threatening climate unsettled UP supporters: "One night they came by," shortly before the coup, one man explains, "throwing telegrams under the leftists' doors." They threw one under his door that said "*Jakarta va, prepárate*" [Jakarta's on, prepare yourself], in reference to the Indonesian anti-Communist massacres of 1965–66. "And," he continues, "they marked the apartments. . . . At night when I arrived home, more than once I found a Chilean-flag stamp stuck on the door, and they were only on leftists' apartments." The intimidation stoked fear because "you didn't know what they were planning, in what moment they would arrive. We knew what had happened in Jakarta, we knew what was happening in Brazil and Uruguay." Who "they" were was unclear, a woman adds: "You never knew if it was the military or the Christian Democrats who went around infiltrating the houses. So, it was a situation in which you were careful, you had to [think] 'ok, this one is leftist, I can talk with him. With this other one, no.'"[20] Nevertheless, the days immediately preceding the coup were relatively calm within a general atmosphere of political tension. The UP leadership estimated that a coup might occur during the week of September 17.[21] For those with an ear to the ground, the timing, not the coup, was the surprise.

The Coup in La Legua

Many pobladores began September 11 going about their usual business, but by midday the pace of life changed. In the morning, children went to school, and adults went to work, attended appointments, and ran errands. One of don Luis's neighbors left La Legua shortly before eight in the morning and crossed downtown Santiago to the northern municipality of Recoleta without noticing anything amiss. When he heard about the coup, he returned home. On the way, he noted how the city had changed: "How they sowed terror, I tell you, seeing the streets like that, dirty, empty, with a silence of death. . . . We were the only people on the streets, until we got to the población." There, in La Legua, "everyone was in the streets."[22] Mothers hurried about collecting their children, men and women returned home from work, children watched from street corners and doorways, and Communist and Socialist Party members discussed the situation. Rumors spread that the Air Force would bomb the poblaciones. The Air Force had bombed La Moneda and the president's residence, and the junta threatened at least three times that day to attack workers, factories, homes, and groups resisting the coup with "land and air forces" using "the same energy and decision" employed in the attacks on its earlier targets.[23] As news of the destruction of La Moneda and Allende's death spread—it was yet unclear whether the latter was true or how it had occurred—industrial workers decided whether to occupy their factories, schoolchildren and workers headed home, and pobladores gathered in the streets of their neighborhoods. Meanwhile, the military surrounded downtown Santiago and occupied thoroughfares, silenced opposition radio stations, and isolated industrial corridors and poblaciones, trapping the civilian population in the web. It was in this context that Juan met the armed strangers in La Legua's Callejón Venecia.

Most of those strangers were members of the Socialist Party's armed apparatus. Early that morning, as don Luis balanced his books and Juan prepared for school, news spread via party networks, telephone, and radio that the coup was in progress: the Navy had invaded Valparaíso. Leaders of the Socialist Party's political commission met that morning at the Fesa factory in Maipú, and at around 8:30 a.m. about 130 members of the Socialist Party's armed apparatus gathered at the Corporación de Mejoramiento Urbano (CORMU, Urban Improvement Corporation) stadium to await weapons and instructions. Surviving participants report that the group possessed 140 AK-47s with 120 rounds each; four RPG-7 shoulder-fired rocket launchers with six rounds each; one .30 machine gun; and personal sidearms. In other words, writes one survivor, they only had enough "for a single battle."[24] Later that morning, the Socialists set out from the CORMU stadium to meet representatives of the Communist Party and the MIR at Indumet, a factory near the northern border of La Legua convenient to industrial corridors San Joaquín, Santa Rosa-Gran Avenida, and Vicuña Mackenna. At Indumet they found approximately three hundred people, among them industrial workers, labor unionists, and nurses. There, the Socialists Arnoldo Camú, Rolando Calderón, and Exequiel Ponce met with Miguel Enríquez and Andrés Pascal Allende of the MIR and Víctor Díaz and José Oyarce of the Communist Party. The Communist Party decided to monitor the situation. The MIR needed several hours to gather fifty fully armed fighters—too late for the Socialists' objectives, which reportedly centered on rescuing Allende from La Moneda and creating a "liberated zone" in popular sector Santiago.[25]

Carabineros from the Southern Prefecture attacked Indumet at about one o'clock in the afternoon, as the Miristas and Socialists—unaware of Allende's death—attempted to coordinate plans. The militants fought their way out of the factory under heavy fire, suffering casualties.[26] One group of Miristas, including party leaders Enríquez and Pascal Allende, skirted La Legua and reached safe houses.[27] The Socialists planned to regroup at Sumar-Polyester. They crossed Ave. San Joaquín (now Carlos Valdovinos), and, according to one participant, approximately two hundred people hurried down Callejón Venecia into La Legua Emergencia, where Juan and his friend saw them and climbed down from Comandari's roof.[28] Soon after, twelve-year-old Delia watched as dozens of armed civilians paused in front of her house. Delia was not afraid because her mother said that "they were the compañeros; they were the ones who were going to fight for us." Delia's mother gave the strangers fruit, water, and a ladder to look out over the rooftops and orient themselves.[29]

The strangers offered weapons, but her mother, María, refused, because "if we didn't know how to shoot, how were we going to take up arms?"[30] María's reluctance to take up arms was a common response.

Despite theories about the revolutionary nature of the working class, the combatants did not have enough weaponry or ammunition to arm a significant number of pobladores or workers, nor did many pobladores or workers have the desire or training necessary to take up arms. Training, without weapons and ammunition, is of little use; meanwhile, those who had training and weapons cite lack of ammunition as a significant problem. The Communist and Socialist Parties' armed apparatuses were prepared to protect leaders, guard property, and repel right-wing paramilitaries.[31] According to Luis Corvalán, general secretary of the Communist Party (1958–90) and senator of the Republic (1961–73), between 1963 and 1973 the Communist Party trained approximately one thousand members in military tactics, strategy, and automatic weapons. Another two thousand received training in small arms, self-defense, and street fighting. How much weaponry and ammunition the Communist Party had at the time of the coup is unclear—Corvalán describes it as "limited"—and the leadership deemed it insufficient to successfully confront the military.[32] The Communist Party's strategy had been to respond to right-wing threats with unarmed, mass mobilization. Nor did the Socialist Party and the MIR possess the means to successfully confront the military. Both the Grupo de Amigos Personales (GAP, Group of Personal Friends)—Allende's bodyguards—and the Socialist Party's armed apparatus (essentially two divisions of the same organization) had weaponry and combatants, some of whom had participated in the Chilean Ejército de Liberación Nacional (ELN, National Liberation Army), an organization associated with the Bolivian guerrilla movement of the same name. Members of the GAP were at the president's residence at Tomás Moro and at La Moneda on September 11. After the Air Force bombed the Tomás Moro residence, some made their way to Sumar-Polyester with weaponry, where they joined workers and Socialists who had fled Indumet. The MIR was unprepared to confront the coup, if its leadership's ability to muster only fifty fully armed fighters late on September 11 is any indication. Throughout the period leading up to the coup, as right-wing violence intensified and US efforts to drive Allende from office continued, Allende refused to arm the *pueblo* or form civilian militias. Notwithstanding fiery rhetoric, the government, UP, and MIR generally refrained from meeting right-wing provocation with violence.[33]

The Left's strategies rested upon the theory that in the event of a coup the military would split between those who supported the coup (*golpistas*) and those who would defend the constitutionally elected government (*constitucionalistas*).

In this scenario, the parties' armed apparatuses would support the constitutionalist forces. The parties were unprepared to repel a military coup on their
own. The Communist Party's central committee decided not to mount armed
resistance to the coup at approximately two o'clock in the afternoon.[34] One of
La Legua's Communists recalls that an emissary from the regional committee
reached the neighborhood that afternoon with news of the decision and
advised them to remain alert. "We waited until four in the afternoon," he
explains, "since the rumor was circulating that General [Carlos] Prats was
advancing on Santiago from San Fernando with an armed column; we would
join them."[35]

Rumors of General Prats's impending advance on Santiago is one example
of the disconnectedness and lack of information that was particularly acute in
poblaciones, where activists lost contact with party and labor networks, media
access was limited, and pobladores had difficulty returning home as public
transportation slowed to a trickle and then stopped. Leo, a UP supporter who
walked from downtown Santiago through the municipality of San Miguel on
the day of the coup en route to a political rendezvous that never materialized,
witnessed the prevailing disorganization. "I had a surreal experience as I was
walking," he recalls, "for example, I reached a plaza and there was a small
población with wooden houses, and the houses were full of bullet holes, and I
found a woman with her child hidden on the ground, and I said, 'No, look,
they're not here anymore.' She didn't dare come out." Later, he passed a Socialist Youth headquarters, and "I asked them what they were doing, and they
told me, 'We don't know what to do, but we have some explosives.'" They gave
him a box of "nails, fulminates, and ammonium gelatine—I mean, you mix
that and it all explodes—so as best I could I took the box, went into a corner,
separated the stuff, and said, 'OK, throw this out.' There you see a little of
how lost people were that day, everything was disconnected."[36] "Of course,"
María Inés, a *legüina* affiliated with the MIR, explains, La Legua "wasn't prepared, as a población, for the coup, no. Because we had contact with compañeros who talked, who just argued a lot about the coup. But we also thought
that something would come from above. Imagine if there was nothing above,
what was there going to be below? Nothing was prepared."[37] Although it is
clear in retrospect that "nothing was prepared"—or, what was prepared was
insufficient and unsuccessful—at the time many pro-UP pobladores expected
something to have been prepared, and they awaited instructions. Should they
march downtown in mass support of the constitutional government as they had
done after the tanquetazo? Should they join workers in occupying factories
and industrial corridors? Would they receive weapons? Would General Prats
muster loyal soldiers? None of these things occurred, and disillusionment,

honed by the years of repression and poverty that followed, remained thirty years later.

Rumors of the imminent arrival of constitutionalist soldiers were widespread but ultimately unfounded. General Prats and loyal forces did not reach La Legua; the armed apparatus of the Socialist Party did. The Socialists who entered La Legua found themselves in unfamiliar territory and depended on locals to make their way to Sumar. La Legua Emergencia boasted a crooked grid, few obvious landmarks, and numerous dead ends. Their decision to cut through La Legua to reach Sumar, while made under duress, was not haphazard. After the September 7 raid on Sumar-Nylon, members of La Legua's Communist Youth had met with workers from Sumar to discuss what to do in the event of a coup. The MIR and the armed apparatuses of the Communist and Socialist Parties also met to discuss options. Drawing on these contacts, before the coup resisters left Indumet, someone called La Legua's Communist Party committee to ask about the possibility of escaping through the neighborhood. "To that we said, 'Well, I don't think it's possible, but . . . OK, I'll let them know,'" recounts Margarita D., who took the call, "because I couldn't make that determination either; at the moment the situation was very murky."[38] Local Communist Youth had been busy "counting how many people could fight, weapons, medical supplies, checking which houses had second floors, telephones, etc., and, especially, seeking information," explains Wladimir.[39] When the phone call came, the youth were walking toward La Legua Emergencia. They intercepted Arnoldo Camú's column near Comandante Riesle and San Gregorio Streets around three o'clock.[40] After a brief skirmish with police near Comandante Riesle and Maestranza Streets, the column reached La Legua's central plaza and crossed paths with the neighborhood's fire engine. They requisitioned the fire engine and sped toward Sumar.[41]

The confluence of armed militants seeking passage to Sumar with La Legua's Communist Youth was born of the exigencies of the moment. It was not entirely spontaneous, but neither did it reflect a detailed strategy or party directive. There is no indication that the Socialists initially planned to enter La Legua, or that the Communist Youth were expecting them before the phone call alerted them to the situation at Indumet. It also went against the Communist Party's official position: the party had not approved armed resistance to the coup, deciding instead to await further developments. Likewise, that morning, Allende had called on workers to occupy factories and remain alert—not to take up arms. On the ground, though, events had progressed beyond what party leadership could contain or channel. The Left's leadership was moving underground, and communication with the rank and file ranged from disrupted to nonexistent. The Communist Party's leadership had lost contact with the Socialists, the Socialist Party's leaders had lost contact with one other, and the MIR was in a similar state of disconnect.[42] In poblaciones and factories, though, labor unionists, pobladores, and party members were in contact with one another, and they variously plotted, cooperated, and quarreled. Despite political and social conflict on the local level, it was not uncommon for pobladores and workers—even on the fractious left—to cooperate in emergencies. This was the case in La Legua, where a diverse network of pobladores assisted, and some Communist Youth joined, the armed Socialists.

Camú's group reached Sumar-Polyester with the assistance of La Legua's Communist Youth and the neighborhood's fire engine, and there they joined workers and members of the GAP who had arrived from Tomás Moro. After shooting down a military helicopter, the approximately two hundred combatants at Sumar divided into several groups to relocate to Madeco, a factory southwest of La Legua. At least one group, led by Camú, crossed La Legua en route to Madeco in hopes of reuniting with combatants who had remained in the población.[43] Some of the latter were with Catimay, a local youngster acting as guide. His group had initially wanted to reach Madeco, but a messenger arrived and instructed them to regroup at Sumar. Catimay turned the group around, but near La Legua's plaza they encountered one of the groups from Sumar arriving with a pickup and weaponry. "They started to hand it out there at [the intersection of] Toro y Zambrano and Alcalde Pedro Alarcón," he recalls. Some of the Communist Youth helped by sorting ammunition, and "afterward," explains Catimay, "we wanted to continue on to Madeco . . . and an infernal firefight breaks out, on Álvarez de Toledo almost to Ave. Las Industrias, against a police bus."[44]

The police were passing through La Legua on their way to Comandari when they crossed the combatants' path. Earlier that afternoon, the police's 12a Comisaría of San Miguel requested reinforcements, reporting that "armed mobs" were attacking outlying police stations. Carabineros from the 22a Comisaría of La Cisterna, under the command of Major Mario Salazar Silva, responded.[45] According to Salazar, as they drove through La Legua "the bus advanced followed by me in the car, when suddenly, while we were going down a street that I think is called Los Copihues, the first vehicle suddenly stopped. I could see that a pickup had stopped at the corner and some eight individuals got out, armed with automatic rifles or machine guns, with which they immediately started to shoot at us." The Carabineros Martín Vega Antiquera and Raúl Lucero Ayala fell dead, and Salazar was wounded. Some policemen managed to flee in the bus, and others fought "until reinforcements arrived and they could abandon the scene."[46]

The Northern Santiago Prefecture answered the call for reinforcements with *tanquetas* (anti-riot tanks) and two shock-troop units totaling fifty-two men.[47] "As we reached Toro Zambrano and the corner of [Estrella] Polar [now Alcalde Pedro Alarcón]," the Carabinero Dante Toledo reported to *El Mercurio* a few weeks later, "they started to shoot at us. Suddenly from an improvised trench, a group shot at us with a bazooka. The rocket hit the front of the bus, broke the windshield, and fell inside. It didn't explode, miraculously. Otherwise, we all would have died."[48] Don Luis, who lived on Los Copihues, explains that "a bus appeared with armed Carabineros, and a youngster appeared—I don't know where he was from—with a bazooka, you understand. . . . He had the luck of I don't know what, the luck of hitting the bus right in the middle. . . . Some [Carabineros] fell down, some ran, the bus [was] destroyed, and others were dead."[49] Then the tanquetas fired indiscriminately, pobladores took refuge indoors, and the fight continued onto Toro y Zambrano, where "some youngsters" shot at the police from rooftops.[50] Garcés and Leiva have established that the principal actors that day in La Legua were armed Socialists, Sumar labor unionists, and pobladores who assisted the armed combatants. They fought against three tanquetas and two police buses—one on Toro Zambrano and another that was hit by a bazooka round near Álvarez de Toledo and Los Copihues.[51]

As the conflict continued, at least five coup resisters from outside the neighborhood fell dead or wounded, and the ambulance crews that entered La Legua aided only policemen. Pobladores provided first aid to coup resisters but were unable to treat severe injuries.[52] Deaths that day also included people uninvolved in the conflict. Earlier that day, pobladores found Juaniquillo, a fruit vendor, dead in the street. Later, during the firefight, Carabineros shot and killed Benito Rojas Miranda near San Cayetano. That same day, a military patrol shot Juan Manuel Lira Morales as he walked down the street with his wife; he died on September 12.[53] The violence terrified many. Seventeen-year-old Alicia was at home waiting for her husband to return from work. The violence threw her into a panic. "I just yelled," she explains. "I just wanted to leave, I just wanted to run away. I didn't know what to do. It was as if I were crazy."[54] The fight in La Legua ended near dusk. As curfew fell, pobladores, Socialists, and Sumar workers lay dead or wounded in La Legua's streets and houses. Surviving combatants from outside La Legua remained hidden in the neighborhood as the electricity was cut and the military isolated the area.[55] Medical personnel at the nearby Hospital Barros Luco/Trudeau received a call from La Legua requesting ambulances at around three o'clock on the morning of September 12. The ambulance crews responded but found only cadavers.[56]

Historias Populares

The battle in La Legua went down in popular history as one of the only instances of armed resistance on the day of the coup. La Legua's reputation as a combative población is partly based on this event, which was not the day's only confrontation between pro- and anti-coup forces but certainly among the largest and most deadly.[57] As inaccurate as some of the stories about the fight in La Legua might be, they signal several points important to researching the history of the coup and dictatorship in poblaciones. In the early twenty-first century, details remained fuzzy and certain subjects were off limits, especially the identities of pobladores who took up arms. The caution is rational: the dictatorship used this event to justify repression, and repression did not end, although it changed, with the transition to civilian rule.[58] Over the years the story of La Legua has been told, retold, and elaborated upon. In the neighborhood, the story includes embellished versions of the destruction of the police bus:

> JULIA: The thing with the bus was the eleventh as well. . . . It was the eleventh because there they ordered everyone inside.
> CARLOS: The bus was like a hot potato.
> MARÍA: They told me they burned it.
> JULIA: Yes, they burned it; the bus belonged to Carabineros.
> CARLOS: But that they grabbed a bus and killed everyone, no.
> JULIA: And they hanged [the Carabineros].
> CARLOS: Now that's a lie.[59]

As we see here, elaborations include hearsay and contested versions of hearsay, including the subject of retribution against police, a recurring theme in coup narratives. While many narratives highlight solidarity between pobladores themselves and between pobladores and coup resisters, few report solidarity with Carabineros. On the contrary, some include stories about withholding solidarity from the police, reflecting a class-based political solidarity that identified enemies of the UP as enemies of the *pueblo*. On the day of the coup, one woman remembers, an ambulance passed her home carrying a wounded Carabinero: "He asked for water, and my mama sent us all inside. She said, 'No, don't give them water; they're killing the pueblo, so let them die.'"[60] Regardless of whether this actually happened, narratives of retribution—active retribution, as in the case of the alleged hangings, or passive retribution, as in the case of withholding assistance—are embedded in many stories about the coup, and they are linked to ideas of justice. This aspect of coup narratives may have multiple origins: Carabineros fired on pobladores that day and repressed pobladores throughout the dictatorship, and, at the time the interviews were conducted, many still viewed the police as abusive and corrupt presences in the neighborhood.[61] They may also reflect an attempt to assert determinative power over events and processes experienced as alienating and uncontrollable.[62]

Stories of coup resistance in La Legua fed popular histories through the years of dictatorship and beyond. They stood to counter, to some extent, the government's demonization of the Left and pobladores during the subsequent decades. In contrast to narratives that express feelings of fear, disconnect, and lack of solidarity, versions of the story picked up and relayed by international solidarity networks focused on the combat in La Legua as a shining example of a solidary pueblo's resistance to tyranny. One example includes several sections on combat in Indumet, Sumar, and La Legua and addresses the destruction of the police bus: "The bus burns in a second; amid the firefight / it looks like a bonfire / or the end of the world. / With a deep roar / they begin the retreat / the soldiers disbanded / because the sovereign pueblo / with rifle in hand / is very respected."[63] The imagery is that of a people in arms, an ad hoc worker-poblador fighting force that sent the military packing from working-class territory. That the pueblo was not armed and that those who were armed drove out the police (not the military, which bided its time) was less important than the poet's objective of encouraging opposition to the dictatorship.

Although stories of the firefight tend to dominate coup narratives in La Legua, most pobladores there and elsewhere did not take up arms. Armed combat was not the only, or even the most important, aspect of poblador participation in the events in La Legua. Margarita D. and Cristina, a combatant from outside La Legua, highlight unarmed pobladores' solidarity with the coup resisters. Pobladores provided directions and first aid, and lent their homes as hiding places and parapets.[64] "The rest of the población participated en masse," explains Margarita D., "opening their doors to the compañeros." It was "an impressive thing, I'm telling you. I never would have expected it from certain people who weren't even leftists, but there was something like class consciousness."[65] Margarita D.'s description of the población participating "en masse" may involve some poetic license—it would have been impossible for one individual to account for all of La Legua's residents. What matters here is the emphasis on the solidarity of people whom Margarita D. did not expect to support the resistance.

Margarita D.'s description of solidarity from unexpected quarters and from more people than she expected is not implausible. Poblaciones were minefields of political conflict and entrenched social problems, but solidarity was not uncommon. The practice of solidarity and overlooking political differences literally created and built Nueva La Legua, the sector in which the battle occurred, and brought infrastructure and services to the población. What Margarita D.'s statement suggests is that in La Legua the coup and local firefight aroused solidarity among neighbors whose political sympathies led leftists to expect the opposite. In extremis, they defied political divisions and protected people who were defending a government that—in Margarita D.'s estimation—advanced their interests as poor and working-class people. They may also have deliberately subordinated politics to personal or community solidarity. In poblaciones, the flip side of narratives about "snitches" and betrayal is narratives about the protection of neighbors despite political differences, and solidarity in the face of a greater enemy.

The Coup in Villa Francia

Residents of most poblaciones experienced the day of the coup very differently than in La Legua. The most obvious difference was the absence of armed combat. Unlike La Legua, where coup narratives frequently include mention of the firefight regardless of whether the individual was an eyewitness, in Villa Francia no such collective core story emerges. Rather, limited encounters with military patrols, uncertainty, shock, lack of information, and political rancor between neighbors are oft-recurring themes. Villa Francia was farther from events downtown and in the dense industrial corridors and poblaciones of southern Santiago. There were few police and military patrols in Villa Francia on September 11.[66] Villa Francia's location placed it out of the main lines of fire on the day of the coup, but the day brought rapid change, uncertainty, and agitation to the neighborhood.

On the day of the coup in Villa Francia, Margarita watched soldiers pound on her neighbor's door. He "had put up a flag at half-mast with a tremendous black ribbon," she says, "and I look, and the *milicos* [a derogatory term for soldiers] were there: 'Take down the flag, *huevón*, take down the flag!' 'No, they killed the President, huevón,'" replied her neighbor.[67] The soldiers removed the flag and left. Margarita remembers this incident as "the first act of resistance, to see that he had the flag up. It was the only mourning flag I saw at half-mast, and he didn't take it down, and the milicos didn't take him away. . . . The next day there was another flag up on the corner . . . there at Juan's place, and they took him away. That was the first detention I saw." While some flew their flags at half-mast, others flew them high in celebration of the coup. Some pro-coup pobladores needled their mourning neighbors, to the latter's disgust. "I flew my flag at half-mast," remembers one resident, "and the woman across the street, who's good and dead, said to me: 'Who died, neighbor?' *Vieja conchesumadre*."[68]

Others felt disbelief, confusion, or the sense that the day's events were not as serious as others seemed to think. When Aida first heard the news, "I thought it wasn't real, that it was like propaganda." Another describes herself as "a little bird! I didn't know anything! I wasn't aware."[69]

On September 11 much of the opposition in Villa Francia involved discussing options, distributing food, and connecting with coup resisters from the Cerrillos-Maipú industrial corridor. In the neighborhood, Irene recalls, "after they overthrew Allende, everyone wanted to do something, to defend, defend."[70] Early that day, writes Eugenio Cabrera, a CAP organizer in Villa Francia at the time of the coup, activists met to decide what to do. There was no organized leadership, and they had little idea of how to resist.[71] "There were meetings here in the school," says Irene, "and they gathered bottles to make [Molotovs]. Pepe [her husband] told me that 'we're going to lay a wire so the jeeps will overturn,' that they were going to pour oil on the streets, so all the people, everyone, wanted to mount defense."[72] Some collected empty pisco bottles and first-aid supplies as activists called over loudspeakers for neighbors to rebel. Leaders of the CAP decided to distribute surplus merchandise. What began as an orderly sale, recounts Cabrera, turned chaotic as consumers crowded the counter and finally sacked the locale. Disorganzation reigned, and resistance fell short of activists' hopes. As in other poblaciones, activists in Villa Francia had little material to work with. Molotovs and homemade first-aid kits of cotton, bandages, and rubbing alcohol were insufficient in the face of well-armed military and police forces. Only as the day progressed did they realize that the coup was not just another "passing event" like the tanquetazo. "They still hadn't measured, internalized, or dimensioned what the full deployment of the Armed Forces' military power meant," writes Cabrera, and "naïveté was a preponderant factor in those moments."[73]

Substantial resistance on the day of the coup never materialized in Villa Francia, but some pobladores became involved with coup resisters from the Cerrillos-Maipú industrial corridor. Organized workers, Miristas, and possibly also Socialists from Cerrillos-Maipú had established contact with campesino and poblador committees and political networks in the municipality of Maipú and in Las Rejas (the subsector where Villa Francia was located), and on the day of the coup they tried to connect with them.[74] According to Guillermo Rodríguez, of the MIR's Military Commission in Cerrillos-Maipú, the military occupied the road running through the industrial corridor early in the day. The Miristas tried to mount resistance but had lost contact with the party. Meanwhile, explains Rodríguez, "there are no resistance foci in Santiago or environs, no armed forces units breaking away from the golpista command, no masses in the street, no information about what is happening in the country, we don't have weapons."[75] Nevertheless, workers from the Perlack and Fensa factories in Cerrillos-Maipú built barricades, coup resisters shot at a helicopter, and workers surrounded a truck carrying air force personnel. In retaliation, military helicopters fired warning rounds. Rumors spread that the military would sweep the corridor and evacuate Fensa where, according to Rodríguez, Communists and workers had occupied the factory. Faced with the impossibility of defending the corridor where whatever organization there was had collapsed, several Miristas set out as darkness approached to contact other party members, poblador committees, and workers (from Perlack, some say). Later that night, small groups of coup resisters gathered elsewhere in Maipú, including in Villa Francia.[76]

When several dozen pobladores, workers, and members of various parties gathered in Villa Francia, "one of the people from outside the población," recounts Cabrera, who attended the meeting, "mentioned the possibility that weapons would arrive, and that they would be handed out to the people, so there was a possibility of going out to fight." Even if weapons had arrived— and they did not—Cabrera writes that "except for one young man who had done his military service, nobody was prepared to take up arms in defense of the government." The meeting came to naught, and the attendees dispersed.[77] "I remember that Pepe arrived [home], very disappointed, and threw himself on the bed," Irene remembers. A militant from outside the neighborhood soon appeared at the house with two young men. He suggested that they try to reach the Sindelen factory in Cerrillos-Maipú, recounts Irene, "and that's when they confronted the jeep carrying the other compañeros. The ones from here shot at it, they shot it and overturned it."[78] The story of the jeep, a friendly fire incident that killed at least one, also appears in Rodríguez's narrative. Two groups of coup resisters operating near Cerrillos-Maipú unexpectedly crossed paths, and the group moving on foot opened fire on the second group, thinking it was a military patrol. Shrinking groups of resisters harassed military patrols on local roads late into the night, before seeking safety.[79]

It was becoming increasingly clear to coup resisters in poblaciones, who had been cut off from reliable information for much of the day, that the coup had succeeded. September 12 dawned with the city under curfew and dead bodies lying in La Legua's streets. La Legua remained eerily free of large-scale military and police presence until September 16, when the military launched a mass allanamiento (search raid) in the neighborhood and imprisoned hundreds of legüinos in El Bosque Air Force Base and the National Stadium. The new circumstances soon became clear to pobladores in Villa Francia as cadavers appeared in the nearby landfill and neighbors disappeared into political prisons. On September 19 several pobladores went to the landfill, where "we saw

The Coup and the Past That Is Present

the driver from the gas station in Plaza Brasil . . . dead! That was the first dead person they dumped here, afterward they came at night to dump them."[80]

Memorias Soterradas and the Past That Is Present

The coup converted poblaciones and factories into territories of violence, strategic nodes of a repressive web whose objective was to destroy the growing political and economic influence of the Left and poor and working-class people.[81] Pobladores were not necessarily strangers to violence: many neighborhoods emerged from land invasions and squatter settlements that met with police repression, and poblaciones were not free of domestic violence and crime. The violence of the coup and its aftermath, though, were unprecedented in the experience of most Chileans at the time. Its repercussions are still rippling through Santiago's poblaciones. As Clara Han has found, "state violence is experienced as a past continuous that inhabits present life conditions."[82] It is Han's "past continuous," Bevernage and Aerts's "irrevocable past" that "rejects the notion of a temporal 'distance' separating past and present," and Rose's "unpast" that highlights the historical continuity and social embeddedness of elite violence against the poor that I invoke with "the past that is present."[83] Memories of the coup—and evocations of the past that is present—coalesce around people, dates, events, and physical locations (or "sites of humanity, sites in time, and sites of physical matter or geography") as social actors struggle to ascribe meaning to these sites, forming what Steve Stern calls "memory knots on the social body."[84] Garcés and Leiva have identified people and events around which memories accumulate in La Legua: the dead and disappeared, the threat of aerial bombardment, the attack on the police bus, "solidary looting" of nearby businesses in the wake of the coup as supplies became scarce, and the September 16 mass allanamiento.[85]

In addition to people, dates, events, and physical locations, memories of the coup in poblaciones quietly coalesce around less tangible themes that rarely find expression or amplification beyond the bounds of poblaciones. These are constituent elements of collective memorias soterradas that circulate outside the bounds of mainstream memory struggles and discourse, in part because they circulate among marginalized social sectors, and because they link the present to a dictatorial past that, pobladores suggest, has not passed. In these underground memories, pobladores levy a trenchant critique of the "democratic" present unwelcome in the elite-dominated, social and political mainstream. The underground memories combine themes of violence and fear, resistance and solidarity, anger, justice, loss, and cross-generational experience to produce a distinctly integrated set of class- and territorially contingent interpretations particular to the urban popular sectors.

Fear is an emotion often mentioned in relation to coup memories in poblaciones, and it was particularly strong in La Legua, where helicopters flew over and rumors of aerial bombardment proliferated. Many recall an apocalyptic terror so acute that they prepared to die together with their families in a last act of self-defense. One mother imagined poisoning herself and her children to spare them the horror of aerial bombardment.[86] As the military repeatedly raided the neighborhood in the weeks after the coup, another mother hatched a plan with her children: "'Here,'" she said, "'we're going to die: if they're going to take someone, we're all going to throw ourselves on top of them, so that they kill us all and no one is left alive.' . . . Even the littlest kid agreed."[87] When police dragged another family from their home at gunpoint, the parents held their children tight against their chests, "so that if they shot us through the back it would take the children too."[88] In La Legua, finding cadavers in the streets and seeing neighbors die were traumatic experiences that resonated with young and old alike.

Withstanding fear, some explain, brought strength of ambiguous value. "This has made us women harder, now we see a death and pay it no mind," a woman asserts; "a cadaver fell next to my house, and I didn't go out to retrieve it for fear they'd kill us too."[89] While this strength served as a survival mechanism, it was also a symptom of community-scarring trauma that—for a time, at least—swept aside cultural practices regarding solidarity, compassion, and death. The violence, part of a general assault on the popular sectors to atomize communities and repress pursuit of further socioeconomic reform, was relatively effective. "I had seen . . . activists they detained during the dictatorship," explains one woman, who grew up south of Santiago and later moved to La Legua, and "afterward I was afraid of joining institutions or organizations," even after the dictatorship had ended.[90] Others, advocating proactive preparation rather than defensive withdrawal, express a sense of urgency born of past experience and concern for the future. Social organizations and the Left should prepare to prevent a coup from happening again, argues a man who survived some of the worst of the dictatorship's atrocities, because "another coup will be even more terrible, alright? . . . They won't pardon anyone; anyone with a whiff of the Left, call it socialist or Christian Democrat, they're going to massacre everyone."[91]

Talk of fear and repression raises the themes of resistance and solidarity in memorias soterradas. Many longtime activists interpret the coup as a hiatus rather than a total rupture in a lifetime of activism. One way to access this

The Coup and the Past That Is Present

fundamental interpretive difference is to pay close attention to how darkness and nighttime appear in individuals' narratives. Night represented fear and uncertainty for some, and dangerous but potentially fruitful opportunity for others. The regime imposed nighttime curfews for years because it wanted to monopolize the dark and the opportunities for dominance and impunity it provided. The dark hours of the first night of dictatorship brought tanks, helicopters, and a shoot-to-kill curfew that would last several days. They also brought the advantages that the dark provides to those with deep knowledge of their local environs: which streets and alleyways intersect, which roofs hang low, which doors might open in an emergency. Activist pobladores tend to trace the beginning of resistance to the first twenty-four hours following the coup, including the dark hours of curfew, despite later interruptions due to repression.

During the night of September 11 and the early morning of September 12, much of the resistance activity in poblaciones shifted to safeguarding people from repression. On the night of September 11, in the darkness of La Legua, where the electricity was out and flares cut the night sky, many tried to dispose of weapons abandoned after the firefight. They discovered that security forces had surrounded La Legua, and they "couldn't get anything out." They adapted, seeking people within the neighborhood "who would agree to store the things. That took us until one or two in the morning."[92] Residents sheltered coup resisters from outside the población who were unable to leave. Others protected strangers fleeing repression in nearby factories and poblaciones. One woman who lived in the area remembers that her family hid fleeing youngsters in their house, "all of them quiet, all around, sitting on the floor, not even in the chair, quiet, there in the kitchen, on the patio, in the other room."[93] On the day of the coup, explains a woman from Villa Francia whose husband was a Communist Party activist, "we said goodbye, he left, and I saw him again about three days later. And from that very moment, he went to work. From then on he was always working, organizing the resistance. And he didn't stop. He never stopped."[94] Nevertheless, unpreparedness remained a matter of frustration in conversations about resistance and solidarity. Don Ernesto, of the Communist Party and La Legua, recalls that "we trusted Allende's masses, and we didn't organize ourselves militarily. I think that here, in La Legua, we had that experience: they caught us with our hands in our pockets in 1973."[95] Consideration of the value of armed resistance is evident in narratives about the coup in poblaciones, even—and perhaps especially—among the Communists whose party's official position, until 1980, eschewed armed struggle. This position changed significantly in the context of the dictatorship, occasioning reassessments of armed struggle, and oral history conversations reflect this process.

Anger is also a potent theme in memorias soterradas. News of the coup "enraged me," reports one woman in Villa Francia. "Lots of rage," a neighbor concurs.[96] Pobladores especially express anger with the police and military. "They say I should call them 'Carabineros,' no, to me they're *'pacos'* [a derogatory term]," a woman in La Legua says. "Half are the biggest murderers in the world. The Air Force is even more murderous," she continues, and the most murderous of all is "that man who unfortunately didn't die in the assassination attempt."[97] The latter refers to Pinochet, who is not often referred to by name but rather as "that man" (*ese hombre*); or, sarcastically, "that gentleman" (*el caballero ése*); "Pinocho" (combining Pinochet with Pinocchio, the lying puppet); "Perrochet" (combining Pinochet with *perro*, dog); or, simply, "the murderer" (*el asesino*). The nicknaming of state agents of repression served several purposes, including dark humor and plausible deniability: "*ese hombre*" and "*el caballero ése*" derive their derogatory spice from tone, not vocabulary. They are brief signals that encapsulate complex messages.

Anger also surfaces in conversations about people who taunted their pro-UP neighbors on the day of the coup or who denounced neighbors to the authorities. During one oral history conversation about repression in poblaciones, participants spent a significant amount of time discussing the matter of betrayal and naming neighbors who acted as informants during the dictatorship, arguing that their full names should be published because "it's good that these names be included in the history of the población, in the interest of the pueblo's dignity, when there were people who were traitors." Nonetheless, conflicts arose over the fine line between informants who acted deliberately and those who provided information without thinking or because they were "cowards." As one man put it, "There's a difference between snitching and being a dumbass." The anger surfaces when discussion turns to those who deliberately served as informants yet are "still walking around free and happy." One participant argues that remembering the names of informants during the dictatorship is just as important as remembering the victims, because "nobody knows what will happen in the future. One could find oneself dealing with this kind of person again."[98]

Talk of dealing justice to informants is part of a broader theme of justice that frequently enters conversations about human rights violations in poblaciones, perhaps because few perpetrators have been prosecuted. Stories—most of which are impossible to corroborate—circulate about covert actions against state agents during the 1970s and 1980s. One elaborate narrative from southern Santiago describes a plot in which attractive young women flirted with policemen or soldiers on patrol in their neighborhoods. When a targeted man was "*hirviendo de caliente*" (so hot-to-trot he was boiling) the woman would propose a nighttime rendezvous in the población. When the policeman or soldier arrived, male collaborators would ambush and kill him. These stories are not celebratory in tone, but they rarely express opprobrium of action against repressors. They focus, rather, on redress for injustice in the form of retribution dealt by pobladores themselves, outside the bounds of the formal justice system that was complicit with the repression.

Talk of post-dictatorship justice in poblaciones also refers to comeuppance achieved outside the bounds of the official justice system. In La Legua, violence associated with narcotrafficking increased during the time of these oral history conversations, and pobladores incorporated this into their analyses. "When I see the pacos in the población," explains one woman, "I say, 'Now they're paying for it, they have to come humiliate themselves so the narcotraffickers will give them money,' that's how I think, with lots of rage." She continues, "They're always going to win, but justice will have to be done before God someday." Yet divine authority alone is not enough, she argues, and must be complemented with human activity. "So just like people have always organized themselves— many have given their lives for their brothers—we still have a lot of organizing to do." "With time," she asks, "how will Pinochet be remembered? As a hero: hero of the murderers."[99] Here, justice is characterized as inevitable and its sources diverse—it manifests as narcotraffickers, divine judgment, and organized pobladores. In contrast to stories about the 1970s and 1980s, stories about the post-1990 period usually do not include tales of violence against repressors. But, like the dictatorship-era stories, the official justice system remains conspicuously absent in talk of justice under the Concertación.

Lost opportunity for social justice is a prevalent theme in memorias soterradas that cuts across generations. "I left Chile with a great deal of hatred for all of us," explains a man from La Legua who went into exile, "because I felt we wasted the tremendous opportunity to achieve the dream we fought so hard for, especially the [Communist Party's] old-timers." "When we were going to be happy," an old-timer interjects.[100] During the UP, many pobladores were able, for the first time in family history, to send their children to college and postsecondary institutes. For the first time, adults and children saw the real possibility that they would have stable, dignified work and educational opportunities. A woman from the Caro-Ochagavía sector who was in high school in 1973 also describes the coup's meaning in terms of happiness and loss. "We were all happy" during the UP, she explains, "our parents had dignified work, and we glimpsed many hopes and dreams to be achieved. We could go to university, we could study, we could do many things that were forbidden to us after the coup."[101] These comments strike at the heart of the sentiments of long-term loss related to the coup and their repercussions across generations, from "old-timer" Communists who had worked toward a more just society for decades, to a schoolgirl who once glimpsed a university education on the horizon. The dictatorship ended many *pobladores'* long-standing hopes and dreams, and social justice had not returned with the Concertación.[102]

Cross-generational experience is important when considering children's place in history. The common idea that children were too young to remember or ascribe meaning to the coup must be examined with care. They did not understand it in the same way as adults, but it did not pass unnoticed. "I was very little, how old was I? Ten years old, it was terrible, it anguishes me," says Alejandra, who lived in población José Cardijn. Family political culture and intergenerational dynamics were important to her experience. Belonging to a "leftist home" influenced her experience of the coup, which she came to understand through changes in her daily life. Before the coup, she recalls, "a very lovely activity leader would gather us together, and we made crafts with recycled paper, we drew on the streets and did things, and this ended." "When you're little and activities are cut off," she continues, "you figure out that the thing isn't good." Her mother lost weight from "sadness, and all that, so, just the same, you see your mom and you say, 'This isn't good.'"[103] María Teresa, who was thirteen or fourteen at the time, also experienced the coup as the end of better times that she juxtaposes against the dictatorship that followed. She remembers the UP as a time of happiness. She participated in the lively political culture: "The marches were marvelous, many people in the house, surely a great deal of conversation about political analysis, and I was always there just listening." She read *Paloma* magazine and learned about dictatorships in other South American countries. The coup "surprised me, because I noted the adults' anguish," she explains. The most salient impression was "the sensation of death. I remember that, I remember the day, and I remember the sensation it gave me."[104] Children watched adults' responses to the coup and noted its effect on their own lives and environments. They were not oblivious to the social and political context in which they lived.

It was often parents who interpreted the meaning of the coup and dictatorship for their children. It was challenging for parents to explain the coup and its aftermath, and few were able to shield their children entirely. The fear that violence generated reached far beyond the period of dictatorship. "If I'm still marked [by the experience]," asks one woman in La Legua, "the children, how must they be? They screamed like little animals. When they remember now, they cry."[105] Lucy, an adult at the time of the coup, explains that her son, whose father is a disappeared detainee (*detenido-desaparecido*), had argued with a neighbor who defended the military. She intervened and scolded the men for "'just spouting nonsense because you don't really know what it was like then; you've heard things from the grown-ups. For example you,'" she said to her son, "'you heard it from me.'" "'Even so,'" he replied, "'I think too, Mom.'"[106] One point of her story is that although he did not experience the dictatorship the same way she did, he observed and listened to her, had his own experiences, and developed his own opinions. Other parents avoided the subject entirely, and their children noticed. "I grew up with a history that became clear little by little," a young person says. "In the streets there were some murals commemorating things I didn't understand. People generally told me to shut up, that that time had passed." With this, his parents "tried to keep such a traumatic situation from happening again." "When we grow up under dictatorship," a man born in 1975 concludes, "we become dictators a bit, we harvest abusive power relations." The coup does not "affect" him, he explains; rather, "it constitutes me, and in that I don't have much to thank it for."[107]

Children were aware of the coup and in some cases tried to resist, but it was mostly older pobladores already active in social and political organizations— elders and young adults of the 1948 and 1968 generations, respectively—who took action on September 11. Family political culture, and family as a place of political education, did not disappear with the coup. On the contrary, their importance increased under the dictatorship as other spaces for political education closed. Young women and men who were children at the time of the coup eventually became the most active and numerous anti-regime street protestors, and their radicalization became a source of intergenerational concern as they joined their elders in political parties and community organizations.

Into the Abyss

Pobladores had few available resources to resist the coup. Myriad futile endeavors are burned into individual and collective popular memory, and they informed later decisions about resisting the dictatorship. But on the night of September 11, with their windows covered with blankets to hide the light of their candles, many families waited for the situation to pass, unaware that it would soon worsen considerably and that the dictatorship would last for seventeen years.[108] In La Legua, the September 11 firefight set the stage for a storm of repression against leftists, UP supporters, and community leaders. The intensity of repression in La Legua would profoundly affect the course of post-coup organization in the neighborhood. In Villa Francia, which maintained a lower profile during the coup, pobladores had slightly more room to maneuver during the following weeks, although many did not escape detention and torture.

Despite local differences, activists in La Legua, Villa Francia, and other poblaciones had coup experiences in common. These included persecution, repression, and the importance of social and political networks to survival and resistance. The coup often appears as a hiatus rather than an absolute rupture in activist narratives. The context changed, activities changed, ways of doing politics changed, and experienced activists adjusted. It was people opposed to the coup, and with previous organizing experience, who created the first opposition organizations in poblaciones under the dictatorship. The majority, however, initially withdrew from social and political activity. After the coup, remembers Gina from Pudahuel, organizations she participated in were "paralyzed by terror, fear, and incredulity. Mostly, looking back, I'd say, from naïveté—'No, this can't be happening; no, how can they be so barbarous; no, this can't happen'—an enormous naïveté."[109] Repression of pobladores was extremely violent and widespread, as the state sought to terrorize the active and organized urban popular sectors into submission. The following chapter analyzes state repression in poblaciones between 1973 and 1978 as the dictatorship sought to "make our compatriots return to the traditional ways," in which the poor and working classes did not pose a challenge to the power of the political and economic elite.[110]

3

The Economy of Terror, 1973–1978

A cold and dirty drizzle fell on that intricate and hermetic tapestry, spectrally lit by the strategic spotlights of the garden, and the light, far from giving the powerful monster life, highlighted the coldness of its construction, its overbearing and abusive volume. I discovered though, for whomever might want to see it, the real character of that excessive creature of multiple, sealed eyes. "It was made to be inaccessible" I thought, while I reread the letters of its frontispiece: Tribunals of Justice. . . . From the impenetrable cracks, there in the windows, appeared a weak liquid line, red and brilliant.

> Leonardo Sepúlveda Toro, "Algo se cuela por los resquicios" ("Something Is Leaking through the Cracks")[1]

P: How did you know [your husband's kidnapping/execution] was exactly like that?
G: Well, because I found out.
P: From some friends or what?
G: Because somebody always sees. Somebody always sees something.

> La Legua, 2000[2]

Something Is Leaking through the Cracks

"What's leaking through the cracks is blood," explains Leo Sepúlveda in 2004, indicating the book's cover art depicting thin red lines creeping down the peaks of the snow-capped Andes. The title story, "Algo se cuela por los resquicios," is a macabre tale of political and socioeconomic injustice in which the protagonist, pounding the pavement in search of work in the alienating atmosphere of downtown Santiago during the recessionary 1980s, notices blood trickling from cracks in the building housing the Tribunals of

Justice. The trickle quickly becomes a flood that inundates the adjacent business district, submerging passersby in a roiling tide of "boiling, frothing" blood. The "Supreme Government" declares the liquid not to be blood and the disaster a "monstrous joke," "terrorist propaganda" perpetrated by "insane authors" against "the dignity of all well-born Chileans." The authorities claim that the liquid's red color—"the color characteristic of international terrorism"—reveals that the perpetrators were leftists. They pump the blood into tanker trucks and transport it "to the north, to some unknown place in the enormous desert, where deep holes contained it. These were carefully filled in afterward. Nobody was able, then, to locate that place, but its existence is a fact known to all."[3]

The story critiques the combination of political and social injustice underlying 1980s society. It depicts a world in which the dictatorship's violence and lies, the neoliberal economy's noxious effects on workers, the justice tribunals' complicity with atrocity, and the general population's acquiescence all worked in concert to mask a deadly reality. Before the blood broke through the walls of the Tribunals of Justice, "people walked, the blood in each of them running its intricate paths, but somehow they were passive, inert, distant from the human tragedy in which, nevertheless, they were inevitable protagonists and accomplices." It pains him, he confesses, "to again feel that throbbing wound my people provoke in me with their hollow dignity, hidden behind that bloody veil that many decided, individually and collectively, to place before their eyes."[4] The story's protagonist addresses a sensitive matter: even before the sea of blood hidden behind officialdom's walls burst forth in stunning revelations of national proportions, his compatriots were aware of the injustice and violence of the society in which they lived. The dictatorship knew this, blamed the Left for the disaster, and buried the blood in the desert to deceive the public and provide plausible deniability for those who preferred to ignore reality. Although the evidence was hidden, the narrator concludes, everyone knew it existed, the subterranean pools of blood irrigating the "vast expanse of desert we're both in now, the enormous, live, and inexplicable garden that surrounds us, made up of thousands of perennial and anonymous red flowers."[5] The political and economic system rested upon the hidden blood of the dictatorship's victims, he implies, but their presence and the truth endured despite society's attempts to pretend otherwise.

As the story suggests, political violence and obfuscatory discourse were key to the implementation and maintenance of Chile's neoliberal economic model. In Chile, lofty philosophical rhetoric—that humankind's freedom depends upon capitalist free markets and noninterventionist states—accompanied the model's implementation. However, heavy-handed state intervention was among that model's central features. The version of monetarist theory imported into

Chile from the University of Chicago to the Universidad Católica, as applied by the Chilean economists known as the "Chicago Boys," was a radically exclusionary, "messianic and dogmatic" ideology that sought a fundamental restructuring of the economy, politics, and society in the name of freedom.[6] Yet "the only freedom they cared about," writes Peter Winn, "was the economic liberty of those Chileans and foreigners with capital to invest and consume."[7] Pobladores were not among those with capital to invest and consume. Rather, they came to occupy a central position within the system as a large un- and underemployed "flexible" workforce whose labor—compensated with paltry wages reinforced by repression, downward moral displacement, and anti-worker labor laws—generated employer profits. The regime did not fully adopt neoliberalism as official policy until 1975, but the coup set in motion a rapid process of political and socioeconomic dispossession that relied on violence to suppress organization and quell dissent as the new authorities rolled back popular sector economic and political gains of the previous decades.[8] The neoliberal transition of the mid-1970s and the maintenance of the economic model afterward relied on the sociopolitical atomization and demobilization that state-perpetrated repression secured. Ongoing violence and lack of transparency in government short-circuited opponents' ability to effectively respond to further structural adjustment measures, such as the 1979 Labor Code, trade liberalization that destroyed national manufacturing industries, and the commodification of health care, social security, education, and low-income housing.

Following the coup, the state combined mass repression in the poblaciones with selective political persecution to exact a high toll in lives and well-being as it centrally planned, implemented, and enforced structural adjustment measures. Repression in poblaciones—the urban working class's place of residence and physical, social, and cultural reproduction—sought to eliminate the Left, labor unions, and grassroots community organizations in its quest to build a "new Chile" organized according to archconservative interpretations of natural law and the ideology of Cold War anti-Communism. This nation-building project sought not a classless society but rather the naturalization of social inequality. The "new Chile" had little room for the urban poor and working class other than as obedient, inexpensive laborers who could be disciplined, exploited, and disposed of as profit-maximizing schemes and political expediency dictated. To this end, the regime used repression and what J. T. Way calls "downward moral displacement"—for example, blaming poverty on poor people's supposed moral failings and character flaws—in order to demobilize and stigmatize the urban popular sectors.[9] Repression and downward moral displacement reproduced and reinforced social authoritarianism, the hierarchies of ethnicity, class, race, and gender that "prevent the vast majority of de jure citizens from even imagining, let alone publicly claiming, the prerogative to have rights."[10] Official discourse and practice portrayed the urban poor as naturally unfit to have a say in the life of the nation or to partake equitably in national wealth and social opportunity.

As part of this process, repression in poblaciones sought to destroy the "social commons" that characterized pre-coup culture and that were a constituent element of community formation and historical memory in many poblaciones. Before the coup, community members openly commented on and mobilized around economic, social, and political matters relevant to their lives, and they did so in places of their own choosing, such as homes, streets, plazas, and community centers.[11] "Social commons," then, refers both to the ways in which pobladores addressed issues and the physical spaces in which they chose to address them.[12] The social commons arose from a shared and historically conditioned sense of neighborhood political culture and social space that included sets of evolving, unwritten rules governing the use of specific places and ways of interacting. It is the culture of the social commons that makes a community a community, something other than an inchoate or externally defined collection of people or city blocks, and Santiago was no exception.[13] Pobladores worked together to acquire spaces such as soccer fields and community centers precisely in order to facilitate deeper levels of social interaction in their neighborhoods, thereby engaging in an ongoing cycle of grassroots social, political, and cultural production in their residential territories. In many poblaciones the social commons were defined to a significant extent by the pobladores themselves, as residents exchanged ideas, intervened in the landscape, and wove themselves and their organizations into the *tejido social* (social fabric) of the neighborhood and the nation. This process was not harmonious—the social commons encompassed both conflict and cooperation. In general, though, and especially compared to the post-coup context, the pre-coup culture of the social commons was relatively open and democratic.

The concept of the social commons is useful for understanding the target, scope, and long-term repercussions of repression in poblaciones. One of the principal objectives of repression was to change the culture of the social commons: that is, to instill fear so that people would effectively police themselves, abandon their past social and political activities, and pull a "bloody veil" over their eyes, to borrow the imagery of Sepúlveda's story.[14] The dictatorship did this by attacking people in the places they inhabited on a daily basis and where their most intimate and public social interactions took place. Repressors used plazas and community centers as temporary prisons. They harassed and detained people for walking in the streets. They tortured people in their living rooms, ripping down curtains to make sure that neighbors would see. As these examples suggest, spectacle and manipulation of visibility were central to the regime's nation-building project. In addition to its practical applications (e.g., the physical elimination of opponents), repression constituted public spectacle in the service of terror: it was meant to be seen, to be heard, and to persuade observers to conform to new social, cultural, and political norms. After the initial spectacular onslaught of the coup—the military occupation of Valparaíso and Santiago and the bombing of La Moneda—among the most ubiquitous spectacles of repression were the mass allanamientos (search raids) of poblaciones and factories. Mass allanamientos served the purpose of terrorizing thousands of poor and working-class Chileans within concentrated, contiguous urban territories.

Selective repression targeting individuals deepened fear of the consequences for nonconformity. While less visible because of the relatively smaller scale of the operations involved, incidents of selective repression in poblaciones were, in their own way, visible matters of community import. Even in the case of disappearance, the most intensely secret repressive practice, the disappeared person's absence was visible, the fact of her absence was tangible, and her silence was "audible" in its conspicuity. In poblaciones, it was difficult for families to hide such an absence from the eyes of neighbors. The absence was visible not only to members of the household and the disappeared person's social and political circles but also to the local community. In this sense, secretive repressive practices such as disappearance were obliquely visible. When one woman's brother disappeared, she remembers, "friends disappeared, surely for fear because they knew he was gone, and others because I stopped visiting them for fear something would happen to them."[15] This type of repression served as terrifying public spectacle and destroyed community relations even as it constituted a secretive practice meant to annihilate and erase without a trace.

The fear generated by this ripping apart of the social commons fed a new culture of the social commons, the culture of the "bloody veil" of Sepúlveda's story. Pulling a bloody veil over one's eyes is strong imagery suggesting a complex sociocultural practice of knowing but not acknowledging, and being at once intimately involved in and profoundly alienated from the milieu in which one lives. The image of the veil underscores the act of simultaneously seeing and deliberately obstructing sight—sight passes through veils but not always in both directions, and never without a certain amount of obfuscation. It can facilitate the practice of secretly seeing, but in a context in which it is very dangerous to speak about or act upon what one sees, the secrecy itself can become oppressive. The veil signifies the interplay of visibility and invisibility and deliberate seeing-but-not-seeing such that a culture of acquiescence, silence, and impunity emerges that implicates broad sectors of society in its maintenance and reproduction. This destruction and reorientation of the culture of the social commons was central to the violence and the imposition of neoliberalism in Santiago's poblaciones: the "bloody veil" masked both political repression and the economic crises that neoliberal policies caused there. Central to the consolidation of neoliberalism was a combination of economics, violence, and downward moral displacement meant to delegitimize popular sector protest and claims to rights.

The Transition to Neoliberalism

Neoliberal ideology borrows selectively from Adam Smith's *Wealth of Nations* and is rooted in nineteenth-century neoclassical economic theory. Friedrich Hayek, Milton Friedman, and other scholars at the University of Chicago developed its contemporary form. The theory rests on a belief in the existence of a pure, natural market possessed of an "invisible hand." Within this market, human beings act as autonomous individuals motivated by rational economic self-interest. The theory's basic premise is that if the market, with its invisible hand, is left to operate freely, it will self-correct to maximize economic efficiency and equilibrium with the supportive action of technocratic economists endowed with the knowledge necessary to read and respond to the market's "signs." In this context, state regulation and collective interest groups such as labor unions represent all that is wrong with the economy: their interventions and pressure tactics distort the purity of the natural market and hobble its self-regulatory mechanisms. The emphasis on the market as a naturally occurring phenomenon set the foundation for neoliberal practitioners to claim that their brand of economic theory constituted a hard science based on laws of nature.

In Chile, neoliberal economists advanced a militantly fundamentalist belief that their theoretical models constituted an objective science providing the only path to "freedom, liberty and progress."[16] The claim to scientific objectivity was an ideological premise that served the political purpose of discounting competing theories, removing economic policy from the realm of public debate, and restricting the scope of people considered qualified to comment upon and intervene in economic affairs. It was difficult for dissenters to gain traction in policy discussions because neoliberal theory rested on deeply political and ideological foundations even as its promotors denied its political and ideological character. Dissenters were discounted as unqualified, ignorant, ideologically driven, and wedded to antimodern dogma.[17] In the Cold War context, this implied that dissenters' theories would lead to outmoded statist policies that could devolve into totalitarianism. Charges of "Marxism" or "communism"—dangerous accusations in Pinochet's Chile—could easily follow.

The thorniest conundrums facing applied neoliberal economic theory arise because its foundational premises are divorced from historical realities. One of the most significant challenges it faces is human behavior. Contrary to the ideology's foundational assumption that human beings are naturally motivated first and foremost by individual, rational, economic self-interest, throughout history people have organized collectively to further their economic interests as a group, sometimes to their own individual detriment, and they respond to both noneconomic and economic desires without necessarily privileging the latter. Because people do not consistently behave and therefore societies do not necessarily exist in ways conducive to the application of neoliberal theory, policymakers seek to create the conditions necessary for neoliberal economies to function. This need for social engineering shapes the state's role in implementing and maintaining neoliberal economies.

As David Harvey has shown, the state is central to neoliberalism despite neoliberals' rhetoric of nonintervention. The state suppresses political parties, labor unions, and other collectives that might protest structural adjustment measures. It privatizes public services, deregulates industries, and negotiates free-trade agreements. The state produces social-welfare, labor, immigration, finance, and tax legislation. State ministries, law-making bodies, judicial systems, and security forces shelter technocrats from political pressure, enforce property regimes, and repress protest. In Chile, as elsewhere, the implementation and maintenance of neoliberal policies have depended upon the state.[18] Contrary to neoliberals' anti-interventionist rhetoric, the question is not whether the state intervenes in the economy: the question is, on whose behalf and to what ends?

In Chile, the junta's ideological objectives of ridding society of the political practices, institutions, and cultures it deemed responsible for social disorder and the Left's ascent to power fit neoliberal policymakers' needs, which included the elimination of labor unions and political parties, the suppression of protest, and the promotion of the individualist consumerism that they thought would unleash the *homo economicus* essential to free-market capitalist success.[19] Ultimately, the junta's and the neoliberals' ideological projects dovetailed in the quest to remake Chilean society such that collective activism contrary to elite interests, conflict between labor and capital, and the popular sectors' involvement in national decision-making processes would end. Under these conditions and ideological assumptions, the dictatorship and its supporters at home and abroad carried out one of the first and most radical neoliberal economic experiments in the world. The self-isolating nature of fundamentalist neoliberal theory, combined with political repression to suppress dissent and alternative policy responses, contributed to severe economic crises in the mid-1970s and early 1980s.

Although analysts usually date Chile's neoliberal crisis to the debt crisis of 1981–84, economic depression hit the poor and working classes en masse in 1975 when neoliberal shock measures applied in the context of falling copper prices and rising oil prices provoked what was at that point Chile's worst economic downturn since the Great Depression. In 1975, as the regime imposed structural adjustment, industrial production dropped 28 percent and GNP 13 percent. National unemployment rose to 16 percent, and inflation remained in the triple digits.[20] By March 1976, national unemployment climbed to 19.8 percent with what analysts described as an "incredible" 12.3-month average length of unemployment, up from 6.4 months in December 1973.[21] Meanwhile, the regime continued to reduce social spending, from US$106 (1973) per capita to US$78 (1977), eviscerating public programs at a time when they were urgently needed.[22] The dictatorship's emergency make-work program, the Programa de Empleo Mínimo (PEM, Minimum Employment Program), paid below minimum wage and failed as a temporary mitigation measure.[23] The economy improved marginally between 1976 and 1981 during the so-called economic miracle. During this period, national unemployment averaged 17 percent, inflation diminished, and the economy grew. However, the official statistics of 8 percent annual growth misrepresented the economic rebound: they were calculated from the lows of the 1975 recession. Corrected for the recession, growth rates averaged 1.4 percent.[24]

In neighborhoods like Villa Francia and La Legua, neoliberal structural adjustment threatened pobladores' physical survival. By 1976, urban laborers' purchasing power had declined to the point that if a family of five earning less than two living wages per month spent its entire income on food, it could acquire only up to 77.95 percent of the basic food basket. If the family spent 80 percent of its income on food, the family's protein deficit would still reach 16.96 to 21.66 percent, and its caloric deficit 39.39 to 42.8 percent.[25] In response to hunger in poblaciones, by September 1977 the Church had opened 329 comedores infantiles (children's soup kitchens) in Santiago, serving 32,900 children, mothers, and senior citizens.[26] Food was not scarce, but pobladores were unable to satisfy minimum nutritional requirements because of the economic structures imposed by neoliberal policies.[27] Compounding the problem, in Santiago's urban environment, pobladores lacked the means to produce food in sufficient quantities to meet their own nutritional needs. Urban food acquisition depended on labor/wage exchange, and unemployment in poblaciones surpassed national averages. When pobladores were under- or unemployed, their access to food declined. This situation was not unique to the dictatorship or to capitalism, but neoliberal policies drastically reduced price controls, public health, and food-distribution programs, subordinating the provision of basic necessities to market logic. Food was a commodity, not a right.

The result was a host of public health crises. In 1978, Church personnel estimated unemployment rates of 40 percent in western Santiago and 30–70 percent in southern Santiago. Health workers in western Santiago reported high levels of pediatric dental problems, lice, food insecurity, and school absenteeism. Health workers in southern Santiago found that of the adults they treated for diverse complaints, 35 percent of men and 79 percent of women of child-bearing age fell below minimum weight standards, and 21 percent of men met only the minimum standard. Of the children in the southern zone's *comedores*, who probably received better nourishment than nonmembers given the widespread crisis, 54 percent were malnourished. Stress-related psychological illness ("neurosis") and alcoholism reached alarming proportions.[28] Meanwhile, between 1973 and 1978 the number of typhoid cases in Santiago tripled, suggesting decreased access to clean water and sanitation.[29] Pobladores, buckling under prolonged unemployment and deteriorating living conditions, found their physical survival in jeopardy not because food and other necessities were scarce but because under the new market logic, by virtue of their socioeconomic status, they were not entitled to them.[30]

By 1982, as the international economy contracted, Chile's economy was in freefall. Growth fell by 14 percent, and national unemployment increased to 26 percent. The situation worsened in 1983, as national unemployment rose to more than 30 percent, inflation exceeded 20 percent, and real wages fell nearly 11 percent.[31] As during the 1970s, unemployment was especially high in poblaciones: in western Santiago unemployment rose to an estimated 73 percent.[32] The economy gradually improved as more pragmatic economists replaced the architects of Chile's economic disaster, yet by 1988 real wages had still not recovered their 1970 levels.[33] The result of the combination of repression and neoliberalization was the reversal of the short-lived trend of downward redistribution during the Allende years and the subsequent upward redistribution of national wealth.[34] From the mid-1970s on, pobladores faced unemployment and hunger as the regime foreclosed economic opportunity and unraveled the social safety net in the absence of effective opposition.

Neoliberalism and State Violence

The transition to neoliberalism represented a return to capitalism writ large—the economic system in place for most of Chile's history—but in the urban popular sectors it was not a return to capitalism-as-usual. This was not a return to the fledgling welfare state of the 1960s, to the industrializing 1950s, or even to the 1920s when mass politics resulted in a new constitution that expanded political pluralism. Moreover, when compared to its capitalist predecessors of the 1950s and 1960s, the dictatorship's economic performance was mediocre at best, and the substandard conditions it generated weighed disproportionately on popular sector households.[35] That the neoliberal transition was from a pro-worker, democratic socialist agenda with a high-employment economy to an anti-worker, authoritarian right-wing neoliberal model with high unemployment made it all the more disorienting, especially for activists facing the scorched earth of the social commons.

The post-coup process of political and economic change represented for many a traumatic rupture with previous lived experience. Many pobladores had survived earlier rounds of economic misery, political repression, labor conflict, and police attacks on squatter settlements. Stories of unionization struggles and labor and political massacres survived in popular sector political culture, but the new regime's ferocity was unprecedented in living memory. Official truth commission statistics compiled between 1990 and 2005 place the total number of people imprisoned for political reasons and tortured during the dictatorship at 27,255 and the number of dead and disappeared at a combined total of 3,197.[36] These statistics also state that 28,913 people were detained between September 11, 1973, and December 31, 1977.[37] These, like other truth commission statistics, are necessarily conservative. The junta's documentation indicates that during the first year of dictatorship alone, from September 11, 1973, to August 31, 1974, 29,976 people were detained for political reasons. According to a 1974 report to the junta by Colonel Jorge Espinoza Ulloa, director of the Secretaría Ejecutiva Nacional de Detenidos (SENDET, National Executive Secretariat of Detainees), an additional, unspecified number were in the hands of "some Intelligence services, among them the Dirección de Inteligencia Nacional [DINA, National Intelligence Directorate] and some belonging to the Air Force, who keep them in silence, and we don't have access to them."[38]

The official truth commission statistics suggest that the poor and working class bore the brunt of state-perpetrated repression. Of the 27,255 victims of political prison and torture accounted for by 2005, at least 14,678 (53.85 percent) belonged to Chile's poor and working class at the time of the coup.[39] Of the dead or disappeared, at least 35 percent were urban or rural workers.[40] Overall, at least 52 percent of all officially recognized victims of these violations were poor or working-class people.[41] A significant number of torture victims (35.2 percent) and most of the dead or disappeared (60.2 percent) were from Santiago.[42] Meanwhile in Santiago, mass allanamientos (unaccounted for in official reports) were routine only in poblaciones.[43] This demographic and geographic distribution of repression suggests that it was especially intense in Santiago's poblaciones. Repression in poblaciones extended political persecution from workplaces, schools, and party headquarters to plazas, soccer fields, and children's bedrooms, spreading terror, contributing to social fragmentation, and disarticulating potential opposition to the regime's policies.

Justificatory discourse linking economics and political violence appeared in the public sphere soon after the coup. Gustavo Leigh Guzmán, one of the junta's hard-liners between 1973 and 1978, expressed the relationship between violence and economics on the night of September 11, 1973, when he declared war on Marxism, a philosophy that treats politics and economics as inseparable facets of the human condition. He declared that the new regime would "extirpate the Marxist cancer"—a metaphor whose violent overtones rang clear in light of the brutality of the coup. Violent biomedical and hygienic references were frequent in state and media discourse at the time. According to this discourse, the country was riddled with cancer, suffering from "moral and economic insanity," in need of "cleansing," and contending with a plague best cured with violent intervention.[44] An opinion column in a national daily paper compared the bullet holes in the walls of downtown buildings to the scars of smallpox survivors: "Smallpox is a plague and the walls are Chile's face. [The face] of Chile that was sick with plague and whose organism reacted well, that was capable of defeating the contagious and cruel illness and came out of it fortified by it. Fortified and immune." The bullet holes, the author argued, were Chile's "certificate of vaccination" and should be left unrepaired as a reminder.[45]

As neoliberalism became state policy in the mid-1970s, official discourse shifted focus to justification of social violence as structural adjustment drove the urban poor to desperation. In 1975, Leigh announced in the press that "to control inflation today in Chile a social cost must be paid," arguing that state retrenchment and privatization were "pillars of action that the current Government will not renounce for any reason."[46] In 1977, after economic shock measures had provoked a severe recession, unemployment, and starvation in the popular sectors, he argued that "political and economic restrictions" were "the inevitable price of recuperation" from "economic, social, political and ethical prostration."[47] For their part, economists responsible for restructuring the Chilean economy admitted that dictatorship was necessary to the implementation of neoliberal policies.[48] Politicians also sought to capitalize on the opportunities repression offered. Ex-president Jorge Alessandri (1958–64), a member of Pinochet's Consejo de Estado (State Council), argued in 1977 that it would be impossible to prohibit strikes in a system "dominated by political parties" but that it was possible and "propitious" under "a government like this one."[49]

The romance with neoliberalism flagged little with the return to civilian rule in 1990. During the 1990s heyday of "Washington Consensus" politics, the newly democratizing Chile was lauded as a rags-to-riches story and regularly appeared in national and international media as Latin America's economic "jaguar" to Asia's "tigers." The centrality of human rights violations to the neoliberal model was a taboo topic as the country became the darling of international finance agencies, analysts, and policymakers who touted the Chilean system as a silver bullet for economic ills. In Chile, significant economic reform during the political transition to civilian rule was unlikely, as the Concertación prioritized "governability" over social and political justice in a context of economic volatility and military saber-rattling. The Concertación hewed closely to the economic platform inherited from the dictatorship, focusing social programs on the elimination of extreme poverty. Poverty rates declined and economic growth improved, but disturbing levels of inequality remained. Quantitative estimates of Chile's inequality levels vary, but all indicate that inequality has remained notably high. By 2011, Chile was the most unequal country in the Organization for Economic Cooperation and Development (OECD), with a "particularly high" poverty rate that placed it third from the bottom of member nations. In early 2015 the economist Thomas Piketty calculated that Chile was the most unequal country in the world, with an estimated 35 percent of national wealth in the hands of the richest 1 percent.[50]

Dominant public discourse after 1990 decoupled the subjects of violence and economics, portraying the origins and costs of Chile's neoliberal economy in a softer light as one of the dictatorship's few positive legacies, a silver lining that set Chile on a path to membership in the "First World."[51] Thousands might have suffered, apologists for atrocity allowed, but to make an omelet some eggs had to be broken. The Concertación—more delicate in its handling of the matter—promoted the idea that neoliberal capitalism was an essential condition for democracy.[52] Meanwhile, successive concertacionista administrations provided limited redress for the dictatorship's most extreme human rights violations, but only as artifacts of the past. The result was restriction of conversation about alternative socioeconomic systems and a widespread perception that human rights violations were an ontological impossibility in democracy. Even so, many people continued to experience social and political injustices that generated dissonance between their lived experience and the forceful naturalizing discourses about neoliberal democracy and human rights that dominated the public sphere and did much to discourage public debate.[53] In this context, to claim that human rights violations occurred under the

Concertación and that these served elite powerbrokers' interests insinuated that the Concertación was not the savior of Chilean democracy it purported to be, that it was not living up to its call for *nunca más* (never again), and that the new democracy was a continuation of authoritarianism by other means. Dissonance between lived experience and dominant discourse manifested itself in polling data. In September 2003, a national opinion poll found that 22 percent of Chileans surveyed claimed that "for people like me," democracy or authoritarianism "makes no difference."[54]

Critique of the violence underlying neoliberalism in both dictatorship and democracy was unwelcome in mainstream public discourse but frequent in poblaciones.[55] Decades of poverty, high levels of social inequality, and a glaring disconnect between dominant discourse and lived experience contributed to discontent. In 1998, Fr. Pierre Dubois, who spent much of the dictatorship in población La Victoria and later served in Lo Espejo, an impoverished municipality in southern Santiago, summarized the situation in his parish for the Spanish newspaper *El País*. "Most believe that the Concertación does the same as in the times of the dictator," he explained to a reporter. "So many young people are convinced that Pinochet, Aylwin, Frei [Ruiz-Tagle] are the same."[56] Similar attitudes existed in the early twenty-first century in poblaciones across the city, including La Legua and Villa Francia, although disagreements arose about degrees of difference between the dictatorship and the Concertación. Pobladores frequently drew comparisons to the dictatorship on two fronts. In neighborhoods subjected to police occupation as part of anti-drug-trafficking measures, as was the case in La Legua, pobladores alluded to parallels with dictatorial repression. The hulking police vehicles posted on neighborhood streets did little to discourage the association. In Villa Francia, pobladores criticized police violence in the población during protests, and persecution of leftists. In both neighborhoods, pobladores pointed to continuities between media reports during the dictatorship and in the twenty-first century that portrayed their neighborhoods as violent ghettos of crime and political extremism. From their perspective, political and social injustice, including derogatory treatment in the flesh and in the media, was part of a single system spanning both periods.

It is not surprising that critique of the relationship between neoliberalism and repression was of relatively long standing in poblaciones, given the conjoined histories of socioeconomic dispossession and political violence. The following sections return to the era of the coup to trace these conjoined histories through a discussion of mass repression and downward moral displacement targeting pobladores, as the dictatorship wove a "bloody veil" of repression, fear, and social stigma in an effort to reorient the social commons in ways amenable to its political and economic ends.

When All Hope and Everything Was Lost

María and her husband stayed up late on the night of September 15, 1973, in La Legua, listening to Radio Moscow for news of Chile.[57] Domestic media was censored, and information of questionable reliability filtered through local rumor mills. Since September 12, when the police conducted a raid in La Legua and the military emptied factories in the nearby Vicuña Mackenna industrial corridor, the neighborhood had settled into an eerie calm. The days-long curfew and temporary market closures created shortages that some legüinos ameliorated by taking goods from nearby stores and factories, episodes frequently remembered as "solidary looting" (*saqueo solidario*).[58] In La Emergencia, members of the neighborhood council distributed flour from a local bakery, selling one or two kilos to each family.[59] In Nueva La Legua, don Luis recalls, "some kids from the [Communist] Youth said, 'We're going to look for food.' They went to look and brought back a sack of nothing." A resurgence of hope was short-lived when "all of a sudden a really happy kid arrived, with a very heavy, half-wet bag. 'Here, I've got a lot,' and he throws it on the ground . . . and it's a bag of salt. The next day we didn't have anything to eat."[60] The days fell into a pattern: wait for news, host visitors and refugees from outside the neighborhood, discuss politics, and search for food.

Glimpses of the worsening political climate occasionally broke the quiet tension, and some prepared for further repression. A police raid on September 12 killed two legüinos, and the mass allanamiento of the nearby industrial corridor Vicuña Mackenna brought heavily armed military contingents into the area. "A big truck stopped in front of the house with a salmon-colored tarp," a woman recalls, "and the only thing I could see were hands hanging down and a ton of flies. It was there for several days. I asked my dad and he responded: 'Look, lamentably they're dead compañeros, compañeros they've killed.'"[61] The truck later vanished with its silent cargo. One woman's parents spent the week training her for interrogations. "My dad said that they would always go for me because an innocent little girl is going to talk," she explains, "so they spent many days preparing me to say, 'No, my dad comes home from work and goes straight to bed.'"[62] In La Emergencia, people knocked on party walls to alert their neighbors to detentions.[63]

In the early morning hours of September 16, warplanes swept low over the roofs of La Legua. Chechita remembers that her family crouched under a cot, waiting to die. At her home nearby, María yelled at her neighbors to take shelter.[64] Meanwhile, soldiers and Carabineros surrounded La Legua and blocked the exits. At seven in the morning, troops entered the area on foot. María's husband saw soldiers with machine guns stationed every twenty meters along the street.[65] After a preliminary sweep, the soldiers returned to specific homes with lists of names reportedly supplied by local informants. "First the soldiers came through here," don Luis explains, "and a colonel very nicely asked me several things about life in the población, and I answered him, and he said, 'Look, sir, try not to get involved in these things anymore. We're going to leave. We don't have anything to do [here].'" The treatment changed as the allanamiento continued. "About ten minutes later a man from the Air Force with the face of a fascist—because his eyes were bulging—came with a list. . . . I was first on the list. He entered, gave the door a kick, and said, 'Who's Luis?' 'I am.' 'Outside!' he said."[66] While one group of soldiers sacked don Luis's home, another forced their prisoners to La Legua's plaza and beat them.[67]

The soldiers marched the prisoners to Santa Rosa Avenue at La Legua's western border. There, the soldiers beat and tortured them as residents of a neighboring población watched through their windows. "So," don Luis recalls, "the soldiers started to spray machine gun fire at the windows so that nobody would see what they were doing there."[68] The abuse continued in the public thoroughfare, to the horror of the captives and anyone who might still dare to look. "They hit us on the knees and wherever they could," remembers don Luis, "and it occurred to one policeman to cut the hair of this neighbor from La Emergencia. . . . They started to cut everyone's hair, and they made them eat their hair."[69] He adds, during a later conversation, "then two trucks came— damn are they evil!—the trucks were full of pig shit, and they threw us all in there, one on top of the other."[70] The trucks took the prisoners to Air Force Base El Bosque, where they endured further abuse before their transfer to the National Stadium, which the military had converted into a political prison and torture facility.[71]

The mass allanamiento in La Legua set an example for pobladores in other parts of the city and damaged legüinos' ability to organize collectively and defend themselves. Many of those imprisoned in the stadium after the first mass allanamiento were leaders and activists in the Communist Party, the Communist Youth, the JOC, the neighborhood councils, and other community organizations. Oral history conversations suggest that all the prisoners were men and boys, reflecting the military's presumption that men were more politically capable and therefore more dangerous than women. In La Legua, thousands of people witnessed the mass allanamiento and hundreds, at least, would have seen the soldiers marching the men away at gunpoint. The men's absence from the neighborhood was conspicuous. Their example and their families' pain served as object lessons to deter resistance. The military returned in October and took more men to the National Stadium, and over the following months the nascent DINA initiated a cycle of deadly repression against local Communists.[72]

The regime's attempt to destroy La Legua's social commons extended to traditional community institutions. From weekend soccer matches to the parish church, nowhere was safe, and nothing was sacred. According to a local Catholic missionary, on September 16 the police and military broke into San Cayetano. The police abducted the priest, Luis Borremans, accusing him of organizing the September 11 firefight and releasing him only when Cardinal Raúl Silva Henríquez and the military intervened.[73] Community members' daily routines and activities were disrupted as security agents policed legüinos' movements and corralled them inside the neighborhood. "There were four consecutive weeks where we had a concentration camp here in La Legua," explains one of the men who remained in the neighborhood. "We couldn't go out to play soccer. We'd go out, we'd reach Salesianos [and soldiers or police would say], 'No, listen, you can't go.' I tell you," he continues, "La Legua was a concentration camp full of people."[74]

After approximately a month in the National Stadium, some legüinos were transferred to northern desert prison camps, the Estadio Chile (now Estadio Víctor Jara), and Santiago's public penitentiary. Others returned home. The prisoners met with varying degrees of solidarity and rejection upon their transfer or release from the National Stadium. In many cases, in addition to the physical and psychological wounds of torture and imprisonment, subsequent discrimination compounded the repression's effect on ex-prisoners. Those sent to the public penitentiary were reportedly well received by the common criminals, don Luis recalls: "The news spread: '*Los de La Legua* are coming! *Los de La Legua!*' And the prisoners gave up all their things: they threw them bread, they threw them everything. Imagine the solidarity those men expressed."[75] Those released from the National Stadium returned home malnourished and disoriented. Prisoners' families waited daily outside the National Stadium, and Carlos remembers his release as a moment of solidarity. "The people hugged me, they touched me, they gave me bread, drink," he recalls. He went home to La Legua, "because my house was in La Legua. I wasn't going to go anywhere else. I wasn't afraid to return to my neighborhood."[76] Don Luis also returned to La Legua, where his neighbor prepared two "tremendously fat" chickens for him to eat.[77] But repression also fueled fear. Carlos's friends integrated him back into their social lives, but many of his older neighbors were afraid to talk with him. When he applied for jobs, nobody would hire him because he had been a political prisoner.[78] Repression translated into stigma that marginalized ex-prisoners.

Sunday, September 16, was the day in which "all hope and everything was lost," says don Ernesto. "Those who weren't [already] prisoners went to the Stadium that day and others of us were in jail that day, and my two boys

The Economy of Terror, 1973–1978

disappeared," he continues, without pause.[79] Here, don Ernesto telescopes several months of repression into a single day, September 16, that in retrospect represented the finalization of the coup, the savage repression to come, and an end to hope. Although they did not know it at the time, the mass allanamiento was an opening salvo in a barrage of repression that over the year ahead would almost eliminate the upcoming generation of left-wing political leadership in the neighborhood as the mass repression of the early months gave way to selective repression that explicitly targeted leftists and their families. Delia, a child at the time, remembers the coup and what followed as "tremendous pain, because in school they teach you about the Day of the Carabinero, that Carabineros take care of the children, they keep people safe," she explains. She had liked watching the annual military parade, and it was a shock "to learn that all those people who paraded, whom I enjoyed, had ordered . . . they were . . . well, they were murderers—because that's how I see them— murderers who killed people, children, youth, elderly."[80] In some ways, the world turned upside down for children like Delia. The shift was also deeply upsetting to adults who had experienced the 1960s and early 1970s as a time of growing inclusion and influence in national political, economic, and social life, through improved working conditions, homeownership rights, and sociopolitical activism. With the coup, they found themselves violently excluded and persecuted precisely because of these experiences.

Weaving the "Bloody Veil"

Mass allanamientos of poblaciones are conspicuously absent from analyses of repression under the dictatorship. Studies usually characterize repression during the last quarter of 1973 as "random and haphazard" to differentiate it from selective political repression perpetrated later by intelligence services like the DINA.[81] However, during this period mass repression was neither random nor haphazard. Mass allanamientos required planning, resources, and cross-institutional collaboration. They were most frequent during the last months of 1973, as the dictatorship sought to "pacify" the population. They peaked again, in sheer numbers, in the mid-1980s as the national protests, which were strongest in the poblaciones, rocked the city. Mass allanamientos targeted pobladores systematically, persistently, and nearly exclusively. Between 1973 and 1990, most occurred in Santiago's southern zone, historically the most extensive and politically active area of poblaciones in the capital. The eastern—and wealthiest—zone of Santiago had the fewest. The operations affected large numbers of people: between 1973 and 1990, in only sixteen of

Santiago's hundreds of poblaciones, an estimated 98,000 men over the age of fifteen were detained during mass allanamientos.[82] The regime targeted poblaciones because poor and working-class Chileans formed the base of support for the UP government, industrial labor unions, and the Left. Many pobladores, in addition to participating in labor unions and political parties, had also been part of the pobladores movement that produced hundreds of squatter settlements. From the new authorities' perspective, poblaciones were "breeding grounds for Marxism" and "bedroom communities of delinquents," dangerous because of the history they represented and the opposition that pobladores could produce.[83]

Mass allanamientos of poblaciones were one of the most visible forms of repression during the dictatorship.[84] They mobilized large contingents of police and military; they disrupted traffic, commerce, and daily life in and around targeted areas; and they attracted media attention. Mass allanamientos varied little in their basic structure across neighborhoods and over time. The raid of La Legua on September 16 was unusual for the number of people taken to detention and torture centers elsewhere in the city. The procedure, though, was typical. During mass allanamientos, military, police, and intelligence agents cordoned off and searched entire poblaciones. The operations often began during curfew, sometimes at three or four o'clock in the morning, to catch as many people as possible at home and maximize fear and disorientation. The raids targeted both men and women, although in different ways. Pobladores would wake to bullhorns, loudspeakers, and shouts ordering all men aged fifteen and older out of their houses. The men, and sometimes the women, would be forced into soccer fields, plazas, community buildings, or temporary corrals. There, while state agents invaded their homes, pobladores endured identity checks, interrogations, and abuse. Women and children were usually imprisoned at home while state agents searched their belongings, destroyed property, and perpetrated physical, sexual, and psychological abuse. During allanamientos, soldiers and police confiscated UP-era publications, posters, pamphlets, books, and artisan or "hippie" clothing and decorations.[85] Survivors frequently report that the invaders stole valuables and destroyed household items by mixing detergent with flour, slashing mattresses, and dismantling appliances. Mass allanamientos demonstrated to pobladores that state agents could enter and destroy their private property at will and search their bodies and belongings with impunity.

These raids were part of a broader context of violence in poblaciones. Their power rested in part upon the threat of death, and pobladores were acutely aware of the new authorities' willingness to kill. One of the most emblematic examples of the irruption of death into daily life during this period is that of the *muertos* (dead people) that floated through downtown Santiago on the Mapocho River. Testimonies and news reports suggest the shock that this caused downtown, but they rarely follow the dead to their final resting place. The muertos tended to wash ashore downstream in western Santiago, where pobladores who lived near the riverbank found and buried the bodies. Aware of where the violence originated, they tended to avoid state authorities and instead reported the deaths to local nuns. Shortly after the coup, remembers Sister Nadine "Odile" Loubet, who lived in población El Montijo with Sister Blanca Rengifo, "a little nun from población Violeta Parra arrived who had seen four muertos at Resbalón Bridge. Since we were closer to the river, she asked us to go see because it seemed that every day there were muertos." Odile found seventeen muertos in fifteen days, and she "saw new crosses marking new burials" on her way to work in the mornings. Her reports fell upon deaf ears. She told "many people, but they didn't believe me. I told the Cardinal, but he didn't believe. I also wrote to the Pope, but he didn't answer me."[86] While doubt swirled around the question of whether the new authorities were systematically killing people, many pobladores already knew that they were.

State agents also abandoned their victims' bodies in and near poblaciones. The Metropolitan Cemetery, surrounded by poblaciones in southern Santiago, was notorious for the dead abandoned along its edges. In northern Santiago, state agents left bodies on población Angela Davis's soccer field, where pobladores would see them.[87] Pobladores also witnessed killings. In Villa Francia, one woman remembers, "they brought a prisoner and made him run— over there where the houses are, on the other side of the canal, those were fields—they made the youngster run, and they fired on him from behind. I remember that all the people were on top of their roofs watching how they killed him."[88] Rumor had it that nighttime was especially dangerous even inside one's own home, because "at night the milicos went around itching for action, they went around at night, it was said, they listened, yes, it was necessary to hide," recalls a woman from La Legua.[89] With nowhere to turn for assistance and no legal recourse, pobladores and allies such as Odile faced the repression as best they could. Eventually, a clandestine network of priests and nuns mobilized to rescue people in danger, and religious leaders formed a human rights organization, the Comité Pro Paz, to help the persecuted. Until then, pobladores without the contacts and financial means to move to lower-risk neighborhoods, seek asylum, or emigrate independently were on their own.

During and between mass allanamientos, everyone was subject to arbitrary detention "for suspicion." Suspicious activity included staring at a house while on a corner, evading questioning, and gathering in groups larger than two.[90] It included men with long hair, untrimmed beards, artisan or "extravagant" clothing, and "hippie-style backpacks," all of which the regime associated with "criminal or extremist groups."[91] Detention for suspicion could occur anywhere in the city, but police targeted male pobladores especially. Again, the explicit targeting of men for physical repression reflected the dictatorship's conservative, patriarchal views. The policing of men's hairstyles and clothing, and publicized vice raids targeting gay men, sent strong messages to a broad audience about the regime's expectations for politically and socially conservative, heteronormative masculinity.

The regime used the physical repression of men to discipline and control both men and women, and it repressed women in an attempt to discipline and control them and their male comrades and loved ones. According to the regime's patriarchal logic, women's lives only had meaning and women could find fulfillment only as mother, spouse, and homemaker.[92] "Good mothers," and therefore "good women," did not raise children who ran afoul of state authorities, and certainly not children who became leftists. They raised children "for the Fatherland" and according to the Catholic right's and military authorities' conservative ideologies.[93] "Good wives," and therefore "good women," created home lives that attracted their husbands to the home and away from opposition politics, drink, and other sources of trouble. Women were to keep an orderly household, raise obedient children, maintain their "honor," and submit to their husbands. State officials abused women with disappeared or imprisoned husbands or children. They denigrated and blamed the women for failing to keep their husbands and children in check. Women political prisoners endured extreme psychological, physical, and sexual torture, sometimes in the presence of their male comrades and family members, as punishment for what their captors considered a double (political and gendered) transgression. The regime's social imaginary portrayed the nation as a large family, with Pinochet as patriarch, and within this construct, men and women who "failed" to uphold traditional patriarchal and heteronormative gender roles were threats to national security.

State agents also targeted youth. In many poblaciones, social life took place in the streets, making youth easy targets. "I was fourteen the first time [I was detained]," explains a man in La Legua, "and they took me every weekend until I was twenty. By then I was tired of it. . . . You'd be coming from school or work and they'd still arrest you. And another thing: When they stopped you they were violent. They pointed the pistol at your head, they didn't just stop you."[94] The police and military treated youth "just like dogs," remembers Delia. When young pobladores were detained, "they treated them super badly . . . legs apart, hands behind the head, and punches to the ribs . . . all that."[95] The repression affected entire communities by spreading distrust among neighbors, and it reinforced fear by demonstrating the authorities' impunity.

Three nested aspects of these public spectacles of violence further highlight the damage that mass repression did to pobladores' social commons. First, the authorities undermined social solidarity on a personal level by seeking, creating, and encouraging collaborators and informants. Second, through techniques such as sending poblador conscripts to repress urban, working-class communities, they exacerbated social divisions by turning pobladores against one another, forcibly manipulating social and political identities in ways that provoked psychological stress and atomized communities. Third, they attacked the social commons through the vehicle of the mass allanamiento itself, in effect making visible and omnipresent some of the hidden terrors of the political prisons.

First was the attack on social solidarity and personal trust. The authorities' encouragement of those who were willing (or too afraid not) to denounce their neighbors both exploited and sowed division within communities, further atomizing them by driving wedges of fear between people who might otherwise find common cause. Two days after the mass allanamiento in La Legua, the junta praised "responsible" citizens who denounced "the extremists who in a suicidal form operated in some sectors of the capital."[96] Shortly thereafter, over the course of one week police and military forces detained 107 people in Santiago for "spreading false rumors." This report, published in a newspaper targeted to a popular sector readership, goes on to praise the "Chilean men and women who, with a high sense of patriotism, concerned themselves with communicating to the patrols the existence of these negative elements."[97]

Pobladores were attuned to surveillance inside their neighborhoods, and distrust of outsiders became a common self-defense measure. "Living in La Legua one always knows at least who is who, one knows the neighbors," one woman explains. After the coup, "some young guys arrived on the corner, flirtatious-like and, since in our house we knew more or less what was happening, ah, well we knew they could be informants." The girls befriended the suspected "sapos" (toads, stool pigeons), which they could do in part because the regime did not consider young girls capable of constituting a political threat, and "in one of my little-girl games . . . I started to investigate a little more, and like a little girl I took something out of his shirt pocket, and it was a military ID."[98] The damage informants sowed in lives lost and pain inflicted continues to reverberate in poblaciones.

Second, the regime used pobladores' multifaceted identities and affiliations against them in an effort to produce further social division. One example is the prevalence of conscripts in the lower ranks of the army. Very little is known about conscripts' experiences during the dictatorship, but there are indications that in 1973 they came from across the political spectrum and that there may have been significant disorientation, existential crisis, and fear among their ranks. Conscripts were often from poblaciones and poor rural areas, and after the coup the military mobilized them with their units to participate in mass allanamientos. This meant that conscripts from poblaciones carried out mass allanamientos in neighborhoods and homes similar to their own. An ex-conscript from La Legua, who was stationed in Arica until his unit transferred to Santiago soon after the coup, recalls that one day "they woke us up at about four in the morning. At six in the morning we were in the poblaciones that we had to search, and other soldiers with heavier weapons, with armor-piercing weapons, were already there." He was assigned to search duties. "In the houses we had to search," he explains, "there were only women and children. There were no men, no grandfathers." When he caught a glimpse of the soccer field, he "saw that they were beating some friends from the JOC."[99] Evidence suggests that at the time of the coup the military reversed the practice of transferring conscripts from Santiago to the provinces for the duration of their military service and instead funneled units back into Santiago. It is unclear whether this was simply because more personnel were needed in the capital or whether it also reflected a deliberate attempt to turn urban working-class conscripts against their own and pobladores against each other. Whatever the military hierarchy's motives, conscripts from Santiago returned to their home city to carry out repressive operations where they were more likely to cross paths with people they knew.

This young conscript was not alone in his double life of repressor and repressed. "Sixty percent of us who came in from Arica were from poblaciones in southern Santiago," he estimates, "and 60 percent of those had problems with their family members: family members dead, family members imprisoned, family members disappeared." Mass allanamientos alienated some young conscripts and caused rifts in communities because of the military's role in the repression, and conscripts with family members in political trouble were at risk of repression themselves. When he would visit his family, one ex-conscript remembers, "my friends were on the corner, my friends from forever, and they asked me how many I had killed. . . . Each time my friends asked the question it hurt me more."[100] The trauma was mutual, one woman's testimony suggests. Her nephew was a policeman, "and once when he came to see me the first thing I said was, 'and how many did you eat [kill]?'" She continues, "at best he didn't kill anyone, but just seeing him in uniform was a thing that hurt me very much, very much."[101] The regime's exploitation of pobladores' multifaceted identities and affiliations, including encouraging denunciations, using conscripts to repress the types of communities from which they came, and intense surveillance, contributed to social atomization and a pervasive sense of being surrounded by an "enemy" who existed both inside and outside the población.

Third, mass allanamientos were public, community events. Highly visible in nature, they were deliberate projects of social engineering by which the state generated collective trauma. These raids made repression visible to entire communities in a way that secretive, enclosed prisons and torture chambers did not. Even in cases of selective repression, pobladores report that state agents put their depredations on public display. They tore down curtains so that neighbors and passersby could see how they were abusing a home's inhabitants. Soldiers beat their captives in yards and streets in full public view and so that the sounds of repression breached visual barriers. The abuse was shocking in its impunity and the helplessness it underscored; its public nature led to crises of indignity, fear, and shame. During these incidents, pobladores were forced into situations in which they were unable to protect their loved ones in their own homes, which violated social and cultural norms regarding the privacy and sanctity of the home and the roles of men, women, and children in family relationships. Mass allanamientos also violated accepted use of the very spaces that lay at the heart of family and community life: modest homes acquired through hard work and sacrifice, kitchens, yards, and bedrooms. They converted community centers, soccer fields, and streets, all places for recreation, organization, and socialization, into places of imprisonment and abuse. They twisted and contaminated spaces central to the pre-coup culture of the social commons, marking them with fear, violence, and death.

The strategies of the dictatorial state bound perpetrators, victims, and witnesses into a dangerous web of violence, pain, and fear. These strategies deployed a perverse and mutually reinforcing relationship between creating public spectacles of violence, using their visibility to terrorize witnesses, and then punishing the witnesses for seeing them. One example is the September 16 incident on Santa Rosa Avenue when military and police tortured community leaders from La Legua in full view of residents of a neighboring población and then turned their guns on the observers. Another is the case of pobladores who saw state agents kill a man they knew, but who deemed it wise to remain quiet for fear of retaliation. In this scenario, the act of seeing is both punishment and punished. The spectacle of violence is meant to be seen, to punish, discipline, and terrorize. However, the very act of seeing becomes its own transgression and motive for punishment because of the implicit acknowledgment it represents and the record it creates in the minds of those who see: they see and record that the violence exists, the perpetrators exist, and the victims exist. Repeated often and broadly enough, the combination of creating a spectacle and creating fear of punishment for seeing it disciplines society to "see but not-see": to see but not acknowledge, to see but deny.[102] This potent combination reinforced the social fragmentation necessary to the dictatorship's political and economic projects.

In this atmosphere, fear accelerated the destruction of the social commons. While some people could perhaps comfort themselves with the hope that they could avoid repression by not becoming involved with anyone or anything that might lead the authorities to suspect subversive activity, mass allanamientos suggested that the mere fact of living in a población was suspicious, potentially subversive, and sufficient grounds for both punitive and preemptive repression. The coup and what followed led to profound economic and sociocultural shifts in how pobladores were able to construct their expectations and live their lives. "It was terrible, I tell you, emotionally, to lose so many things," says a man from La Legua. "Everything was lost, all the rights, the little and nothing poor people had in those times. In those three years [of the UP] we saw that we could have a dignified life, the right to go to the Municipal Theater, the right to go downtown, to feel that it wasn't only wealthy people's right to go downtown, rather we could all go."[103] The combination of physical and social violence drove despair deep into social and political culture, magnifying repression's direct physical effects.

The monument to "the pueblo's heroes and martyrs" that stands in La Legua's central plaza lists seventy-six people of the municipality of San Joaquín whom the dictatorship killed outright or disappeared, an estimated forty-eight of whom were from La Legua. Villa Francia and its organizations lost at least fourteen people to state violence between 1973 and 1990.[104] A significant but uncalculated number of people in both neighborhoods suffered political prison and torture, sometimes more than once. "The dictatorship did us so much damage," don Luis recalls. "Some people had to leave, others are dead, disappeared. So many people disappeared. And so much weight fell on the población: they didn't let you live here, allanamiento after allanamiento," he explains. "So," he concludes, "people who don't withstand much withdraw and say, 'this isn't for me,' and few remain, few remain."[105] As a corollary of violent physical repression, the dictatorship used downward moral displacement to reproduce and reinforce social authoritarianism in the interest of facilitating pobladores' social and political disfranchisement. As repression devastated the social commons, officials and the media criminalized and denigrated pobladores, variously portraying them as "antisocial," pathological elements to be eliminated or as upstart social inferiors requiring discipline to "learn their place."

Downward Moral Displacement
in the "New Chile"

Poblaciones and factories, with their "filth," "offensive political slogans," and "bastions of political thought," represented the antithesis of the hierarchical, depoliticized society the dictatorship sought to construct.[106] During the 1960s and the UP period, pobladores had transgressed what the dictatorship considered appropriate bounds of behavior, breaking with their supposedly "natural" place in the social order by organizing in their own interests, making demands, and disputing traditional power arrangements through mobilization, community organization, labor unions, and leftist political parties. In the regime's estimation, the popular sectors needed to peaceably accept a subordinate place in the social hierarchy, and this required enforcing social authoritarianism and delegitimizing the urban poor as sociopolitical actors.

As part of this process, downward moral displacement became a key corollary of repression and socioeconomic dispossession in poblaciones. Downward moral displacement, J.T. Way writes, occurs when "the dominant logic makes it imperative to impose punishment, social engineering, and repression on the victims of the system's very nature by shifting the blame for the badness onto them and thereby avoiding a discussion of the problems' real origins." It works "both because the culture industry promotes it and because people buy it. Its formula is deceptively simple: bad neighborhoods with bad cultures, revolving around bad drugs [in the case of 1970s Chile, "bad" political ideologies], produce bad people who do bad things." It is a potent tool that creates and mobilizes fears and prejudices against people whom the powerful identify as racial, ethnic, socioeconomic, gendered, and/or political others. It criminalizes even the places these others inhabit and frequent, through an environmental reductionism that "endow[s] even spaces with the magical ability to generate evil." In Santiago, poblaciones were portrayed as places that by their very nature, as territories of the poor and working classes, "generate[d] evil" (leftist political "extremism") and "social ill" (crime, vice, and social degeneracy).[107] Downward moral displacement blamed pobladores for their poverty, poverty for crime, and the Left for both poverty and crime in poblaciones.[108]

Soon after the coup, and with increasing frequency as selective political repression moved further underground, the media reported on mass allanamientos in poblaciones as "cleansing operations" against "antisocials" and "delinquents" in addition to or instead of searches for "extremists" and weapons. This targeting of dissidents writ large—of people who did not conform to legal, social, and cultural and not just political, norms—was common to

Southern Cone, Cold War national security regimes. "Theirs was a war not only on communism," Jean Franco writes, "but also on all forms of dissidence including socialists, hippies, women, gay men, and children who became the 'homo sacer,' the dispensable noncitizens."[109] In Chile, officials and the media announced "cleansing campaigns" with fanfare. In late September 1973, the newsmagazine *Ercilla* reported on a mass allanamiento billed as an anti-crime sweep in Quinta Bella, in northern Santiago. The article reported that "the operation permitted the detection of hundreds of men who at that hour, 10:00 [a.m.], should be at work. However, the fact that they were in their homes without justified cause means that they act in the terrain of delinquency."[110] The authorities and media declared that the regime would "liquidate the delinquents," in a "total struggle to the death against delinquency," and that "common crimes [would] be drastically repressed until their total extermination."[111]

The targeting of "antisocials" threatened a broad swath of the urban popular sectors. "Antisocial" was a flexible category that included but was not limited to leftists, criminals, "potheads," "suspicious elements," unlicensed beggars, drug addicts, drunks, gay men, fences, habitual recidivists, and the unemployed homeless, "those who, not having a fixed home, or living in that of another person by mere tolerance or complaisance, lack licit means of subsistence, and, without being impeded from working, do not habitually exercise their profession or trade."[112] In practice, "antisocial" referred to anyone who did not act in accordance with the regime's preferences and dictates. Media reporting on these raids peaked in mid-1974, as the junta sought to burnish its law-and-order image for the first anniversary of the coup.[113] Between July 21 and December 19, 1974, at least twenty-one poblaciones in Santiago suffered mass raids. Among those affected were two hundred people from João Goulart, El Pinar, and El Esfuerzo who were detained by the "Brigade against Vice," and thousands who endured a six-hour allanamiento in Pablo de Rokha and San Rafael, in which agents of the Air Force, Carabineros, and Investigations searched five thousand people and eight hundred houses.[114] The raids against "delinquents" and "antisocials" in poblaciones differed little from mass allanamientos to find political opponents and weapons. Both types of raids were designed to maximize repression and fear in the neighborhoods and portray pobladores as dangerous undesirables.

What this meant in poblaciones was that leftists and community activists continued to run high risks by remaining in their homes and neighborhoods. It also meant that people with police files, criminal records, men with tattoos or scars on their arms or stomachs (assumed to indicate criminal affiliation and knife fighting), and anyone else state authorities might decide to categorize as "antisocial" lived in a persistently dangerous environment.[115] In La Legua,

pobladores explain, during the dictatorship the authorities "dedicated themselves to killing delinquents."[116] Following the coup, while activists in La Legua
burned and hid evidence of their political affiliations, neighborhood criminals
"poured boiling water or anything they could on tattoos," a man remembers,
"because in the old days delinquents had to get tattoos, and this condemned
them because the soldiers said, 'Pull up your shirt, let's see, show your arms,
if you have a cut you die, if you have a tattoo you die just the same.'" "They
killed them anyways," he concludes, with or without scars or tattoos. Some
testimony contends that security forces publicly executed petty criminals on
the streets of La Legua.[117] That this narrative remained in circulation nearly
thirty years later suggests that human rights violations against common delinquents made a deep impression on neighborhood residents despite delinquents'
exclusion from mainstream human rights discourse as a social group specifically targeted for abuse.

The results of several "cleansing" raids came to light in 1975, when human
rights workers investigated the case of pobladores rounded up in mid-1974.
During these raids, security forces detained 301 men and deported them to
prison camps in the Atacama Desert.[118] Some of the prisoners had completed
prison sentences, and others were free on bail or on probation. Most had never
been convicted of a crime.[119] Described in the press as "evildoers," the men—
most of whom were from poblaciones La Legua, José María Caro, La Pincoya,
Quinta Buin (formerly Quinta Bella), and Los Nogales—were supposedly
deported to "work camps" in northern Chile to build public infrastructure.
They were reportedly receiving salaries, clothing, housing, and rehabilitation.[120] Investigators found instead that the men had spent two months in the
basement of Investigations' general headquarters in Santiago before being
transferred to Pisagua and Chacabuco, where military personnel physically
and psychologically abused them. There was no rehabilitation or employment. The men were barefoot, in rags, and malnourished. Several were very ill,
and many suffered insomnia and depression. At least one attempted suicide.
Others reported that the jailors treated with particular brutality prisoners
suspected of being gay. At home, their families endured extreme economic
hardship. When their wives sought help, state agencies and the Catholic charity Caritas Chile denigrated them for their association with alleged criminals.[121] The Comité Pro Paz (COPACHI, Pro Peace Committee) filed a writ
of habeas corpus on behalf of 203 of the prisoners and secured their release.[122]
Nonetheless, the raids continued into the late 1970s. In October 1977, police
and detectives invaded La Legua Emergencia and detained approximately five
hundred men and boys. Most were released, but the repression weighed heavily on affected communities.[123]

The discursive trope of pobladores as lazy incompetents requiring discipline paralleled the rise of "cleansing campaigns" against "antisocials." As raids in poblaciones continued, regime representatives visited Santiago's poblaciones with reporters in tow to press the flesh, inaugurate infrastructure, and announce donations. One of the most popular visitors was the interior minister, General Óscar Bonilla.[124] He admonished pobladores that "we don't want lazy people. . . . When [pobladores don't help the neighborhood council] the authorities will remove the bad pobladores."[125] Officials visited poblaciones to "pull pobladores' ears," as if they were badly behaved children, and to "eradicate laziness from squatter settlements."[126] In other instances, officials and the media portrayed public housing as a "gift" and pobladores as leeches addicted to free handouts at society's expense, rather than as citizens seeking affordable housing for which they were willing to pay.[127] Officials' and the media's repeated insinuations that the urban poor were lazy or incompetent affronted pobladores' dignity. Many had worked for years to save money and acquire housing. In fact, poblaciones were largely built by pobladores themselves, from home construction to public infrastructure. Pobladores, many of whom worked in construction, industrial manufacturing, and transportation, literally built Santiago for rich and poor alike. To impugn pobladores' work ethic devalued their contributions to society and stigmatized them as a social sector.

The scope, target, and procedural aspects of mass repression and downward moral displacement in poblaciones suggest that the authorities considered everyone in poblaciones potential political extremists and criminals. In 1974, Colonel Vicuña, retired from Carabineros and the Consejo Nacional de Menores (National Council on Minors), seconded by the minister of justice, told the junta that 10 percent of the population, including an estimated 650,000 children, lived in an "irregular situation" (lacking adequate access to education, culture, food, and healthcare) and therefore constituted a "breeding ground for Marxism." He warned that another 65,000 children "live in a truly animal state, that's to say, we have primitive man in the very center of the city." Economic trouble created these conditions: "The upper class, when it goes badly, transforms into middle class, and the middle, when it goes badly, transforms into lower class, and the lower descends to a stratum that has never been studied: the animal stratum." Without intervention, Vicuña argued, poor children were destined to become criminals or Marxists.[128] Ideas about pobladores' criminality were widespread. In a 1977 letter to the minister of foreign relations, then-colonel Manuel Contreras Sepúlveda, director of the DINA, called La Legua a "Población of Delinquents."[129] These attitudes contributed to the dehumanization and criminalization of pobladores from cradle to grave.

Mass allanamientos and downward moral displacement served an expressly political purpose as security forces repeatedly invaded poor and working-class residential territories and media accounts criminalized and conflated pobladores, leftists, criminals, and others the regime considered socially or politically undesirable. Pobladores were well aware of the damage these raids and media portrayals caused and that they were discriminated against because of their socioeconomic status and places of residence. In 1982, as allanamientos and derogatory media portrayals of pobladores increased in the context of the debt crisis and rising popular sector protest, a poblador from northern Santiago commented to the opposition press, "I would ask the president of the Supreme Court if people's honor doesn't matter in these cases. Or is it that honor depends on the income level of he who presumably has it? What," he asked, "would the residents of Vitacura or Las Condes [Santiago's wealthiest municipalities], where some bank and industry executives live who are now detained or wanted by the police, think if a nighttime raid was done to find them and the papers said these were 'bedroom communities of criminals'?"[130] As he suggested, repression was differential by both political orientation and social status.

It is perhaps no surprise then that the dictatorship had difficulty generating support among pobladores. During the first years of the dictatorship, pobladores had few avenues of contact with the new regime beyond repression and punitive security measures. Civic action campaigns, usually clustered around politically convenient anniversaries and holidays, appear to have had little effect.[131] The Right lacked a significant party base in poblaciones, and the Christian Democrat Party was in political recess, so there were few cooperative party structures in poblaciones for the dictatorship to co-opt.[132] The Left had significant networks in many poblaciones, but these were precisely what the regime sought to destroy. When the dictatorship took over mothers centers and neighborhood councils, many pobladores began to avoid them. Between February 1974 and July 1975, the authorities dissolved at least 177 community organizations in Santiago, most in popular sector municipalities.[133] It reconstituted some, replacing their deposed directorates with regime-approved representatives.[134] The renovated neighborhood councils were to be run "with military discipline" with assistance from retired military personnel living in poblaciones, and they were to coordinate neighborhood "surveillance and security squads."[135] Likewise, the regime expelled dissidents from mothers centers and monitored members through attendance records and dues collection. These policies rendered pobladores' traditional community organizations dangerous for dissenters and useless as places for meaningful community interaction. The junta therefore rightly feared that it lacked legitimate, nonviolent lines of communication and influence in poblaciones.[136]

Although the media attempted to show that many pobladores actively supported the regime and participated in its programs, by mid-1974 it was clear to the junta that many did not, and official social-action discourse became increasingly punitive.[137] In July 1974 *La Tercera* announced that pobladores "must cooperate to the maximum in all efforts that will be made in their favor, because this is not occurring."[138] The junta member Gustavo Leigh favored forcing participation: "We'll ask the Junta de Gobierno for authorization to institute certain obligatory requirements for pobladores to join the neighborhood councils, so that they're obligated to participate in the community," he proposed.[139] The ideological construction of pobladores as a social sector best dealt with coercively was not limited to the military authorities. Pobladores who failed to cooperate fully should be punished, proposed the civilian director of the Dirección Nacional de Industria y Comercio (DIRINCO, National Industry and Commerce Directorate), during a discussion with the junta about establishing state-run stores in poblaciones. "The status that [the poblador chosen to manage the store] receives is that of a man who wins the lottery," she explained. "The man receives a benefit that falls from the sky, which he never in his life expected. First," she continued, "everything he'll receive during the time he can exploit this business is pure benefit. And because of that we're so drastic, so that the moment he fails us, we can take everything from him, without him having any right to appeal." She concluded, "Simply, it's enough to know that there is a person who is going to be lucky enough to administer [the store] and is going to have to serve the rest, and if he doesn't behave well, we liquidate him."[140] In the "new Chile" it was not pobladores' place to make decisions about their lives and labor; the poor and working-classes' proper place was as subordinate, disposable labor inputs to be "liquidated" at the whim of their superiors. In this sense pobladores became central to the functioning of the neoliberal economy as a large, fragmented, un- or underemployed labor force with little choice but to tolerate low wages and oppressive working conditions. This system depended, in turn, on state violence to enforce this social order by exacerbating sociopolitical fragmentation and hampering collective responses to political and social inequities.

Flowers in the Desert

During the post-coup 1970s, pobladores experienced a rapid and simultaneous rise of political and social injustice as political repression deepened, unemployment and hunger skyrocketed, and neoliberal policymakers laid waste to labor protections, social welfare measures, and public programs in health, education, and housing. The Tribunals of Justice—the "creature of multiple, sealed eyes" of Sepúlveda's story—were complicit with the repression and inaccessible to the poor and politically persecuted, allowing state security forces and policymakers to act with impunity. The dictatorship truncated popular sector Chileans' traditional avenues for claiming rights and improving living and working conditions, and political and social dispossession fed one another in a cycle of violence. Collective, public opposition to the dictatorship emerged slowly in poblaciones, but when it did, activists denounced the regime's acts of political and social violence in myriad ways, fighting against the "bloody veil" to build a new culture of the social commons in pursuit of social justice and political freedom.

4

Solidarity and Resistance, 1973–1978

We met, in those times, in religious services that were Catholic meetings, spiritual, as they say. We met in an old, very dilapidated house and talked about things that were prohibited at the time. It was a very frightening atmosphere because the repression, the DINA, was terrible, it was feared, and we were there talking about prohibited things: freedom, the people's rights, and how to reorganize ourselves and fight.

Juan, Communist Party, Villa Francia[1]

What does it mean for a dictator to declare himself "Catholic" and "defender of Western, Christian culture," while he deepens exclusionary capitalism in his country? If we go beyond suspecting "instrumentalization of religion," isn't there a problem of compatibility between the Gospels and capitalist values? In other words, the actual social and political practice of Latin American dictatorships—whose motor is a process of capitalist accumulation—isn't this a practice of negating Christian values, the human vocation of transcendence, faith in a liberating God, faith in the Kingdom of God as "mankind's integral liberation?"

"El ateísmo del capitalismo," *Cristo Dialogante*, Santiago, 1978[2]

The Cold and Icy Night

Hermana (Sister) Dolores moved to Villa Francia in early 1974. The post-coup atmosphere in western Santiago, a veteran social worker recalls, was as if "a very cold, very icy night arrived, where people took refuge in their homes from many things, first from an enormous fright, to save their lives, and others because many, very many people, especially men in this zone, were detained."[3] Hermana Dolores remembers that she and her colleague, Sister

Angélica, "realized that this place was very persecuted, very repressed, there was a lot of suffering. . . . The people were panicked, they were afraid," she says, "but along with the fear it was necessary to hide those who had been organizers, who had been leaders in this process that was aborted overnight. So Angélica and I, during this first period, were always alert to who needed help, who needed food delivered, who needed clothing." The religious sisters acted in solidarity with the persecuted left, helping people in need. They lived on edge, often going to bed fully dressed, "because the murmur spread, '*tonight they raid*.'"[4]

A mass allanamiento did not materialize in Villa Francia as in La Legua, but widespread selective repression did. "The first to suffer repression here," explains one man, "were the leftist union leaders." State agents also targeted leftist community activists, he recalls: "The president was communist and the secretary was socialist, so we had the hand that ruled here, in the first neighborhood council. They took them, and several more fell, people who worked with them."[5] The violence damaged the social commons. "We had entered a period in which public space was emptied of all types of expression," explains one political activist, "and not only expression in the street, but also in meeting places, gatherings, everything was very controlled, very reduced."[6] The media, says another activist, fanned fears and discouraged resistance. "[Opposition] radio still hadn't come on the air," he remembers, "so the media bombarded us all the time: 'wanted: so-and-so, reward.'" As a result, "we started to be more careful with the neighbor or others that came around, the pressure was like that, and we started to lower our profile a little more" by avoiding neighbors, withdrawing from organizations, and changing appearances. And so, he concludes, "it falls apart."[7]

How far apart "it" (capacity for political resistance) fell and how opposition emerged in Santiago's poblaciones is a complex topic. The early years of dictatorship are often portrayed as a time when popular sector organization and the Left were destroyed and "nothing" was happening. Public discourse sympathetic to pobladores' plight under dictatorship portrays them as voiceless victims for whom the Church spoke as *la voz de los sin voz* (the voice of the voiceless). These interpretations conceal as much as they reveal. The image of an inert Left elides the dedicated work of party activists who organized against the dictatorship during the dark years of the 1970s, often from within Church-affiliated organizations. Similarly, the trope of the "voiceless" poblador reduces pobladores to passive objects rather than active historical subjects. It paints a "safe" portrait of the urban poor palatable to status-anxious middle classes and dominant elites by erasing pobladores' political experience and histories of collective action. While these characterizations were useful during the dictatorship to protect the persecuted and deliver urgent human rights messages to a broad audience, they are damaging in a democracy. The Left was victimized, but leftists were much more than victims. They were the only political sector to unambiguously oppose the dictatorship throughout its tenure, and they spearheaded the struggle for rights and democracy. Pobladores were not voiceless; the dictatorship repressed their voices. Despite state terrorism and poverty, they were active sociopolitical subjects—a role that the figure of the voiceless poblador-victim occludes. Ignoring the Left's and pobladores' centrality to the struggle for democracy warps historical interpretation of the period. Too, insomuch as history informs practice, it limits expectations of and possibilities for democracy.

Opposition organization in poblaciones emerged from a complex process of cooperation between anti-regime Catholics and the secular Marxist left. It was not social organizations *or* leftist parties that gave rise to anti-regime mobilization in poblaciones. Rather, as a social worker from Santiago's Vicaría Zona Oeste explains, anti-regime organization and mobilization arose from cooperation between clandestine political activists and "public actors" like the Catholic Church.[8] The what, when, and how of this process have long circulated in what Elizabeth Jelin calls the "catacombs of history": the places where "other stories, other memories, and alternative interpretations . . . endure in spaces of resistance."[9] Regime opponents undertook relentless, overlapping *trabajo de hormiga* [ant's work]—small-scale, detailed labor contributing to a whole. This trabajo de hormiga laid the foundation for mass protest in Santiago's poblaciones. In the poblaciones, the principal point of convergence between Catholics and the secular Marxist left was the concept of "solidarity," which had roots in both Catholic social doctrine and Marxist political tradition. Grassroots activists interwove these traditions to organize opposition around a vision of a social commons based on democratic ideals, ideological pluralism, and respect for social and political rights. This concept of solidarity offered an alternative vision for society, one diametrically opposed to that of the dictatorship and the prescriptions of neoliberal ideology. Rapprochement between Catholics and the secular Marxist left defied prevailing Cold War political ideologies, generated social commons antithetical to the dictatorship's goals, and facilitated collective organization. This chapter begins with an examination of early political resistance and human rights defense, moving then to the histories of solidarity in Marxist and Catholic traditions that informed popular sector resistance during the dictatorship. It concludes with an examination of solidarity at the grassroots and the rise of ideologically pluralistic, anti-regime organization in Santiago's poblaciones.

The Little Flame of Opposition

The Left reacted quickly to the coup, and each party formed clandestine resistance networks in its wake. Leftist parties continued functioning during the 1970s albeit in diminished circumstances. The UP coalition persisted until 1980, and its members cooperated with one another. Meanwhile, the Communist Party sought alliances with the Christian Democrats and gradually mended fences with the MIR. Of the Left's principal organizations, the Communist Party was best able to weather repression. Although the DINA assassinated two of its internal directorates in 1976, the party maintained structural integrity.[10] The Socialist Party and the MIR were less able to withstand repression. Their networks cracked and retracted inward, leaving many grassroots activists disconnected. By 1977, the MIR's only "centralized structures" were in Santiago.[11] The Socialist Party suffered internal conflict and splintered in 1979. Juan C. recalls that after the coup, the MAPU restricted internal communications and halted recruitment.[12] Many grassroots leftists continued working against the dictatorship, but the scope of early resistance activities was narrow. Very few people were willing even to meet, explains don Luis of the Communist Party in La Legua.[13] In Villa Francia, writes Eugenio Cabrera, leaders of the UP-era CAP threw themselves into neighborhood-league soccer in a different población, to "divert the repression's attention."[14] In Villa Francia, estimates one man, "there weren't even eight of us" active in his political circles.[15]

Oral history conversations about political resistance in poblaciones reflect the social and political fragmentation of the post-coup 1970s, a time when the Left was clandestine and pre-coup activists "went home" or drastically lowered their profiles. The secretive nature of resistance during this period has contributed to the idea that "nothing happened" at the time. The result is a caesura in the narrative of Chile's social movements between the spectacular mass mobilizations of the UP that preceded the coup and the national protests of the 1980s. Much of what happened during these understudied years of the 1970s was invisible by design. Repression, poverty, and fear combined to drive resistance in poblaciones underground, but it never disappeared entirely. On the Left, grassroots political organization emerged immediately following the coup. Although it did not prevent the dictatorship from consolidating its power, it kept a "little flame" of opposition alive.

In the early twenty-first century, residents of Villa Francia disputed the idea that "nothing happened" during the dictatorship's early years. During one oral history conversation in 2004, a man described how pro-regime media discouraged resistance. In response, another participant hypothesized, "so what you're saying is that at least during '73 and '74, nothing happened in the población." "That, that," the man assented, but a woman interjected: "Yes, things happened." The man retracted his initial assertion but qualified her statement: "They happened, but how did they happen? In '74 [party contacts] summoned me to talk. Damn, I said, 'should I go or not?' I said, 'I'm going,'" but with immense caution. In this case, "nothing" was a relative, not an absolute, characterization. In absolute terms, "things" *did* happen in 1973–74, as the conversation revealed, but they paled in comparison to the pre-coup period and the 1980s. Conversations about political resistance in the popular sectors during the 1970s are rife with "nothings" that become "somethings." The possibilities for political work improved somewhat with access to information, the man continued. When the "media came on air a bit more, and Radio Moscow gave us information, we started to listen a little at night, and to begin to build ourselves up a bit more among Chileans."[16]

The coup did not spell the end of leftists' ideals and commitments.[17] "It seems as if everything fell apart," recalls Alba during a group oral history conversation, "but the sensation [my family has] is different." Her husband's political work continued despite the coup, she explains, "and days and days passed when we wouldn't see him, and he was always up to something, things were always happening inside the Villa or elsewhere in the sector . . . there was a movement." The Left was "always here. They were always here," one of her neighbors affirms. "In all the sectors," he continues later, "those of us who were here participated, but minimally, for security reasons, but the little flame was there, the resistance was there, small, and it was like that everywhere."[18]

Poblaciones were full of "little flames," and they housed various layers of resistance. "The participation at the level of social organizations was perhaps the most damaged," explains Sandra, from Villa Francia, "because of the climate of terror that people lived in at the time. The climate was sufficient for people to take precautions and withdraw from social and political organizations," an evaluation that many share. Regime opponents not directly involved in political resistance nevertheless expressed themselves culturally and socially "by talking with the neighbor, listening to Radio Moscow." Indirect forms of resistance also occurred among non-activists. Pobladores often knew their neighbors' political orientations, and this was dangerous. Activists' survival often depended upon neighbors' willingness to feign ignorance. For all those who denounced activists in poblaciones, many others simply looked the other way. Community relations in neighborhoods where residents' lives intersected in multiple ways could be dangerous, but they also allowed activists to function after the coup. In Villa Francia, party activists kept working. "I grew up being a link for my father," recounts Sandra, "where I had to give signals, where I had to call him by a different name." She remembers that her father met with Communists and Miristas, "no fewer than ten people from [población Robert] Kennedy, Las Rejas Norte, from the sector across the Alameda too, General Bonilla perhaps, and Cerrillos."[19]

The Communists in Villa Francia, recalls Juan, "never stopped existing here as a party, of course in difficult conditions." They held their first meetings after the coup in the municipality of Quinta Normal, "pretending we were out on an excursion, and we were in a clandestine meeting over there." From there they began "to rearticulate the party and see how we could struggle against the dictatorship."[20] A similar process occurred in La Legua. Amid repression, leftist legüinos tried to reconnect. Before the coup, estimates René, perhaps forty Socialists from La Legua and the surrounding area met on a regular basis. After the coup, they met as they could, but "the party was completely disarticulated, because the Socialists were well known here, they were already old-timers."[21] One of the only places they could meet was in local sports clubs. They met after curfew in an "isolated fashion," but it was difficult to expand their numbers.[22]

La Legua's Communists began reorganizing soon after the coup, explains don Enrique. He escaped the población on September 11 and returned "when the party told us—the clandestine apparatus was already being built—'we're going to show our face, we're going to take a position and what of it' said the party's *viejos*, 'we're flesh and blood of the pueblo and we can't separate ourselves from what happens to the pueblo. Everyone to their places of residence!'" he remembers. He came home in October 1973 and "opened the workshop until curfew, and I planted myself here until they [state agents] took me away."[23] After his own release from the National Stadium in October, remembers don Luis, "sincerely, one remains afraid, at first I didn't go out much, then later . . . the thing returned to normal. Of course we had meetings but very cautiously."[24] The idea that anything could return to normal under such conditions might seem counterintuitive, but, as another political activist emphasized in an informal conversation, everyday life continued. People carried on with normal activities in abnormal circumstances.

The Communists in don Luis's circles "of course" had meetings—meetings were a normal part of party life. During the dictatorship, regime opponents hid political work behind the façade of acceptable social activity. "Sometimes the military showed up and we told them that they were pobladores' meetings, and they left," remembers don Luis. Another time, the Communists wanted to meet at his house, "so I said, 'look, compañeros, we're going to meet here, but we're going to bring a bottle of wine and we're going to bring a deck of cards, because if they catch us we're going to tell the milicos that we're playing cards and drinking wine.'" One neighbor "was always a snitch, so we'd just started the meeting when some agents show up thanks to him, some Dinos [slang for DINA], and they catch us here playing cards and drinking wine, and one of the Dinos says, 'no, these are just some old drunks.' They came, and they left."[25] In the Caro-Ochagavía sector, Juan C. and his MAPU colleagues pretended to study for university entrance exams in the Metropolitan Cemetery, but among the study materials were microfilmed political documents. Studying in the cemetery was normal, he explains, because "in the poblaciones, the houses are small, the families are big, and there isn't room to study with friends, so one finds places to study, especially in summer, outside."[26] Clandestine political work often occurred in the open, behind a façade of legal activity.

Party reorganization during the early years was precarious and slow, remembers Juanita, a member of the MIR's Frente de Estudiantes Revolucionarios (FER, Revolutionary Students Front) at the time of the coup, and playing on multifaceted identities and affiliations and manipulating visibility were strategies that activists used to keep "the little flame" alive. After the coup, she explains, "militants remained on all sides, from all the political parties. . . . We started to organize ourselves, just to meet, to ask, 'how are you, how are people, how are the detainees, who died?'" These early meetings developed into more systematic resistance: "Then, from there, the Resistance was formed, the 'R.' Everyone signed with 'R.' If you went out to graffiti it was with the 'R,' you didn't put MIR, or MAPU, or PS [Socialist Party], no, nothing: the Resistance." Work with the Church was one of her responsibilities as a Resistance member: "[for] all the people who were in the Resistance it was like an obligation to work with a group affiliated with the Church or whatever, but to work within a group to have as a screen that you were in that group, from that sector, and not that you were in a political party. So that's how it began, at least in the sector where I lived."[27]

As Juanita's story suggests, leftists cautiously made dissent visible soon after the coup. Urban spaces—walls, bathroom stalls, the backs of city bus seats, and street signs became places for anonymous political dissent. It was a time, says Silvia, who was in the Communist Party, "of working alone, ah, because people on the Left never stopped working, never, because I've spoken with compañeras and they did the same: in every bathroom I found I wrote with rouge, for example, 'here they assassinate,' '[political prison] camps exist.'" She was not the only one writing on bathroom walls. "Others went to neighborhood restaurants to eat something, alone," to graffiti the bathrooms, she explains. Men also participated, she points out: "The men have told me, 'I went alone, compadre, to the bathrooms and wrote,' and incredible," she concludes, "but all of this was making us lose our fear."[28] Silvia and her comrades were not the only people to spread ideas contrary to the regime by writing on walls in public places. Later in the 1970s, young people went out after curfew to "hang posters, graffiti the streets," explains Juanita. She went out "many times during curfew to do propaganda, super afraid, but we did it."[29]

The Left's battle for visual presence in the urban landscape was meaning-ful because it spread political messages that challenged the regime's project of historical erasure. After the coup, the regime's cultural "cleansing campaigns" erased visible traces of associations between the Left and the urban popular movement. The authorities ordered pobladores to eliminate political graffiti from neighborhood walls and fly Chilean flags outside their homes.[30] Students from the Universidad Católica's Student Federation erased political slogans from major avenues, the Mapocho River's floodwalls, and poblaciones.[31] Crews painted the factory walls along the Vicuña Mackenna industrial corridor to erase the "bastion of political thinking" they represented.[32] The erasure of working-class and leftist history from the urban landscape extended to the names of streets and poblaciones. The authorities renamed streets and neigh-borhoods bearing names of people, places, and events associated with the Left with new names honoring independence heroes, the military, and the police. The dictatorship also seized the opportunity to rename campamentos (squat-ter camps) as "poblaciones" or "villas," superficially erasing a linguistic indica-tor of some of the country's worst housing conditions.[33]

Pobladores reasserted the power of naming in their neighborhoods in oppo-sition to the regime's erasures. In La Legua, pobladores began calling the cen-tral plaza "Salvador Allende" in 1977, a dangerous time to invoke the deposed president's name. "We started with 'Salvador Allende' to irritate the pacos," remembers one woman. Youngsters would write the name in chalk on the plaza, the police would erase it, and the kids would return to write it again.[34] The conflict over the plaza's name was a local manifestation of memory strug-gles and competition for control of public space that takes on a deeper dimen-sion when we consider that, at the same time, the women had set up an *olla común* (common pot, a type of soup kitchen) in the plaza, making their strug-gle against hunger visible in a public space outside the bounds of Church property.[35] Women from población Angela Davis remember that the authori-ties renamed their neighborhood "Villa Héroes de la Concepción," but, they laughed, "we said we were the Heroes of the Mud," in reference to the poor infrastructure, and continued calling their neighborhood Angela Davis.[36] In simultaneously ridiculing the regime's choice of name, critiquing the state of public infrastructure, and continuing to call their neighborhood Angela Davis, the women asserted control over meaningful political and historical symbolism, exerting a small measure of power over local memory struggles and the urban environment.

Similar stories of subterfuge, improvisation, ad hoc collective action, and even verbal aggression—which appears especially in women's narratives—often surface in stories of local resistance. When DINA agents turned Irene's house in Villa Francia into a *ratonera* (mousetrap)—a repressive practice in which they occupied a home and detained everyone who entered—she protected her husband's political comrades with subterfuge. "Since we had a business," she explains, "I caught them and said, 'No, we're out of eggs, we're out of milk, get out of here because there isn't any.' So other compañeros arrived and I said, 'No, no, no, the milk is already gone, they didn't deliver milk, the truck didn't come by today, so there isn't any.' I caught them and threw them out."[37] Thwarting repression required improvisation and cunning. "We had a compañero who had a bar," says don Luis, "who sometimes thought up nonsense, and sometimes it worked. So one time," he continues, "the Dinos arrive, and one looks and says—excuse the language, but I'm going to repeat it just as it was—'Hey, so you're the *comunista conchetumadre*.' "So [the bartender] said [to the agent], 'Of course I'm communist, and you're communist too, *huevón*, don't you remember?'" The agents left, "because in those times everybody was afraid of everyone."[38]

Because of gendered patterns of repression rooted in traditional cultural mores, women had more leeway than men to berate security forces, especially when fighting on behalf of children or spouses. After the DINA disappeared her husband, security agents kept raiding Lucy's home in La Legua. "I just swore at them," she remembers, "because they wanted to take me that day, and I said, 'You know you can't take me; what are my children going to do?'" Fed up with harassment, she confronted the agents: "I said, 'What are you looking for if he isn't here? You wretched dogs took him from me, you took my children's father from them, and you still have the nerve, wretched dogs, to come look for him here!'"[39] For the first anniversary of the coup, another woman recalls, some youngsters went through La Legua "taking down flags. We watched them: well done, taking down the flags! Why should flags fly for the eleventh, right? I know they burned them." The police rounded up suspects, including her son. Neighbors gathered at the police station to demand the boys' release, and "some [women] got good and bold, J. yelling obscenities to the world there," she says. The police demanded "ten bottles of pisco and ten well-made sandwiches" in exchange for the boys' release. The women made the rounds of stores to request donations of bread, ham, and liquor. They delivered the ransom to the police, "and J., she says, 'Here you go, pacos, *conchesumadres*, pathetic wretches' . . . and what *didn't* that woman say?" Meanwhile, more neighbors arrived, swelling the crowd to about fifty people who waited to make sure the boys were released.[40]

Many such tales of small-*r* resistance circulate in the "catacombs of history." Their subtext is often one of empowerment and resistance in the face of repression. Resistance, however, did not eliminate the problem of repression. The woman who confronted the police at the station had to send her son away from the neighborhood for his own safety shortly thereafter. Although Lucy confronted the agents stalking her home, their abuse of her family continued. Despite Irene's initial success at thwarting the ratonera in Villa Francia, the DINA captured her husband later that evening. Don Luis's laughter while recounting some of his exploits stands out against a backdrop of pain: he survived political prison, torture, and the horrific abuse of family and comrades. During the mid-1970s, political resistance networks faced crisis as repression disrupted their organizational structures and communication channels. The DINA had a chilling effect on party activists' ability to mount opposition. It is important to remember that the regime's strategy for eliminating left-wing parties as political organizations and intergenerational vehicles of social ethics, ideology, and political culture relied first and foremost on destroying human beings. Lethal political repression was not new to Chile, but the sheer scope and profundity of the dictatorship's quest for human destruction was unprecedented in the experience of those living at the time. Most people did not fathom how far the dictatorship would go to carry out its vision for a new society, and the depths of cruelty and cowardice to which its agents and collaborators sank were a perennial source of shock for observers in Chile and abroad. The practice of what ultimately came to be called *solidaridad* initially arose in response to this human rights crisis in all its facets: physical, economic, political, and social. It united diverse faith communities and the secular Marxist left in pursuit of an alternative, anti-regime social commons that protected human rights and advocated democracy.

The Human Rights Emergency and the Seeds of Solidarity

As leftists in Santiago's poblaciones kept the "little flame" alive, religious organizations mobilized to assist the persecuted. International onlookers watched post-coup developments with alarm. The World Council of Churches (WCC) and affiliates of the World Jewish Congress expressed concern as repression spread and as Pope Paul VI took a "neutral" stance suggesting that he considered the coup a "necessary evil."[41] The WCC worried that pro-regime sectors of the Chilean Catholic Church, buoyed by the pope's position, would silence the institution's Left.[42] As an institution embodied in the Conferencia Episcopal de Chile (CECH, Episcopal Conference of Chile), the Chilean Catholic Church was slow to denounce the regime, waiting several years to do so.[43] Across the religious spectrum in Chile, leaders' and congregants' opinions on the dictatorship were mixed. However, with secular institutions incapacitated, religious institutions were best able to respond to the crisis—especially the Catholic Church, an institution the regime was reluctant to openly attack.[44]

Human rights organizations emerged quickly in the wake of the coup. The first was the Comité Nacional de Ayuda a los Refugiados (CONAR, National Committee for Refugee Assistance, est. October 3, 1973), formed by the United Nations High Commissioner for Refugees in cooperation with the dictatorship and the Chilean Catholic, Methodist, Christian Orthodox, and Evangelical Lutheran Churches. Under Allende, Chile had provided refuge to leftists fleeing repression elsewhere in Latin America, and the coup put them in immediate danger. The junta authorized CONAR because it wanted foreign political refugees to leave Chile and sought to burnish its reputation with the gesture.[45] But CONAR's work excluded persecuted Chileans, and regime authorities' access to its internal affairs discouraged some refugees from seeking assistance. CONAR's limitations motivated WCC representatives to seek new alternatives.[46]

The Comité Pro Paz (Pro Peace Committee) was born of WCC representatives' recommendation to the auxiliary bishop Fernando Ariztía that the churches establish an organization to defend persecuted Chileans. The Comité formed in early October 1973 at the instigation of Protestants, with WCC money and the Chilean Catholic Church's cooperation.[47] Ariztía and the Lutheran bishop Helmut Frenz co-directed the Comité in representation of the Catholic Church and WCC, respectively.[48] The leadership also included representatives of the Chilean Methodist, Methodist-Pentecostal, Christian Orthodox, Baptist, and Jewish faith communities. The Comité Pro Paz and its successor, the Vicaría de la Solidaridad (henceforth Vicaría), practiced notable religious and political ecumenism. Leftists were the most willing to work with the Comité and Vicaría. Most of the Comité's initial staff were MAPU militants, and others were nonreligious Socialists and Communists.[49] In December 1975, under pressure from Pinochet to close the Comité, Cardinal Raúl Silva Henríquez opened the Vicaría to continue the Comité's work on firmer institutional footing.

Despite the CECH's ambiguous position toward the dictatorship, many popular sector pastoral workers helped persecuted leftists. Soon after the coup, anti-regime priests, including Rafael Maroto, Sergio Nazer, and Roberto Bolton, took up residence at Fr. Mariano Puga's home in Villa Francia, several blocks from where Hermana Dolores would come to live in 1974. Bolton writes in his memoirs that "I convinced myself that we, at least, didn't have to wait for the Church to adopt a new, more prophetic attitude to tackle the dictatorship's absolute excesses."[50] With likeminded clergy and religious sisters they formed a clandestine network to help the persecuted. When they learned of the Comité Pro Paz, "each of us went downtown to establish links with the people who worked there." The Comité Pro Paz's official purpose was to provide juridical support to the politically persecuted. But, Bolton recalls, "naturally, in this work people often appeared who needed much more than juridical assistance." In these cases, the Comité connected persecuted individuals to the clandestine rescue network, whose members helped them reach asylum in foreign embassies.[51]

Cooperation between Catholics (leftist and otherwise) and the secular Marxist left began in an ad hoc fashion but became more systematic over time. Shortly after the coup, recalls Silvia, she and other Communists met in Villa Francia to arrange safe havens for UP leaders. "Desperate," she remembers, "we saw that we were alone, and . . . because this is a Catholic pueblo, and we've all received Catholic education although I'd forgotten about the Church—I remembered at that moment what the Church preached." The outlook was bleak, and "we said, 'Well, the Church, don't they say they defend the persecuted? Let's go there.' And that was spontaneous in many people. The Church never sought me out or offered me protection. I went." She was an atheist, and "all I respected was Cardinal Silva Henríquez and the priests I knew."[52] Meanwhile, members of Villa Francia's comunidad cristiana popular, Cristo Liberador, also tried to help the persecuted.[53] Cooperation in response to the human rights emergency materialized in La Legua as well, where the mass allanamiento of September 16 left many families without breadwinners. The day after, remembers Anita, a Catholic missionary in the neighborhood, prisoners' wives informed her that their children were hungry. She helped organize what may have been the first post-coup comedor (soup kitchen) in Santiago. The first day, fifty children attended. The number quickly increased to one hundred in La Emergencia alone.[54]

Pastoral workers also responded to repression, as Frs. Luis Borremans and Guido Peeters did when in late 1973 they held a public funeral service at San Cayetano for young men associated with La Legua's Galo González communist committee whom the DINA had tortured and killed. Publicly mourning the young leftists thwarted the dictatorship's attempts to dehumanize the victims and their families by denying funerary rites. The priests helped to preserve the cultural and social cohesion that the regime sought to destroy, but repression continued. In January 1974, the DINA again kidnapped many of La Legua's Communists and Communist Youth, imprisoning them in the Londres 38 and Tejas Verdes torture centers and disappearing the brothers Gerardo Rubilar Morales and Eduardo Salamanca Morales. After this on-slaught, Church personnel and the Comité Pro Paz helped survivors reach asylum outside Chile.

Solidarity between Catholics and the secular Marxist left initially occurred in an ad hoc fashion in response to the human rights emergency. In the popular sectors it deepened and spread as anti-regime Catholics and secular Marxists forged solidary relationships in pursuit of human rights and democracy. Silvia's comments and developments in La Legua offer an important clue to how this was possible. As these stories suggest, the secular Marxist left and the Catholic Church might have been estranged, but they were not strangers. In the pobla-ciones, solidarity was a potent organizing concept because it had deep roots in Catholic social doctrine and Marxist political tradition that had intertwined in popular sector political and religious cultures since the nineteenth century.

Histories of Solidarity in Marxist and Catholic Traditions

After the coup, pastoral workers and members of the secular Marxist left were among the first to put into practice what later came to be understood as "solidarity" by cooperating with one another and assisting the persecuted regardless of political or religious beliefs.[55] Jessica Stites Mor defines solidarity as a process of constructing "relation[s] of proximity." In other words, it is a process by which "social others enter into our social conscious-ness as people to whom we owe responsibility."[56] This is an apt description of the dynamic relationship-building process that developed in poblaciones dur-ing the dictatorship. Solidarity, as an organizing concept and strategy, was not spontaneous or natural. It was developed, taught, learned, and actively constructed. The process was fluid, negotiated, and punctuated with conflict. The result was an ideologically pluralistic concept and practice that shaped underground organizing. In the poblaciones, *solidaridad* established the foun-dation of a new social commons that valued the promotion and practice of human rights and grassroots opposition to the regime.

The idea of solidarity drew upon deep histories that resonated across politi-cal and religious divides. On the international Marxist left, solidarity tradition-ally referred to unity among the industrial proletariat. According to Steinar

Stjernø, Marx rarely used the word "solidarity," but the term was common in nineteenth-century European social democratic and anarchist traditions. The social democrat Karl Kautsky, writes Stjernø, "utilised *solidarity* both as a general concept, meaning the feeling of togetherness in general, as 'servants may have in the families in which they live,' and more particularly as the feeling of community that develops among workers when they recognize their common interests."[57] Anarchists such as Mikhail Bakunin used the term "solidarity" as a concept in its own right and were primarily interested in it as a practice: "The first [step in achieving revolution] is by establishing, first in their own groups and then among all groups, a true fraternal solidarity, not just in words, but in action, not just for holidays, but in their daily life. Every member of the International must be able to feel that all other members are his brothers and be convinced of this in practice."[58] The International was heterogeneous, divided by nationality, ethnicity, gender, race, language, and industry. Many of its members perceived one another as social others. Solidarity—or relationships of responsibility—Bakunin suggests, could not remain limited to consciousness and mere words. Solidarity existed only to the extent that people put it into practice.

Chile's long tradition of leftist organizing drew on international currents of thought but developed within the national context. Historians disagree on the details of anarchism's arrival in Chile, but it is clear that socialism, anarchism, and the labor movement developed in close relation to one another.[59] In 1897 members of the ideologically diverse Centro Social Obrero and Agrupación Fraternal Obrera formed the Unión Socialista to promote socialism in Chile. Meanwhile, anarchist workers organized mutual aid societies and resistance societies to support strike activity, and in northern Chile, workers formed *mancomunales* that organized workers by geographic location. By 1919 socialists and anarchists ran ideologically pluralistic national worker federations. The socialists took over leadership of the Federación Obrera de Chile (FOCH, Workers Federation of Chile, est. 1909), and the anarchists formed an Industrial Workers of the World affiliate.[60]

The Catholic Church also participated in turn-of-the-century labor ferment. The first national labor organization, the FOCH, formed under the auspices of conservative Catholics. Workers in the FOCH would have been exposed to anarchist and socialist ideas and to priests who followed the precepts of Pope Leo XIII's 1891 Encyclical on Capital and Labor, *Rerum Novarum*. This papal letter articulated ideas echoed in later understandings of solidarity, arguing that "[among the earliest Christians] those who were in better circumstances despoiled themselves of their possessions in order to relieve their brethren; whence 'neither was there any one needy among them.'"[61] Leo

XIII supported the principle of private property, accepted social inequality as natural, and rejected Marxism and class struggle. Yet he praised unionization and criticized capitalist exploitation and greed, laying theological groundwork justifying struggles for social justice. He argued that the "working classes" were "citizens by nature and by the same right as the rich."[62]

In turn-of-the-century Chile, anarchism's, socialism's and Catholicism's respective utopias were irreconcilable. However, cooperation on common, shorter-term goals such as unionization and social reform was possible because all three ideologies recognized the existence of socioeconomic inequality and class conflict, the exploitation and oppression at the heart of contemporary capitalism, and the need for reform. Coexistence and interaction between Marxists and Catholics continued throughout the twentieth century, and ideas about solidarity developed in this context.

Within Catholic social doctrine, the word "solidarity" first appeared in the 1961 papal encyclical *Mater et Magistra*.[63] Proponents of solidarity with the poor and working classes in post-coup Chile identified with Chilean-Catholic precursors dating to the early and mid-twentieth century, before *Mater et Magistra* was written. Clotario Blest (1899–1990), a leftist Christian labor leader and anti-regime activist during the dictatorship, was legendary for his role in creating the Asociación Nacional de Empleados Fiscales (ANEF, National Association of Public Employees), the Central Única de Trabajadores (CUT, Unified Workers' Center), and the MIR. Blest's activism combined Catholic and anticapitalist ideals as evidenced in an early organization, the Grupo Social Cristiano Germen. "'*Germen*' means 'source or emergence,'" Blest explained to his biographer, Mónica Echeverría Yáñez. "We wanted our group to be the 'source' of the true Christian principles and the 'source' of the worker's struggle for his rights. Our symbol was the sickle, hammer, and the cross: the sickle and the hammer, symbols of the agricultural and industrial workers, presided over by the cross," he explained, concluding, "why should the Communists be the workers' only representatives?"[64]

The organization put its ideals into practice, organizing workers and calling for unity between Christians and Marxists. Germen, writes Echeverría, offered both a "new perspective on the Catholic Church, Christianity, and mass movements" and a platform for political action, although its quest for unity between Christians and Marxists met with little success.[65] The group agreed with socialist economic doctrine but disagreed with socialism's "philosophical roots and ultimate goal, which are essentially materialistic in contraposition to ours, which are essentially spiritual." Despite opposition to Marxism, Germen sought rapprochement in pursuit of an alternative to capitalism: "[we're] decided to definitively and radically break the clumsy ties that have inconsistently bound

Catholics to the criminal capitalist regime in which we live, a regime of exploitation and scourge of the sacred human personality."[66] Germen was an early example of the growing tensions in modern society that the Catholic Church addressed with Vatican II. For Chilean Catholics it set an example of Christian political action in alliance with the working class. For Marxists, argues Echeverría, "Germen has a prophetic scope that transforms it into indispensable catechism for the future workers' struggle, especially here, in Iberoamerica," a majority-Catholic region rife with social inequality and exploitation.[67]

Throughout the mid-twentieth century, an ongoing tension among Catholic social activists revolved around Catholic concepts of charity. Although the papal encyclicals *Rerum Novarum* and *Quadragesimo Anno* inspired conservative Catholic elites to improve conditions for the poor, these activities often reproduced structures of oppression. The Jesuit priest Luis Alberto Hurtado Cruchaga (1901–52) laid the groundwork for later Chilean-Catholic understandings of solidarity by criticizing traditional Catholic charity. "[Many are] willing to give alms but not to pay a just wage," he observed; "Catholics' social attitudes seem more oriented toward impeding the communist advance than de-proletarianizing the masses. There is no visible effort to achieve [or apply] the Encyclicals' teachings, and even in the exposition of this doctrine [the Church] is too 'prudent' so as not to oppose the ruling classes."[68] Hurtado's work among the poor earned him the epithet of "communist" in mid-century Chile.[69]

During the 1950s and 1960s, in Santiago's poblaciones and factories, the MOAC (Catholic Action Workers' Movement) and JOC (Catholic Worker Youth) fused Catholicism with labor activism. During the 1950s the movement was "self-consciously apolitical," explains Tracey Jaffe in her study of the JOC. It avoided official affiliations with the Left but was not strongly anti-communist.[70] As popular sector organization and political participation expanded in the 1960s, JOC members entered the political fray. By 1970 JOC members were joining Marxist political parties and cultivating "double militancy" in the JOC and their parties.[71] The Catholic Workers movement left a significant legacy. Many Catholic leaders within post-coup human rights organizations and comunidades cristianas populares were involved in this movement. During the decades preceding the coup, the work of Catholics dedicated to improving living and working conditions for the poor transformed the terrain of pastoral activity and sociopolitical commitment in Chile. These activists' work established a foundation for later movements rooted in liberationist interpretations of the Bible.[72]

Most immediately relevant to post-coup concepts of solidarity was the 1968 Latin American Bishops' Conference in Medellín, where the Latin American hierarchy interpreted Vatican II for Latin America and declared that lack of solidarity leads to "the committing of serious sins, evident in the unjust structures which characterize the Latin American situation."[73] To profit from the unjust structures or to be complicit in their maintenance through act or apathy constituted sin, and liberation from sin required active effort for structural change. Although conservative detractors saw in this theological interpretation an unholy amalgamation of Church doctrine and Marxist ideology, the bishops criticized both capitalism and Marxism as systems that "militate against the dignity of the human person"—capitalism because it puts capital and profit before human well-being, and Marxism because "although it ideologically supports a kind of humanism, [it] is more concerned with collective man, and in practice becomes a totalitarian concentration of state power."[74]

If Vatican II and Medellín displeased conservative elites who feared a changing status quo, the emergent liberation theology of the late 1960s was beyond the pale, alarming even some supporters of Vatican II. Liberation theology recognized the value of Marxist analysis in understanding the modern world and posited an indivisible relationship between the temporal and spiritual realms, arguing that only profound structural change could bring about liberation and spiritual salvation. The theologian Gustavo Gutiérrez proposed that Christian solidarity was meaningful insomuch as it constituted practice (praxis). "Solidarity" meant joining *with* the oppressed in their struggle to "[conquer] their liberty."[75] His theory of solidarity critiqued and combined legacies of Catholic approaches to poverty, proposing a new approach for the contemporary context.[76] "No one should 'idealize' poverty," Gutiérrez states, "but rather hold it aloft as an evil, cry out against it, and strive to eliminate it. Through such a spirit of solidarity we can alert the poor to the injustice of their situation. When Christ assumed the condition of poverty," he asserts, "he did so not to idealize it, but to show love and solidarity with men and to redeem them from sin. Christian poverty, an expression of love, makes us one with those who are poor and protests against their poverty."[77] The class-sensitive nature of liberation theology, which argued that the Bible "is to a great extent the expression of the faith and hope of the poor" and that "it reveals to us a God who loves preferentially those whom the world passes over," was revolutionary and deeply meaningful to many in the popular sectors who struggled for better lives but had previously experienced the Catholic Church as yet another institutional pillar of the status quo.[78]

What set liberation theology and its potential consequences apart from earlier Christian movements for social justice was that it found common cause with Marxism. Its conservative detractors in Chile and elsewhere feared and condemned it for its use of Marxism as a tool of analysis and its assertion of radical structural change as moral imperative. Unlike Germen's 1933 call to radical Catholic action that drew a stark line between the spiritual and material, liberation theology rejected separation of the spiritual and material as antithetical to authentic Christianity. Rather, the spiritual and the material, and the religious and the political, were directly related. "The minimal conclusion of Liberation Theology," writes anthropologist Roger Lancaster, "is that ['retrieving the souls of the lost' and 'engaging in radical social action on behalf of the poor'] are complementary activities; its maximal conclusion is that they are identical tasks."[79] Not all clergy and religious sisters who embraced liberation theology were maximalists, but the theory's emphasis on social justice resonated with socially conscious pastoral workers, the poor, and the Left.

Pastoral workers' dedication to social justice for the poor drew them into the political fray of the 1960s. When the possibility of socialist revolution materialized in the form of Salvador Allende and the UP coalition, many of these pastoral workers supported his candidacy. Following the UP's victory, eighty pastoral workers expressed support for the socialist experiment and created Cristianos por el Socialismo (CPS, Christians for Socialism), to the displeasure of the CECH.[80] The CPS encouraged Christians to support the socialist revolution, arguing that "if Christians form a 'group apart,' we divide the working class and betray the Gospels."[81] After the coup, the CPS dissolved, but many members living and working in Santiago's poblaciones remained there in congruence with their religious and political commitments.

The historical trajectory of activist Catholicism had a significant effect on post-coup pastoral work in Santiago's poblaciones. From the mid-twentieth century on, pastoral workers had moved into poblaciones, including La Legua and Villa Francia, to live among the poor.[82] Particularly important to the post-coup context were those with experience in movements for social change such as the MOAC, JOC, CPS, and a liberationist experiment called the "Calama Experience" led by Fr. Juan Caminada. Inspired by Vatican II and liberation theology, during the UP years the "Grupo Calama" attempted to build a new theology and a church born of the popular sectors.[83] They lived in poblaciones, subsisted on wage labor, and joined Chile's Socialist- and Communist-dominated labor unions and Marxist political parties in solidarity with the poor.[84]

Although workers were sometimes surprised to find a priest or religious sister among their ranks in the workplace, their presence as Catholics in leftist organizations did not necessarily cause much surprise. While some Marxists were atheists or estranged from the faith, others partook of sacraments like baptism while otherwise maintaining distance from the Church.[85] This aligned with broader trends in Chilean Catholicism. Citing the *Plan pastoral del Episcopado chileno*, Jaffe found that in the 1960s, 80 percent of Chileans were baptized, but 70 percent identified as "nonpracticing" Catholics who did not regularly attend Mass.[86] A 1981 survey of eighty-two residents of seven poblaciones in western Santiago found that 91.4 percent identified as "believers" (86 percent as Catholic), 3.6 percent as "doubtful," and 2.4 percent as "nonbelievers." Believers' tenets diverged significantly from Church doctrine. For example, 38 percent of "believers" doubted or did not believe in an afterlife. Only 12 percent "identified God with Christ," and most harbored what the Church considered "magical-superstitious" beliefs in miracles, vows, and soothsayers.[87] Pobladores engaged with priests as individuals, foregoing Mass and most sacraments. "One approaches [the Church] through affinity with the priest," explains Juan R., a consecrated layperson from San Cayetano. "There's not a consciousness that 'I go to Mass for the sacraments.' I go because the priest is tough, the priest is cool, he plays soccer, drinks with the boys, chats with the girls, get it?"[88]

Despite historical legacies of distrust between the Catholic hierarchy and the Left, at the parties' bases and in popular religiosity the Church and the Left were not mutually exclusive or always antagonistic. Before the coup, Catholics and secular Marxists coexisted and cooperated in families, neighborhoods, labor unions, and community organizations, despite conflict. In popular sector political and religious culture, Christianity and socialism were not irreconcilable. Catholic pobladores could join the MAPU or the Christian Left, Christian Marxist parties that splintered from the Christian Democrat Party in 1969 and 1971, respectively. However, the Communist and Socialist parties were strong in Santiago's poblaciones and factories, and self-identification with both Catholicism and Marxist ideals was not uncommon. The MIR did not require its members to eschew religious beliefs, and neither the Socialists nor Communists excluded Christians from their ranks. "My leftist militancy in the Socialist Party and [being] a Catholic Christian was never a problem for me," explains Luis, a poblador active in Villa Francia's comunidad cristiana, "because in Chile we've had a Christian formation in general, and many Communists baptize their children. Here there hasn't been an atheist Marxism or socialism," he continues, "and [in] the Socialist Party, furthermore, there's room for all these currents."[89] "The people didn't have a problem with being Christian Marxists," remembers Juan C., "at least people at the base. At a more political level perhaps, because the philosophical questioning begins, but at the base there was no problem being Christian, being leftist, being revolutionary, wanting socialism."[90]

Nor were secular Marxists ignorant of Catholic cultural practices—they permeated Chilean society. Many atheist leftists had grown up as Catholics, with Catholic family members, or at the very least with Catholic friends and neighbors. All leftist parties counted "believers" among their ranks, and not all Catholics understood their faith in a way that precluded membership in secular Marxist parties. In 1971 Communist leaders Luis Corvalán and Volodia Teitelboim told Cardinal Raúl Silva Henríquez that "[the Church's] credibility among the poor was unmatched; among their own [party] bases there was respect for and attention to the clergy." Mireya Baltra, a Communist legislator and politician, "went even further: she said that in her estimation 70 percent of the Communist bases were Catholic or identified as Catholic."[91] After the coup, the unorthodoxies of popular sector political and religious cultures combined with Catholic and Marxist histories of solidarity, providing a foundation for cooperation between anti-regime Catholics and the secular Marxist left. Solidarity provided a conceptual and practical framework for an ideologically pluralistic, anti-regime movement that emphasized the collective pursuit of common cause. In the poblaciones, grassroots opposition coalesced around this nexus.

Solidarity at the Grassroots

As the regime's attacks on the Left intensified and the human rights crisis worsened, grassroots solidarity emerged in poblaciones. Shortly after the coup, some Catholic churches opened their doors to the persecuted left, and as the mid-1970s economic crisis deepened, the Comité Pro Paz promoted the formation of social organizations such as comedores (soup kitchens) and bolsas de cesantes (unemployed people's collectives). Cooperation between anti-regime Church personnel and leftists (Catholic and otherwise) was central to this process, and the social organizations enacted a practice of solidarity that brought disparate social actors into contact with one another. In doing so, the organizations provided spaces for political expression and community interaction that encouraged dialogue and collective action. The organizations also provided a place for leftists to communicate with one another and facilitated rapprochement between the secular Marxist left and the Church, fortifying the social commons and capacity for anti-regime resistance.

Social activists and human rights workers quickly learned that solidarity required attitudinal and tactical shifts. In late 1974, Auxiliary Bishop Fernando Ariztía reported that residents of western Santiago faced escalating unemployment, alcoholism, prostitution, and domestic strife. In Barrancas Norte alone, one-third of children under the age of six were malnourished. Many unemployed workers, accustomed to providing for their families, were loath to seek assistance because they equated it with charity, which they found offensive.

This reaction was frequent enough, and the misery widespread enough, that in a widely disseminated bulletin Ariztía admonished readers to rethink their approach to material assistance. He cited the example of a poblador who yelled at local activists, "I want work and not a plate of food for the little kid; I don't want charity!" Ariztía explained that offering assistance "requires a profound delicacy so as not to wound him who has always lived from his work," and he chastised those with patronizing or complacent attitudes: "Some people become enthused [when they hear about the comedores] and say 'how lovely!,' but in truth what we should say is 'How sad, how lamentable that we've come to this.'" Ariztía proposed instead relationships based on "solidarity," which he defined as "sharing what one has, it indicates equality between people."[92]

Comité Pro Paz collaborators learned that the human rights situation in the poblaciones was extremely complex. They found that low socioeconomic status exacerbated persecuted families' problems. "In this sense, the first thing we saw was unemployment. Then there were health problems, which everyone who sought our help had," writes Sandra Rojas in her testimony of social work in the popular sectors. The combined violation of social and political rights was acute and of paramount concern in poblaciones, she concludes: "We said that the most violated human rights were the rights to health, work, and the possibility of talking with one's neighbors."[93]

In poblaciones, as neoliberal structural adjustment spread violations of social rights well beyond the ranks of the persecuted left, the Comité promoted social organizations that addressed hunger and unemployment. Although neoliberal tenets called for such privatization of social welfare and championed private initiative over public provision, the dictatorial state did not view these organizations kindly. While in one sense they were bootstrap organizations in which private individuals sought to assure their economic subsistence independently of the state, they were also vehicles of collective action outside the state's purview, a thorn in the dictatorship's side whose existence highlighted the regime's economic failures. They also formed part of a strategy to motivate collective action based on principles of solidarity antithetical to the dictatorship's and neoliberal ideologues' attempts to create an individualistic, "apolitical" society.

The social workers focused on food distribution, remembers Rojas, "but what really interested us was training [activists]." The tactical logic of these organizations was that the bolsas de cesantes would attract experienced labor and political activists, most of whom were men, and the comedores would attract women and children. The two types of organization would then form a platform for anti-regime socialization and collective action.[94] The Comité's approach assumed that the bolsas de cesantes would become the motors of sociopolitical organization in the poblaciones, but many priests balked at sheltering them because they distrusted ex-political prisoners' motives and feared repression.[95]

Ultimately, the most numerous and active adult participants were the women of the comedores. Although women rarely occupied leadership positions in labor unions, political parties, or local government, they were a driving force behind the land takeovers that established many poblaciones, and women were solid fixtures in neighborhood life. Pobladoras participated in housing committees, neighborhood councils, youth clubs, mothers centers, and political parties. Community health organizations and JAPs consisted almost exclusively of women. By 1973 there were 20,000 mothers centers in Chile, most in popular sector neighborhoods, with a total of 1,000,000 active members (10 percent of Chile's population).[96] Nor were pobladoras strangers to the world of paid labor. One 1968 study of fifty families in poblaciones San Gregorio and José María Caro found that 86 percent of women had worked outside the home.[97] During the first years of dictatorship, women's access to wage labor decreased as the economy declined. In 1974 and 1975, women's unemployment rate surpassed men's for the first time since 1967, driving both men and women to seek alternative means of subsistence.[98]

The women's focus differed from the men's. "Many [men] came [to the bolsas] after their release from prison camps," Rojas writes. "We got them together with the members of the comedores, and it turned out that the women didn't understand them at all. It was a different language. The women kept up their subsistence work, trying to gather a few pesos. We criticized [the women]," she admits, "because they didn't concern themselves with 'what's important.'" Despite the rocky start, a change in approach was underway that had the potential to achieve both ends: "We realized that what was important was how to distribute and how to receive that food with the goal of strengthening people's own capacity to promote organization."[99] They did this by valuing participants' perspectives and drawing on traditions of collective action rooted in popular sector political culture.

Rojas's story reflects an attitudinal shift from charity to solidarity that was underway in the Catholic Church. Paternalistic attitudes associated with traditional charity were coming to be understood as offensive, and they clashed with the idea of solidarity emerging in the context of cooperation between Christians and the secular Marxist left. In La Legua, participating in social organizations led some women to change their approach from charity to solidarity. Some women joined social organizations "on party orders," says Juan R. Others, though, "participated because they saw it as Christian charity and many, as they joined the groups, awoke to a greater promotional consciousness, a greater commitment to the people and not this thing, 'Son, for God's sake,' the little head-pat, like that. No. It was my moral obligation, and a commitment to those who were in that situation."[100] Concretely, this meant acting in solidarity with the poor and the persecuted left regardless of ideological differences, and it included rejecting downward moral displacement that blamed the poor for their poverty and the Left and women for their own oppression. "When a woman starts to participate in a group," explains Winnie Lira, who worked with the Vicaría, "first she realizes that it's not her that's bad, that she's not a worthless being, undignified, a dog that can be kicked when it's down. No." "And," Lira continues, "they were capable of understanding that the causes lay elsewhere and were provoked by others. As clear as that." The Comité and the Vicaría, she recalls, "never hesitated to point out where the error was. They never said: 'They're different points of view.' No." Rather, "We were very clear that dictatorship is an evil, that trampling human beings is an evil, that nobody should suffer the loss of their liberty because of their political ideas."[101]

Solidarity meant protecting leftists' lives, and it also meant cooperating with them in organizations. The Comité Pro Paz's "essential criteria" for carrying out its human rights work (and that it bequeathed to its successor, the Vicaría) emphasized "ecumenism," because "he who suffers does not distinguish between Churches or theologies, but clearly knows who is with him." Ecumenism, it stated, "extends to nonbelieving sectors who, for different motivations, find a common path." The Comité also rejected the separation of social and political rights, stating that "all the human rights should be assured jointly, because they guarantee the integral development of people and communities." The Comité emphasized commitment to sociopolitical organization, asserting that "serving mankind is not only supporting his individual and collective efforts to face a conjuncture; it's also continuing to support him in his human community to favor his integral liberation."[102] The new language of "human" rights entered the poblaciones via the Church and Comité Pro Paz, and it resonated with long-standing ideas about rights—universal suffrage, social justice, and workers' rights—that originated in nineteenth-century socialism.[103] In Chile, leftist concepts of "the pueblo's rights" embraced these historical principles and others that coincided with the Comité's concerns, including freedom from repression and the rights to assembly, association, and dignified working and living conditions.

The Comité's acceptance of "nonbelievers" enacted the principle of solidarity, and it responded to a de facto situation. By 1975, Juan C. recalls, the Left realized that the dictatorship stood to last. Leftists then began a process of "social insertion," joining popular sector social organizations linked to the

Church, the Comité Pro Paz, and the Vicaría.[104] Before the coup, Juan R. explains, in La Legua "the neighborhood was more at the vanguard than the parish," but afterward the local left and the parish community began "to mix rapidly, absolutely rapidly" because San Cayetano "opens its doors, by and by, to the entire social contingent." In La Legua, the organizational process "started to boom because the parties threw themselves into the church, get it? So, the priest gave them space, and they organized in such a way that they made all the organization theirs."[105] The Left's involvement in social organizations facilitated the turn from charity to solidarity. Historically, the Left was not in the business of charity: it empowered people to act collectively to solve shared problems, and it had a long history of organizing around bread-and-butter issues in the politically pluralistic milieu of Santiago's workplaces and poblaciones. Far from the halls where the powerful negotiated legislation, many leftists were primarily involved in social activism.[106] They created cooperatives, labor unions, and community organizations, improved neighborhood infrastructure, and planned squatter settlements. *Trabajo social* (social work) and *trabajo político* (political work) were mutually inclusive aspects of leftist political culture and revolutionary strategy. The post-coup social organizations were the popular sector left's natural environment, but now they operated almost exclusively under the auspices of the Catholic Church.

In Villa Francia, Cristo Liberador became the neighborhood's center for organization and regime opposition. Cristo Liberador was a concrete manifestation of liberationist Christianity that included Marxists among its congregants. "Already in October [1973]," explains the group's published historical testimony, "a number of people approached the locale, among them wives and family members of detained people. Many young people also came, most of them seeking a place to express themselves."[107] In December 1973, members held a Christmas celebration "with a fear that chewed our stomachs and dried our mouths," remembers the Lizama Ávalos family. "In front of a big bonfire and a hanging pike that served as a bell," they explain, "we denounced the crimes that were being committed in those moments, the suffering of the persecuted and tormented pueblo, and we announced the hope manifested in That Boy, nascent, who gave meaning to Life in a situation of Death."[108] A few months later, on the Saturday of Holy Week, 1974, Cristo Liberador held a Vía Crucis procession in the streets, denouncing "events [we] experienced and while a patrol of Carabineros followed us."[109] At the time, because of its religious identity Cristo Liberador was the only organization that could carry out such sustained public protest—the police stalked the procession but did not attack.

Meanwhile, young leftists drew close to Hermana Dolores, whose precoup experience included living among pobladores and advising students at the highly politicized Universidad de Concepción. Margarita C. recalls that she and a friend "introduced ourselves [to her] and said that we wanted to do something for people of the población in bad economic straits, but we wanted nothing to do with the religious thing. She agreed, and our presence pleased her, so she invited us to the next week's meeting, and of course we went." Although they initially approached the group with trepidation, they found UP activists there, and "we found out that Dolores was a nun, that she was leftist; the group became much more political." Hermana Dolores was "always very respectful and never mentioned to us the possibility of joining the comunidad [cristiana]. This lasted until [priest] Mariano [Puga] scolded the nun. She told me that Mariano asked her how it was possible that she had all the youngsters on that team instead of in the Comunidad Juvenil (Catholic Youth Community). Of course she spoke up and told him that we wanted nothing to do with that Comunidad, because it was lame and didn't resonate with us." The priest invited the young activists to the Comunidad Juvenil, says Margarita C., "and from that point on we integrated ourselves into [it]."[110] Cristo Liberador's inclusion of UP activists, Miristas, and leftist youth contributed to its development as a place for anti-regime organization.

Although affiliation with the Church offered a measure of protection, it did not guarantee safety. In mid-1974, the DINA imprisoned Puga and disappeared three members of Cristo Liberador: Enrique Toro Romero and Eduardo Lara Petrovich of the Communist Party, and José Villagra Astudillo of the MIR. All three were husbands and fathers active in their political parties, labor organizations, community, and church. By the end of 1974, recalls Irene, José's widow, there "were already three families of the disappeared, and there were other people who no longer had anything to eat, their children were malnourished." "We formed a children's comedor," remembers Enrique's wife, "with the support of the comunidad cristiana. Our children helped. So we struggled and forged ahead," she continues, "since the children had to eat. My son asked: 'Why do we have to eat lunch at the comedor?' Very needy children went. I calculate between fifty and one hundred children, but ours initiated it."[111] "Later," Irene explains, "[it] expanded much more, because the unemployment was enormous, and people had to be given food. Then, it wasn't just the children who went, it was entire families."[112]

The search for Eduardo, Enrique, and José drew the secular Marxist left closer to Cristo Liberador. The comunidad cristiana fought for health care and employment, recalls Juan, "things as simple as that," that the Communist Party traditionally supported. There had been no outlet for complaint or redress since the coup, and "that's when this situation arose in which people started to become conscious and also a little brave, and to feel themselves a little supported" by the Church. When Communists joined Cristo Liberador, "we were recognized as Communists, and what's more, sometimes we weren't looked upon very kindly by some people in the comunidad cristiana, or maybe by most," he opines. The Communists' intentions were clear: "We were pursuing the principle of social justice, seeking to clarify the [situation] of the detained-disappeared, and the Catholic Church was taking up that banner." "Most [of the disappeared] weren't Christian," he continues later, "they were Communists and some Miristas, but, let's say, they didn't belong [to the Church]. Fundamentally they were political [activists]," he argues, "so it was our banner of struggle, and if [the Catholics] were taking it up, they were welcome, but we were going to support that situation." "Don't forget," interjects Alba, "that two members of the comunidad cristiana, who today are disappeared detainees, were Communist militants."[113] Discrepancies over whose "banner" it was arose in part because of the disappeared men's multifaceted identities and affiliations. Both Cristo Liberador and the Left legitimately claimed them as their own. They bridged the divide between the Church and the Left precisely because they were active members of both. As such, they posed a threat to the regime. By attacking Catholic leftists in an activist comunidad cristiana, the regime sent the message that not even the Church could guarantee protection, and opening itself to the Left could bring repression upon its congregants.

The repression led to further organization. In 1974 or 1975, explains Irene, Mariano Puga helped create a bolsa de cesantes, "with all the people leaving the industries who were unionists and were organized," including women. The bolsa divided its income in such a way that, in addition to individual earnings, the group could buy scaffolding, assist with medical expenses, contribute to the comedores, and help the community.[114] One organization led to another, because repression and unemployment contributed to alcoholism and depression. The pastoral workers noticed that many of the unemployed were "sick from alcohol, alcoholic," says Hermana Dolores. She found that men "gathered in the *clandestinos* [unlicensed alcohol vendors], where they sold wine, to mourn their sorrows, vent their anguish. Sorrows in the sense that they had undertaken a process, they were subjects, and they became nothing, nobody. They lost their leadership, they lost everything, the organizations were broken." Alcoholism, continues Hermana Dolores, "was a social illness, it wasn't only individual. Usually the wife was neurotic, the teenager was getting high . . . so we said, 'We have to integrate the whole family,' and that's how it grew."[115] Between 1975 and 1979 the resulting rehabilitation club, Renacer a la Vida, grew from seven to nearly sixty men and women plus family members.[116]

The deleterious effects of repression and unemployment affected the comedor as well. "There were no fathers," explains Hermana Dolores, "and where are the fathers? Unemployed, at home, failed. 'Ah, no,' we said, 'maintaining a comedor for children and their fathers aren't responsible,' you see?" The organizers "made a conscious effort to gather the fathers and make them responsible for the comedores." Food preparation rotated among households, "and the pot passed through the población on the way to the comedores, and there the fathers got involved. A lot of people got involved who didn't have children but wanted to solidarize."[117] Some who wanted to solidarize were atheists and leftists estranged from the Church. Villa Francia's Communists, remembers Juan, used party contacts to the organization's benefit. "We had a president of the street markets," he recalls, "he was a party comrade, and we asked him as a favor to give us a certificate authorizing participants in the *olla común* [common pot] to pass through the markets asking the stall owners to cooperate with us. So," he explains, "we took that authorization, signed and stamped by the president of the street markets, and we went through with a cart— several compañeros did this, there were about four of us . . . and asked for donations." They delivered the donations to Cristo Liberador "and made a big pot of food."[118] It was through quotidian activities like these that popular sector social organizations became more pluralistic and ecumenical, and it was through the daily grind of survival that activists built a new social commons. In the process, people who had not considered themselves allies found themselves cooperating in pursuit of shared goals.

Talking about Prohibited Things

As local churches and social organizations brought people together, political relations shifted within the churches and neighborhoods. This process was not free of conflict, despite points of convergence between Marxist and Catholic traditions. Some pastoral workers in poblaciones tacitly supported the coup or defined their mission as purely "spiritual" in an effort to avoid any activity that the state might construe as politically motivated. At Espíritu Santo del Pinar, a church near La Legua, Juan R. recalls, "the guys [the priests] closed the doors. And they started to open them little by little, but we generated the opening, it wasn't the [clerical] congregation's attitude."[119] In La Legua, though, San Cayetano "opened much more, and it opened to everyone, and between them they started the human rights committee, the health team, all the organizations: the *olla común*, comedores— there were comedores in every chapel—there were health teams, women's committees."[120] Tensions occasionally arose between secular leftists and priests. "The Church itself had a clear global plan," Juan C. explains, "but it also wanted, at least the neighborhood priest wanted, this to be the Church's, and the Church's base, and that was how it had to be. On the other hand," he continues, "sectors of the Popular Unity, the Popular Unity parties, most of us aren't Christians, and here we were headed for conflict. There were tensions and contradictions at first, but these things were corrected with time. The Church understood that it should work more broadly, and sectors of the Left also broadened their perspective, being less dogmatic, and that's where all the work known as solidarity [happened]."[121] The Church's outreach bore fruit. In 1973, 20 percent of Santiaguinos attended Mass once or more per month. By 1979 this number had more than doubled, to 42.8 percent. Additionally, by 1975 the Church counted at least 20,000 "actively committed" lay participants in comunidades cristianas nationally, and by 1978 more than 10,000 young people had joined related programs. Although the Church's umbrella provided protection, it had limits. The Church's activities attracted the DINA's attention. The secret police spied on popular sector comundades cristianas and paid unemployed pobladores for information.[122]

The opening of local churches to the secular left brought new people into their orbits, but not all congregants agreed, arguing that their pastors were straying from their spiritual mission, taking too many risks, or becoming too political. Repression targeting comunidades cristianas exacerbated these tensions. Still others worried that the Left would "use" the Church, disrespecting its religious purpose and exposing congregants to danger. Along with the influx of new people came an exodus of others who withdrew or changed churches. In Villa Francia, explains María Teresa, "many people left, in fact, in terms of the Catholic-Catholics of Villa Francia, none participated in Cristo Liberador, no. I mean, they went to Santa Isabel de Hungría, and if they had to baptize their children they baptized them there, if they had to marry, they married there, and they didn't come to the comunidad cristiana to receive the sacraments because those who came had to be super brave," she recalls. "If they came to baptize the kid and ran into Mariano, he demanded, 'You have to commit yourself here, you have to support this and that' . . . and even more, and not dress the child in white for the ceremony, get it?"[123] Pastoral workers in San Cayetano, a longer-standing congregation in an older población, faced similar challenges. "La Legua is different," says Juan R., "because the Christians were always committed Christians with a much more holistic formation. Nevertheless," he continues, "this break between Christians and party people occurred, and many Christians left because at one point Guido [the priest] dedicated himself to the social movement rather than the doctrinal movement." The priest's doctrinal approach was controversial, he remembers: "'There's no faith without deed,' says San Pablo, and in this sense Guido is quite radical, he embraces in one way or another everything having to do with liberation theology." Some people abandoned Sunday Mass, "because Guido's homily is powerful, it's a denunciatory homily, it's a homily to make us react to the dictatorship."[124]

Others welcomed the liberationist approach. "It was very special," Luisa recalls of sacraments in Cristo Liberador, "not just anyone took communion, it wasn't given to whomever just came to stick out his tongue to receive the host, no. . . . Mariano said, 'I don't want people who come here to swallow hosts, I want people committed to the suffering pueblo.'" Communion "was to gain strength to continue working on what one was doing, so it was very striking, very strong, and very rich, even very attractive to the political people." The religious culture of Cristo Liberador emphasized life commitments to social justice. "Mariano said, 'Here I don't want you coming [to confession] to tell me that you stole a candy or beat up the guy next door, here the gravest sin is to not be participating in the liberation of the Chilean pueblo, that's what I want to hear, if somebody wants to tell me that, I accept, the rest can go home,'" Luisa remembers. This approach to faith and practice was new to her. She and her husband had participated in the MOAC, but the liberationist church opened new horizons.[125]

The political potential of liberationist Christianity was attractive to the Left, and the religious aspects resonated with leftists as well, Manuel explains. "I believe it has also been discovered, over time," he says, "that all these 'Marxist' compañeros and compañeras, [had] an entire religious education or formation. . . . So in [Villa Francia's] comunidad it's as if the religious part of these political, Marxist people is reborn, and they start realizing that there are fundamental elements in Christianity and Marxism that are similar and point in the same direction." This rapprochement facilitated communication and tolerance.[126] Silvia, an atheist member of the Communist Party, remembers that "[in Cristo Liberador] we even prayed, we went so far as to pray. We respected, let's say, the place where we were, because we couldn't just go to use it, and it did us good too, so I even prayed." When her young children expressed fear of her going to meetings, "I told them, 'Look, the Christians in there say that God accompanies them. Ask him to accompany you while I'm not here. I don't believe in that, but those who do say he comes, they feel him.' I still didn't want them to believe," she says, "because I don't believe in that, but I felt that it was a very important weapon for a child."[127]

Priests mediated tensions between secular leftists and Catholics within comunidades cristianas and social organizations. When in the late 1970s political conflict arose in Cristo Liberador, Mariano Puga promoted communication and cooperation between members.[128] In La Legua, when San Cayetano opened its doors to the persecuted left, "One knew whom one was dealing with, we knew who was Communist, we knew who was Socialist, we knew who was radical," says Juan R.[129] Juanita, who joined the MIR in the late 1970s, explains that political activists "were free in the rooms [the priest] gave us to organize ourselves as we could," with the understanding that weapons were prohibited on Church property and that they were to help with expenses and activities.[130] Ecumenical practices and liberationist approaches resonated with socially conscious Catholics and the secular Marxist left. Some liberationist comunidades cristianas alienated congregants who preferred more traditional approaches. Nevertheless, although they rejected certain religious practices derived from conservative tradition and folk Catholicism, they were otherwise remarkably democratic islands of refuge in a sea of violent dictatorship.

The generalized damage to the social commons troubled both the Church and the Left. To counter obstacles to unity and collective action, the Church propelled the idea of solidarity through its affiliated social organizations. In this context, leftist and Catholic concepts of solidarity converged to contradict the regime's exclusionary vision for society, as reflected in its repression and demonization of the Left and others who objected to the neoliberal economic policies sowing misery in poblaciones. In July 1975, the cardinal and vicars of Santiago emitted a pastoral letter to explain the doctrinal foundations of solidarity as a practice and provide guidelines for its implementation.[131] A related educational pamphlet circulated in the poblaciones. It emphasized the difference between solidarity and charity, interspersing cartoons with quotes from the pastoral letter. Solidarity, it explained, "is mutual dependence between people that makes it so that some cannot be happy if the rest are not." The fundamental difference between solidarity and charity was that between sharing and distributing, "and not only sharing material things but also joy, pain, and enthusiasm . . . solidarity is not distributed like heating gas, rather it is shared with broad fraternal sensibility."[132] Sharing marked a shift from traditional charity in which the privileged donated castoffs to the poor rather than systematically sharing the wealth. The negative connotation was clear: recipients of charity were themselves castoffs and unworthy of a fair share of the wealth. In poblaciones, where few had surplus to distribute, sharing was also a way to engage as many people as possible in mutual assistance to alleviate the effects of economic crisis. Children who ate at comedores, for example, learned that they should help the organization provide for even more people.[133] From this perspective, well-being was not a zero-sum game. The concept of solidarity encapsulated a set of values and practices to help reverse the social atomization tearing communities apart. It meant providing assistance where needed, regardless of political or religious differences, and working together to solve collective problems.

Solidarity's explicit goal was justice, and its practice encompassed more than just Church-sanctioned activity. "The duty of solidarity does not stop with simply sharing with the needy," read the pastoral letter. "The struggle for justice is also an authentic form of solidary love that can exist in the sphere of social and political conflict just as in the path of nonviolent action and performance in the public opinion."[134] Solidarity, then, a desirable and "Christian" practice, was not confined to religious or apolitical pursuits. Given the pamphlet's intended audience, the reference to social and political conflict appears to be a veiled nod to the clandestine left and an invitation to rapprochement. Illustrations in the pamphlet depict Chile's heterogeneous popular sectors as a group with shared interests. In one, two characters discuss their respective poblaciones and what they have in common. Another illustration shows men, women, and children, poor, blind, and wounded, one man with a shackle trailing from his ankle, walking together toward a point off-page. The caption reads, "Solidarity is received and offered by men, women, and children, emerging from it life and hope born of pain, that guides itself in search of a more just and fraternal society animated by the spirit of the Gospel."[135] This call for liberation through class solidarity and active struggle was clear to both Catholics and leftist "nonbelievers." It was also legible to the authorities, who might view it for what it was: a call to organization and action.

The junta considered itself a defender of Western Christian civilization and its members were Catholic, but it attacked the Catholic Church for its defense of human rights and its social activism.[136] In addition to repression, there were other obstacles to solidarity. Some conservative Catholics disagreed with Vatican II and Medellín; the Left was internally divided; some Catholics feared or abhorred leftists and atheists, and some on the Left rejected the Catholic Church as a historical agent of oppression. Conflicts unrelated to politics or religion, such as property disputes, could also thwart solidarity. To address such obstacles, the document emphasized the transcendent nature of the struggle: "Because these aren't words of today but of always."[137] It also cited the Bible, "[The Spirit of the Lord] sent me to bring the good news to the poor. To announce to the captives their liberty. To return light to the blind and free the oppressed (Luke 4:18–19)." The Church's decision to couch its calls for social justice in language that evoked internationally recognized, historically significant principles such as liberty, equality, and fraternity was strategic. This laid the groundwork for political and religious pluralism within grassroots organizations. The emphasis on the universality of the struggle for liberty and freedom from oppression provided a point of convergence with the ideals of the Left, offering a common ground for cooperation between estranged secular and religious actors. It also extended a measure of protection: activities inspired in transcendent ideals, carried out under the shelter of the "universal" (Catholic) Church were more difficult for the authorities to attack.

Leftist leaders recognized the importance of the social organizations and the Church's orientation toward the popular sectors. In September 1974, the MIR had called for militants to work within community organizations and to form resistance committees.[138] In a July 1975 document prepared in East Berlin, the UP leadership in exile highlighted the importance of the Church's work in poblaciones, commenting favorably on "expressions of solidarity developed in the worker and popular sectors to mitigate the effects of unemployment and hunger." They called for the formation of a Popular Front against the regime that would be "much broader, politically, socially, and ideologically, than the Popular Unity," incorporating "the humanist values of Christians, lay people and Marxists . . ." and implementing "superior and true, honest and egalitarian ideological pluralism in relations between members." They explicitly called for Christians' participation: "In this new patriotic, revolutionary and libratory enterprise, an active role corresponds to the Christian masses together with the rest of the pueblo's organizations. They have a place now and in the future in the struggle to bring down the Junta and establish a new society."[139] Inside Chile at least one clandestine publication, *Pueblo Cristiano*, reprinted the document several months later. It exhorted readers to discuss the document and urged them to struggle against the dictatorship alongside the clandestine left.[140]

As previously estranged sociopolitical actors encountered one another in comunidades cristianas and social organizations, clergy encouraged solidarity. Priests used the parable of the Good Samaritan (Luke 10:30–37) to explain solidarity as an integral part of moral ethics dating to ancient times. In this biblical story, a priest and a Levite bypass a man of their own faith who has been attacked by robbers and lays injured beside the road. Instead, an enemy Samaritan comes to his rescue. "Which of these three do you think was a neighbor to the man who fell into the hands of robbers?" Jesus asks. His listener replies, "The one who had mercy on him." Jesus responds, "Go and do likewise." The story was relevant to the Chilean context, where the most well-positioned people within the government and economic system did not assist victims of oppression. On the contrary, many perpetrated or were complicit with it. In the context of Marxist-Christian relations, the enemy "Samaritan" unexpectedly revealed himself as the injured man's metaphorical neighbor when the Chilean Catholic Church assisted the persecuted Left and when atheist Marxists joined with Christians to feed hungry neighborhood children. It was the Samaritan's act of "establish[ing] this *experience* of the *face-to-face* with those robbed, injured, or abandoned *outside the path*," writes Enrique

Dussel, that made the Samaritan "good" and constituted the act as one of "solidarity."[141] Therefore, everyone was encouraged to think twice about who their "neighbors" really were. Were pobladores' "neighbors" regime supporters who expected them to silently bear the brunt of structural adjustment while their children starved? Might atheist Marxists find "neighbors" among the religious? Shouldn't Christians "Go and do likewise," as Jesus commanded? The parable encouraged everyone to think about who their real allies might be and in doing so to critically examine their own prejudices and behaviors. It offered a guide to solidary praxis that had the potential to counteract the fear and enmity permeating post-coup society, and it provided a framework for an ideologically pluralistic movement for change.

The tenets of the Good Samaritan parable initially played out most visibly in growing support for the Agrupación de Familiares de Detenidos-Desaparecidos (AFDD, Association of Family Members of Disappeared Detainees). In the newsletter *Cristo Dialogante*, of the Chilean Catholic Church's Secretariat for Nonbelievers, a priest who joined the AFDD's hunger strike in 1978 described his experience of solidarity with nonreligious Marxists. "We were well aware that this call [for solidarity] did not come from the Catholic camp," he explained. "It came from them, the AFDD of dominantly Marxist tendency. . . . We discovered in them a marvelous faith. They believe, in spite of their terrible experiences, they believe in mankind, they believe in humanity. They believe in the power of truth and justice. They believe in the efficacy of love and pain. They believe that there is something great for which one can give one's life and they feel the pleasure of the total gift. Isn't this really a religious faith, an 'implicit Christianity?'" he asks, eventually concluding, "We all have faith that something or Someone is moving, and that the structures of vested interests and oppression should cede. Because solidarity will triumph and love is stronger than death."[142] Some secular Marxists resented insistence on their "implicit Christianity" and with good reason; under normal circumstances it suggests profound disrespect for others' beliefs. In this context, though, the priest's comparison was astute. It offered Christians a religious justification for solidarity with the Left, emphasizing similarities rather than differences in such a way as to cast Marxists as essentially Christian. The priest does not ask Christians to accept Marxism but to recognize their own humanity and values in others.

That same year, some members of the Chilean Catholic hierarchy also challenged the compatibility of Christianity with neoliberal capitalism, the system the repression made possible. "In truth," wrote Bishop Jorge Hourton, "the praxis of a competitive, 'liberal individualist' economic system that subordinates everything to its domination and expansion, transforming social life, politics, culture, customs, values, people's aspirations, etc. in function of the economy is merely a form of materialism." This materialism, he continued, "apotheosizes money, pleasure, or power and therefore 'de-apotheosizes' . . . the Christ of the Gospels, of truth, of love, of liberty, of peace: for authentic Christian faith, it is just another form of practical atheism, regardless of individual freedom of worship and its representatives' devotion." He challenged regime supporters' claims to Christianity, asking, "isn't there another case of nonbelieving—and even materialism and atheism—in the soul of regimes of force, that for not believing in true man, cannot truly believe in the living God of Jesus Christ?"[143] These calls for solidarity and critiques of powerful Cold War discourse linking capitalism and Christianity informed resistance organization in poblaciones, as did the Comité's, and later the Vicaría's, promotion of rights that resonated with the popular sectors and the Left: the right to food, work, fair pay, assembly, association, unionization, and political freedom.[144]

Meanwhile, the practice of solidarity provided opportunities for community building, empowerment, and political organizing in the poblaciones. Cristo Liberador's methods, explains Mario, at the time a Mirista organizing in Villa Francia, "opened Old Testament themes, it wasn't restricted to the Gospels, but rather it opened up strongly, I'd say, to more than one prophet, to more than one text of the Old Testament, but especially Exodus." The story of the Israelites' liberation, he remembers, "that, definitively, was the pueblo in which we wanted to see ourselves, that served as a mirror for this pueblo subjected to oppression who wants to forge a path to liberation and that in some way has Yahvé as an ally who is interested in the liberation of his people, interested in his people's lot." This theological approach had profound effects, he recalls, "in the sense that the comunidad had not only the opportunity to see it and problematize it, to feel supported by the word of God, but also [to feel] supported by their own experience of community. To feel that you're not alone in the world, you're not just a *loco* on the loose whom the dictatorship hasn't yet managed to eliminate, but that life had more meaning and could be lived in other ways."[145] The story of Exodus buoyed the spirits of regime opponents, as did Old Testament tales of divine wrath against oppressors. Cristo Liberador's pedagogical methods encouraged sociopolitical analysis and political education. The comunidad's leaders "sought methodological, educational forms so that people would understand well and quickly," explains Manuel. "For example, one person would lie on the floor and another would put a foot on him, step on him, then Mariano would say, 'What do we do in a situation like this, what does a person do when stepped on?' [The person] either allows him- or herself to be stepped on, or the person gets up, with dignity," he concludes.[146]

The practice of solidarity in a context of ideological pluralism and ecumenism built individuals' self-confidence and capacity for sociopolitical activism. "You know, that word, [solidarity], is very important," says Rosa, a teenager in población José María Caro during the 1970s. In 1974 the DINA disappeared her brother, Pedro Merino Molina, a Communist Youth activist. Rosa's mother, Ana, joined the AFDD, and the oldest children helped her and cared for their younger siblings. The children ate at the local church's comedor, and during the mid-1970s, remembers Rosa, "They started to talk a lot about 'solidarity.' I heard it and heard it." "One week," she continues, "my mama was so sick that I went to stand in line [at the comedor] with my sister, and she said, 'We have to go [to the Catholic meeting too],' and I went, not very pleased. When I arrived, I felt, one feels it in her heart that she shares the feeling that the other is experiencing. And I've never forgotten that moment, because it was the moment in which I was capable of stating an opinion." Stating her opinion was difficult, "but afterward I felt such relief when I stated an opinion about what solidarity was, and I felt the other people's support. They shared my opinion, and that made me feel good, as if I had done something positive."[147] A wide range of people found in these organizations religious and political pluralism and freedom of expression and association—cornerstones of democratic society that the regime repressed but that were not forgotten. These fragile but significant spaces allowed an alternative social commons to take root, one opposed in its diversity and values to the dictatorship's exclusionary practices and attempts to form obedient, apolitical citizens in service to the neoliberal economy.

As the dictatorship began to institutionalize its rule and cement its neoliberal model amid the so-called economic miracle of the late 1970s, the party-based political opposition struggled to maintain forward momentum. In poblaciones, though, activism accelerated. There was no economic miracle in the poblaciones but rather growing sentiments that high unemployment, repression, and economic crisis were the new normal. In this context grassroots activists expanded and solidified organizational networks, and political parties—especially the MIR and the Communist Party—surfaced more openly in the popular sectors. Meanwhile, youth began to assert themselves within neighborhood social organizations and comunidades cristianas. They formed organizations of their own, and some joined the clandestine left, taking local regime opposition in new directions. Rather than a period of crisis, 1978 marked the end of five years of retreat, kicking off a resumption of popular sector mobilization that reached a climax with the national protests of 1983–87.

5

Miracles, Mirages, and Mobilization, 1978–1982

The authorities, for their part, have acknowledged [that people have disappeared]. Of course they haven't acknowledged—because they can't—that disappearance is due to actions attributable to the Government.

Sergio Fernández Fernández, minister of the interior, 1978[1]

We are sincerely sorry for you all because the Lord will charge you the price of the truth, and the price has been very high: the life, blood and disappearance of hundreds of people, human beings, detained by government Security Services. . . . The truth is simple: we're a great mass of people who suffer hunger, unemployment, lack of social security, we don't have access to health care, we're marginalized from education, we're denied access to recreation, we're prohibited from thinking and we're prohibited from speaking . . . on pain of disappearance.

Letter to Lucía Hiriart de Pinochet from Comunidad Cristiana Popular Cristo Liberador, Villa Francia, 1979[2]

The Price of the Truth

"The Lord will charge you the price of the truth" for violating the pueblo's human rights, members of Cristo Liberador warned First Lady Lucía Hiriart de Pinochet. The letter's authors did not draw a line between the violation of political and social rights. Rather, they describe them as constituent elements of the same project of dispossession and subjugation. They charge that the regime used gross human rights violations—in this case disappearance—as a means to suppress the exercise of the political rights necessary to fulfill social rights. Their warning was not idle, and the bill collectors would not necessarily come from on high. Within the liberationist Christian traditions at Cristo Liberador's roots, "the oppressed pueblo is the Lord of history," and human struggle against worldly injustice would establish the Kingdom of God.[3] In September 1979, when Cristo Liberador's letter appeared in the press, the struggle had already begun. Mobilization against the regime had risen over the previous year. The 1978 International Women's Day (March 8) and May Day (May 1) demonstrations drew an estimated 10,000 protesters apiece, and a seventeen-day, AFDD hunger strike later that May galvanized solidarity in Chile and abroad. The revelation that November of the horrors of Lonquén, where the corpses of disappeared campesinos were found in abandoned lime ovens, provided concrete evidence of state-perpetrated disappearance. The protest pilgrimage to the atrocity site in early 1979 produced powerful images, as photographers captured the ovens' stark brickwork and the 1,500 protesters.[4] Members of Cristo Liberador had participated in the May Day demonstrations, the AFDD hunger strike and solidarity activities, and the pilgrimage to Lonquén, and now, in a different form of protest, they directly challenged Hiriart de Pinochet. The letter was not an ingenuous petition for intercession, which its authors knew better than to expect, but rather a blistering denunciation of atrocity and an example of audacious free speech: it was partially reproduced in the Vicaría's magazine, *Solidaridad*.

This rising tide of mobilization addressed political and social rights in similar measure. Some of the largest protests were the AFDD's hunger strikes in 1978 and 1979. They birthed street protests, fasts, assemblies, solidarity strikes, and other expressions of support in Chile and abroad. Other mobilizations, such as annual protest demonstrations in September—traditionally, the month of national independence (Sept. 18), presidential elections (Sept. 4), and now also the coup anniversary (Sept. 11)—and on December 10 (Human Rights Day), referenced political rights and democracy with their timing and focus. A third type of mobilization addressed social rights more explicitly in the form of labor actions and strikes; hunger marches; protests on March 8 and May 1; and petitions, assemblies, and land takeovers in pursuit of affordable housing. Continuing economic crisis and political repression were bringing frustrations to a boiling point in the popular sectors. In Villa Francia, Hermana Dolores remembers, "The situation became unsustainable." When a border conflict over islands in the Beagle Channel broke out in late 1978 between Chile and Argentina, she did a survey in the población, asking, "'Listen, what happens if they call you to fight Argentina?' I asked one, I asked others, I asked many. They all gave me the same answer: 'I'll go to La Moneda, but afterward I'll throw myself against Pinochet, not against Argentina.' They all told me the same," she recalls, "so I realized the internal state people were in, to respond with weapons, I mean, willing, if they had weapons, if given an opportunity. The disparity was very large, but look what they had in mind." Hermana Dolores uses this story to make the point that by the late 1970s, in Villa Francia contempt for the regime had begun to outweigh fear, and "people's only aspiration was to end the dictatorship, they couldn't stand it."[5]

The escalating unrest stood in sharp contrast to the regime's triumphalism; 1977 to 1981 were the dictatorship's glory years, the years of "economic miracle" and political institutionalization. When in July 1977 Pinochet gave his (in)famous Chacarillas speech on the homonymous Santiago hilltop before a crowd of right-wing, torch-carrying youngsters of the Frente Juvenil de Unidad Nacional (National Unity Youth Front), what most struck anti-regime listeners, beyond the event's fascist aesthetic, was Pinochet's announcement of plans for political institutionalization. These would project the dictatorship's neoliberal system into the foreseeable future through a new political constitution and a gradual transition to a "protected" (partial and limited) democracy. Along with the proscription of the political parties "in recess," including the Christian Democrats, these developments put to rest remaining hope among moderate liberals that the regime's grip on power would be transitory or elections forthcoming.

Nevertheless, hopes for international pressure against the dictatorship ran high as the United Nations' Ad Hoc Working Group on the Situation of Human Rights in Chile sent an investigatory commission to Chile, and the Carter administration pressed the regime for information about the 1976 assassination of Orlando Letelier and Ronni Moffitt in Washington, DC. To cultivate an image of legality and stability necessary to lessen the pressure and attract political support at home, the dictatorship dissolved the DINA in 1977, replacing it with the Central Nacional de Informaciones (CNI, National Information Center); orchestrated a "national consultation" in 1978 to demonstrate citizen opposition to international human rights observers; instituted an amnesty law for political crimes committed between 1973 and 1978; and ended the state of siege, downgrading to a lesser state of emergency. Meanwhile, to produce an image of political opening, the junta incorporated more members of the civilian right into high government posts, including Mónica Madariaga as minister of justice (1977) and Sergio Fernández Fernández as minister of the interior (1978). Throughout, the regime proceeded apace with its plans and soon basked in the glow of the "economic miracle," the promulgation of the 1980 Constitution, and the election of dictator-friendly Ronald Reagan to the U.S. presidency. Falling inflation, improved economic growth, and a shiny veneer of imported consumer goods and conspicuous consumption attracted positive international attention. It also generated domestic support, or at least complacency, among middle- and upper-class sectors that benefited from financial deregulation, easy credit, and an overvalued peso. With renewed airs of legitimacy, regime technocrats forged ahead with the so-called seven modernizations, including judicial reform, the privatization of health care, education, agriculture, labor, and social security, plus administrative decentralization that fragmented the targets of popular sector demands in areas such as housing, health, and education.

By the early 1980s, the regime would be touting the virtues of a radical neoliberal economic model built on foreign credit and short-term speculative ventures, constructed at the expense of a heavily repressed, immiserated population. As it crafted this mirage of economic success, however, the marginalized people whose misery underpinned it were organizing in a time of profound and rapid change. The years from 1978 to 1982 were a complex time of agitation and strategic reorientation, and it was no longer possible to claim that "nothing" was happening in poblaciones as popular sector protest multiplied in frequency and size. Popular sector activists' multifaceted identities and affiliations contributed to mobilization.[6] They also account for the difficulty of fitting the rise of poblador protest into either "old" or "new" social movement paradigms. The "old social movement" paradigms that emphasize the role of labor, the Left, and class identity falter when faced with the post-coup 1970s and 1980s when these elements did not appear to dominate popular sector organization. The rise of what appeared to be new modes of organization and sociopolitical identity (e.g. nonparty-affiliated women's and youth organizations) complicated theoretical paradigms drawn from analyses of pre-coup political practice. Yet the multifaceted nature of popular sector identities and affiliations also makes the "new social movement" paradigms an uneasy fit in the Chilean context. Several factors complicate the narrative of the "new" in terms of both identity and affiliation: (1) the presence and influence of leftists and labor unionists within "new" social organizations, (2) the ways in which individuals' "old" political and theoretical frameworks informed their "new" identities and organizations, (3) the class-based nature of "new" organizations and subjectivities in Santiago's poblaciones, and (4) organized labor's and the Left's continuing influence in popular sector political culture.

Pobladores and their allies used their multifaceted identities and affiliations with the Church, political parties, labor unions, and social organizations to build and mobilize "social movement webs" of dissent. The term "social movement webs," more so than "networks," write Sonia Alvarez, Evelina Dagnino, and Arturo Escobar, "conveys the intricacy and precariousness of the manifold imbrications and ties established among movement organizations, individual participants, and other actors in civil and political society and the state." The concept of social movement webs is rooted in new social movement theory but offers a useful corrective to the binary of "old" and "new" because it recognizes this greater complexity and does not exclude "old" class-based movements and their activists from consideration of "new" collectives organized around identities not primarily defined by socioeconomic class. Yet it allows for the inclusion of socioeconomic class and class struggle as constituent parts of identity formation and cultural politics, ameliorating new social movement theories' tendency to downplay class as a superseded category of analysis supposedly rendered obsolete with the decline of Cold War–era socialism and the rise of neoliberalism.[7] Combining the idea of social movement webs with those of "subsidence" and *fin del reflujo* (end of the ebb), two concepts derived from Chilean theories of social history to be discussed later, is useful in reconciling some of the theoretical disjunctures between the old and new social movement paradigms. The concepts of *fin del reflujo* and subsidence suggest that the "historicity, social bases, and origins" of Chile's social movements had not fundamentally changed during the 1970s and early 1980s, and that a combination of both culture and political economy underpinned the rise of anti-regime, popular sector social movement.[8] The concept of social movement webs is especially appropriate in the Chilean case because, like a floating fishing net moving with waves and tide, a social movement web can be simultaneously visible and invisible, as some of its segments move below the surface, out of sight, while others move visibly upon the surface.

These grassroots dynamics reveal a new periodization of activism and protest in Chile. Economic crisis and revelations of gross human rights violations spurred protest well before the economy crashed in 1982. The post-coup solidarity-building that we saw in chapter 4 laid the basis for the reemergence of large-scale popular sector protest after the five-year ebb between 1973 and 1978. Although dominant interpretations of the 1978–82 period most often highlight the sense of stagnation and strategic crisis that the regime's economic and political consolidation produced among opposition elite and party strategists, in poblaciones this was a time of organizational effervescence and rising protest.

Stories of Stagnation and Mobilization

The regime's political institutionalization and neoliberalism's seeming successes accelerated a period of critical reflection within the UP and

MIR as party leadership confronted the limitations of current strategies and instituted profound, divergent changes based on analyses of the Allende administration's downfall, the dictatorship's power, and exiled party leaders' experiences with Eastern European socialism. By 1980 the UP coalition ended as the Socialist Party fractured and the Left's strategies changed. Following the coup, the parties of the UP had followed a broad "Antifascist Front" strategy led by the Communist Party, cooperating with one another, seeking alliances with the Christian Democrats, and calling on "all the men, women, and youth of our pueblo" to join together to overthrow the dictatorship and "retake, with majoritarian support of the pueblo, the path of revolutionary change."[9] The MIR and a sector of the Socialist Party had advocated a combination of armed resistance and grassroots sociopolitical struggle to form a popular movement capable of overthrowing the dictatorship.[10] During the late 1970s, these orientations shifted. The MIR instituted its Guerra Popular Prolongada (Prolonged Popular War) strategy and began Operación Retorno, an ill-fated project to return militants to Chile from abroad to reinvigorate the party and form guerrilla fronts. In 1979 the Socialist Party fractured as "renovated" factions accepted capitalism and sought alliances with the Christian Democrat Party, whose recent migration into the opposition in 1977 expanded political opportunities for moderate liberals. The MAPU and Izquierda Cristiana also broke with orthodox Marxism. A divergent MAPU faction joined the armed resistance, forming the Movimiento Juvenil Lautaro (Lautaro) in 1982.[11] In 1980 the Communist Party announced its Rebelión Popular de Masas (Popular Rebellion of the Masses) strategy and accepted the legitimacy of "all forms of struggle," drawing closer to the MIR and building what would later become the Frente Patriótico Manuel Rodríguez (Manuel Rodríguez Patriotic Front, FPMR/Frente).[12] The Christian Democrat Party's new presence among the opposition and the Left's improved operational capacity generated a hardening breach between the regime and the opposition such that by 1981, underlying social, economic, and political tensions arguably reached levels similar to those of 1973.[13] Still, the regime's success in cultivating legitimacy at home and abroad with lower-profile repression, political institutionalization, and the "economic miracle" presented challenges for the divided political opposition, generating a sense of stagnation and strategic crisis.

In poblaciones, though, this was a time of organizational momentum, sociopolitical effervescence, and rising protest, as pobladores and their allies expanded and mobilized social dissent rooted in the politics and practice of solidarity developed between 1973 and 1978. The complexities of Christian and Marxist subjectivity and practice were but some of the many ways that pobladores and their allies defied simple categorization and used their multifaceted identities and affiliations to mount resistance to the regime. During the late 1970s and early 1980s, the same people might mobilize as workers or unemployed workers on May 1, as pobladores in land takeovers, or as Christians in anti-regime Vía Crucis processions. Party activists joined social organizations, and members of social organizations joined political parties. Members of armed groups participated in nonviolent organizations, including those that practiced nonviolent resistance. Activists practiced solidarity across organizational lines, and the relative fluidity of their identities and affiliations facilitated this process, making them nexuses in expanding webs of dissent that crisscrossed Santiago.

The protests of 1978–82 broke through the "bloody veil" by eroding walls of silence, insularity, and fear. Seeing protest held the potential to revert the silencing effects of the regime's spectacles of repression in poblaciones. Seeing protest offered observers and participants the opportunity to change their perceptions of the potential for opposition, and to connect the individual to the collective and the personal to the political.[14] Seeing others' public expressions of dissent opened vistas of possibility for expressing one's own opposition, and seeing substantial numbers of protesters made joining them seem more possible. In Villa Francia, the comunidad cristiana made dissent visible by taking protest activities outdoors. In a context in which public gatherings attracted suspicion and often ended in arrests, beatings, and worse, the presence in the street of dozens, sometimes hundreds, of demonstrators was powerful. Numerous factors contributed to the rise of public protest: feelings of frustration and unsustainability, a sense of urgency and righteous outrage, the examples set by earlier protestors such as the AFDD, and the end of the state of siege. The Church also provided opportunities for public expressions of dissent, as *Soldaridad*'s report on Cristo Liberador's letter to Hiriart de Pinochet demonstrates.

Between 1978 and 1982, with the support of local churches and the Left, protest increased in size and frequency. Leftist militants noticed and shared responsibility for the rise in protest activity, and trabajo político (political work) surfaced more explicitly in Santiago's poblaciones as party activists stepped up efforts to support and influence what many thought could be an incipient anti-regime social movement. Juan C. recalls that "you beg[an] to compete to lead the social movement . . . the MAPU competing with the MIR at the youth level, the MAPU competing with the Communist Party for the unemployed, or allegados, homeless. And also these militants made themselves known to the clergy, priests, nuns. . . . They're no longer so clandestine, you start to have public people, and they're the spokespeople and representatives of those parties." Political activists' more open presence was generally accepted, he remembers, "if it was an honest form of contributing. If there was manipulation and the name of the organization was used in other instances without the organization's authorization, it produced friction and problems."[15] Meanwhile, the easing of restrictions on professional associations and access to international aid created a growing number of NGOs critical of the regime. Some took the form of research institutes, where intellectuals produced analyses and policy studies. Others, such as Educación and Comunicaciones (ECO), combined research with outreach and political education.

Maintaining cohesion within and among the organizations and people in the webs of dissent was a contentious process. It became more so as impatience grew in poblaciones, as the Left operated more openly, as the PC, MIR, and Lautaro channeled resources into armed struggle, and as the Church moved rightward under Pope John Paul II. Clergy and religious sisters tried to guide and support their parishioners through sociopolitical decision-making processes, ever wary of political instrumentalization by the Left and the dangers of repression. Many of the breaches that widened within the opposition after 1983—between the grassroots and political parties, between liberationist Christians and the Church, and between regime opponents who accepted armed struggle and those who condemned it—first arose in the late 1970s and early 1980s. The conflicts stemmed from historical rivalries, incompatible long-term objectives, and disagreements about strategies and tactics. However, despite intra-opposition conflict, this was a period of growth and acceleration within popular sector social movement webs.

The 1978–82 period holds a privileged but overlooked place in memorias soterradas. It is sometimes overlooked because, in retrospect, it was a transitional period between the suffocatingly repressive years of 1973–78 and the explosion of the first national protests in 1983. The terror of 1973–78 and the exhilaration of the national protests tend to overshadow these intermediate years of transition, which nonetheless generate positive associations because many popular sector activists saw their efforts bear fruit as public protest gained momentum. Certain events hold special places in memorias soterradas, including perennial March 8 and May 1 demonstrations, the AFDD hunger strikes of 1978 and 1979, the urban land takeovers of 1980, the mass Vía Crucis processions of the early 1980s, and the Hunger Marches of 1982.[16] Rising labor unrest, including miners' protests and the 1980 Panal strike helped crack the stifling political climate of the previous five years, signaling that the labor movement, a traditional bulwark of popular sector power, was expanding its repertoire of resistance. The Left played an increasingly visible role in these grassroots processes. There was also a notable rise in anti-regime political violence and confrontational protest tactics. In retrospect, many popular sector activists credit the continuing ant's work and momentum of these years with paving the way for the national protests.[17] Cristo Liberador's letter to Lucía Hiriart de Pinochet was but one of many public acts of public dissent that marked a gradual turn from defense to offense. It was the "fin del reflujo," when the tide of popular movement ceased its retreat and reversed its flow.

People in the social movement webs of dissent set an example for others by exercising rights despite prohibitions. Organizations produced petitions, manifestos, letters, and speeches setting forth their understandings of and demands for rights. Direct action was one of the most visible means by which pobladores claimed rights. Homeless pobladores not only petitioned the housing authorities for shelter; they also took over land. People with political ideals contrary to the authorities' did not wait for the regime to recognize the right of free association; they joined organizations. Pobladores did not ask the authorities' permission to express their ideas; they gathered and spoke their minds. Youth did not wait for an end to censorship to produce art and newsletters. The practice of claiming and exercising rights despite prohibitions, although not without adaptations born of the dangerous political climate, undermined the dictatorship's authority. Those in power knew too that they had much to lose should popular sector opposition spread. The Vicaría's monthly reports demonstrate that the state continued to repress pobladores, social organizations, and liberationist comunidades cristianas. Abuse of power, intimidation, abduction, interrogation, and torture continued as the regime attempted to restrict and control the newly (re)constituted social commons. Pobladores knew from experience that economic misery, social authoritarianism, and political repression were the flip side of the regime's "glory years," despite dominant discourse and image-making to the contrary.

The Glory Years: Miracles and Mirages

In 1980 economist José Piñera, architect of Chile's social security privatization and 1979 Labor Code, stated in an interview with the pro-regime magazine ¿Qué Pasa? that the coup gave the ensuing dictatorship "salvationist and revolutionary" legitimacy. "Salvationist legitimacy," he contended, "to liberate us from communism and rebuild the country, [a legitimacy] which ends precisely with its success. Revolutionary legitimacy," he went on, "which is fully valid today, to achieve profound transformations with the finality of not repeating the cycle that ended in Marxism." The seven modernizations would constitute a "true liberating revolution" that was neither liberal nor Marxist.[18] The dictatorship's greatest challenge, he opined, was to make "the ultimate revolution, the liberating [revolution], which in wresting power from the State and returning it to individuals, will end all revolutions."[19] In 1980 Piñera and fellow regime economist Miguel Kast made spectacular predictions: by the 1990s Chile would "break the development barrier," "by the 90s we will have eliminated extreme poverty," and in the 1990s "Chile will have a labor shortage, and we'll have the great satisfaction of bringing back not only the professionals who are already arriving but also unskilled blue-collar Chilean workers who work abroad."[20] The predictions were premature, but with inflation and unemployment falling and growth indicators improving, it appeared to some that the neoliberal model might fulfill its boosters' promises.

This was to be the revolution to end all revolutions, achieved through the depoliticizing power of the neoliberal authoritarian state. The 1980 Constitution, ushered in on the heels of a fraudulent national referendum, was the political keystone of this project. It institutionalized neoliberal tenets and provided a framework for a "protected" form of capitalist democracy designed to avoid what its architects considered the pitfalls of western liberal democracy as practiced in the US and Europe. From the hard right's perspective, these systems were weak and fatally flawed: their permissiveness and political pluralism rendered them dangerously vulnerable to Marxist influence if indeed they were not already irredeemably infiltrated. If Chile were to return to civilian rule, it would not be to a US- or European-style system that could lead to another Allende. The 1980 Constitution reserved a powerful place for the Armed Forces as the overseers and arbiters of civilian politics in the interest of safeguarding the anti-Marxist, neoliberal system. The constitutional restrictions especially disadvantaged the Left and also reined in moderate liberals who might seek to regulate the private sector or erode the privatization and commodification of education, social security, health care, and other social welfare measures.

For regime supporters, the twin peaks of the "economic miracle" and the 1980 Constitution stood as monuments to success and legitimacy, and the authorities did not hesitate to leverage their triumph to garner further support at home and abroad. The outward appearance of order, economic dynamism, and political institutionalization polished the dictatorship's image among supporters, sympathizers, and those willing to grant it the benefit of the doubt. However, appearances were deceiving, and continuing political repression and economic crisis generated opposition in poblaciones, where the mirage of progress faded.

There was no economic miracle in the poblaciones, to the consternation and frustration of poor and working-class people who read and heard about an economic boom but saw little improvement in their own lives. A November

1978 Vicaría report on an area of southern Santiago comprising the municipality of La Granja and southern San Miguel provides an example of what the boom looked like in poblaciones. This area was home to 400,000 people living in fifty-two poblaciones and seventeen campamentos. Of these 400,000 people, 51.4 percent lived in extreme poverty and 15 percent "lacked means of subsistence." Of a workforce of 80,000 people, 25 percent were unemployed; 70 percent of housing in the poblaciones lacked sewage service, and many families were without water and electricity because of inability to pay. In the campamentos, most homes lacked utilities altogether. The five health clinics serving the population reported high levels of "neurosis" among adults and pediatric diarrhea and malnutrition, all preventable maladies stemming from economic misery, repression, and inadequate food and sanitation.[21]

Pobladores had few opportunities to improve these conditions. In June 1978, the real unemployment rate in Gran Santiago remained high, at 15 percent. Many of the unemployed in La Granja/San Miguel were textile workers, shoemakers, and construction workers, all industries hit hard during the crisis of the mid-1970s. The panorama for young people was similarly bleak. The primary schools could seat 38,212 students, leaving 120,000 children without access. The area's three high schools served only 3,462 students, and the one commercial institute served 1,323.[22] With blue-collar occupations collapsing and without access to schools, youth had few prospects for upward mobility. In 1978 the PEM continued doing little to ameliorate unemployment, employing only 31,992 people in Gran Santiago and at 65.6 percent of 1975 PEM wages, which were already below the minimum.[23] The report also highlighted heavy political repression. Of the 613 cases of disappearance between the years 1973 and 1976 that the Vicaría filed with the Supreme Court, eighty-two of the victims were from southern Santiago and nineteen from this particular sector. Repression and economic misery, the Vicaría's report suggests, damaged pobladores' ability to address collective problems. Before the coup, pobladores in this sector had a "high historical degree of participation and organization," but after the coup traditional community organizations had become authoritarian and alienating.[24] In the 1980s, the forcible relocation to La Granja of squatters from elsewhere in Santiago would further complicate community relations and place additional pressure on overtaxed municipal institutions charged with funding and administering public education, health, and housing in the newly decentralized state-administrative structure.

The negative effects of the neoliberal model weighed heavily on the urban poor. The combination of unemployment, underemployment, low wages, and rising prices meant that falling behind during periods of under- or unemployment made it difficult, if not impossible, to catch up with debts and deficits in better times.[25] Some deficits could not be made up. For example, malnutrition's effects on adults' health and children's development could be irreversible. Although it does not address differential distribution according to socioeconomic class, a 1978 study of caloric intake and protein consumption illustrates the systemic nature of the problem. In 1977 FAO/WHO guidelines recommended that children consume 798, 1,595, 2,380, or 2,690 calories daily, according to age.[26] In 1978 caloric consumption in Chile had fallen to 88.6 percent of its 1970 levels, from 1,745 calories per capita to 1,546, an amount sufficient only for a small child. Chileans were eating less wheat, sugar, beef, eggs, pork, and milk than in 1970 but more potatoes and oil. The rise in starch and oil intake, together with the decline in meat, grain, sugar, and dairy consumption, reflects a decline in the variety and quality of nutrients being consumed. Per capita protein consumption showed a similar pattern of deterioration. Relative to 1970, in 1978 Chileans were eating more potatoes and less wheat, beef, pork, poultry, eggs, and milk, reducing per capita protein consumption to 81.8 percent of 1970 levels. In short, Chileans were eating starch-heavy diets low in calories and protein. Not all social strata experienced the same drop in caloric and protein intake. Like unemployment, in urban areas malnutrition was concentrated among the poor. Falling caloric and protein consumption can indicate declining food availability, and indeed, food imports dropped quickly after 1974, reaching 44 percent of the 1971–73 average by 1977. The Vicaría's analysts found that the drop in food imports was not because domestic production had displaced imports—noting also that domestic production was oriented to export markets—but because falling purchasing power lowered the economic (although not the biological) demand for food.[27]

Although food imports declined, in 1977 the importation of inedible consumer goods increased 232 percent relative to 1976 and 74 percent relative to the 1971–73 average. Many of these imports were luxury goods that analysts noted "could only be acquired by high-income groups."[28] As Heidi Tinsman found among agricultural workers in Aconcagua, the import boom did not begin and end with upper-class consumption.[29] The rise of consumer credit and the availability of relatively cheap imported goods meant that pobladores could participate in consumerism. The 1982 census found that in 106,608 urban households in the Santiago Metropolitan Region that sheltered in *mejora-emergencia* homes—low-income housing usually located in campamentos and poblaciones—the most common items (of a list of ten) were black-and-white televisions (75.6 percent), radios/radio-cassettes/record players (75.1 percent), bicycles (33.8 percent), refrigerators (29.8 percent), and sewing/weaving machines (24.9 percent).[30] The census does not consider when or how households acquired these items, their condition, or their make—during the UP period pobladores could acquire factory-direct electrodomestics and Chilean-made Antú televisions that would have appeared in this census. The presence of such goods in low-income households was not necessarily a case of pobladores privileging them over necessities such as food, utilities, or mortgage payments. Some household items, such as radios and, increasingly, televisions, were modern cultural necessities. Others, such as bicycles and sewing/weaving machines, had long been important for transportation, household maintenance, and wage work. Some items might have been secondhand or refurbished, and others might have been purchased because durable goods can retain value in unstable, inflationary economies.[31]

Pobladores' consumerism was uneven across families and over time. In the mid-1970s, a woman in La Legua explains, "the shop windows were full of things, and we didn't have money. There's no work, there's no money." Later in the 1970s, "all the merchandise started to appear," she continues, "manufactured goods, lots of shoes, lots of everything, and at least people began to adapt, they started to open these *casas comerciales* [nonbank issuers of credit], and so now many of us have a little something more, a stove, a refrigerator." Buying on credit was not new. It was not uncommon for local shopkeepers to allow customers to run a tab and pay the balances at periodic intervals, but negotiating debt with the neighborhood shopkeeper was different from negotiating with impersonal casas comerciales whose credit schemes perpetuated debt to generate profit. Although pobladores acquired goods during the "miracle years," many went into debt, and memories of consumerist gain are often tempered by memories of the economic crash that followed. During the early 1980s economic crisis, explains another woman from La Legua, "*la volvimos a ver verde*" (we were in for it again).[32]

Around the turn of the decade, the regime and its propagandists pointed to falling inflation and rising economic growth rates as proof of the radical free-market model's efficacy and neoliberal economists' prowess. Pobladores, though, perceived the inconsistencies between their lived experience and officialdom's claims. A 1978 survey of 581 unemployed workers in bolsas de cesantes in the Santiago Metropolitan Region found that a vast majority of respondents reported that people stopped looking for work because "there isn't work" (84 percent). Most did not think that jobs were scarce because entrepreneurs lacked money, perhaps because money's presence was apparent in the high-end construction boom and the rise of conspicuous consumption among the wealthier classes. Instead, the most frequent responses were that job scarcity was due to industries closing and economic policies that were bad for workers.[33] Indeed, the closing of manufacturing industries did not necessarily mean that entrepreneurs were broke (although industries did go bankrupt). Many switched their enterprises from production to importation, leaving manufacturing workers unemployed.[34]

At the time, dissenting economists pointed out the short-term nature of the economic gains and the model's unsustainability. A 1977 study by analysts associated with the Vicaría warned that the new system left the national economy dangerously dependent on external credit and foreign investments, and that private investment was not replacing declining public investment. Likewise, the study warned, foreign capital investment in production was not occurring, "despite the unusually favorable conditions granted [to this sector]." In addition, by 1977 military spending reached historic highs, consuming "around 20 percent of total foreign exchange earnings, 18 percent of total expenditures, and nearly 30 percent of total export income, not including costs covered by bank financing." The military and debt-financing expenditures meant that the foreign exchange budget could not support "a process of accelerated investment, nor income redistribution, nor internal reactivation capable of eradicating existing unemployment."[35] In 1978 economists warned that unemployment remained well above the 6 percent historic average and again pointed to a lack of investment in production, noting that capital goods investment was down 22 percent from the UP period (or more, relative to pre-UP periods).[36] The "miracle," they warned, hinged on foreign loans funneled into speculative ventures and imported luxury goods.

Reliance on foreign credit and private investment did not pay off as Pinochet's economists had predicted. Between 1977 and 1981, Chile's foreign debt tripled, from US$5.2 billion to US$15.6 billion. Capitalizing on deregulation, financiers borrowed abroad and made unsound loans, often within their own consortia. Meanwhile, a fixed exchange rate masked the peso's 30 percent value loss between 1979 and 1982. When the economy crashed in 1982 amid falling copper prices, rising international interest rates, and currency devaluation, it became even clearer that the miracle years had been more mirage than miracle. By 1983 Chile's foreign debt obligations were 113 percent of GNP, inflation rose to more than 20 percent, and national unemployment topped 30 percent. International factors exacerbated the crisis, but domestic policymakers bore responsibility for its severity in Chile.[37] Although shoppers greeted full display windows, consumer credit, and the array of imported products with satisfaction, and many observers may have considered this a sign of development and modernity, it was the economic equivalent of empty calories. The "miracle" was a house of cards built on a foundation of crass economic exploitation and social authoritarianism enforced through state-perpetrated repression to quell opposition and maintain the mirage of prosperity and citizen satisfaction. It rested on low wages, high unemployment (helping to drive down labor costs), and suppression of opposition. The regime, the Vicaría noted, considered "demands for certain basic rights incompatible with the imposed development plan—such as the right to affordable, dignified housing," to be threats to national security.[38] State security forces persecuted beggars, street vendors, ollas comunes, bolsas de cesantes, dissatisfied PEM workers, the Left, squatters, and labor unionists to keep visible manifestations of poverty and discontent off the streets and out of sight as state economists and regime supporters trumpeted Chile's imminent entry into the "developed" world.

In poblaciones, there was also little sign of political opening or the return to the rule of law that "political institutionalization" rhetoric portended. In 1978 the auxiliary bishop of Santiago, Jorge Hourton, wrote to his colleagues that "the effective fact that there are no new registered cases of disappearance during 1978 and a certain greater legality in some formalities tends to make people believe that 'things are much better' and that human rights violations are only a thing of the past. The truth is that, despite appearances, degrading and arbitrary procedures, official lies, and insufficient judicial safeguards persist." The security forces remained "very repressive, arrogant, operating on mere irresponsible denunciations or suspicions, with very little respect for legal formalities, tending to threaten and terrorize, especially the poor and defenseless."[39] The Vicaría noted in 1979 that Carabineros and the CNI—still popularly referred to as the DINA, suggesting that few saw much difference—continued persecuting students, the Left, and people associated with comunidades cristianas and parish organizations.[40] In these circumstances, the regime's triumphalism and conspicuous consumption among the wealthier classes only highlighted the political, personal, and economic losses, the widening social disparities, and the violence that many pobladores suffered under the prevailing political and economic system. These realizations contributed to the expansion of social movement webs and the mobilization of public protest.

Complexities of Subjectivity and Practice

Activists and scholars on the Left identified the increase in popular sector activity between 1978 and 1982 as the "fin del reflujo."[41] "Fin del reflujo" encapsulates an understanding of popular sector social movement that differs substantially from some analysts' tendency to focus on peaks of protest mobilization and to treat intervening periods of invisibility as times of apathy, apoliticism, or social anomie that in turn generate periodic explosions of disorganized, rage-fueled protest with little social utility and few political prospects. At worst, this latter approach robs popular sector sociopolitical actors of their human agency, reducing peaks of mobilization to Pavlovian reactions to external stimuli. At best, it provides too narrow a window onto sociopolitical forces that, like plate tectonics, underlie the popular sectors' periodic irruptions onto the national political scene. In Chile, these peaks of mobilization and protest are sometimes colloquially described as *terremotos* (earthquakes): they might take observers by surprise, but they are the visible manifestation of deeper, less visible processes.

The concept of fin del reflujo acknowledges that there was a retreat from 1973 to 1978, but it does not imply apathy, dissolution, or acquiescence. It suggests an ebb and flow of popular movement, a shift in location, energy, and visibility rather than cessation of existence. The ebb between 1973 and 1978 can be understood as what Gabriel Salazar calls a "period of subsidence," a sinking below the surface, a period of movement "below the flotation line." During periods of subsidence, he writes, popular movements move on "submerged planes, within subjectivity, in intersubjectivity, in the center of privacy, in verbal exchanges, according to accumulated memory and lived experience." Here people deliberate, formulate new approaches, and accumulate "social capital," moving slowly and almost imperceptibly, "weaving new social and cultural plots. Tuning new voices and outlining new behaviors." Periods of subsidence, Salazar argues, are as much a part of "social movement" as periods of open mobilization.[42] These are not times during which activity ceases. Instead, they are periods of diminished, veiled activity, often shaped by disadvantageous conditions not of dissenters' own making.

The concepts of post-coup subsidence and fin del reflujo rest upon the well-supported premise that a popular movement existed in Chile prior to 1973. The two concepts also hinge upon a particular understanding of the relationship between popular movements and popular sector organizations in which organizations change over time according to context and contingency; organizations are the indicators and bellwethers of the health, priorities, and direction of deeper, longer-term movement. Activist-scholars writing in 1983 under the umbrella of ECO, a popular-education NGO located at the crossroads of the liberationist church and the Left, identified a popular movement as one consisting of "popular action or struggle, popular organization, and the pueblo's vision of the world."[43] This perspective assumes that popular sector sociopolitical actors are agents of history, that they respond rather than just react to historical context and contingency, and that they accumulate learned experience, produce and elaborate upon sociopolitical ideals, and pass these on to others.

A popular movement is therefore an ongoing, constructive process rather than a discrete collection of specific organizations and mobilizations. Organizations and mobilizations are but the tip of the iceberg: they are the visible contact points between the overarching political, social, and economic environment and longer-term movement beneath the surface. The rise of new types of organizations between 1973 and 1978, ECO's analysts found, did not "comprise an 'alternative model' of organization but rather an amplification of [pre-coup ways] of understanding and developing popular organization."[44] The repression and destruction of popular sector organizations after the coup were not the end of the popular movement. On the contrary, the decline and reemergence of organizations between 1973 and 1978 suggest that the popular movement entered a period of subsidence after the coup as activists sought and tested ways of confronting the new context. The reemergence of popular sector protest in 1978 was not unusual. There are patterns of retreat, subsidence, and reemergence throughout Chilean history.[45] What was unusual was the relatively short, five-year retreat.

The idea that social movements are greater than the sum of their component parts and run deeper than their peaks of public mobilization suggest is rooted in Chilean history and political culture, as an experienced Communist activist in La Legua explains. "The objectives of the social movement have to change as new satisfactions are achieved," he writes, and "the revolutionaries, the people with the most *conciencia*, have to understand that they have to dominate, in each period of human experience, the problems of the moment." He concludes that "the old-timers understood that it was necessary to raise consciousness, since it wasn't enough to fight for conjunctural problems; rather, their participation should also involve seeking the solution to the general problems of the población, the region, and the nation, and this formation of consciousness is what has permitted, through the years, organization to stay alive, not as active as in those years, but the spirit is alive."[46] The combined concepts of subsidence and fin del reflujo allow movements to move. They allow continuity and rupture to coexist, including the overlap of different organizational types and differential paces of organization and mobilization among various movement sectors. They recognize that people, with their ideas and values, bridge and move through multiple historical subperiods and organizations, adjusting to contingencies and bringing their experiences and ideas to bear in new contexts. They also allow for new people, ideas, and values to arise and coexist with the old, not without conflict but not necessarily in irreconcilable contradiction.

The social organizations that the popular movement produced between 1973 and 1978 (bolsas de cesantes, comedores, and the like) changed between 1978 and 1982 to address new conditions and in response to activists' sense that these organizations had stagnated politically. By 1980 activists realized that what they had thought would be a brief period of popular sector political and economic crisis was a constituent part of the regime's politico-economic model and not just a passing emergency. Activists saw that authoritarianism and economic crisis were becoming the new normal, marking a potentially irredeemable rupture with pre-coup paradigms that would render "normal" ways of politics obsolete.[47] In response to changing conditions, the Catholic Church and the Left sought to support popular sector struggle on a more institutional scale. The Church opened the Vicaría Pastoral Obrera in 1977 to assist organized labor. In poblaciones, the Vicaría de la Solidaridad's Social Department de-emphasized comedores and began promoting ollas comunes connected to bolsas de cesantes. Organizers hoped that the ollas comunes would become more autonomous than the comedores.[48] New organizations for women and youth also formed during this period. They opened more space for political organizing, as their emphases on gender and culture did not attract repression in the same way that more traditionally "political" organizing did. Activists valued them because of the consciousness-raising and political opportunities they provided and because they allowed participants to work outside traditional party/labor paradigms with a broader kaleidoscope of people and issues. Meanwhile, the Church and the Left also channeled resources into support for affordable-housing committees and debtors collectives, traditional types of organization that addressed bread-and-butter issues.

The rise of new types of organizations (or in this case old types of organizations in a new context) generated hope and conflict. Their reemergence was, on the one hand, a promising sign, because of the political opportunities they presented and their potential to ameliorate subsistence problems. While grassroots alliances between the Church and the Left sometimes generated tension, increasing organization and mobilization fanned hope that the social organizations were seeds of new forms of democratic power generated from below, an incipient, autonomous poder popular (popular power) free from hierarchical, clientelistic relationships with political parties and the state. On the other hand, these organizations' emphasis on bread-and-butter issues prompted activists focused on the political long game to worry that organizations emphasizing short-term, material goals diverted attention and resources from the greater priority of ousting the regime. Another concern was that such initiatives would attract masses of people *sin conciencia* (without consciousness) who would demobilize and perhaps even support the dictatorship if it met their demands, limiting the organizations' utility as vehicles for achieving longer-term political goals.

The Left formed coordinators (*coordinadoras*) such as the Communist Party's Coordinadora Metropolitana de Pobladores (METRO, Metropolitan Coordinator of Pobladores) and the MIR's Coordinadora de Agrupaciones Poblacionales (COAPO, Coordinator of Poblador Associations) to direct, support, and harness to party interests the renewed movement for affordable housing. Other coordinadoras organized workers, women, and youth, while national-level commissions, such as the Comisión Nacional de Pobladores (National Commission of Pobladores) that linked METRO and COAPO, established yet higher levels of coordination. From a grassroots perspective, the rise of coordinadoras was another hopeful yet controversial development. For some, the coordinadoras represented political parties' attempts to dominate grassroots organizations and therefore aroused suspicion. For others, the coordinadoras elicited positive memories of territorial organization during the UP, such as *cordones industriales* (industrial cordons) and *comandos comunales* (muncipal commands) and their political potential as foundations for poder popular. The new coordinadoras were not territorially based, and one of their problems, according to some critics, was that they were vertical organizations that did not mesh well with movement dynamics in poblaciones—a critique later leveled at political parties during the transition. Coordinadoras organized and grouped people by social function (laborers, women, youth, unemployed, homeless), but in individual poblaciones people often organized transversally across these functional lines rather than along them. The coordinadoras helped spread and expand webs of dissent, but their structure worked at cross-purposes with the transversal coordination within poblaciones. Transversal, territorially based coordination, some argued, would give the poor and working classes more cohesive power, in all their heterogeneity, at the level of the municipality and beyond. As it was, the dispersion of people who lived side by side into functional categories—women, youth, workers—diluted their collective power as people with shared problems derived from their socioeconomic status and place of residence. Juan C. argues that territorially based coordinadoras could have served both peaceful and insurrectionary purposes, but the question of organizational form was sidelined as strategic debates over forms of struggle took precedence, and so momentum faltered.[49]

This strategic conflict became most acute after 1983, but it began in the late 1970s as the Communist Party and MIR began incorporating or privileging armed struggle, respectively. Aside from the obvious dangers, the exigencies of armed struggle conflicted with the Communist Party's and the MIR's historical practice of social activism as a central component of grassroots political organization.[50] While the coordinadoras reflected this more traditional method of using bread-and-butter issues as a vehicle for political consciousness-raising and movement building, armed struggle required different structures and methods. The turn toward armed struggle sometimes clashed with social activists' work, generating tension among party activists, grassroots organizations, and the Church as the parties implemented their strategies.

Analysis of the long-term outlook in light of the "economic miracle" and the regime's political consolidation, and the experience of working closely with pobladores within local organizations, had changed many grassroots activists' ideas about how to achieve revolution and what ways of doing so were desirable and feasible. While some activists turned to armed struggle as a means to revolutionary power, others privileged grassroots organizing and popular education as vehicles of revolutionary change. The latter gained currency among activists based on a combination of grassroots organizing experience, positive revaluations of democracy, and reconsideration of revolutionary theory that shifted attention from Lenin and Ho Chi Minh to ideas about the role of culture in revolution derived from Gramscian theory.[51] "The idea began to emerge," wrote ECO's analysts, "that it was no longer so much a question of 'setting upright' what was knocked down [an objective between 1973 and 1978], but rather of building 'something new.' This 'something new' was coming to be understood as a 'popular political subject.'"[52] This meant empowering the urban poor as "popular political subjects" to build a movement beyond traditional party-poblador/state-poblador relationships. These reconsiderations generated newfound attention to devalued subjectivities and struggles that orthodox Marxism had long considered secondary.

The activists behind post-coup organization in Santiago's poblaciones during the 1970s were people with pre-coup experience in popular sector organizations—party, labor, community, or otherwise—who adapted to the new context. Activists were frequently involved in more than one type of organization and harbored multifaceted identities. Juanita, for example, was a youth, pobladora, Mirista, woman, student, worker, and participant in social organizations. "We had these groups," she recalls of her work with women's organizations linked to the Vicaría, "where we taught embroidery, knitting, how to make *arpilleras* (patchwork tapestries). That was our . . . how should I say, the legal part. And within those groups were women who helped us distribute pamphlets, paint graffiti, and everything." Social work and political work were not mutually exclusive, and one was a means to another. "During the day you could be in a social organization," she explains, and "we made handicrafts that were sold [through the Vicaría]. But at the same time, the same group also participated politically, not in the beginning, because first you have to teach them, see where they're coming from, who they are. Afterward they participated."[53]

Church-affiliated social organizations attracted a wide variety of participants, including people new to sociopolitical organization. Although women, as a category of social actor, were not new to popular sector sociopolitical activism, during the economic crises of the 1970s and 1980s many individual pobladoras joined sociopolitical organizations for the first time. New arrivals encountered women like Juanita with long activist trajectories, not all or even most of which revolved around traditionally feminine concerns even when "the legal part" of their work, as Juanita puts it, occurred within women's organizations. Experience gained through one facet of identity and affiliation informed people's experiences with respect to others (and vice versa) in a complex feedback loop, as their imbricated social positionalities marked their lived experiences and informed their decision-making processes. Juanita's presence as a young but experienced activist woman working within a political party and social organizations created links between different generations of women, between adult women and youth of both sexes, and between social organizations, the Catholic Church, and the clandestine left, contributing to building social movement webs of dissent.

The complexities of subjectivity and practice were central to the expansion of social movement webs and the rise of protest in poblaciones. Politically experienced activists were significant knots in growing webs of dissent in poblaciones. They channeled dissent through social organizations and political parties, using trabajo social (social work) as an element of political strategy—as was traditionally the case on the Chilean left—and blurred the lines between social and political mobilization. Solidarity between activists, political parties, social organizations, the Church, and others in the social movement webs was the stuff of which mass mobilizations were made. When the AFDD went on hunger strike in 1978 and 1979, the relationships that the strikers had with activists in poblaciones catalyzed protest, strengthening ties among regime opponents.

Our Lives for the Truth

By the end of the decade, Cristo Liberador was the nexus of a vibrant social movement web that stretched beyond Villa Francia into city-wide Church, human rights, and political party circles. Cristo Liberador supported many organizations, including a bolsa de cesantes, rehabilitation club, senior citizens club, comedor, youth pastoral organization, preuniversitario (university admissions test prep group), and a cultural group. The AFDD members from the neighborhood participated in Cristo Liberador and social organizations, establishing connections locally and outward into broader political and human rights circles. Through the Vicaría Zona Oeste, Cristo Liberador connected to other comunidades cristianas. The Communist Party was active in the neighborhood and for a time operated a clandestine printing press in one of the apartment complexes, and leftist party militants of all sorts participated in social organizations and Cristo Liberador, including Miristas from outside the neighborhood.[54] Many of the neighborhood's sociopolitical leaders had pre-coup experience in political parties, the Church, community and labor organizations, or in all of the above. Villa Francia was in many ways an exemplary case of social movement formation, and Cristo Liberador's role was perhaps unparalleled elsewhere. Nevertheless, a look at Villa Francia reveals a microcosm of processes common to popular sector, anti-regime organization and mobilization across the city.

Mario, at the time a Mirista from outside Villa Francia, remembers that when he first visited the neighborhood in the late 1970s the pobladores' level of sociopolitical mobilization impressed him. His arrival there was a product of his relationships with others already involved in anti-regime work. "A community of religious sisters that I knew from Concepción had installed themselves [in Villa Francia]," he explains. "So on one occasion," he continues, "[one of the sisters] called us and told us that Clotario Blest was going to participate [in an activity]. And yes, I was interested in going to see him, and there I had the first contact with a very active comunidad cristiana, in those times, in very poor accommodations. It operated out of an old school that was falling down all around, but with great mystique, great presence." He returned again for a public health meeting with neighborhood youth, "and that was a gathering with youth that also impressed me very much, for its massivity." A gathering of sixty to seventy young people in those times was notable, "almost a demonstration." It was "very attractive in terms of the capacity that had developed to reconnect people, to open spaces for new organization . . . and above all I think the existence of the comunidad itself as a space of popular gathering during that period seemed to me of impressive value."[55] Across Santiago, the activism and effervescence of the social movement webs rooted in the poblaciones attracted the attention of experienced leftist party activists. Mario's observations piqued his interest in doing political work in Villa Francia, which "during that stage was basically to set up resistance committees," small groups that discussed politics and produced anti-regime propaganda.

The difficulties of reaching into a población from without, and creating inclusive organizations without compromising clandestinity, were challenges political militants faced throughout the city. Mario remembers that he "spoke with the religious sister. . . . I made it explicit, we knew each other: 'I'm interested in doing a more political type of work here . . . and I need your support, the people don't know me, I have to figure out how to reach them.'" She responded, "'Think of a service you can give the community, and that way you approach and do what you want to do.'" He and his colleagues created a *pre-universitario* to help poblador youth prepare for university admission exams.

The preuniversitario achieved its objectives. Several of its students entered universities, and the Miristas set up several resistance committees. The Communist Party maintained its cell structures and crossed paths with the Miristas and resistance committee members in social organizations and Cristo Liberador. The cross-hatching of party structures and the neighborhood's constellation of social organizations created opportunities for pobladores to discuss politics, analyze their experiences, and expand social movement webs.

In May 1978, remembers Mario, "teaching [preuniversitario] class on a Saturday, a pair of young people came to tell us that the AFDD had begun a hunger strike and that it was very important in the comunidad cristiana, that it was very important to act in solidarity, so they invited us as professors, and the students, to join a fast in a nearby church that night." The opportunity was enticing, but, Mario explains, "this caused me some doubts, above all because it implied another, more public, step that could mean risks, in the sense that I wasn't from the población. Also, some of us were militants and leftists and so were very cautious about our security. But curiously," he continues, "there, of that base of militants who were in that zone, I was the leader and my subordinates said, 'no, no, we have to go, if the población says so we must.' I doubted and didn't go the first time, but fifteen or nineteen days later, there was a new invitation and yes, it seemed necessary to go, so that was the first time I fasted in a western-zone church, and many people joined, nearly a hundred people fasted and we finished the following day, Sunday, with the church full, four hundred, five hundred people in solidarity with the strike."[56]

Members of the AFDD, many of whom were from poblaciones, were the first to stage public protests that attracted national and international attention. The AFDD formed in 1974, and it held its first large demonstration in 1975 in response to Operación Colombo, an attack on the Left and the AFDD in which the regime published—in fake foreign magazines created for this purpose—lists of 119 disappeared Chileans supposedly killed in internecine political conflict abroad, including Villa Francia's Enrique Toro, José Villagra, and Eduardo Lara. However, many of *Los 119*, as they came to be called, had been seen during their kidnappings or in political prisons, belying the media montage that human rights activists soon unmasked as crude, and cruel, political propaganda. The AFDD's 1975 protest in Santiago's Iglesia de Lourdes numbered in the hundreds. In 1977, as an influx of Communist Party family members changed the organization's political makeup, the AFDD embarked on a series of direct-action protests, including hunger strikes and an audacious demonstration in which AFDD members chained themselves to a fence outside the ministry of justice in downtown Santiago. According to Hernán Vidal, long-standing communist traditions of family political education meant that although families associated with the Communist Party suffered no less the loss of their loved ones, they could situate their trauma within a broader collective history of struggle. This, he argues, fueled a shift in the AFDD's protests, transforming them "into dramatic convocations to the entire nation for democratization in Chile. In Marxism-Leninism," he continues, "there is an optimistic, utopian dimension that impels human beings to concretize in reality a mode of life based on material and spiritual justice. The new Communist members of the Agrupación placed emphasis on the hope of life to protest against the Authoritarian State."[57] This emphasis on hope resonated with Christians, other leftists, members of the AFDD, and people uninvolved with anti-regime organization but who privately abhorred the repression.

The AFDD's 1978 hunger strike mobilized people across Santiago, Chile, and the world. In Villa Francia, pobladores mobilized in support of truth and justice for Enrique Toro, José Villagra, and Eduardo Lara. Fr. Mariano Puga and Hermana Dolores joined the AFDD's strike in accordance with the dictates of their consciences, although hunger strikes (as suicides in the making) contradicted Catholic doctrine. Hermana Dolores remembers that in making the decision to join, "'Yes,' I said, 'give life for life.' They were requesting an answer from the government; they felt protected in a church. 'I'm Christian,' I said, 'so to struggle for life . . .' I was young, I was forty, so I was full of life, I didn't have any difficulty." She joined the strike at Jesús Obrero parish church, where participants included fourteen women and men of the AFDD, seven priests, and six other religious sisters. Hermana Dolores remembers that the nuns and clergy "were with the strikers for seventeen days. Every day we celebrated the Eucharist among ourselves, but many of them [nonreligious AFDD members] came to join us, and we let them."[58]

In Villa Francia, pobladores gathered at Cristo Liberador to organize a solidarity action. Fr. Roberto Bolton arrived to find the building besieged by police. Bolton and the assembled pobladores decided to protest with a Vía Crucis procession. They marched past the police and walked through the neighborhood praying the rosary. But, Fr. Bolton remembers, they changed the words: "We said, 'This mystery,' for example, 'the second painful mystery, the lashes that our Lord suffered: at this station we pray for those who are on hunger strike so that they don't fall ill and so that they achieve their objective. . . .'" They wound through Villa Francia and returned to the chapel without incident.[59] The protesters expressed their discontent through the strategic use of Catholic prayer and ritual. This approach was meaningful to those who understood their political positions in religious terms, and it was politically astute. Couching political speech in religious language and ritual created a conundrum for the police. If they attacked a Catholic religious procession, they would worsen tension between the Church and the regime and incite criticism when the world's eyes were already on the hunger strikers.

Villa Francia's Communists mobilized in support of the hunger strikers by taking over a church near the población. "So we got there, we hung up our banners and installed ourselves," Juan recalls, "and we explained to the priest—who didn't agree much with this—that we wanted to fast and hunger-strike for a few days in support of the principal strike that these *religiosos* were doing." The Communists recognized that the hunger strikers from the Villa included "two who weren't religious and, on the other hand, Mariano Puga and the nun Dolores." The Communists and other allies in Villa Francia "met every day at the nuns' house, every day to analyze the issue, act in solidarity with the people."[60] The Communists respected the Catholic Church's importance to the AFDD's cause, and they acknowledged the *religiosos'* sacrifice in solidarity with the disappeared and their families. The shared experiences of collective action arising from the hunger strike forged new relationships of solidarity and new organizations, contributing to the expansion and strengthening of social movement webs in Villa Francia.

Closer organizational ties also generated growing pains. "When the strike was over," remembers Juan, "I personally proposed preparing a reception, after they recuperated, for the strikers. An homage, a recognition, something, let's say, in gratitude for the sacrifice they made." Others in Cristo Liberador didn't agree "because the people in the comunidad cristiana, when a Communist proposes it, oppose it," Juan concludes. "And still do today," laughs another participant in the conversation. Mariano Puga, Juan continues, played the role of mediator and organized a retreat to discuss faith and politics. "We as a party prepared ourselves to confront this bothersome situation," he recalls, "that 'Ah, that one's a Communist,' and what have you, and getting looked at with suspicion," by preparing in advance what they were going to say during the meeting. But, he explains, "we didn't have to open our mouths, because Mariano Puga said it all. Mariano Puga made a master case for what socialism is, and what social justice is, and what solidarity should be."[61] Mariano Puga and Hermana Dolores were skilled at balancing the political situation within Cristo Liberador, remember Irene and Jorge, who were not affiliated with the Communist Party. "If everyone came [to Cristo Liberador] it's because Mariano told them that politics and religion were the same," says Irene, but the priest met with political activists to "make clear to them that the [comunidad] wasn't for . . ." "For doing politics directly," finishes Jorge. He remembers that political discussion was allowed in Cristo Liberador and that "there were moments in which Mariano asked how we would like Chile to be under socialism—we were in dictatorship—and that lasted for two Masses, two *cultos* [religious assemblies], as they were called . . . on how we wanted Chile to be, no?" Cristo Liberador's pedagogical approach encouraged collective leadership and open discussion of social and political issues. "All the social organizations that were in the población or close to the comunidad," Jorge remembers, "could direct [assembly] on Sundays. . . . Those who understood a little more about the Bible, read the Bible. Others presented a labor topic for discussion, and there were arguments, but in good faith. There were big arguments but not rejection."[62]

On the heels of the hunger strike, a cultural group formed that united anti-regime activists of various ages, including especially youth from Cristo Liberador. The cultural group was more explicitly political than other social organizations. "We did marvelous activities in the comunidad cristiana," Juan remembers, "like an exposition of paintings about what we were experiencing, about torture, with the theme of the disappeared, there were poems, songs."[63] The cultural group, says Leonor, who participated in Cristo Liberador as a young woman unaffiliated with a political party, was new and different. "It's a group that gathers people of different political tendencies, principally it's people linked to the comunidad cristiana, but other people from the Communist Party, people from the MIR, also participated." In the cultural group "the idea was, for example, to read documents, present them to the compañeros, reflect on that, draw conclusions."[64] The skills that youth developed in the cultural group made them influential in Cristo Liberador. While developing young people's leadership and critical-thinking skills was among their elders' objectives, the youth became increasingly assertive within the comunidad and, some would argue, radical and uncompromising, arousing concern among the adults. This increasing youth activism was not unique to Villa Francia.

Like Fr. Mariano Puga in Villa Francia, Fr. Guido Peeters expected people to act in solidarity with one another to address collective problems. In La Legua, under the shelter of San Cayetano, women sewed arpilleras (patchwork tapestries) to express themselves, denounce repression, and earn money.[65] San Cayetano also sheltered a *taller laboral* (labor workshop), a cultural group, several comedores and an olla común, a human rights committee, a congregation organized into several comunidades cristianas, and sacramental groups.[66] Since September 1973, state agents had kept close watch on La Legua, and the rise of social organizations did not go unnoticed. As the organizations multiplied, the CNI and Carabineros turned their attention to repressing them outright. In 1978 the CNI began to openly surveil and intimidate people who entered and exited the parish grounds and those known to participate in social organizations. In July of that year, Carabineros attacked the olla común in the central plaza and took at least ten pobladores and Peeters prisoner, the latter supposedly because he allowed pobladores to store food on church property.[67]

In 1980 security agents raided San Cayetano, scaring many people away from the church and social organizations.[68]

San Cayetano was a center for anti-regime activity, sociopolitical education, and sanctuary. Fr. Peeters protected the persecuted, motivated organization, and managed conflicts among those who crossed paths on church grounds. The Communist Party was the largest organization in La Legua, and Communists there recall that the Church was key to their ability to organize during the dictatorship.[69] In La Legua, don Luis remembers, party members met in private homes and other locales, in precarious conditions: "Three or four, maximum five people would meet, but always three or four. They met in cells, as they're called. And, like I tell you, everything memorized, nothing on paper."[70] By 1978 local Communists gathered every week with other leftists in San Cayetano's taller laboral to discuss politics, resistance, and how to help people in need.[71] It was called "taller laboral," explains don Luis, "so as not to show our hand. . . . Of course, it was a façade. . . . So someone would come and ask, 'What's that?' 'Taller laboral, *pues*, we do work.'"[72] The taller laboral prepared protests, assisted the needy, and supported the persecuted. In its meetings, members discussed divisive topics: the UP, the coup, and how to confront the dictatorship. "There we had problems with the Communist compañeros," remembers María, of the MIR, "but we kept on. It even gave me a stomachache when I went to that meeting because it was just pure arguing, we had different positions."[73] In the taller laboral, says another participant, "the Miristas and Communists recriminated one another, the Socialists, then they blamed each other for the coup." Fr. Peeters helped calm the waters. "One of Guido's gifts," the man remembers, "was to centralize the opinions: 'Well, whatever your opinions of what happened, now is what matters, now we have to resist.' So this is one of Guido's great merits. He has to appear in the history of La Legua, he should have a special place."[74]

San Cayetano also became a center for human rights education and promotion. One man remembers that after a rash of repression, "I joined the party's regional committee to replace the fallen compañeros, so clandestine meetings in this sector were held in the parish church."[75] Allowing outlawed political parties to meet on parish property was part of church personnel's commitment to human rights, as well as a moral imperative given the lethal consequences for anti-regime activism. "The vision that the parish priest of La Legua, Guido, had of commitment to human rights," says Juan R., "meant that [San Cayetano] was the center—at the level of the diocese, at the level of the five or six parishes that made up the diocese—the center of formation. Because we didn't have formation in human rights—everything that was promotion of justice, equality—there were fora with human rights lawyers." As parish personnel acquired training in the concept, practice, and legal formalities of human rights, they also worked with people who suffered hunger, unemployment, and political persecution. The idea that respect for both political and social rights was necessary for freedom, democracy, and justice was particularly strong in the poblaciones, where economic crisis and political repression were greatest, and where analysis of the relationship between political and social rights was part of the education that the Church and the Left provided.

It was in this context that on September 8, 1979, legüinos participated in what was perhaps the largest protest yet to occur in the población since the coup. On September 3, the AFDD had launched its fourth hunger strike, this time to demand the remains of fifteen disappeared campesinos found in Lonquén in November 1978. A military court had dismissed charges against the eight Carabineros implicated in the kidnapping-murders by invoking the new 1978 amnesty law, and the authorities were now withholding the remains from the families. The hunger strikers, most of whom were women and children, occupied the Danish embassy and Catholic churches across Santiago: Jesús Maestro, Recoleta Franciscana, San Roque, and San Cayetano. The strike soon spread to the cities of Temuco, Viña del Mar, and Concepción. In addition, Monsignor Alfonso Baeza and the bishop Enrique Alvear, along with 130 religious personnel, fasted in solidarity with the hunger strikers.[76] As they had in 1978, the social movement webs of dissent in poblaciones mobilized in support.

Guido Peeters supported the hunger strikers in San Cayetano and encouraged local organizations to do the same. On September 8, regime opponents from across southern Santiago, including clergy, nuns, leftist party activists, youth with party and Church connections, and representatives of the Vicaría mobilized in solidarity with the strikers. Many were from La Legua, La Granja, and Caro-Ochagavía. They gathered at the church of Nuestra Señora de los Parrales, several kilometers south of La Legua. They marched to San Cayetano through the poblaciones located between Nuestra Señora de los Parrales and La Legua, many of which also had histories of anti-regime struggle. When they arrived in La Legua, the marchers joined pobladores in peaceful protest outside San Cayetano. "The pacos arrived and they gave us a beating," remembers Juan R. "They didn't respect habit, priest, nun, children, nothing. They hit us, and hit us, and hit us. . . . Afterward there was another activity—they were generally on Sunday afternoons—and the same thing happened. The parish church was the point of encounter for things like this."[77]

During the attack, some 150 protesters took refuge inside San Cayetano. The police tried to enter the church, but Guido Peeters stopped them. The vicars Juan de Castro, Ignacio Ortúzar, and Cristián Precht arrived at San

Cayetano to negotiate the release of the refugees and the religious personnel in police custody. The mainstream media reported the incident as a clash among protesters in La Legua that provoked police intervention, invoking the tired trope of violent pobladores, violent leftists, and violence in La Legua. The regime, for its part, accused the protesters of violating the Ley de Seguridad del Estado (State Security Law).[78] Across southern Santiago, pobladores expressed solidarity with the prisoners. In población Santa Adriana, youth who had participated in the protest took up a collection to help the prisoners: "It caught [our elders'] attention. They even counseled us, asking, 'Aren't you afraid, kids?' We weren't afraid. At best we didn't know what fear meant. We did what we thought was right."[79] Many young people did not carry the same burden of fear as their elders, a phenomenon that accounts in part for young people's notable presence in public protests. The hunger strikes of 1978 and 1979 were some of the first and largest protests that young people were old enough to participate in first-hand. In poblaciones, a new generation was coming of political age, and their political education was important to their elders. They and their elders were aware that the economic model and the regime's political institutionalization were to their detriment and that theirs was an uphill battle.

The Rise of the Youth

Since 1975–76, youth cultural groups like Villa Francia's had been spreading across Santiago's poblaciones, with the support of the Left, the Catholic Church, and ecumenical and Protestant organizations such as the Fundación de Ayuda Social de las Iglesias Cristianas (FASIC, Social Assistance Foundation of the Christian Churches) and the Servicio Evangélico para el Desarrollo (SEPADE, Evangelical Service for Development).[80] In Villa Francia, Hermana Dolores paid close attention to local youth, many of whom faced more than the usual challenges of adolescence given the prevalence of poverty and repression. She and other adults in Cristo Liberador created spaces where young people could exercise free expression, engage in discussion, and receive social and political education unavailable elsewhere.

For some, joining Cristo Liberador was life-changing. In the 1970s and 1980s, Villa Francia suffered poverty, malnutrition, alcoholism, drug use, and school abandonment. When children and adolescents joined Cristo Liberador, they were assigned counselors—either religious personnel or specially prepared lay adults—to guide them through an educational process. When they demonstrated special skills or interests, the counselors guided them toward social organizations where they could further develop them. "For me," says Leonor, "joining the comunidad was a radical change, absolutely radical. Until then I had a group of friends I smoked marijuana with sometimes, so entering [Cristo Liberador's] youth community meant leaving that other group, but it was my decision, nobody asked me to do it, *I* did it. But it was also a change in all senses," she continues, because "for me Dolores was a very significant person, she was a person who worried about me, who motivated me, for example, to work, to continue studying. She paid attention to whether I went to meetings, if we got up [in the morning], if we didn't get up, if we needed economic help, if we had a serious problem at home." Through participation in Cristo Liberador's organizations, she developed her leadership skills and acquired social, religious, and political education.[81]

One of the most outstanding features of the new generation's discourse was the nearly seamless connection young people drew between religious faith, leftist politics, and anti-regime action. The youth appear to have translated religious faith into political commitment more readily than their elders, by-passing many of the arduous debates adults faced after the coup as the Church opened its doors to the persecuted left. Instead, many young people considered their political commitments an extension of their religious faith. Around 1980, youth in the cultural group began producing a newsletter called "Horizonte." "Horizonte" reported on economic issues, culture, religion, politics, other organizations' activities, and the importance of community engagement. The authors' commentary ran from the local to the national. In one 1981 issue, they published a hand-drawn board game, "Let's Play at Coming Out of Reclusion!" to promote community participation. Ways to advance around the board included going to church with a new neighbor or holding a family meeting to discuss a problem. Ways to fall back included alcohol or drug use, machista behavior, and going into debt for a color television. Everyone advanced when a player landed on a May 1 event.[82] In another 1981 issue, they addressed political stagnation, arguing that the bolsas de cesantes and comedores "didn't become organisms of denunciation, on May 1 workers weren't in the streets, housewives weren't present either, and the leaders of the big organizations started to fight over who would represent the workers, without asking whether the pueblo wanted to be represented by them. On the other hand the 'more advanced' groups haven't united and don't have clear which path to follow." They then take responsibility for enacting change: "It's our duty to create a movement that identifies us, that unites us, to build in that way the Kingdom that Christ promised us."[83] Their political commentary expresses the influences of the anti-regime religious and political circles in which they grew up, and they explicitly link religious faith with political action. "Because Christ demands that we, as people of faith, fulfill his word," another early 1980s piece reads, "which means that we must seek, in our environment, here and now, the construction of the 'Kingdom' that Christ offers us, but that it is our responsibility to build. To do that, we should seek out those organizations, those values, that we see (companionship, friendship, loyalty, etc.) that most closely resemble the true path of justice, equality, and fraternity."[84] This excerpt has a strong religious component and evokes Enlightenment ideals at the heart of liberalism and socialism. Many members of the group had grown up in Cristo Liberador where they imbibed the teachings of liberation theology in close proximity to the political left and other pro-democracy pobladores. Religious language was also a locally, socially acceptable way to exhort others to oppose injustice.

Like Cristo Liberador, San Cayetano offered several options for restless youth. By the early 1980s, young people in San Cayetano's organizations were well versed in sociopolitical issues. There were two types of youth under San Cayetano's umbrella, remembers Juan R., "those who came for the sacraments and everything else, and those who came above all because of a social attitude." He and Guido Peeters evangelized the youth, "but from a libratory perspective. We worked a great deal with liberation theology, which made the youth become conscious of their surroundings and their social reality, and from there, [we] evangelized." "We've always said, 'from the world, for the world,'" which meant sensitizing youth to their own surroundings, lives, and histories, "to motivate them such that Jesus Christ carries them to a permanent commitment toward life."[85]

Other young people received political education at home and in political parties but also participated in church-affiliated organizations. "I believe the people of the Frente were coming from the Jota [Communist Youth]," says Juan R., "so they stared there, in the Communist Youth, and the Youth are the children of the old historic Communists, the oldest. Of course there are young people who, through friendships or sensibilities, through music, sang protest songs and were also politically committed. The youngest," he remembers, "were children of militants or people with leftist inclinations who had records of Quilapayún, Víctor Jara, etcetera, so they managed to sensitize [them]."[86] At their high point, an estimated 80 to 120 young people participated in San Cayetano's organizations, and there were approximately 40 to 60 young people and adults with religious responsibilities such as maintaining the chapel and teaching catechism. Organized youth in La Legua and Villa Francia knew about human rights abuses through conversations, neighborhood history, and personal experience, and they were well aware of their exclusion from the benefits of the economic model. The sociopolitical education available through San Cayetano, Cristo Liberador, and leftist political parties provided them with frameworks for interpreting their environment.

Church-sheltered organizations became recruiting grounds for leftist political collectives, and they were nexuses of webs linking political parties with popular sector bases. As parties of the Left rebuilt and reconsolidated between 1978 and 1982, poblador activists began asking themselves how to best channel their efforts for change. As youth became more socially and politically aware, they raised questions and examined their political options. In Villa Francia, María Teresa explains, "people who had taken many steps started to say, 'So where is the true commitment to change society?' It's not in the Church, because the church that Mariano represents is the church [in Villa Francia] and maybe in other poblaciones, but it's not the official Church," which she deemed too conservative, patriarchal, and hidebound to support structural change. "So," she asks, "where does the commitment have to be? In a party. It couldn't *not* be in a party."[87]

Cristo Liberador, like San Cayetano, was a "trampoline" to political commitment. Young people also joined parties through contacts with friends and peers in social organizations, school, or other places. "So my friends, youth, started to become party militants," remembers María Teresa, "but since it was clandestine, you didn't catch on, you only got a few things when you snooped around asking questions. So you had a conversation with someone: 'Ah no, you have to go talk with so and so.' And that person sent you to talk with someone else, and you got involved, and you went clandestine. It was part of your commitment."[88] Not all young people joined political parties. Some were unconvinced that political parties were a desirable vehicle for change, and others were unsure of which party to join. Others believed that the path to change was through autonomous community activism or the Church. Despite differences, young party militants and nonmilitants worked together in social organizations, comunidades cristianas, and, later, protest committees.

Tensions arose between generations and among adults regarding the exigencies of commitment in Cristo Liberador. Many youth viewed sociopolitical engagement as an evolutionary process that required increasingly ironclad, radical commitments. They perhaps inherited this intensity from their elders. The exigencies of participation in Cristo Liberador were already a source of debate among the adults, especially in terms of the extent to which they limited the organization's ability to attract new members. Comunidad activists sought to lead exemplary lives, congruent with their political and religious beliefs, in terms of personal responsibility, social habits, and accountability. Cristo Liberador, recalls Mario, "was the heir of people, ex-militants, with very grave demeanors, and, when things didn't work, with a tremendously great [tendency] toward self-criticism: we were bad, we hadn't fulfilled our commitment, we had failed everyone, very radical." "In a way," he explains, "such strict, such Christian, militancy separated the members of the group from the rest of the población." He and others argued that they should make an effort to engage more in the routine sociability of daily life.[89]

Young people were also demanding of themselves and one another. "The [attitude] of Christian social commitment was such that if you weren't committed to something you were worthless, and your commitment always had to grow," explains María Teresa. "I'm talking about more or less sixty committed people and from there on down diverse degrees of commitment. And that, in Villa Francia, was absolutely massive. It wasn't a group of ten people, it was *many* people. . . . Sometimes there were fifty or sixty young people together," she remembers.[90] Their elders understood the significance of critical attitudes that led youth to question the Church and explore other options: "Mariano said, 'The comunidad cristiana is never going to change the system in which we are living, that's not its job. . . . It has to be the political parties that take those reins,'" remembers Luisa. "So those things made people think, made them make decisions. That was important."[91]

The influx of youth into political parties ignited debate among the adults about whether and to what extent to support youngsters' political decisions. María Teresa, who was active in Cristo Liberador and had joined the MIR, remembers that "there was a contradiction [among the adults] in the sense of the people who said, 'These jerk kids are just screwing around,' and the people who said, 'This is a true commitment and we have to support it.' It was a vital contradiction that was never overcome."[92] In some cases parents and pastoral workers did what they could to support young people in making their own decisions. Luisa explains that when in 1982 her son told his parents that he was joining the MIR, she knew that "the repression was prepared precisely to eliminate the militants of these parties. . . . So it was a very heavy blow that [he] had committed himself to the MIR, because we knew what that meant, but this was already happening all over Santiago." They had raised their children "with the freedom to seek their own paths. So [his commitment] was very special . . . since we saw that participation in the MIR was so dangerous we held a Eucharist here in the house, with a priest who accompanied us, and there [my son] decided to participate in the MIR."[93] In La Legua, Juan R. remembers, pastoral workers tried to modulate the influence of political activists from outside the población. "There was a great deal of intervention by young people from outside, university boys or rich boys, who came to the poor to tell them that such-and-such a party was worthy, or another was more worthy. So there, as a church, we tried to achieve a balance. And when I talk about balance," he explains, "I mean, 'Faith leads us to participation congruent with the gospel.' So we'd enter into profound discussions about violence and that when the moment to take up arms arrives, some do, and some don't. And, if they do, why? And then we'd discuss why, for hours."[94] Discussion of the entire panorama of political options available to them helped young people make decisions for themselves in a way that refusing to address the complexity of controversial subjects like the armed left did not.

Cristo Liberador also played an important role in young people's political decisions. While the comunidad was a trampoline to leftist political activism it may also have helped to temper youngsters' decisions to join armed groups. "The comunidad," remembers Mario, who left the MIR during this period, "acknowledged a certain degree of autonomy in the political realm, in the sense that in Chile, politics on the Left were always pluralistic. [This was] the only political answer that could restrain the youngest members who thought, 'If the gospel was radical, then I'm obliged to become a militant, the most radical of them all,' and 'The most radical militancy is the most heroic, and so it's the one with the most risks and inevitably has a military component.'" The comunidades cristianas, he continues, "could buffer it to the extent that they permitted a larger debate about politics . . . facilitating the idea that there wasn't a single answer to the existing problems."[95] Liberationist comunidades cristianas played a double-edged role. They provided venues for political education and radicalization, but they faced challenges when young people joined armed groups that put them directly in harm's way and that, according to some opinions, were strategically or morally mistaken. For its part, the institutional Church advocated nonviolence, and the Vicaría denied legal assistance to militants involved in assassinations or armed assaults.[96]

In Villa Francia, youth who joined political collectives tended to join the MIR, the Communist Youth, or the FPMR.[97] In La Legua, they tended to join Lautaro or the FPMR, and some joined the MIR. However, participation in comunidades cristianas that encouraged diverse types of political and social organization taught a certain level of tolerance and respect for others' commitments. Many young people who were not in political parties put their energy into cultural and social activism, often alongside friends and peers who were party militants. They also participated actively in protests and political discussions. By encouraging engagement in many different types of opposition groups, liberationist churches showed young people that there were a variety of outlets through which to further their interests. Despite arguments and competition for influence, young party militants and nonmilitants alike generally continued to put into practice the idea of solidarity that their elders developed in the early years of the dictatorship.

By the late 1970s and early 1980s, shared rejection of dictatorship and support for political and social rights drew people together in a vibrant, popular sector social movement. Several of the Catholic Church's vicariates—the Vicaría de la Solidaridad, the Vicaría de Pastoral Obrera, the Vicaría de Pastoral Juvenil (Youth Pastoral Vicariate), and the Zonal Vicariates—facilitated this process, as did connections between young people in the grassroots opposition movement. One man involved in youth organizations in La Legua remembers he and a friend "spent entire nights talking about opening spaces for people who put themselves on the line. . . . We met in the Vicaría de Pastoral Juvenil, we met with young people from different parts of Santiago, from different poblaciones, and that gave us an idea of what was happening in Santiago, because television stations and radio didn't inform."[98] Women from población Angela Davis recall "a contact with [población] La Victoria, and some youngsters came here to work. And then we started to hold music festivals, to do cultural work, so that people would start to meet together, to gather, to talk, etcetera."[99] In poblaciones, anti-regime activists in the Church, social organizations, and political parties worked to forge alternatives to the dictatorship, its neoliberal model, and the society these were creating.

The Divided City

"Adam and Eve were Chilean because they went around naked, they didn't work, they believed in Paradise, and when they complained they were thrown out," went a joke circulating at the 1981 annual meeting of popular sector comunidades cristianas. Another joke making its way through Santiago in 1982 took aim at Pinochet:

"You know the one about Pinochet, when they found him dead in La Moneda?"
"No, I don't."
"Me neither, but damn, it starts out good, no!?"[100]

As this underground humor suggests, by 1982 discontent with the conditions underpinning the mirage of neoliberal economic progress and political institutionalization ran high. The schism between dominant discourse and conditions in the popular sectors was also apparent in the media. A comparative survey of two magazines, the pro-regime *¿Qué Pasa?*, designed for a well-to-do audience, and the Vicaría's *Solidaridad*, which circulated widely (though not exclusively) in popular sector comunidades cristianas, provides a snapshot of disparities in experience and perception of the "miracle" years as relative to socioeconomic class. In 1980 *¿Qué Pasa?* published admiring interviews with neoliberal economists and the head of the CNI, photos of well-heeled youth and businessmen, and reports on novel frivolities like roller rinks. It ran editorial screeds against Christian Democrats and Marxists, others in favor of neoliberal "modernization," and although its reporters lightly questioned some economic policies, its reportage was overwhelmingly pro-regime. The dull newsprint magazine featured glossy full-color ads for cars, commercial banks, high-end real estate, and airlines flying to international vacation destinations. That same year, *Solidaridad* reported on housing shortages, poor conditions in tenements, homelessness, urban land takeovers, and abuse of power and assassinations in poblaciones. It also reported on an immense Holy Week Vía Crucis in which pobladores took to the streets, invoking the name of the martyred Salvadoran archbishop Óscar Romero and concluding with a ceremony at Patio 29 of Santiago's General Cemetery, a place correctly rumored to be a clandestine burial site of the disappeared. The two magazines represent what came to be known as "the two Chiles" or *la ciudad escindida* (the divided city): one comfortable, complacent, and oblivious (if not complicit), and the other impoverished, violently repressed, and struggling.[101] Growing collective consciousness of gross injustices and activists' tenacious ant's work catalyzed the expansion and mobilization of anti-regime social movement webs in poblaciones during the years of "economic miracle" and political institutionalization. Enactment of social and political human rights had grown close to the heart of oppositionist political culture. When the economy crashed in 1982 and worsened in 1983, pobladores took to the streets en masse to demand an end to the dictatorship and a return to democracy.

6

National Protest and Possibility, 1983–1990

The kids asked my permission to go out. Sometimes they said to me, "Papa, we're just going over there," and I'd tell them, "Sure, just go ahead." "We're going to meet up with a kid, we're going to the stadium." Lies! They were going to organize themselves for the struggle, they felt trampled, they were victims of the dictatorship. So from there, they organized themselves, participated in really important organizations, and later the moment came when times got harder, and there they were participating in everything. And those testimonies are etched in my mind because their mother, may she rest in peace, always said to me, "But, *viejo*, you always give them permission." "Yes," I told her, "they have to be given permission because they're the ones who are going to take this country into the future. If we don't let them participate, they won't amount to anything in the future."

Father, La Legua, 2000[1]

"The dead in the dispute for power, in how we transitioned from Pinochet to democracy, are ours." And I think that's right, and I believe that there was the outcome there was because of the work that was done—good, bad, deficient—I believe that, yes, without the protests, without anything, I believe we'd still have Pinochet or a right-wing replacement. . . . But the Christian Democrats never would have taken so much power if we hadn't been at it for four years, with the workers in the streets, the students, the unity between students and pobladores. They're things that for better or worse paved the way.

Alejandra, José Cardijn and Villa Francia, 2005[2]

Death, Democracy, and Dreams

In Villa Francia the header of a four-story mural on an apartment block reads: "*Aquí nadie muere, compañero. Aquí cada día es continuar*"

(Here nobody dies, compañero. Here each day is to carry on). The mural abbreviates the lyrics of the song "Compañero," by Marcelo Puente: "Here nobody dies, compañero / Here nobody stops struggling / Here nothing ends, compañero / Here each day is to carry on."[3] The lyrics and mural express the idea that the ideals of leftists who died in the struggle for democracy live on in those who continue fighting for a better world. The mural, painted sometime between 1986 and 1988 and restored at least once since, commemorates the life and death of Miguel Leal Díaz, an eighteen-year-old FPMR militant from Villa Francia killed by police on September 5, 1986. Its dominant image is a full-body portrait of Leal, rifle in hand, draped with a Chilean flag. The mural resignifies the flag as a national symbol of patriotism and *chilenidad*, reclaiming it from the dictatorship by wrapping it around a young poblador, anti-regime activist, and member of the Communist armed left. During the 1980s, this image directly challenged the "new Chile's" elitist, anti-Communist conservatism, vacuous consumer culture, and "modern" neoliberal system anchored by a terrorist state that apotheosized wealth and denigrated the poor. In the early twenty-first century it challenged the injustices of the post-1990 neoliberal state and the erasure of pobladores and the Left from the dominant narrative of the struggle for democracy. In reappropriating national symbolism and associating it with people and ideals contrary to those espoused by the neoliberal state in both dictatorship and democracy, the mural remained a potent symbol in the early twenty-first century. Its heading linked past and present, allowing observers to project their own struggles for social justice into its message about legacy and continuity and to feel themselves part of an ongoing history.

The mural is also point of entry into complex memorias soterradas regarding the 1980s and the dictatorship's aftermath. A double helix of empowerment/protest and repression/death profoundly marked Villa Francia's political culture. So too did the experience of having enacted direct political protagonism in the struggle for democracy, only to face continued social and political marginalization after 1990. During the national protests Villa Francia became known as a combative población because of the strength of its protest culture and the presence of the armed left (especially the MIR and the FPMR), all of which contributed to notably high levels of mobilization and confrontational audacity.[4] In Santiago's combative poblaciones, organized youth from political parties, social organizations, and comunidades cristianas were at the forefront of the protests and bore the brunt of the repression. In Villa Francia, of the fourteen people the state killed or disappeared between 1973 and 1990, eight died between 1984 and 1988. Seven of the eight were between the ages of thirteen and twenty-five. The strength of anti-regime, pro-democracy activism in these neighborhoods and the pride associated with resistance coexists with a legacy of loss, as the mural suggests. During the 1980s and 1990s, the youth who formed the backbone of the popular sector protest movement experienced exhilarating moments of power and possibility but also profound dislocation. They lost loved ones and compañeros to repression, they lost their political protagonism to the elite-pacted transition, and they lost their imagined futures to the new neoliberal democracy.

The measure of a social movement, Robin D. G. Kelley writes in *Freedom Dreams*, is not merely whether it achieves its ultimate goals. "By such a measure virtually every radical movement failed because the basic power relations they sought to change remain pretty much intact. And yet," he continues, "it is precisely these alternative visions and dreams that inspire new generations to continue to struggle for change." Their importance lies in the "merits or power of the visions themselves," regardless of whether these were achieved in a movement's historical moment.[5] In Chile, popular sector regime opponents' struggle to achieve their "freedom dreams" materialized, in explosive and visible fashion, in the streets of Santiago's poblaciones during the twenty-two national protests that began on May 11, 1983, and persisted, with varying degrees of frequency and intensity, until 1987. Their most powerful period, what Tomás Moulián calls the "period of assault," stretched from May 1983 to November 1984, ending with a state of siege lasting from November 6, 1984, to June 16, 1985. Pinochet justified the state of siege as necessary to "save democracy and liberty" and "put an end to the criminal increase in terrorism" after a national strike shut down much of Santiago on October 30, 1984.[6] During the strike, as they had many times since the national protests began, pobladores blocked access to broad swaths of the capital, calling for Pinochet's ouster, for justice, and for an end to hunger, repression, and unemployment. The protests were "basically identical" from one población to the next, reported the opposition newsmagazine *Cauce*, with "barricades, vociferous crowds, occasional confrontations with public [security] forces." "Vast sectors of the capital," the magazine reported, "resemble virtual liberated zones." Western Santiago was inaccessible, and the southern districts were "a single broad and extended band of fire."[7]

The national protests were especially powerful in poblaciones. They were not only a reaction to the debt crisis, nor were they spontaneous.[8] They marked the climax, not the beginning, of anti-regime protest in poblaciones. By 1983 organized pobladores had accumulated substantial experience protesting under dictatorship, most notably in the Church-affiliated Vía Crucis marches of the early 1980s and the Left-sponsored Hunger Marches of 1982. Activist pobladores' experiences informed their responses to the Confederación de Trabajadores del Cobre's (CTC, Copper Workers' Confederation) call to national protest on May 11, 1983, as they mobilized social movement webs built in the 1970s that expanded in the early 1980s as the economic crisis worsened. Preparing for national protests in poblaciones required a substantial amount of time, energy, and labor, from acquiring materials for barricades and persuading neighbors to protest, to equipping first-aid posts and identifying safehouses. Smaller demonstrations took place between national protests, creating momentum.

The prevailing "protest climate" provided an opening and a platform for the resurgence of political parties. The Left, especially the MIR and the Communist Party (and in some areas of southern Santiago the MAPU), had an organizational foothold in poblaciones and enjoyed a certain level of respect within popular sector social movement webs. Party activists' ability to motivate, organize, and execute protests contributed to the national protests' power and longevity. Churches staffed by liberationist priests continued to serve as sanctuaries and to shelter organizations. Finally, a new generation of mobilized, energized youth (*jóvenes*) quickly moved to the forefront of the pro-democracy struggle. Some had grown up in liberationist comunidades cristianas, social organizations, and in contact with older anti-regime dissidents, and their sociopolitical commitments matured in the context of the protests. Others' commitments to sociopolitical change emerged in the context of deepening economic crisis and repression as they gained political empowerment through protest.

Jóvenes' activities often departed from the Christian Democrat–led, centrist opposition's and the Church's emphasis on peaceful protest. Protests in poblaciones aligned more closely with—although they did not necessarily obey— the strategies of the insurrectionary left, whose strongest proponents were the Communist Party and the MIR. The insurrectionary left sought to topple the dictatorship through massive popular uprisings backed by armed cadres. Years of violent repression had sharpened pobladores' interest in self-defense, and they displayed a willingness to tolerate defensive political violence, although few were willing to take up arms. In addition to nonviolent action, protest in poblaciones included barricades, fire, Molotovs, noise bombs, trenches, booby-traps, rock throwing, and sometimes armed resistance by the armed left.

In early twenty-first-century oral history conversations, interpretations of the meaning and import of the 1980s are closely tied to the experience of protest, the Left's setbacks, and the disappointments of the post-1990 period. The 1980s were a time of hope and renewal for the popular sector left, as the Sandinistas came to power in 1979 on a wave of mass insurrection that overthrew the Somoza dictatorship in Nicaragua, and as the national protests in Chile suggested that Chileans might be able to do the same. Yet revolutionary dreamers soon faced a series of setbacks that included a "second defeat" of the

Left (the first was the 1973 coup) when the "decisive year" of 1986 wore on without the regime's capitulation, and when hopes for a more radical solution flickered out with the regime's discovery of an FPMR weapons cache that August and the FPMR's unsuccessful attempt on Pinochet's life that September.[9] The splintering of the MIR between 1985 and 1987, conflict within the Communist Party as a faction of the Frente broke away in 1987, and dissolution of the USSR in 1990 as Chile's pacted transition took hold sharpened the sense of defeat, further deflating prospects for an alternative to the neoliberal status quo.

Pinochet's defeat in the 1988 plebiscite and the Concertación's triumph in the 1989 presidential elections hold a special place in collective memories of the end of the dictatorship. The idea of defeating the sword with the pen was, and continues to be, a powerfully attractive depiction of the transition to democracy. But viewed from the perspective of the poblaciones, the transition to democracy began with the national protests in the 1980s, not with the plebiscite. This transition was not peaceful, and it was not won only, or even primarily, at the ballot box. Yet the concertacionista narrative that has become the dominant interpretation of the transition emphasizes the Christian Democrats and renovated Socialists of the centrist political elite, and the technocratic aspects of the 1988 plebiscite and 1989 election campaigns. This now-accepted narrative obscures a deeper history of resistance. It was the Left and the strength of poblador protest that drove the dictatorship to pursue dialogue with the centrist opposition as part of a divide-and-rule strategy adopted after the second national protest, in June 1983. The "insurrectionary potential" of the mass mobilizations and the rise of an armed left also worried the Reagan administration—which feared Left-led regime change—into pressuring centrist politicians and the dictatorship to negotiate a center-right transition governed by the 1980 Constitution.[10] The concertacionista version of events that became the dominant historical narrative elided the popular sector protest movement that forced the regime to the negotiating table, provided Christian Democrat and renovated Socialist politicians the opportunity to position themselves as influential political actors, and brought the Concertación's "No" campaign to victory in the 1988 plebiscite.

Similar to the role it played after the coup, downward moral displacement facilitated the consolidation of this dominant narrative well into the early twenty-first century. The dictatorship excoriated poblador protesters, especially youth, as vandals, extremists, lumpen, terrorists, and *violentistas*. The centrist opposition—embodied first in the Christian Democrat–led Alianza Democrática (AD, Democratic Alliance, est. August 1983) and later the Concertación—tended to characterize poblador youth as violent victims of social anomie.

After the first national protest, Christian Democratic leader Patricio Aylwin argued that peaceful protest was the "only civilized way" to express dissent in the absence of an elected, representative government.[11] Poblador protest, which often included elements of political violence, was therefore by definition "uncivilized" and pobladores unsuited to share in political decision-making. The confluence between the regime's and the centrist opposition's portrayals was not lost on poblador youth and their allies. By 1988, reported a participant in a workshop coordinated by the popular-education organization ECO, poblador youth felt a "deepening sense of exclusion. A social image has been generated that could be characterized as barbaric, violent, and this doesn't only appear in the regime's discourse, more importantly, it also appears in the opposition press."[12] The regime, the Church, the Right, and the centrist opposition also derided armed struggle, which was present in poblaciones and had a young membership, as *terrorismo*. The Church emphasized nonviolent resistance and condemned political violence from all quarters, although the CECH made ethical distinctions between state terrorism and armed resistance without condoning the latter.[13] Nonetheless, the idea of condemning violence "from wherever it comes," a soundbite selectively culled from the Church's more complex position and magnified through the echo chamber of the centrist opposition's rhetoric, discursively equated the violence of rock-throwing adolescents with that of the terrorist state. These attitudes alienated protesters in poblaciones whose patience with political and economic conditions had run out, where state-perpetrated repression was extraordinarily violent, and where few had reason to believe that nonviolence was sufficient to confront the challenges they faced.

The poblador youth of the national protests were not irrational actors, although they indeed were angry and had few prospects. "One looks and realizes that a political way out of this crisis that we're living, which goes beyond the crisis of dictatorship, is not going to prioritize the needs and interests of popular youth. We'll still be eternally postponed," a young poblador and popular-education activist reported in 1984.[14] "The kids in the población are tired of being hungry, of not finding work, of being beaten and killed, and of being detained even while just dating in their neighborhood," said a young community activist in 1985.[15] Poblador youth responded to their circumstances in complex ways, from peaceful mobilization to armed struggle. Activist youth made difficult political choices under conditions over which they had little control, drawing upon their ideals, experiences, and hopes for the future. With the Concertación's rise to power, they were shut out of the decision-making processes of the transition and reduced to the role of voters tasked with choosing among options presented to them. Pobladores' sociopolitical and economic prospects were subsequently circumscribed to the disadvantageous status quo of the "limited," neoliberal democracy.

The tropes of a violent urban underclass, enraged youth with nothing left to lose, and barbarians raging at the gates of political propriety tell us more about their creators' political interests and social prejudices than they do about the protesters. For the centrist politicians and newly minted neoliberal democrats of the AD and later the Concertación, poblador protesters were useful allies in the streets and at the ballot box: they had blown open the political arena in 1983 and carried the Concertación to victory in the 1988 plebiscite. The centrists rode the protest movement to political prominence and consolidated their brand by positioning themselves against the backdrop of mass protest and an insurgent left as the safest political alternative and the only one capable of healing a divided nation. As popular sector protesters pushed for deeper social and political reform than the Concertación and the Right were willing to countenance, the Concertación disinherited its erstwhile allies as retrograde, violence-prone rabble who posed a danger to democracy. This shift was a cornerstone of the ascendant "neoliberal democracy" as subsequent concertacionista administrations limited political and economic change in the interest of consolidating power, appeasing military saber-rattlers, and preserving the outcome of the elite-pacted transition. This turn was especially hard on leftist poblador youth who saw their revolutionary dreams foreclosed and their imagined futures mortgaged to a national order that, at best, discounted their role in the struggle for democracy and, at worst, held it against them.

On May 11, 1983, though, the first national protest raged across Santiago, proving that massive multisectoral mobilization was possible. A democratic future appeared ripe for the taking. The poblaciones exploded in protest, far beyond what even organizers dared to expect. Middle- and upper-class Santiaguinos also protested in substantial numbers, showing that opposition to the regime had spread among its old supporters. On one level, the protests in poblaciones revolved around resistance to and rejection of the regime: pobladores protested against Pinochet, against dictatorship, against repression, and against the economic situation. Chants such as *"fuera Pinochet"* (get out Pinochet), *"y va a caer"* (and he's going to fall), and *"morir luchando, de hambre ni cagando"* (die fighting, of hunger, not even shitting [never]") capture some of this spirit of rejection. Yet on a deeper level, protest in poblaciones was not only about rejection. The protests encouraged visions of a Chile without dictatorship, conjuring a world of possibility that people populated with their own dreams of what democracy would look like. Poblador youth protested in favor of political and social rights, and for a sociopolitical system that would allow them opportunities for food, employment, education, housing, and political freedom. This world of possibility would permeate the protest climate of poblaciones for the rest of the decade, only to erode with the pacted transition and the disappointments of neoliberal democracy.[16] This chapter discusses the rise of mass protest in 1982 and the making of the national protests in poblaciones. It continues with an examination of the divide-and-rule strategy that the regime adopted in 1983. It then examines the generational shift in poblaciones that brought youth to the forefront of pro-democracy struggles in their neighborhoods. It closes with a consideration of memory, loss, and contemporary challenges.

The Rising Tide of Protest

The national protests' immediate precursors were the mass Hunger Marches of 1982. Poblador protest escalated throughout 1982, a year featuring debt crisis, economic meltdown, and spectacles of state-perpetrated political violence as the regime assassinated centrist opposition leaders Tucapel Jiménez and (investigators learned much later) Eduardo Frei Montalva. The escalating protests were due in part to the rising strength of the Communist Party and the MIR. The UP coalition had dissolved in 1980–81, but the Communist Party—the strongest party of the Left—maintained relationships with the parties of the ex-UP and sought alliances to the Right and Left, with the Christian Democrats and the MIR.[17] The Communist Party's *trabajo de masas* (mass work) had continued uninterrupted during the late 1970s and accelerated in the early 1980s, contributing to rising grassroots resistance. Meanwhile, the Communist Party's embrace of "all forms of struggle" in 1980 brought it closer to the MIR, providing opportunities for alliance with its old rival.[18]

The Left's reconsolidation contributed to rising protest activity throughout 1982. On March 8, 1982, International Women's Day, the Comité de Defensa de los Derechos de la Mujer (Committee for the Defense of Women's Rights), the Frente Unitario de Mujeres Pobladoras (Unitary Front of Poblador Women), youth groups from the Caro-Ochagavía sector of southern Santiago, and organizations from poblaciones across the city mounted protests against unemployment and hunger. At ten o'clock that night, the clanging of pots rang out across popular sector Santiago, in a form of protest called *caceroleo* that would become a hallmark of the national protests a year later. One of the women involved explained, "We're clear that hunger won't end with this little bit of caceroleo. But there's no doubt that the struggle isn't limited only to this. Today we begin like this. Tomorrow, when many of our neighbors who are staying home today join the fight, we'll be doing even bigger things."[19] The bigger things were soon to come.

On March 31, 1982, hundreds of pobladores carried out the first "March Against Hunger" in downtown Santiago. Protesters demonstrated, fought with police, and temporarily cut traffic on the Alameda—Santiago's principal east-west artery—with a burning barricade that reportedly shot flames several meters into the air. On August 19, 1982, the Communist Party, METRO, and COAPO sponsored a second Hunger March. In the poblaciones, the principal political parties involved were the Communist Party, MIR, MAPU, and assorted Socialists. As would be the case in the national protests, activists mobilized social movement webs in poblaciones, drawing participants from political parties, social organizations, and comunidades cristianas. A coalition of left-wing parties called for a third Hunger March on December 15, to follow up on the December 10 International Day of the Declaration of Human Rights (Article 25(1) of the Declaration establishes the right to food and other basic necessities). The protests began several days before December 15 in the poblaciones with marches, cultural events, effigy burnings, and barricades. Clandestine radio broadcasts encouraged pobladores to join the Hunger March, refuse to pay utility bills, occupy vacant land, "expropriate" food from stores, sabotage electric lines, and set up ollas comunes.[20] The December 15 Hunger March attracted the long-standing core opposition to the dictatorship—organized pobladores, workers, and the Left—plus students and middle-class protesters. It also spread to the provinces. Protesters in Concepción, Valparaíso, Viña del Mar, Lota, and Talca marched against the regime's economic policies and demanded civil liberties and democracy. They built barricades, printed pamphlets, flew banners, blocked streets, and cut electricity. Simultaneous protests occurred across popular sector Santiago, in Pudahuel, Américo Vespucio Sur, Renca, Conchalí, La Feria, La Granja, and in poblaciones La Legua, La Victoria, and La Bandera.[21] The MIR reported with optimism that the December 15 Hunger March yielded positive results, including cooperation within the Left, capacity for mobilization, and widespread expressions of anti-regime sentiment. The party concluded that "without doubt it was an experience . . . that will be repeated in the future."[22] The Hunger Marches had served as a test, a *sondeo* (probe), that suggested to the leftist opposition that mass protest was possible.

Participants in the burgeoning social movement webs engaged in rights talk that did not separate social from political rights. They also combined leftist and liberal rights traditions with broadly inclusive concepts of rights derived from the post-conciliar Church's interpretation of natural law that, Daniel Levine writes, "brought together a range of social, economic, cultural, and personal rights (to health, work, land, assembly, movement, education, etc.) in a coherent whole."[23] *La Nuez*, a newsletter written by youth affiliated with Santa Cruz parish in población Nogales, drew links between violence and injustice, drawing upon the tenet of Catholic natural law that all humans are reflections of God: "All injustice is also a form of violence: because it's a trampling of others' rights and of God himself."[24] Meanwhile, youth from Cristo Liberador in Villa Francia explicitly associated injustice, or trampling of rights, with unemployment, hunger, and persecution.[25] An interview that they conducted with a peer in Villa Francia's Comité de Trabajadores (Workers' Committee, the former "bolsa de cesantes") revealed a similar association: "It's unjust that human beings lose their rights as workers and as people," the young worker stated.[26] Although in the popular sectors the term "human rights" was often reserved for situations of political repression, participants in these social movement webs talked about a broad range of rights as something to which they were entitled as human beings.

The growth of social organizations and the quest for rights were not disconnected from or contrary to street protest. The rising tide of protest spurred community organization, and vice versa, as street protest provided a new venue for political education and solidarity. In taking dissent to the streets, activists disputed the regime's dominance of public space. They used the streets of their neighborhoods, which had become sites of abusive state dominance, to make dissent visible. These anti-regime spectacles reestablished neighborhood streets as contested—and contestatory—space, and they further expanded the reconstructed social commons into public territory, beyond the shelter of churches and private homes. Mass protest in the 1980s was the result of a long history of ant's work to build political cultures of solidarity and dissent in poblaciones. Church-affiliated demonstrations had done much to open public spaces of dissent—during the 1970s these were often the only types of protest that authorities (reluctantly) allowed.[27] In Villa Francia, remembers María Teresa, Cristo Liberador "did the famous Vía Crucis in which we literally took over the streets of Villa Francia, but with little candles and songs: 'They'll arrive with light, hope, and liberty' to the max, alright, with candles and hundreds of people in the población." Villa Francia's political culture was relatively permissive of public demonstrations in part because residents had become used to anti-regime activists' presence, and the activists were their neighbors, their children's friends, and people they saw at the soup kitchen, at church, and at weekend soccer matches. For years, activists in Villa Francia had gone door-to-door collecting food for activities and items for clothing drives, explaining to their neighbors the reasons for their work and the purpose of the donations. "So people in Villa Francia had experience in that sense, door to door, I mean, everyone knew," remembers María Teresa. "So afterward people see the Vía Crucis march go by with candles, praying for the disappeared, praying for the tortured, [and] it didn't surprise them, they peeked out. Then later, during the protests, they opened the door, obviously."[28] A man in La Legua describes a similar phenomenon in which repetition and visibility normalized anti-regime activity and made it easier for others to participate: "When we began there were people who looked out their windows, and then later they stood in their doorways, then they spoke with us and joined the march."[29]

Before 1983, political disagreements and disorientation generated by the regime's institutionalization hampered possibilities for larger protests. The leftist coalitions that called the Hunger Marches were influential in many poblaciones, but broader calls to protest could fail among middle- and upper-class sectors if the Left were openly involved, given the class-based nature of political affiliations, the controversies and taboos surrounding the UP period, and the effect of years of anti-Marxist repression on national political culture. Yet a broad anti-regime movement was gradually emerging. In 1982 the Vicaría de Pastoral Obrera tried to facilitate coordination between pobladores and the labor movement.[30] In late 1982, Monsignor Alfonso Baeza, head of that vicariate, reported, "The conviction has grown among people that this government has failed, but the expected reaction does not occur for reasons internal to the movement, where diverse tendencies struggle. Unity has not been achieved." Nevertheless, he observed: "I believe that the fact that a popular movement exists is always positive. The repression and the severity with which the authorities act is proof that this movement exists, and it is feared."[31]

Making the National Protests

The stunningly successful first national protest was on May 11, 1983. On April 21, 1983, the CTC, with the support of the Coordinadora Nacional Sindical (CNS, National Trade-Union Coordinator), had called a general strike for May 11. On April 25, the CNS initiated discussions with affiliated labor and poblador organizations and held joint meetings with "national organizations" (presumably including the clandestine left), students, and professional associations.[32] When the CTC and CNS announced the strike, activists in poblaciones began planning to support it. The annual May Day protests were quickly approaching, and the national strike would follow fast on its heels; this was an opportunity to produce momentum. In the Caro-Ochagavía sector, Juan C. remembers that activists held strike-planning assemblies and that their preparations accelerated after the May Day protests.[33] In La Legua, activists formed a Comando de Protesta to coordinate May 11 activities. Youth made the rounds of local businesses, factories, street markets, and bus routes to persuade shopkeepers, factory workers, shoppers, merchants, and bus drivers to participate.[34] The regime and the national copper company, the Corporación Nacional del Cobre (CODELCO, National Copper Corporation), responded to the call to strike with threats and a show of military force at the mines.[35] Divisions within the labor movement also weakened the strike's prospects. On May 7, the CTC canceled the strike and called instead for a "social protest."[36] Social protest lowered the bar for participation and encouraged creativity. Instructions directed the general populace to avoid purchases and bureaucratic transactions; to stay home; to drive slowly and honk car horns at one and six o'clock in the afternoon; and for caceroleo at eight in the evening. The instructions suggested that workers slow down, stop work briefly, and boycott company cafeterias. It urged employers not to retaliate, for bus drivers to stop plying their routes, and for shopkeepers to close for the day, enforcing disruption of normal daily activity. Rodolfo Seguel, leader of the CTC, called for an "active and peaceful protest. We don't want anyone to expose themselves to repression."[37]

Activists in poblaciones considered the call to protest an opportunity to escalate their struggle. From his perspective in La Legua, Juan R. remembers, "there was already a movement generated" under the shelter of the Church, and when "our sociopolitical leaders, at the national level, call a protest it's because there had already been a probe among the population." This accounted for the protests' enormity across several social sectors as people in the social movement webs responded to the call.[38] Juan C., from his vantage point in Caro-Ochagavía, noted that among pobladores the worsening economic crisis provoked deja vú, not disorientation. "We had the objective problem of hunger, similar to 1975," he explains, but this time they were prepared to confront it and protest against it, mobilizing the social movement webs they had already built. "There was a rebirth of bolsas de cesantes," Juan C. recalls, "but now we also denounced the hunger and organized Hunger Marches in downtown Santiago, to protest." He reaches conclusions similar to Juan R.'s regarding the first national protest. "The protests don't come out of nowhere," he explains. "Before them were the Hunger Marches, May firsts, and many things." When, for the first national protest, the CTC called on the population to "stay in their houses, not send the children to school, it was a peaceful convocation," he remembers. "The pobladores transformed it into a protest. We took over the poblaciones, we made the barricades and all that."[39] Activists in poblaciones created opportunities for others to protest. They spread information, planned protest activities, persuaded family members and neighbors to join them, started cacerleo at the appointed hour, and went first into the streets. They made protest visible, audible, and palpable, thereby challenging and changing the collective imagination of what was possible.

In general, as a social sector, pobladores responded to the CTC's call to protest. In practice, as individuals, they responded to the call of people they knew: familiar local activists, family, neighbors, and friends. At the household level, everyone had to decide for themselves whether and how to participate. Silvia, a member of the Communist Party and Cristo Liberador, remembers, "People thought of things on their own. I saw to that. To going to see the señora who had never done anything, to see what she would do." "That's why the cacerleo was so successful," she explains, "because this didn't scare them, because they did it in their room, with the kids held tight, or they stuck the kids under the cot." Others preferred the bathroom, she remembers, "because they felt that it was solid, the bullets couldn't pass through. So they stuck [the kids] in there and stood next to the window to hit [the pots and pans]." Juan, one of Silvia's comrades, remembers that he convinced his "whole family to just hit [the pots and pans], that we shouldn't be afraid. In any case I was in my house, and in my house I can do what I want. That was the principle of liberty," he ironized. "I have private property and all that they talk about: well, let's exercise it."[40] Even cacerleo, one of the most common and spontaneous-seeming protest methods, required some premeditation. While some reveled in using cacerleo to turn the tables on wealthy right-wing women who had used the tactic against the UP, others chose not to use pots and pans because they did not want to replicate what they deemed a tainted right-wing protest tactic. Still others preferred not to damage their kitchen utensils. Instead, they used sturdier propane tanks, pipes, or tools.[41]

Local party activists had significant influence within the social movement webs that mobilized to "make" the first national protests in poblaciones. During the 1980s, the borders between social organizations and political parties remained diffuse, but disagreements escalated as political parties gained strength. Party activists sometimes attracted criticism for trying to dominate or manipulate the groups for their parties' political purposes. Clashes of organizational culture and purpose occurred regularly and produced conflict, but party activists' experience and skills also played an important role in successful protest mobilization. "There was a super-quotidian contribution of commitment, of saying . . . 'Listen, if we have to do this, those of you who are organized have to take the step, you have to continue,'" María Teresa recalls. The protests did not surprise her, she remembers, "because I saw that work being done, which was to say, 'Listen, I believe we have to express ourselves in some way,' get it? If you start to say that beforehand, although it provokes crisis in some people, they prepare themselves."[42] Juanita's experience suggests, likewise, that the national protests were born of relationships within the organizationally diverse and politically pluralistic social movement webs. "It's not something that was born [spontaneously]: 'Oooh, we're in bad shape.' No," she explains, "the organization is otherwise."[43]

The first national protests attracted mass participation because they were tailored to the repressive conditions and the collective concerns of broad segments of the population. Participation "didn't imply great costs," explains Mario, "because you could make your discontent visible in various ways." Protest response differed by socioeconomic sector. He recalls that there was "obviously a more middle-class logic" in the first call to protest that emphasized keeping children home from school, avoiding bureaucratic transactions downtown, and boycotting commerce. School absenteeism was already high in poblaciones, there was little money to go downtown, and, as a woman from población Lo Hermida commented to a reporter, on May 11, 1983, "we didn't buy anything, but that's not unusual."[44] In the popular sectors, says Mario, the protest "rapidly took the form of marches through the población, demonstrations, or shouting together, then when the police arrive, building barricades to give the notion that the neighborhood belongs to us." The barricades created a space for "socialization, where people sang, danced, did rounds. The children were there, the women, the elderly, in other words, everyone was in the street."[45] Although the nighttime protests were the most extensive, pobladores also protested during the day, often in creative ways: they staged funerals for empty cooking pots, and women marched through street markets with empty shopping bags.[46] Pobladores also participated in student and labor protests, according to their multifaceted affiliations. At night caceroleo and chants filled the air, and the barricades circled Santiago with fire.

Y Va a Caer . . .

At eight o'clock on the evening of May 11, 1983, don Enrique stood near the window of his home in Nueva La Legua listening for the caceroleo to begin but heard nothing.[47] The first national protest in La Legua had begun the night before, on May 10, when youth lit barricades at strategic intersections. They kept the barricades burning until midnight, and then the neighborhood was quiet until 5:30 on the morning of May 11, when protesters scattered *miguelitos* (bent nails used to puncture tires) across the roads.[48] Alán remembers that "La Legua was one of the first poblaciones to kick off the protest. I remember that on my block some kids, neighbors from Toro y

Zambrano—I'm not going to give their names—started to come by the house." The protest was a neighborhood affair, its rhythm and routine an extension of local political culture and conditions. He remembers that "one of the kids went around with a black hood and on a bicycle in that first protest, and there was always the jerk who recognized him and shouted his name in front of everyone. We were burning tires; others went around throwing Molotovs at the corners, at the barricades people were preparing." In La Legua "we knew there was going to be a protest, and everyone knew that on their block specific people were going to be involved, and they worked with them trying to, how shall I say, avoid being noticed . . . because there were people snitching."[49] On May 11, the Álvarez de Toledo and Toro y Zambrano barricade was burning by nine o'clock in the morning, and protesters threw rocks at city buses to stop them from running their routes.[50]

Don Enrique and his fellow organizers in La Legua worked hard to convince others to participate in the evening caceroleo. "[We'd say], 'R, bang pots and pans.' [R. would say], 'Noooooo.' [We'd say], 'Do it at the very back of your property so they don't hear you in the street, and H. will be right next to you. He's going to bang a pot at the back of *his* property.'" Shortly after eight o'clock that evening, don Enrique still heard nothing. "So here, for the first protest, shoot, five or ten minutes passed and nothing was happening, damn it," he remembers, "so then I go bananas, and I take an empty propane tank upstairs, and I hang it there . . . and I get a tool from the workshop, and TA TA TA! And desperately," he emphasizes, "because the [Communist] Party is taking a big risk for this protest, the Party went all in, with everything, and I was a regional leader." People soon gathered in the street outside. A speech ensued, a march set out, and "there the old guys got fired up."[51]

As caceroleo spread and the march wound through the neighborhood, more people joined them. Many others stayed inside their houses, afraid of what would happen. Some kept barricades burning by throwing their own household items on the fires. Groups formed around bonfires inside the barricades' protective perimeter. Similar scenarios unfolded that night in poblaciones across Santiago. Juan C. remembers that during the first protest in his neighborhood, "the repression couldn't enter the población for four hours with all its armored equipment, the población was taken over by us pobladores." The police retreated because "the cost was high, the people were fired up, venting their rage, their energy. It could have been a massacre. In many poblaciones they had to evacuate the Carabineros because they couldn't repress, they had to withdraw them."[52] The temporary pockets of freedom—what party militants referred to as "liberated zones"—nurtured a festive, world-upside-down atmosphere. When he was a child, remembers a man from La Legua, "for me it was fascinating to have my own pot [for caceroleo], to see the people singing, it was a *fiesta social*, and suddenly whistles to attract the pacos, and it was all a game of hide and seek, because everyone [said], 'the pacos are coming, everyone to your houses,' or wherever you landed, so I lived in a corner house and thousands of people fit in there." As his recollections demonstrate, though, repression tempered the festivities. When the police came, "I was speechless, frozen, looking for my mom, with everyone scattered, and the gunfire started, pa pa pa pa, and I was desperate. Somebody grabbed me, threw me. I was in my house, but I was crying because I couldn't find my mom. In the end she was right behind me. I always remember that. I remember that they came shooting indiscriminately."[53] Around midnight on May 11, Carabineros reached La Legua with tear gas, firearms, and a helicopter but eventually retreated. A group of youth later went to the nearby poblaciones El Pinar and Germán Riesco to join protesters there, traveling along the threads of the social movement webs to lend a hand beyond La Legua.[54]

For Carlos, in Villa Francia, the first national protest was a moment of catharsis. He was active in the Socialist Party and community organizations before the coup, but after the coup he withdrew and participated only very selectively. It was the first time in ten years that he saw so many of his neighbors openly express their discontent. Even those who avoided street protest stood in their doorways or banged pots and pans indoors.[55] Leonor, who did not join a political party but was active in social organizations and Cristo Liberador, remembers that during the protests in Villa Francia, "at first we all participated, everyone in the comunidad [cristiana], everyone in the social organizations, but those who organized the activities were people linked to the political world, sectors of the MIR, sectors of the Communist Party who later rearticulated themselves in the Frente."[56] During the weeks leading up to May 11, youth cooperated across party and organizational lines to plan the protest. Adults went door to door persuading their neighbors to participate in the caceroleo. Through Villa Francia's social movement webs, "everyone" knew that a national protest was at hand; the question was whether and how to participate.[57] Other areas of western Santiago where the liberationist church and the Left were influential, such as Pudahuel, were also active protest zones. In some areas of Pudahuel, on the first night of national protest pobladores continued the caceroleo and threw rocks at police until three in the morning.[58]

Villa Francia, like other poblaciones with strong anti-regime political cultures, was enmeshed in social movement webs that intersected beyond the poblaciones with the labor movement, political parties, and the Catholic Church. Villa Francia's social organizations formed part of the Coordinadora de Organizaciones Políticas y Sociales de Las Rejas that organized protests in that part of the city.[59] Protests required a substantial amount of work, from collecting tires and gasoline for barricades to making miguelitos, digging trenches, and planning marches, ollas comunes, and cultural activities. The Coordinadora connected multiple poblaciones, "planning, communicating, and assigning tasks," explains Jorge. "Each población organized how to defend itself," says Irene, "so it assigned tasks: some [people] found tires to make barricades. . . . Others, in the bolsa [de cesantes] made the miguelitos." "We bought the wire," remembers Jorge, and "we cut it, soldered it, bags full." "The next day at five in the morning we went out to block the streets," continues Irene. "And," interjects Jorge, "we planned how to defend the barricades. . . . Those who got the tires were up almost all night getting tires out of the sand pits and hiding them in the houses, throwing them in the high grass over there. The next day at six, five-thirty in the morning, the barricade had to be built, and everyone went out with the tires, blocking, cutting off [the streets], well organized."[60]

The first national protest raised hopes among the opposition for an imminent end to the dictatorship and a quick transition to democracy. News of its success spread by word of mouth, opposition press, and clandestine publications and pamphlets. In the May issue of the clandestine Catholic opposition paper *Policarpo*, an article titled "Time to prepare for the June protests!" encouraged readers to think of May 11 as a model. It suggested foot dragging, caceroleo, assemblies, school absenteeism, commercial boycotts, traffic jams, and further protest planning.[61] For the second protest, organizers in Villa Francia prepared more carefully and included more people. "It was 'You, stand here, you stand there, do this, [do] this other thing,' and have doors open at the houses, and the *vieja* who had to lend support and hide [people, materials], [and] well, the barricade," María Teresa remembers.[62] The protests became more organized in southern Santiago as well, Juan C. recalls. During the first protest, "we intentionally built the barricades, but we didn't manage to plan or make or scatter the miguelitos like we did for the second one, or to open the canal at the Lo Espejo underpass, to flood it, which we did for the second one to stop more traffic."[63]

Pobladores' inter-protest ant's work and their local knowledge were key elements of the national protests. The physical and human geography of the poblaciones and local political cultures shaped the ways that pobladores protested. The barricades were a protest tactic and symbol that is still used today. Barricades' "particular virtue," writes Eric Hazan, "is to proliferate and form a network that crosses the space of the city. This faculty of rapid multiplication can make it an offensive instrument: victorious barricades . . . are those that pin down the forces of repression, paralyse their movements and end up stifling them into impotence."[64] The barricades of Santiago's poblaciones were no exceptions; they were both defensive and offensive. The barricades stopped traffic, bringing normal urban activity to a halt; they discouraged police from entering neighborhoods; they were gathering points for protesters; and they demarcated territory that pobladores claimed as their own. Fire was a key element of Santiago's barricades, and flammable materials like tires had to be replenished. Between protests, activists had to collect and store tires and accelerant without being caught.

Protesters used their local knowledge to the police's disadvantage, cutting electricity and laying traps. Police sometimes avoided entering La Legua "because they knew they'd lose, because they had no idea where the flying rocks, the explosions, were coming from, because they ended up snout-down on the ground," Juan explains.[65] Like barricades, booby-traps, and ambushes, cutting the electricity at night was a self-defense tactic that protesters used to amplify the advantages that local knowledge provided. "In those times we had cables," explains one man, "those old cables that you could pull together by throwing a chain around them and cut the current. It was a question of logic," he says, "we knew the población, so if there's going to be resistance the first thing to do is to cut the electricity, because I know where to run, the pacos have no idea, so I come out ahead in that sense."[66] These types of self-defense tactics meant that on some protest days, "this was free territory," says a poblador from Villa Francia.[67] Under those conditions, María Teresa remembers, "inside [the población] one did what one wanted."[68]

Local political cultures also shaped the contours of the protests. Because of differing intra-neighborhood political cultures, in La Legua protesters tended not to gather in La Emergencia, and protesters from La Emergencia went to other parts of La Legua to protest. In La Emergencia "some people built bonfires, for example those from the chapel," explains one woman, but the professional thieves would "get angry at people who did things . . . because they were assuring their liberty [by avoiding the police]." A man explains that in La Emergencia, "there were neighbors who even came out with buckets of water to douse the barricade."[69] Some residents of La Emergencia wanted to confront the police. Juan remembers that he and others "all went up there [to Nueva La Legua] because the pacos didn't come in here [to La Emergencia], they were afraid. So we went to find them there at Salesianos and Copihues. That was the fight headquarters."[70]

The protests persisted despite and because of repression. Although repressive forces had withdrawn from some neighborhoods, on May 11, 1983, state agents killed two pobladores, injured dozens of people, and detained hundreds.[71]

Most of the people killed in the national protests were pobladores, a pattern originating much earlier in the dictatorship that continued into the 1980s. In wealthier residential sectors of the city, repressors used tear gas, water cannons, and beatings to dissuade protesters. In poblaciones, they relied on tear gas, base brutality, and live ammunition.[72] Most of the arrests during the first protest occurred in the popular sectors of Santiago near the intersection of Aves. Grecia and Pedro de Valdivia; in poblaciones Santa Julia, Lo Hermida, La Victoria, João Goulart, La Castina, and Yungay; and in the working-class municipalities of La Granja, San Miguel, Pudahuel, La Florida, and Renca. Repression and resistance continued between protests. On May 13, police occupied población Santa Adriana with water cannons and tear gas trucks and attacked a thousands-strong funeral procession for Andrés Fuentes Sepúlveda, one of the pobladores killed during the first national protest. In response, pobladores lit barricades and threw rocks at police in poblaciones La Victoria, Lo Valledor, José María Caro, and Dávila.[73] On May 14, the dictatorship unleashed mass allanamientos in poblaciones La Victoria, La Castrina, João Goulart, and Yungay, detaining at least 6,000 families. Pobladores viewed the allanamientos as a repeat of the regime's repressive tactics following the coup.[74] As it had after the coup, the pro-regime press billed the allanamientos as campaigns against criminals and "subversives," but official rhetoric now met with suspicion and open opprobrium as people overcame their fear. As one artisanal bulletin stated, "We're in June of 1983, not October of 1973."[75]

The first national protest stunned the opposition and regime alike, changing the collective imagination of what was possible. Protest activity continued between national protests, leading to a "state of permanent protest" that endured for the next three years. Between May 11 and June 14, the date of the second national protest, pobladores, artists, women, students, and professionals demonstrated in Santiago. Labor federations formed the Comando Nacional de Trabajadores (CNT, National Workers' Command). The CNT set a second national protest date for June 14 with the objective of reestablishing democracy and "the free exercise of labor and civil rights."[76] The protest movement—born of the Left, organized labor, and pobladores—was by now attracting people from beyond the Left and the popular sectors. Discontent spread even to the pro-regime right, as the economic crisis worsened and right-wing politicians noticed that middle- and upper-class sectors, where they had historically enjoyed the most support, had joined the protests. They hoped for a controlled *apertura* (political opening) that would preserve the regime's upper hand.[77] When the second national protest exploded on June 14, the dictators (Pinochet and the junta) read the writing on the wall.

"Useful Fools" and "Those Who Will Never Forgive Us"

At five thirty on the evening of June 16, 1983, the junta discussed whether to authorize a state of siege. Two days earlier, the second national protest had shaken the dictators' confidence. In its aftermath, Pinochet submitted to the junta a draft law declaring a state of siege, arguing that political parties were using organized labor to exacerbate the economic crisis and provoke political instability. He charged that "concerted action among groups opposing the government," sought to "destabilize the constitutional regime" and that such activity "could have unpredictable consequences for the national social and economic order."[78] During the meeting, the junta—José Toribio Merino (Navy), Fernando Matthei (Air Force), César Benavides (Army), and César Mendoza (Carabineros)—discussed their options. If they allowed the protests to continue and the political opposition to operate with impunity, they risked being forced from power under conditions not of their own making. If a state of siege failed to quell the unrest, they would have wasted their trump card with similar results. They worried too that a state of siege would require the military to "again take charge of the dirty part of the problem," as Merino referred to repression, to the detriment of their international image, with negative results for foreign debt negotiations.[79]

The junta greeted Pinochet's draft law with frustration, not because its members wholly disagreed with his rendering of the circumstances and their potential consequences but because the many-headed hydra of economic disaster, debt negotiation, and mass protest put them between a rock and a hard place. In its call to protest that May 11, the CTC had roundly rejected the dictatorship's project: "our problem is not one law more or one law less, or one modification or another to an existing one, rather it is much more profound and fundamental: it's about a complete economic, social, cultural, and political system that has us bound and oppressed, that contradicts our idiosyncrasies as Chileans and workers, that has tried to asphyxiate us with weapons such as terror and repression to bind us even more, because it was imposed upon us by force and with trickery."[80] The dictatorship's constitutional framework for a transition to civilian rule kept Pinochet in power until at least 1989, but the opposition was now pushing for an immediate transition and the derogation of the 1980 Constitution, while the Left and labor also sought an end to the neoliberal economic model. The second national protest signaled to the dictators that a transition was underway, and it was not one to their liking.

The junta's concerns following the second national protest centered on the relationship between economic and political crisis, and the possibility that the junta itself would fall from power. The economy's abysmal performance made this a distinct possibility. In 1982 industrial growth fell by 21 percent and the GDP by 14 percent, while unemployment rose to 26 percent. Bankruptcies multiplied at an alarming rate as the overleveraged conglomerates of the "miracle" years crumbled: 810 companies went bankrupt in 1982, well above the annual 277-company average of 1975–81. Inflation climbed to more than 20 percent nationally and to 37 percent for the urban poor, and currency devaluation decimated commercial and household economies. In early 1983 the regime liquidated three major banks and took over five others, and the Central Bank bailed out other failing financial institutions. In Santiago, median family incomes dropped by 28 percent. Real wages fell nearly 11 percent, and unemployment continued its upward trajectory, eventually rising to over 31 percent nationally and as high as 60–80 percent in Santiago's poblaciones.[81] The most pressing concern for the junta in this context of neoliberal economic meltdown was that the Communist Party would use the economic crisis to spark a political crisis that could compromise foreign debt negotiations. If the junta authorized a state of siege to control the protests, it risked projecting an image of political instability that could stymie negotiations with England, Germany, Japan, and Israel. In this scenario, argued Merino, to declare a state of siege was to pen a "death certificate for the current regime." If the junta authorized a state of siege, stopping the protests but spooking creditors, Merino asked, "What do we do if this year we keep paying the 1,240 million dollars we owe? . . . There's nowhere to get them. Then we fall not because of politics but because of the economic part." Matthei agreed that a state of siege might ruin debt negotiations. "Internally," he stated, "I consider it explosive. Externally, I consider it deadly."[82]

Although the regime's spokespeople, including Pinochet, minimized and delegitimized the protests in public, the junta realized that they represented a powerful political sea change. The dictators were therefore wary of declaring a state of siege too soon. "If the state of siege is the employment of the reserves," Benavides asked rhetorically, "what's after that?" "Nothing. Just to leave," interjected Merino.[83] Matthei argued against the state of siege, pointing out that the regime's "system for doing away with the political parties" was a "complete failure . . . because the Christian Democrat Party has a president, it has this and that and activists, and they're functioning. As far as the Communist Party, all you have to do is look to see that it's functioning. What's not functioning is our own parties." Anything the regime did to "sit on the lid of the pot," he warned, would blow the lid off, and "if the pressure is so great that it explodes, we're going to fly far."[84] Matthei proposed to divide and rule. "Why don't we face the reality that there's an opposition, that there are people who aren't happy, that there are people who in a certain way are within more or less legitimate canons, and there are others who are unpardonable enemies to the death who have declared war on us, like the Communist Party and the armed struggle. They're two different things. Why do we treat them like the same thing?" The regime had created the conditions for a unified opposition, he argued, "because we force them into the same sack, we push them to stick themselves into the same sack, everyone who doesn't agree with everything we propose. That was the first mistake of all," he charged: "a mistake that began on the very eleventh of September [1973] and that we still haven't corrected today."[85]

Matthei had reason to believe that divide-and-rule tactics would bear fruit, and he was thinking historically when he proposed to disaggregate the opposition. Unlike the Communist Party and "the armed struggle"—the only opposition, along with the Christian Democrats (PDC), that the junta deemed relevant—the PDC had repeatedly proven willing to cooperate. The party had opposed the UP and supported the coup and the fledgling dictatorship.[86] Following the coup, the ex-president Eduardo Frei Montalva attended the national Independence Day Te Deum ceremony, an act that communicated support for the coup. That October he made international declarations of support for the regime. On October 10, 1973, Patricio Aylwin, an ex-senator and PDC party president, met with the junta. According to the meeting minutes, he expressed concern about the loss of university autonomy, the dissolution of municipal governments, and the quantity of political prisoners. He spent much of the meeting, however, currying the dictators' favor. He reminded them of the role that the PDC played in "anti-Marxist struggle" during the UP. He offered Christian Democrats' collaboration, as individuals, with "the junta's work" (the party, as such, was supposed to be in political recess). He expressed his support for the coup, talked about his party's recruitment moratorium and reorganization, and extended his wishes for the junta's success. Much of the meeting revolved around his concern that the PDC could not compete with the outlawed Communist Party during the political recess. He worried that the Left would "increase its forces in clandestinity" such that when "the situation normalizes" the PDC would have lost political ground. He closed by requesting that the party's directorate be informed of any charges against Christian Democrats, so that matters could be "conveniently clarified." The party directorate, he informed the dictators, knew that "vested interests" sought to create the impression that it had "anti-junta attitudes."[87]

Although by 1983 the PDC had moved into the opposition, it was clear from the junta's point of view that in calculating how to divide the opposition, the PDC was less likely than the Left to threaten the dictatorship's legacy. The Left had defied the regime from day one and now sought a breadth and depth of social and political democratization that the PDC had joined with the Right and the military to destroy in 1973. The Christian Democrats fell into the category of "people who are not happy" but "who in a certain way are within more or less legitimate canons." Co-opting the political center by luring the Christian Democrats into negotiations held the promise of preventing an alliance between the Communist Party and the PDC and thwarting the protests by peeling off the centrist opposition.

A corollary of this divide-and-rule strategy involved distinguishing between protesters by social class. The protests in well-to-do neighborhoods, historical bastions of the Right, were "grotesque" and easily handled, Matthei argued. They were "a concertation of some 'useful fools' who go around honking their horns and everything in Mercedes Benzes, which is almost grotesque; that's to say, not almost, it's absolutely grotesque, and in luxury apartments banging pot lids." "With imported pots!" interjected Merino. "With imported pots," affirmed Matthei, "the most grotesque there is and that should just be laughed at. It's best to laugh at them and make them look ridiculous, like the fools they are." Unlike the "grotesque" protests of the well-off, Matthei continued, "there is another part that is perfectly directed and orchestrated by the Communist Party and that takes place in other, completely different areas and with other people," where "lumpen" purportedly ran amok. These different areas were the poblaciones—where the Left had a historical base, where the protests were strongest, and where the regime presumed lumpen to reside. These "other people," Matthei's comments suggest, had reason to protest but should be prevented from doing so. He did not refer to them as deserving of ridicule but discursively linked these "completely different areas" and "other people" to criminals and the Communist Party in order to justify cracking down on protest in poblaciones. "There's another thing," he said, "they'll never stop. Corks will sink and stones will float, but these guys will never stop. So we can implement a state of siege: just the same, they won't stop." The situation was only "explosive," Matthei concluded, to the extent that the authorities failed to "manage" it. To declare a state of siege would be "playing right into these *señores*' [the Communist Party's] hands," argued Matthei. That's not what "the vast majority of Chileans [want]," he continued, "although at best many of them have legitimate problems with this government, and they don't agree, and they'd like something else, but there are others who will never forgive us and whom we will never be able to attract. Against that only one thing fits: a firm hand."[88] The junta concluded that a state of siege was unwarranted and instead advocated the divide-and-rule strategy.

The strategy of opening dialogue with amenable centrists and crushing the Left and poblador protest exacerbated tensions between centrist opposition leadership and the popular sector protesters who had driven the regime to the dialogue table.[89] Dialogue did not stop the protests, because of the regime's intransigence and because the AD pursued an ambiguous dialogue/protest strategy and had less influence than the Left at the grassroots, where fed-up pobladores organized protests and cooperated across political divides.

The disconnect between centrist opposition elites and popular sector protesters became especially apparent in September 1983. For the August 1983 national protest, the AD had unsuccessfully attempted to persuade pobladores to change their protest methods to better complement its political agenda.[90] The regime, for its part, sent eighteen thousand soldiers into Santiago's streets to repress protest with much violence and little success. Shortly thereafter the AD entered into talks with the regime representative Sergio Onofre Jarpa. When a divided opposition called for various lengths and types of protest that September, poblador protest surpassed all elite control, continuing for nearly a week. On September 15, the traditional pobladores' movement for affordable housing, which, like the protest movement, was rooted in the social movement webs of popular sector Santiago, burst into the national spotlight with the largest two land takeovers in Santiago's history, totaling approximately fifteen thousand people. The explosion of the traditional pobladores movement back onto the national scene alongside the protest movement highlighted the strength of the popular movement's roots in the poblaciones.

In the wake of the September protest, the Communist Party, MIR, and the Socialist Party-Almeyda formed the Movimiento Democrático Popular (MDP, Popular Democratic Movement), which sought the regime's ouster through mass insurrection. The Communist-led MDP called the sixth national protest for October 11, 12, and 13.[91] The Christian Democrat-led AD canceled its protest plans, splitting openly with the MDP. As the protests continued and the AD played both sides, the opposition leadership repeatedly failed to forge a united front, and the dictatorship reestablished its hold.

Protest continued after the AD-Jarpa dialogue broke down in late 1983, leading to relatively unified protests through May 1984 that included a de facto general strike in March.[92] On May 16, 1984, the junta finally granted Pinochet a ninety-day authorization to declare a state of siege, with Merino and Mendoza arguing that "if only Pudahuel [a western Santiago municipality dense with poblaciones] could be under a state of siege it would be ideal" because "Pudahuel requires it urgently."[93] The junta renewed the unused authorization on August 30 although Matthei distrusted Pinochet's motives. The authorization, Matthei commented, should be used to actually impose a state of siege, "not so that he has an ace up his sleeve."[94] Pinochet declared the state of siege that November following the national strike of October 30.

The divide-and-rule approach, combined with the state of siege, contributed to the isolation of popular sector protest and centrists' willingness to soften their demands. In August 1985, the center-right opposition produced the Church-backed Acuerdo Nacional para la Transición Plena a la Democracia (National Accord for the Full Transition to Democracy).[95] The Acuerdo accepted the dictatorship's framework for transition and did not address the regime's human rights abuses, the illegitimacy of the 1980 Constitution, or the dictatorship's origins.[96] The AD, in the spirit of the new accord, canceled its September 1985 national protest plans and instructed its supporters to remain indoors.[97] As centrists withdrew support for protests to pursue negotiations with the dictatorship, protest became increasingly isolated in the poblaciones. "They didn't consult the youth [when designing the Acuerdo]," commented young community activists in southern Santiago, "and if we want pobladores to participate in [the spirit of] this document we have to make them feel that they participated in its generation."[98] Patricia Richards has found that in poblaciones, "participation" meant "being present rather than merely being represented."[99] According to researchers at ECO, pobladores placed high value on participatory democracy and understood democratization "as an instrument to assure more authentic participation." Activist pobladores did not perceive democratization as a "phenomenon or task" of the 1980s. Rather, they understood democratization as "a long-term process that—with advances and setbacks—began the moment that pobladores began organizing themselves and reconstituting themselves as actors after the 1973 coup."[100] Representation without participation became especially problematic when those who arrogated to themselves the task and privilege of representation failed to consult those they claimed to represent.

The tension between elite-led representative democracy and grassroots participatory democracy and the tenuous relationship between the political elite and the grassroots contributed to divisions within the opposition. The dictatorship ultimately rejected the Acuerdo, stonewalling dialogue, driving the centrist opposition into a virtual dead end, and reinvigorating the Left's insurrectionary strategy. Party leaderships on both Left and Center doubled down on their competing political strategies—mass insurrection, armed struggle, and overthrow, on the one hand, and political negotiation with the regime, on the other—marginalizing the grassroots social movement in poblaciones to the extent that its localized, politically pluralistic, and relatively horizontal political culture did not lend itself to party directive or cooptation.[101] Throughout 1985 and 1986 repression and political violence in poblaciones peaked in deadly fashion, falling heavily on poblador youth and the insurrectionary left, the boogeymen of the transition for the dictatorship, the US, and the centrist opposition alike.[102]

Taking the Country into the Future

The national protests were the province of poblador youth. Youth repeatedly took to the streets of their poblaciones, calling for democracy and the right to food, employment, housing, education, and political freedom. These demands represented desires for profound social, political, and economic change, up to and including socialist revolution. Youth were not monolithic in their purposes and goals, but they converged in the streets during protests, forging an action-based collective that influenced and mobilized others in their neighborhoods. As a man from La Legua remembers, "The adults made us become conscious, but the great struggle . . . the strong fight in the times of the dictatorship and, as they say, those who got their butts wet [*los que se mojaron el poto*], were the youth."[103]

The generational shift in which organized poblador youth took the helm of anti-regime, pro-democracy activism in their neighborhoods is one of the most notable aspects of the 1980s. In practical terms, the category of "youth" was popularly understood to mean people aged fifteen to thirty, or who were under the age of twenty at the time of the coup. Popular education initiatives in poblaciones and articles in opposition media, NGOs, and Church publications tended to focus on teenagers and people in their early twenties.[104] Chilean researchers attuned to the construction of "youth" as a social category eschewed age ranges in favor of culturally defined social parameters. Irene Agurto wrote during the 1980s that "youth" was a "period marked by the search for identity and the definition of a future life project" and shaped by material conditions, "socializing agents," and "ideological apparatuses."[105] It was a "moratorium" in which experimentation and errors were permitted as people acquired "social and psychological skills that imply a process of understanding and acknowledgment of themselves and the social environment in which they live." The moratorium depended on delayed workforce entry, families' permissiveness, and society's willingness to grant youth legitimacy as people with goals and futures.[106] This life phase was both violated and prolonged in contradictory ways during the dictatorship as social and cultural marginalization, deteriorating living conditions, and political exclusion became the "new normal." These conditions were "not the product of an 'emergency,'" Agurto stated, "and young people do not perceive them as something transitory. Increasing deterioration of quality of life has become internalized as a 'normal aspect' of youth's daily lives and those of the popular world in general, producing a situation that, years before, would have been considered abnormal." This new normal created a future crisis, a *"crisis de futuro,"* by indefinitely delaying adulthood. Youth found themselves trapped in a neoliberal system that neither "contemplates the incorporation of new workforce contingents into the economic structure" nor "expands the educational system," thereby preventing them from assuming the social responsibilities associated with adulthood.[107] Jóvenes responded to these conditions by constructing their lives in various ways, grouped loosely into subcultures including *patos malos* (hoods/delinquents), *volados* (stoners), *lúcidos* and *puntudos* (politically "lucid" or "sharp" ones affiliated with the Church and/or political parties), and *los que no están ni ahí* (the sociopolitically apathetic, "those who couldn't care less"). With the exception perhaps of *los que no están ni ahí*, this heterogeneous collective of popular sector youth converged at the barricades, forming a circumstantial, fractious coalition that materialized on protest days and disassembled in the interims.

It was the organized lúcidos/puntudos who planned the protests and maintained group cohesion in the interims. Organized 1980s-generation youth often recount the national protests with pride: this was a time when the pueblo took its destiny in hand, said *¡basta!* (enough!) and made history, facing down the dictatorship in the streets and eventually at the ballot box. Powerful visions of possibility swirled at the heart of the protest movement in poblaciones. Young activists' affiliations, motives, and goals were generally linked to subsistence, resistance, and a quest for dignity broadly understood as an end to poverty, hunger, unemployment, and repression as foundational, inalienable elements of democracy.[108] Democracy meant a society in which political and social rights would apply to all. These ideas about democracy represented explicit rejection of the dictatorship's authoritarianism and neoliberalism but not necessarily a wholesale acceptance of liberalism, which, historically, had not proven itself a reliable promotor and guarantor of political and social rights for the urban poor and working class. Among youth protesters were those who rejected the dictatorship and desired inclusion in neoliberal capitalism's benefits, albeit in ways that would have required substantial changes to its fundamental structures. Others rejected both the dictatorship and the economic system and desired profound political and economic change up to and including socialist revolution. Still others sought to oust the dictatorship posthaste, with details to be resolved later. In diffuse and often utopian fashion, youth incorporated into their "freedom dreams" elements of pre-coup developmentalism, liberation theology, and democratic socialism.[109] In doing so they expressed a loosely articulated set of ethical values and projects for post-dictatorial society that ultimately clashed with the AD's emphasis on elite-led political representation and the Concertación's embrace of neoliberal, limited democracy.

What David Scott identifies as "memory" and "postmemory" were key elements of the generational shift that brought youth to the fore of anti-regime, pro-democracy struggles in Santiago's poblaciones. Some jóvenes had "direct remembrances" of pre-coup democracy and the coup, but others remembered neither. Many harbored what Scott calls "postmemories," which are not "literal memories inasmuch as they are the direct remembrances of a *previous* generation. They are therefore mediated less through recollection than through imagination." In his study of the fall of the Grenadian revolution, Scott found that the "affective force" of traumatic memory transformed from one generation to the next, from memory to postmemory, such that the new generation could "act upon it—or with it—*differently* than their predecessors did."[110] Postmemory, though, is not only at work in historical trauma. Chilean youth inherited postmemory of the coup and also of pre-coup democracy, especially the period of democratic socialism and its benefits for poblador families. This generational interplay of memory and postmemory of pre-coup democracy, democratic socialism, and coup-related trauma shaped 1980s youth activism.

One example of the affective force of memory transforming as it passes into the postmemory of a new generation comes from a young man from La Legua who recounts the story of his political life in terms of his relationship to his parents. He knew that during the UP his father had furthered his studies and sympathized with Allende. "But I remember that at home" after the coup, he says, "I never heard any kind of commentary, any kind of analysis of that. I saw, rather, fear, a lot of fear, and they transmitted that fear." He imagined how terrifying the coup must have been for his parents' generation: "I imagine in those times the airplanes passing over the roofs of the houses and shooting, how the bullet casings would have fallen on the roofs. People weren't accustomed to that. I imagine the terror it provoked." For his parents, memories of the UP and the coup carried an affective force of secrecy, taboo, and fear. Nonetheless, this force lost its paralyzing effects in its transformation into postmemory as it crossed generations, and their son constructed his life in a different way as he combined postmemories of the UP and the coup with his own "direct remembrances" of life under dictatorship. At school, he "realized that many of my classmates didn't have anything to eat. I saw classmates eating onions, there was no lunch in their homes." Motivated by the injustices he saw, he joined social organizations and eventually the Communist Youth. Sensitive to his elders' fears, he organized in ways that respected their experiences. "We started to do activities, to camouflage [politics] by doing activities with children, going out to the plazas, having hot chocolate and drawing," he remembers. When parents picked up their children, he "took advantage of the opportunity to talk and reconnect people."[111] As his story suggests, jóvenes who had not directly experienced democracy, the terror of the coup, and the destruction of revolutionary dreams had a different relationship with fear.

They sensed their elders' fear, but they did not internalize it in the same ways. Alejandra, who experienced the coup as a child, remembers that during the 1980s "we were young, we were at the barricades, and we were indestructible. I mean, that sense that [despite] the repression you went out, and, I believe, nobody thought they were going to die. Well, you shit yourself a little with fear if the pacos came and all, but I think there was a very strong sense that nothing was going to happen to you."[112] Jóvenes' postmemories combined with "direct remembrances" of their own experiences in ways that informed their interpretations of the context in which they lived and their place within it.

Youth acquired ideals and values contrary to the regime's through interaction with elders, peers, and involvement in social movement webs. Their own experiences figured prominently in their decision-making processes. One man remembers that his parents avoided politics and warned him against "*haciendo cagadas*" (fucking up) but that he had many "uncles," adult friends of his parents, who set examples of what it meant to be leftist and committed to social justice by doing political work and sharing what they had with others. "The important thing is that they left an idea, they left an ideal, and I had it right here, close to me. I didn't have to buy books to hear it. I didn't have to buy a book to understand things."[113] Parents' involvement in their children's political lives—which sometimes meant stepping aside to let them go forth—was important to the intergenerational transmission of ideals and values contrary to the regime's. The father whose quote opens this chapter did not object to his children's political activities "because I had a childhood different from this one. I lived surrounded by delinquents . . . alcoholics . . . vagrants, among marks, sharks, thieves, and was involved in that environment. But I had a north that was a worker's orientation, which my parents taught me, and I'm thankful for that. So, one shouldn't lose sight of that horizon because we must keep struggling for a more just society. My kids did that, and they're doing it. I'm proud of them because they keep struggling, in a different way but nonetheless."[114] Political education and permission provided by parents and other influential adults in young people's lives allowed ideals that the regime sought to uproot to survive into the present.

Local churches with liberationist priests continued as centers of social and political education during the 1980s, and they played an important role in young people's political choices. In Villa Francia, Cristo Liberador propagated ideals and values contrary to the dictatorship's by what Daniel Levine describes as "mediat[ing] between everyday life and big structures" both materially (by facilitating connections with national and international human rights and aid networks) and conceptually (by teaching participants to draw connections between their everyday lives and larger social structures).[115] "You became conscious of your reality," remembers María Teresa, "and you said, 'Ya, I'm going to change it because I can do this' . . . and you realized it was a structural problem, not a social problem, that was causing this situation of poverty and inequality, and you get involved in the structures. And when you get into the structures then 'Ya,' you start to say, 'no, what has to happen is structural transformation.' And there," she concludes, "you start to realize that this was a whole process of consciousness-raising."[116]

Many of the youth who joined the Left, including the MIR, Lautaro, and the FPMR, explains Manuel, came from popular sector comunidades cristianas. Many left comunidades cristianas as they became more involved in their new political roles, but they remained affiliated with local churches in other ways. Manuel remembers that Cristo Liberador was the center of sociopolitical activity in Villa Francia, but "when the political parties start to organize themselves [political militants] stop going to the comunidad cristiana and just Christians remain, the most assiduous ones. But the contact wasn't lost," he points out. "There was always a relationship between the political youth and the comunidad cristiana."[117] Some popular sector priests supported their parishioners' decisions to join the Left, and in the political context of Santiago's poblaciones this often meant the armed left. Many of the young people who joined the Left considered their political commitments a logical continuation of the social commitments they developed in liberationist comunidades cristianas and social organizations.[118] In La Legua during the 1980s, Juan R. recalls, "The kids were recruited from the parish youth center, where they were shown options for beginning their party life, and several of them joined the MIR or Lautaro. Look, I had twenty-five kids in Confirmation, and they were all militants, except for a few of the women." Those with ties to the Communist Party tended to join the Frente.[119] "It didn't shock us," recalls Juan R. "On the contrary, we believed we had triumphed in those youth who achieved militancy. Now, the militancy wasn't pacific. It was always armed militancy, the majority, in the MIR, in Lautaro—groups that were confrontational in a big way—the Frente." Very few, he recalls, "were militants in more traditional youth organizations like the Jota or the Socialist Youth."[120] Cristo Liberador, explains Luisa, an adult in the comunidad cristiana at the time, was a "trampoline" to sociopolitical commitment that prepared people to "open new spaces" beyond the Church.[121] In Villa Francia, youth tended to join the MIR and organizations affiliated with the Communist Party (the Brigadas Rodriguistas, the Communist Youth, and the FPMR). Still others never joined political parties but participated actively in protest activities alongside their party-affiliated peers.

As the national protests continued, intergenerational relationships and currents of influence changed, but adults remained important sources of support and protection for activist youth. "I had a ton of white sheets, and the kids made short work of them," Margarita remembers of her children and their friends. "They didn't ask our permission for anything anymore, and you didn't [expect it], either. You'd get up in the morning and find ten, twenty kids sleeping and eating." Youths' political activity drew their elders into the streets with them. Women in Villa Francia ran an olla común to feed the protesters, remembers Silvia. "We began to hand out homemade bread and milk, to feed the combatants—that's how we talked, 'We have to feed the combatants'—in the streets," she explains, "because they spent the whole day absorbing the smoke from the barricades." Margarita remembers that as her children became more politically active she "began participating, for terror of leaving them alone, and I told them, 'If something happens to you I'm going to continue for you.' I got involved for them." "I had them in an iron grip, held very close, because obviously they're my children," she continues, "and I'm going to have them as long as I can, and when I don't have them they're still my children." Alba found parenting activist children to be a process of letting go. "The people who were militants always, with much pain, had to just let them [go forth], but, also, a little like [Margarita], with even more reason I participated alongside them and waited for them to return, or you went with them to what they were going to do, or you were the lookout." "Well," she concludes, "there we saw many fall," including her son, "and we had to keep on living, but it was letting go, it was always letting go of them."[122] In La Legua, recalls don Luis, older activists helped younger ones, and generational divisions of labor emerged with the protests and the rise of the armed left. Many youth joined the Frente, an organization that "we viewed with much enthusiasm, with great strength because we saw that they were going to play, and they played, a very important role in making war—if one can put it that way—on the dictatorship." The Frente was a young organization in its origins and membership, but the older generation "did certain work in people's favor, or we had the mission of delivering messages, because to do what the kids did you had to be young and fast."[123]

Solidarity between young activists and older neighbors, especially women, was integral to protest culture in poblaciones. Carmen, an adult resident of Villa Francia who participated in social organizations and the comunidad cristiana but "wasn't involved in politics at all, at all," disagreed with youngsters' protest methods and use of church space for protest preparations, but, she says, "I made pots of beans and took them outside, or bread and milk" to feed them. "I did things anonymously," she explains. "I don't like people to know what I do. When they came by asking for money for their candlelight vigils, I gave the kids money, when I had it." She found common cause with the young activists in rejection of the dictatorship and desire for democracy.[124] Juanita's experience in the Caro-Ochagavía sector was one of young activists drawing older women into collective resistance, and of older women protecting them. As a social activist and Mirista, Juanita worked within women's groups linked to the Vicaría. "We started out saying, 'What's happening here? What have you found out? What's going on?'" she recalls. "Besides, the women started to talk on their own: 'They searched the neighbor's house, they took him away.'" She would ask about their responses to the situations they described—"'But did you help him? Did you alert someone?'"—opening an opportunity to talk about experiences of injustice and potential courses of action. She also worked with youth and adults from other organizations. "To get a person to commit was very slow work. . . . You had to go very slowly with people so as not to scare them. They all had an enormous fear of repression," she remembers. The strongest allies were "older women from the area who participated with us and helped us. They bought us gasoline, they transported things for us, they found houses where, in case of repression, we could stay, and they also participated directly in all the protests."[125]

Even adults with reservations about youths' activities faced a de facto situation: jóvenes they had known from children were now at the epicenter of the national protests. Many were joining the Left, even more were protesting in the streets, and state security forces were shooting to kill. "Snitches" and the secret police were constant sources of concern. Solidarity remained of paramount importance, and it was often adults who stepped into the role of protectors. The solidarity of social organizations and neighbors extended to include activist youth in part because they were known to reciprocate. Many had been or still were involved in social organizations in their neighborhoods.[126] Víctor Hugo, who joined Lautaro and later the MIR, recalls too that clandestine political activists built reputations as good community members on principle and as a security measure.[127] As in the 1970s, during the 1980s solidarity ran from turning a blind eye to protecting adversaries in the face of greater enemies. Walking with me on a cold winter afternoon in July 2005, Alba pointed to a house down a side street, home to a woman who disagreed with Alba's family's politics and did not participate in the protests. Alba explained that one day when police were chasing protesters through the streets, she saw the woman blocking an officer from entering the house. Alba later learned that it was her own son who had hidden in the woman's home that day.

Church personnel also continued to offer solidarity. They were nodes in human rights defense networks that ran to the Vicaría and the international arena. They lent space to political activists and provided sanctuary on church grounds. Some, under the extreme conditions of the poblaciones in which they worked, provided protection far beyond their official duties. In La Victoria, Fr.

Pierre Dubois stood between protesting pobladores and the police. In La Legua, certain parish personnel were integrated into political organizations' structures as emergency contacts.[128] If, after carrying out political actions, militants failed to check in by a certain time, the emergency contacts alerted human rights organizations and took other safety measures. "We as a church," says Juan R., "although it wasn't an institutional thing, had to go see if these kids were at home, because these kids were militants of the Church in addition to being militants in their parties, and you knew they had more than a little something in their houses. Besides pamphlets there were other things. So you had to go to their families and say, 'Look, you know what, so-and-so has something in his room, a book I need right away. Can I go into his room and get it?' And I'd go in," he explains, "and instead of getting a book I had to remove the grenades, the Molotovs, whatever."[129] Neighbors, family members, and others who had known activist youth as children and who had played a role in their upbringing often continued to support them as they moved more deeply into political activity. Neighbors, priests and nuns, and sometimes local delinquents would warn young activists when state agents were spotted in the area or came around asking questions.[130] Even though the Vicaría did not defend people associated with the armed left, grassroots Church personnel in poblaciones often continued to defend the lives of all those persecuted by the regime as they had during the 1970s.[131]

Youth also acted in solidarity with one another as they had learned to do as children in comunidades cristianas and social organizations. Pobladores' multifaceted identities and affiliations, a feature of pre-coup political culture that had continued into the 1970s, passed to the new 1980s generation of organized youth. Among the 1980s generation, social organization and Church affiliation often predated political militancy, and many youth followed in their elders' footsteps in that they were "militants" of several organizations at once: party, social organization, student movement, Church. Affection also played an important role in cooperation. "The young Communists and Miristas started to date each other," explains one mother in Villa Francia. "For me the cooperation was very visible. It wasn't by party accord, it was without banners. All the same, when they met to discuss politics they fought, they had different points of view. But they could never break completely because there were couples, there was too much affection." The stress and danger of the circumstances, she adds, contributed to bonds of affection.[132] Dreams of freedom, democracy, and, for some, revolution, also exerted a powerful emotional force that drew activist youth together.

Youth also entered into disputes with each other and their elders. Disagreement surfaced over the role of political parties in social organizations and protest leadership. People of different political affiliations clashed over strategy and influence. The vertical and mechanistic form that party culture sometimes took, remembers Alejandra, generated conflict. "I didn't find much sense in doing all the things they did," she explains, "and I think we were very *pendejos*, very young, and if your party says to you, 'Look, you have to build a barricade in this street,' and another person in the group says to you, 'Listen, no way are you doing it there,' you as a militant don't have much power to decide, 'Well we won't do it,' because what you have to do as militants is DO. So, personally, I pushed back against these ideas of doing things to be doing them."[133] In other instances conflict arose between poblador youth and activists from outside the poblaciones—for example, university students from more privileged backgrounds—who found in poblaciones a venue for political activism and in poblador youth a ready workforce experienced in the heavy lifting of protest. Outsiders who planned and directed protests but did not put their own bodies on the line, and outsiders who marginalized poblador youth during meetings, generated rancor.[134] The vertical, sometimes authoritarian, relationships that developed between political militants and nonmilitants within social organizations, and between outsiders and poblador youth, disrupted the relatively horizontal and pluralistic organizational cultures generated during the 1970s and weakened cohesion within social movement webs.

As the Left gained strength and as political violence increased, tensions mounted within liberationist comunidades cristianas. In Villa Francia, party militants began leaving Cristo Liberador as the protests opened political space and as the comunidad cristiana was still finding its feet as a lay-run organization. Fr. Mariano Puga had left the comunidad in the early 1980s to allow it to function without a priest, in hopes of creating a grassroots church run by its congregants. Fr. Roberto Bolton remained in Villa Francia to support, but not direct, Cristo Liberador. Puga was a strong and charismatic leader, and remaining participants felt his absence as factionalism reared its head. Leonor explains that during this period, "what the more traditional Christians say is: '[The Left] came to occupy the comunidad cristiana, they used us all that time, and now they leave,' or 'They want to keep using the building, but for their own purposes.' The way things were done was what caused the disagreements: for example, storing tires in the comunidad's yard, gathering in the comunidad to make Molotovs, or asking the comunidad to hold a *peña* [folk-music event] and then using the money to buy gasoline," she recalls; "so all of this strained relationships, until they finally broke."[135] In La Legua, political activists remained associated with San Cayetano "for security reasons," explains one man.[136] This relationship deteriorated when in 1986 repression and the Church hierarchy's lack of support drove Fr. Guido Peeters from the parish. Peeters' replacement, opines one leguïno, had a "more fascist mentality," and others remember that he alienated many people by trying to banish nonsacramental activities—including subsistence organizations—from church grounds.[137] The hierarchy's diminishing support for liberationist comunidades cristianas and the appointment of more conservative priests to popular sector parishes during the 1980s reflected the Vatican's conservative turn under John Paul II, as did the institutional Church's turn toward a "mediating role" between the regime and the opposition. This shift contributed to the gradual unraveling of popular sector social movement webs, a process that accelerated after 1989, and growing disaffection with the Church among grassroots laypeople.[138]

As the Church moved rightward, as young people moved to the forefront of the protests, and as party militants expressed themselves more forcefully as such within the social organizations to which they belonged, currents of influence shifted within social movement webs. These shifts were both generational and political. Youths' new political activities wrought changes in local organizations and drew adults into serious conversation and disagreement about whether or how to support their activities. Some disagreed with young people's specific political choices, especially when those choices included an armed component. Some elders worried that the jóvenes did not understand the risks. Others thought the youngsters were not serious enough to rise to the challenge. Still others encouraged radical choices, which drew criticism from those who thought encouragement irresponsible given the political context. Others tried their best to support young people in making their own decisions.

Some of the most contentious debates about youths' choices revolved around the question of political violence. The national protests marked a historical peak of popular sector political violence, much of it concentrated in poblaciones.[139] Political violence, from barricades and rock-throwing to armed struggle, did not necessarily provoke opprobrium in poblaciones, nor was it dismissed a priori as inappropriate behavior.[140] Rather, it roused debates about strategy, ethics, and efficacy. That youth became involved with the political organizations operating in their medium was neither unexpected nor unusual. Political parties were traditional venues for popular sector politics in Chile, and, because of that history, priests and other anti-regime authority figures often depicted them as the predilect vehicles for political and social change.

Organizations of the Left attracted anti-regime poblador youth for good reason. The Left was associated with positive memories and postmemories of political and social gains during the 1960s and the Allende years. The Left had never supported the dictatorship. The Left had supported social organizations in poblaciones throughout the 1970s. Since the coup, the Left had also undertaken a process of internal reflection and self-criticism that resulted in a higher valuation of democracy, including that of the "bourgeois" variety. As the dictatorship wore on, exacting a high cost in human lives and well-being, and inspired too by the Nicaraguan revolution (an event that represented, at its most fundamental level, the successful overthrow of a brutal, entrenched, US-backed dictatorship), the Communist Party, MIR, and a segment of the MAPU adopted insurrectionary strategies that combined mass mobilization with armed struggle. The Left did not view the role of political violence in the reestablishment of democracy as an exclusive or monolithic strategy. The embrace of "all forms of struggle," as the Communist Party called it, included nonviolent action and social organization; it meant that all forms of struggle against the dictatorship were legitimate. As Víctor Hugo recalls, this meant that members of parties that used political violence also participated in and respected the methods even of organizations that practiced only nonviolent resistance, such as the Movimiento Contra la Tortura Sebastián Acevedo (Sebastián Acevedo Movement Against Torture).[141] In theory, "all forms of struggle" were complementary, not contradictory, and this resonated with jóvenes accustomed to the political pluralism and multifaceted sociopolitical affiliations of popular sector social movement webs.

Much attention to the armed left, and to the Church's and centrist opposition's reactions to it, revolves around leftist party leaderships' strategic decisions and the question of acute political violence—guerrilla operations, assassinations, military and combat training in Cuba, the Eastern Bloc, and Central America. But at the local level in poblaciones, armed militancy generally took a different form. Militants' responsibilities varied depending on their positions in their respective organizations, but youth associated with the armed left often painted graffiti; built booby-traps, trenches, and barricades; dissuaded "snitches"; and occasionally committed political theft by "expropriating" or "recuperating" goods from businesses. They worked among social organizations, mobilized anti-regime activity, and politicized peers. Some, remembers Juan from Villa Sur, were tapped for training and disappeared from local organizations to join the ranks of military cadre, but most poblador youth who joined the armed left did not enter those ranks.[142] Many joined *brigadas* (brigades) or *milicias* (militias) associated with the Communist Party and the MIR that focused on protest and local resistance activities. As one Mirista brigade member reported in 1982: "If the social organizations carry out a march to protest hunger, or if they need to submit a petition to the dictatorship's representative in a given locality (the mayor), at the same time the brigades build barricades and spread propaganda in support of our brothers of the pueblo; or they block the streets with miguelitos so that the repression can't reach the pobladores' gathering place."[143] They also kept order during protests. During the national protests in La Legua, Victor Hugo remembers, the armed left kept order by preventing "lumpen," who accorded the *políticos* a certain measure of respect, from thieving and destroying property.[144] In Villa Francia, recalls Silvia, pobladores "hoped that the Frente would appear when the pacos were repressing. Everyone watched, hoping that the Frente would appear so that they could take over the confrontation and [the pobladores] could retreat." "The Frente," she opines, "played a tremendous role in the poblaciones. . . . Without the Frente the massacre would have been much greater, because they imposed themselves and ordered you to retreat, they told you it was time to leave." She remembers too that a Frentista helped protesters overcome their fear of anti-riot tanks by climbing onto one and demonstrating that it could not fire at close range. Protesters also learned that with international eyes trained on Chile, the gunners would not destroy an entire población. "With that," recalls Silvia, "all the *viejas* who never came out, came out, and other people started to come out." At the local level, members of the armed left played a role in reducing pobladores' fear, organizing and directing protest activity, and mitigating the effects of repression during protests.[145]

Political violence in poblaciones, from rock throwing to armed resistance, obeyed certain codes and logics. According to Gabriel Salazar and Julio Pinto, popular political violence "adhered to a diffuse project for a new social order."[146] During the 1980s, Chilean researchers found that organized poblador youth reflected on the ethics of violence as part of their political decision-making processes and expressed complex interpretations of violence and its legitimacy. In general terms, they understood violence as action that harmed people or property and nonviolence as action that did not. However, the distinctions that youth drew between legitimate and illegitimate violence were tied to consideration of context and just intent. For example, building barricades with paving stones damaged public property but with the just intent of protecting the public from police violence. In this case the context and just intent legitimated the lesser act of property violence. The jóvenes also believed that one person's rights ended where another's began, so damaging neighbors' private property to build barricades was unjust and therefore illegitimate. They considered violence just and legitimate if it was used in self-defense, especially when under attack by a stronger force. Approaching the subject of violence through an ethics of legitimacy rather than moral absolutism (all violence is bad therefore all violence is illegitimate) allowed for historicism and the weighing of options in a way that recourse to universal absolutes and prohibitions did not. The researchers found that organized poblador youth did not exhibit "destructured, disarticulated or indefined consciousness," nor were they "defenseless victim[s] of the individualism, conformism, and social and political disinterest" that the neoliberal system generated. The youth had adopted, in contradiction to authoritarian neoliberalism, "cultural elements that come from democratic traditions and those that have emerged from alternative practices during these years [of dictatorship]."[147]

Youth resisted the regime and pursued democracy in many different ways. Their outlooks and decisions were deeply intertwined with postmemory, "direct remembrances" of their own concrete experiences, and local political cultures and relationships. Many had grown up in the politically pluralistic and some-times radically democratic worlds of neighborhood social organizations and comunidades cristianas, where political parties were present but not domi-nant, and where critique, debate, and collective leadership were encouraged. While the political and generational shifts within social movement webs gen-erated conflict, there was also cooperation and solidarity. Youth collaborated openly, although not always harmoniously, across organizational lines in soli-darity with one another and with their elders, as their elders had done during the dark years of the 1970s. Youth protest in poblaciones combined rejection of the current social and political situation with hopes and dreams for the future.

Lost in Transition

The youth who "made" the national protests frequently speak of the 1980s as their 1968: this was the moment in which they, as a generation, took the political stage and brought the house down. The outcome was not what many had hoped, especially in the cases of those who sought socialist revolution, but neither was the outcome of 1968. Memories of the 1980s, as recounted in the early twenty-first century, evince similar parts pride and pain, a consequence of the historical moment's promise, its human costs, and its later denouement into an elite-pacted transition, the popular movement's demobilization, the Church's rightward turn, and the opportunities and dis-appointments of the new democratic era.[148]

Repression took a heavy toll on the 1980s generation of popular sector youth and their elders. Mourning changed political culture within social move-ment webs in ways that still echo in poblaciones and bleed into evaluations of the post-1990 era. In Villa Francia, the deaths of young people in street dem-onstrations and the political assassinations of young local activists Eduardo and Rafael Vergara Toledo of the MIR in 1985, Miguel Leal Díaz of the FPMR in 1986, and Pablo Vergara Toledo of the MIR in 1988 shook their peers and elders to the core, provoking reconsideration and further disagreement about youths' political decisions and adults' support for those decisions.[149] The deaths of young activists here and in other areas of the city, many of them also members of the Left, punctuated the popular sector protest climate with a litany of loss such that youths' political activities came to include mourning and memory struggles via the production of murals like Miguel Leal's and commemorations such as the March 29 Día del Joven Combatiente. In 2004 María Teresa voiced some of the effects that this dual turn to protest and mourning had for her during the 1980s:

> MARÍA TERESA: And after, I went to all the funerals, of all those who died.
> AJB: From Villa Francia?
> MARÍA TERESA: No, all of them, of all Santiago. All of those that could be made public. . . .
> AJB: . . . How did you . . . overcome [the fear] because, it seems it wasn't easy . . .
> MARÍA TERESA: It was more difficult for me to overcome the pain than the fear.[150]

Among the older generation, oral history conversations about the 1980s elicit mixed feelings. Jorge comments that there was "a great deal of suffering, but there were also, how can I say it, moments of happiness because when there were these immense marches it was an immense happiness, no?" Yet there was also "bitterness, sadness," he concludes, "because things were achieved, but people were lost who could have served now. All those kids who fell would have made a great contribution."[151]

The end of the dictatorship in 1990 brought elation, relief, and hope. Many young people, finally able to rest after years of dangerous struggle, found an opportunity to tend to studies, work, and family. Even so, a mother recalls, many suffered depression brought on by political demobilization, disorientation within the Left, and the dashing of expectations. "The great depression hit. I'm telling you the jóvenes suffered terrible depression, kids drinking to excess, others unemployed," she remembers. Her daughter went from leading a busy, politically active life to one in which she "didn't do anything, sitting hours and hours watching, with her compañero, indignant at this, until they picked themselves back up."[152] Popular sector youth who sought profound political and social change faced triple alienation in the new democracy—political, social, and generational. The protests, explains Alejandra, "make the political parties and social organizations say, 'Shoot, we're in better shape than we thought,' but then there's negotiation, of course, because there's attrition, and that negotiation is capitalized upon by the party elite and not just the party elite, the old members of that elite." In the new democracy, "it wasn't the young party militants who landed in parliament or other places, it's the old ones: I mean, you have Zaldívar, who was around in 1973, you have Gabriel Valdés. . . . And that's something that's still there." she concludes. "The youth from that generation who participated in the student struggles didn't come to power either."[153]

The new civilian administrations revolved around two political coalitions, the Concertación and the right-wing Alianza, both neoliberal in practice and both dominated by political parties with little presence in poblaciones during the dictatorship.[154] Concertacionista political elites projected themselves as "experts" in democracy and modern political techniques, foreclosing inclusive debate about what democracy should be in the new era. The rise of this technocratic class of "democracy experts" further alienated concertacionista administrations from the popular sector grassroots.[155] As the years passed, both the Concertación and the Alianza emphasized "governability"—a term that in its negative connotation came to mean the exercise of authoritarianism to uphold the status quo—over deeper democratization and social and political justice.

The euphoria of the new democratic times soured as the repercussions of this "alienated transition" took hold.[156] The end of the dictatorship ushered in positive change in multiple areas of national life. Yet the Concertación did not deliver on its promises of "growth with equity."[157] The neoliberal democracy, opined Silvia in 2005, continued in its own way the dictatorship's project of dispossession and marginalization. "Of course there isn't blood in the streets," she explains, "but there's pain, there's masked poverty, there's unemployment, and drugs have gained strength because of the lack of opportunity. . . . At least for me, it's the result of the betrayal of those who reached this agreement and marginalized us."[158] Centrist politicians "used the social protest to reorganize themselves to return to the State," writes Mario Garcés, "excluding the social world from the 'arrangements' of the transition, and, above all, from political participation." It was an elite-pacted transition to the elites' benefit, "a pact at the heights, without the pueblo," that failed to deliver on its democratic promise.[159] These critiques are not the sour grapes of revolutionary dreamers denied. In the early twenty-first century they reflected discontent with the neoliberal economy, disgust with the Concertación's repression of protest, and frustration with impunity for human rights violators past and present. From this perspective, the politicians who negotiated the transition and took over administration of the neoliberal state in 1990 betrayed those who had made their victory possible through organization and protest during the most dangerous political times in living memory.

Epilogue

And the Joy?

¡La alegría ya viene! (Joy is coming!)
> Campaign slogan, Concertación de Partidos por el No, 1988

Here what's not understood is that not only the laws must comply with
international law, but also the practices.
> Nelson Caucoto, human rights lawyer, 2016[1]

Human Rights in the Neoliberal Democracy

In 2015 the Instituto Nacional de Derechos Humanos (INDH),
Chile's state-funded national human rights institute, released a study of violence and human rights in La Legua.[2] The INDH undertook the investigation
at the behest of social activists in La Legua who were concerned about police
violence in the neighborhood. The police had long been a source of violence
there, and both their presence and their violent behavior increased with the
implementation in 2001 of an intervention plan whose purported aim was
to quell violence and drug-trafficking. The plan included educational and
urban planning initiatives, but in practice it emphasized punitive policing
and created an *estado de sitio policial* (police state of siege) in La Emergencia.
Police detained and strip-searched people in public and without cause, raided
homes without warrant or explanation, and tortured, intimidated, and ver-
bally and sexually abused legüinos with impunity. As one resident told INDH
investigators, the police's attitude was that "you live in La Legua and we can

do anything, and anything we want, with you, because in this población we have orders and it's intervened."[3]

What set the INDH report apart from usual discourse about human rights in Chile, and certainly from dominant discourse earlier in the twenty-first century, is that it placed the contemporary situation within the context of historical legacies of political and social violence in La Legua and analyzed the violence's effect on pobladores' ability to exercise "fundamental rights."[4] It acknowledged the importance of social inequality to violations of rights, citing the United Nations special rapporteur Philip Alston's declaration following a 2015 visit to Chile, in which he stated that Chile's high poverty and inequality levels were "neither sustainable nor acceptable in a society that prides itself on its strong and profound commitment to respect for human rights for all its peoples."[5] The INDH report did not, as earlier official efforts tended to do, limit its focus to gross human rights violations committed during the dictatorship. It cast a broader net, using concepts of rights contained in the Universal Declaration, the American Declaration of the Rights and Duties of Man, the American Convention on Human Rights, the International Covenant on Civil and Political Rights, the General Comments of the Committee on the Rights of the Child, and the Chilean Penal Code to explore the extent to which the state's failure to "guarantee democratic security" infringed upon legüinos' fundamental rights on a daily basis. The INDH found that residents of La Emergencia, especially, collectively suffered violations of rights to adequate housing, health, work, equality, nondiscrimination, physical and psychological integrity, education, individual security, personal liberty, and access to the judicial system.[6] The INDH investigators demonstrated the complexity of human rights violations at the grassroots and revealed that questions about what human rights entail, what it means to "have human rights," and how they should be put into practice are far from settled. The INDH study effectively breaks through the restrictive association of human rights abuse with dictatorship, and the report recommends measures to prevent police abuse and ameliorate the effects of social inequality on housing, health, education, and access to the judicial system. As perhaps is necessary for an agency dependent on the neoliberal state, it stops short of recommending structural reform to target the causes of the social inequities at the heart of the matter. To do so would challenge the foundations of the neoliberal system.

According to Samuel Moyn, human rights as movement and utopia date to the 1970s and were born as "other [utopian] visions imploded."[7] Yet the concepts and ideals underlying the contemporary human rights movement drew heavily upon much older currents of rights-thought and rights-talk.[8] In Chile, the movement for human rights did not arise in the wake of utopias that collapsed under the weight of what Moyn describes as "mistrust of more maximal plans for transformation—especially revolutions but also programmatic endeavors of any kind."[9] Rather, it came about in direct response to the state's programmatic attempt to destroy the utopia that the UP represented by killing, torturing, exiling, and otherwise trying to erase the people and ideals that gave it life. The human rights movement in Chile arose because people, not ideals, were dying.

Nor did the human rights movement in Chile represent a shift from "the *droits de l'homme*" that "implied a politics of citizenship at home" to newer concepts of "human rights" that "[implied] a politics of suffering abroad."[10] The human rights movement in Chile responded to a politics of suffering at home, as political repression and economic misery destroyed human lives. It drew upon long-standing rights claims and combined them with the newer idea of universal human rights. The human rights movement in Chile did not seek to supersede the nation-state with an international order of universal rights and governance. It strategically appealed to ostensibly higher moral authorities than the state—international law, the Catholic Church, God—in the interest of returning to a domestic system in which the state would act as protector and guarantor of rights.

It would be an exercise in anachronism to label the popular movement that this book is about a "human rights movement" as the term is generally understood. This was a much more fluid and ideologically diverse movement than retrospective application of a universalizing human rights framework can adequately explain. Members of the anti-regime popular movement fought for and promoted ideals that form part of the human rights canon, but they did not necessarily draw their ideals from these international conventions and documents or use human rights talk in their own descriptions of their struggle, although they strategically invoked it in specific situations. The explicit movement for human rights in Chile (embodied in the Comité Pro Paz and Vicaría de la Solidaridad, FASIC, the Comisión Chilena de Derechos Humanos, CODEPU, grassroots human rights committees, and organizations like the AFDD) intersected with this popular sector movement that was initiated and sustained by liberationist Catholics and a Left that had not abandoned its ideals or desires for revolution. The "human rights movement" proper arose in response to the intense, albeit unequally matched, social and political conflict of the 1970s and 1980s in the interest of protecting and assisting the victims of the dictatorship and those who mounted resistance to it.

The popular movement in resistance to the dictatorship had its widest webs and deepest roots in Santiago's poblaciones, where violations of political and social rights were visibly manifest and closely intertwined. With the coup, pobladores found themselves at the center of a storm of rights violations and existential danger as political repression fell upon the Left and the poor, and as the transition to neoliberalism generated mass unemployment and hunger. Documentation from the period and later oral history conversations reveal substantial slippage in the use of rights terminology in popular sector discourse. Although pobladores often used the term "human rights" to refer to gross human rights violations, ideas about fundamental or inherent rights remained fluid and inclusive of a broader range of political and social rights, and the language and concept of "human rights" did not displace earlier currents of rights talk. Pobladores invoked "the pueblo's rights" and "rights" derived from liberal and socialist philosophies, as well as the newer "human rights," as rights inherent to all human beings and that the state had the duty to promote and protect. The fluidity of this conceptual framework clashed with the Concertación's narrow framing of human rights as successive administrations sought to put the past to rest and to administer, with minimal disruption, the neoliberal system inherited from the dictatorship. During much of the 1990s and the early twenty-first century, the politically weakened Left, grassroots organizations, and a dwindling number of NGOs remained to pursue the promotion and defense of human rights in a fickle, and sometimes hostile, political environment.

Examination of the grassroots struggle against the dictatorship also disrupts dominant narratives about cycles of popular protest and activism, and the transition to democracy. During the dictatorship, popular sector activists associated with the Left and the liberationist church mounted a mass struggle for rights, democracy, and, in some cases, renewed socialist revolution. The periodization of this struggle does not map neatly onto dominant narratives traditionally defined by changes in presidential administration, in which both the coup and the 1990 transition to civilian rule appear as profound ruptures between one era and another.[11]

The framework shifts if we look to the grassroots and decenter the focus from traditional chronological markers. The dictatorship began on September 11, 1973, but neither the UP nor the MIR died that day. The UP remained a political coalition until approximately 1981, when it dissolved itself in accordance with the parties' changing strategies. However, the UP had deep roots and support in the popular sectors, many militants of the UP and the MIR had substantial organizing experience, and many continued cooperating with each other at the grassroots. A shift of perspective reveals continuities within the context of rupture and many experiences of *construcción de izquierda* (building the Left) at a time when the parties appeared prostrate. These histories are far from triumphalist—they are often tinged with pain and frustration—but they suggest that the Left had ignited imaginations and hope in the popular sectors during the 1960s and 1970s, and they demonstrate that this world of imagination and hope did not end with the coup. People who survived the repression passed their ideals to new generations, generating new cycles of organization and mobilization, especially among popular sector youth. As María Teresa remembers, from the late 1970s through the 1980s, "It was a vibe like, the revolution would begin tomorrow, it was a vibe like, I mean, for those who were committed, living the thing, as if 'Yes, tomorrow, kids,' if everything was moving in that direction, *cachái*? It was super-like that," she says. "I'm trying to put myself into the mentality of that era, not looking at it now, but how I believed before."[12] The double-layered historicity expressed in oral history narratives like hers provides a glimpse of continuities and ruptures that force reconsideration of dominant paradigms. From a decentered perspective that takes the grassroots into account, the post-coup blackout (*apagón*) of mass protest lasted only five years, from 1973 to 1978, and the national protests were the climax of the anti-regime protest cycle, not its beginning.[13] From this perspective, the greatest rupture in Chile's post–World War II cycle of popular sector movement was not the 1973 coup, although its impact was determinative; it was the Concertación's rise to power and the consolidation of neoliberal democracy.

Shifting the analytical framework provides insight into deep sociopolitical processes that shape popular political culture and historical memory. In reference to state-perpetrated human rights abuses in La Legua, a poblador commented to INDH investigators that "one, too, comes at this with the logic that we have a democratic state and that these things don't happen anymore, that they're in our sad past. But, nevertheless, it's really astonishing when one raises histories from La Legua" that reveal contemporary official attitudes and state-perpetrated abuses redolent of the dictatorship.[14] The end of the dictatorship was a watershed moment in national and individual histories that ushered in positive change and a better quality of life for many, yet continuities with the dictatorship persisted well into the twenty-first century.

At the time of writing, extreme social inequality, disturbing levels of impunity, political corruption, the militarized police occupation of Mapuche communities and urban poblaciones, and the violent repression of student protest all pointed to persistent authoritarianism and anti-democratic practice that political rhetoric no longer sufficed to conceal, and for which the political elite could no longer evade responsibility by pointing to an outgoing dictatorship's saber-rattlers. The activist pobladores who organized opposition during the most brutal days of dictatorship, and whose work was pivotal to removing the dictatorship from power, were acutely aware of the "betrayals" or "partial nature" of the transition. At the outset of the new millennium, many continued their work in pursuit of bread, justice, and liberty.

Notes

The oral history interviews cited appear in the endnotes with initials (some pseudony-mous) or group indicator and date. All interviews took place in Santiago, Chile. All interviews were conducted in Spanish, and all translations into English are my own. Between 2003 and 2006, I conducted interviews independently and as a member of the now-defunct Colectivo Memoria Histórica José Domingo Cañas. Mario Garcés generously shared transcripts in his personal archive (PAMG) from projects that he directed in La Legua with support from ECO, the Red de Organizaciones Sociales de La Legua, the Fundación Ford, and the Vicerrectoría de Investigación, Publicaciones y Extensión de la Universidad ARCIS. I quote and cite those transcripts with his permis-sion. Published interviews are cited as such in the notes.

Introduction

1. BSI, "Lo que vimos y oímos (apuntes): 1° de Mayo: El pueblo sale a las calles," *No Podemos Callar*, no. 30 (May 1978): 3–5. In response to a recommendation by Fr. Rafael Maroto, José Aldunate and several other priests produced the clandestine news-letters *No Podemos Callar* (1975–81) and *Policarpo* (1981–84). José Aldunate Lyon, SJ, *Un peregrino cuenta su historia* (Santiago: Ediciones Ignacianas, [2002?]), 124–25. Unless otherwise noted, all translations are mine.

2. Juan Ávalos, "Odas al pueblo humillado," in *Poesía de Villa Francia: Andarás en el bosque de los aves que somos,* by Grupo Amistad por un Mundo Mejor (Santiago: Grupo Amistad por un Mundo Mejor, 2008), 29.

3. Peter Winn, "The Other 9/11: My Coup Diary," *ReVista: Harvard Review of Latin America* (Spring 2004), https://revista.drclas.harvard.edu/book/other-911; *Fuer-zas Armadas y Carabineros: Septiembre de 1973: Los cien combates de una batalla* (Santi-ago: Editorial Gabriela Mistral, [n.d.]), 14; J.S, Jan. 15, 2003, PAMG.

4. Poblaciones are the result of urban public housing programs or a combination of these programs and land takeovers.

5. J.S., Jan. 15, 2003, PAMG.

6. The Concertación was the coalition of centrist political parties, anchored by renovated Socialists and Christian Democrats, that led the campaign to vote "no" against Pinochet in the 1988 plebiscite, ran against the regime's candidate in the 1989 presidential elections, and held the presidency of the republic from 1990 to 2010. Its rival, the Alianza por Chile (Alianza), gathered the pro-regime right. In 2013 the center-left parties of the Concertación allied with the Communist Party and created a coalition called the Nueva Mayoría. The Alianza persisted until 2015 (although between 2009 and 2012 it was called Coalición por el Cambio). In 2015 it rebranded itself as "Chile Vamos." For more on the Concertación, see Steve J. Stern, *Reckoning with Pinochet: The Memory Question in Democratic Chile, 1989–2006* (Durham, NC: Duke University Press, 2010); Julia Paley, *Marketing Democracy: Power and Social Movements in Post-Dictatorship Chile* (Berkeley: University of California Press, 2001); Brian Loveman and Elizabeth Lira, *Las ardientes cenizas del olvido: Vía chilena de reconciliación política, 1932–1994* (Santiago: LOM, 2000); and Edgardo Boeninger, *Democracia en Chile: Lecciones para la gobernabilidad* (Santiago: Andrés Bello, 1997).

7. Lists of people assassinated by the state during the concertacionista period range from sixty to upwards of seventy, plus one *detenido-desaparecido* (disappeared detainee). At least thirty were "youth" (under thirty years of age), and many were leftists, Mapuche, and/or pobladores. Felipe Ramírez Sánchez, "Chile: Muertos en 'Transición a la Democracia,'" *El Ciudadano*, no. 83, http://www.elciudadano.cl/2010/08/02/25053/chile-muertos-en-transicion-a-la-democracia/; Felipe Gutiérrez Ríos, "La lista de asesinados por la 'democracia' Chilena," June 16, 2011, reproduced by http://mapuche-montreal.blogspot.com/2011/06/la-lista-de-asesinados-por-la.html; and Ana Vergara Toledo, "Los Otros Muertos," *The Clinic*, Oct. 18, 2010, http://www.theclinic.cl/2010/10/18/los-otros-muertos/.

8. Ávalos, "Odas al pueblo humillado," 29–31.

9. The radical neoliberal model of the 1970s underwent a shift in the mid-1980s, generating a second "economic miracle" as more "pragmatic" neoliberals gained influence in government circles after the economic crisis. Peter Winn, "The Pinochet Era," in *Victims of the Chilean Miracle: Workers and Neoliberalism in the Pinochet Era, 1973–2002*, ed. Peter Winn (Durham, NC: Duke University Press, 2004), 42.

10. Conversations with H.M.D. (2008) and L.T. (2004).

11. These narratives of continuity dissolve temporal distance between past and present. They reflect experiences at odds with what Berber Bevernage and Koen Aerts call the "dominant regime of historicity": "the specific manner in which a culture relates to time and the temporal dimensions of past, present, and future." Instead, the narratives express an experience of "irrevocable past": experience of the past "as a persistent, enduring and massive depository that is vitally present." The "irrevocable" does not deny the "inalterability of the past, but . . . [it] rejects the notion of a temporal 'distance' separating past and present." Berber Bevernage and Koen Aerts, "Haunting Pasts: Time and Historicity as Constructed by the Argentine *Madres de Plaza de Mayo* and Radical Flemish Nationalists," *Social History* 34, no. 4 (2009): 393–94. For some, the past has not passed. Representatives of mainstream culture—the media, government

officials, political commentators—frequently dismiss as anachronistic, and even pathological, the actions of people who are living an experience of irrevocable past, marginalizing actions and interpretations born of this experience of time as a manifestation of psychological illness, thirst for revenge, or misplaced nostalgia that prevents sufferers from "turning the page" and moving on.

12. Micheline R. Ishay, *The History of Human Rights: From Ancient Times to the Globalization Era* (Berkeley: University of California Press, 2008), 2.

13. Ishay, *History of Human Rights*, 2.

14. Steve J. Stern and Scott Straus, "Embracing Paradox: Human Rights in the Global Age," in *The Human Rights Paradox: Universality and Its Discontents*, ed. Steve Stern and Scott Straus (Madison: University of Wisconsin Press, 2014), 3.

15. International human rights activism regarding Brazil pre-dated the Chilean coup. James N. Green, *We Cannot Remain Silent: Opposition to the Brazilian Military Dictatorship in the United States* (Durham, NC: Duke University Press, 2010).

16. Luis Van Isschot, *The Social Origins of Human Rights: Protesting Political Violence in Colombia's Oil Capital, 1919–2010* (Madison: University of Wisconsin Press, 2015), 14.

17. Several studies explore historical memory and discrepancies between dominant interpretations of Chilean history and those of populations whose experiences have differed significantly from traditional historical narratives that elide the centrality of violence and marginalization to Chile's nation-building processes. See Florencia Mallon, *Courage Tastes of Blood: The Mapuche Community of Nicolás Ailío and the Chilean State, 1906–2001* (Durham, NC: Duke University Press, 2005); Lessie Jo Frazier, *Salt in the Sand: Memory, Violence, and the Nation-State in Chile, 1890 to the Present* (Durham, NC: Duke University Press, 2007); and Thomas Miller Klubock, "Ránquil: Violence and Peasant Politics on Chile's Southern Frontier," in *A Century of Revolution: Insurgent and Counterinsurgent Violence during Latin America's Long Cold War*, ed. Greg Grandin and Gilbert M. Joseph (Durham, NC: Duke University Press, 2010), 121–59.

18. With few exceptions, the study of pobladores' experiences and political activity during the dictatorship centers on the 1980s and has been the nearly exclusive province of sociologists and political scientists. Pobladores' experiences under dictatorship receive some attention in later historical overviews, such as Gabriel Salazar and Julio Pinto's *Historia contemporánea de Chile*, vols. 1–5 (Santiago: LOM, 1999–2002). The few historians who prioritize pobladores' experiences under dictatorship emphasize historical memory of the day of the coup, repression, neoliberalism, housing policy, and grassroots activism. See Mario Garcés and Sebastián Leiva, *El golpe en La Legua: Caminos de la historia y la memoria* (Santiago: LOM, 2005); Alison J. Bruey, "Neoliberalism and Repression in *Poblaciones* of Santiago de Chile," *Stockholm Review of Latin American Studies*, no. 5 (Sep. 2009): 17–27; Alison J. Bruey, "Limitless Land and the Redefinition of Rights: Popular Mobilisation and the Limits of Neoliberalism in Chile, 1973–1985," *JLAS* 44, no. 3 (2012): 523–52; Alison J. Bruey, "Transnational Concepts, Local Contexts: Solidarity at the Grassroots in Pinochet's Chile," in *Human*

Rights and Transnational Solidarity in Cold War Latin America, ed. Jessica Stites Mor (Madison: University of Wisconsin Press, 2013), 120–42; and Edward Murphy, *For a Proper Home: Housing Rights in the Margins of Urban Chile, 1960–2010* (Pittsburgh: University of Pittsburgh Press, 2015).

19. See Vicente Espinoza, *Para una historia de los pobres de la ciudad* (Santiago: SUR, 1988); and Eugenio Tironi, ed., "Marginalidad, Movimientos Sociales y Democracia," *Proposiciones* 14 (August 1987).

20. Eugenio Tironi, "El fantasma de los pobladores," *Estudios Sociológicos* 4, no. 12 (1986): 392. Mónica Iglesias Vázquez argues, in *Rompiendo el cerco: El movimiento de pobladores contra la dictadura* (Santiago: Radio Universidad de Chile, 2011), that these ideas were most developed in Tironi, "Marginalidad, Movimientos Sociales y Democracia." Many of the ideas underpinning the 1987 publication appeared in earlier articles. See Eugenio Tironi, "La revuelta de los pobladores: Integración social y democracia," *Nueva Sociedad* 83 (May–June 1986): 24–32; and Tironi, "El fantasma de los pobladores." Iglesias Vázquez's critique disputes the assertion that pobladores did not form a social movement.

21. Tironi, "La revuelta de los pobladores," 25.

22. Tironi, "La revuelta de los pobladores," 24, 25, 28–29; Tironi, "El fantasma de los pobladores," 391, 396–97.

23. Tironi, "La revuelta de los pobladores," 33.

24. See Iglesias Vázquez, *Rompiendo el cerco*. In 1990, after pobladores swept the political opposition to victory in the 1988 plebiscite on Pinochet's rule, Tironi published a more nuanced argument in *Autoritarismo, modernización y marginalidad*. He found that—with the exception of "young pobladores of the opposition" and those who were "educated, young, students, or unemployed"—pobladores were not especially prone to violence. Rather, he concludes that pobladores were not "indifferent to democracy" but that they were conformist, resigned, politically apathetic, fatalist, individualistic, and considered the state an antagonist. Eugenio Tironi, *Autoritarismo, modernización y marginalidad: El caso de Chile, 1973–1989* (Santiago: SUR, 1990), 184–204, 225–26, 270, 280. While the conclusions shift somewhat from his earlier work, they echo schools of thought from the 1960s and 1970s that pathologize poverty.

25. See Cathy Lisa Schneider, *Shantytown Protest in Pinochet's Chile* (Philadelphia: Temple University Press, 1995), for an "old social movement" approach and Philip D. Oxhorn, *Organizing Civil Society: The Popular Sectors and the Struggle for Democracy in Chile* (University Park: Penn State University Press, 1995); Mario Garcés, *Tomando su sitio: El movimiento de pobladores de Santiago, 1957–1970* (Santiago: LOM, 2002); Teresa Valdés, *Venid, benditas de mi padre: Las pobladoras, sus rutinas y sus sueños* (Santiago: FLACSO, 1988), and Teresa Valdés and Marisa Weinstein, *Mujeres que sueñan: Las organizaciones de pobladoras en Chile: 1973–1989* (Santiago: FLACSO, 1993), for examples of "new social movement" approaches. For a recent critique of new social movement theory, see Timothy P. Wickham-Crowley and Susan Eckstein, "The Persisting Relevance of Political Economy and Political Sociology in Latin American Social Movement Studies," *LARR* 50, no. 4 (2015): 3–25.

26. Jessica Stites Mor, "Situating Transnational Solidarity within Critical Human Rights Studies of Cold War Latin America," in Stites Mor, *Human Rights and Transnational Solidarity*, 5.

27. Jeffrey N. Wasserstrom, "The Chinese Revolution and Contemporary Paradoxes," in *Human Rights and Revolutions*, 2nd ed., ed. Jeffrey N. Wasserstrom, Greg Grandin, Lynn Hunt, and Marilyn B. Young (New York: Rowman and Littlefield, 2007), 41.

28. For the movement in the U. S., see Margaret Power, "The U.S. Movement in Solidarity with Chile in the 1970s," *Latin American Perspectives* 36, no. 6 (2009): 46–66.

29. In Latin America, the Left was instrumental in the democratization of society during the twentieth century. Greg Grandin, *The Last Colonial Massacre: Latin America in the Cold War* (Chicago: University of Chicago Press, 2011), 4–6.

30. Greg Grandin, "Human Rights and Empire's Embrace," in Wasserstrom et al., *Human Rights and Revolutions*, 198.

31. Samuel Moyn argues that the concept of human rights did not emerge on the world scene with any force until the 1970s, when activists began to make systematic appeals in the name of human rights in support of Eastern European dissidents and victims of political repression in Latin America. He downplays the Universal Declaration's multicultural origins, characterizing its framers as a predominantly Christian "global diplomatic elite, often schooled in Western locales." Samuel Moyn, *The Last Utopia: Human Rights in History* (Cambridge, MA: Harvard University Press, 2010), 220, 66. Micheline Ishay, Lynn Hunt, and others stress the various historical processes and intellectual and legal traditions that have contributed to modern human rights concepts. See Lynn Hunt, *Inventing Human Rights: A History* (New York: Norton, 2007); Lynn Hunt, "The Paradoxical Origins of Human Rights," in Wasserstrom et al., *Human Rights and Revolutions*, 3–20; Jeffrey N. Wasserstrom, "The Chinese Revolution and Contemporary Paradoxes," in Wasserstrom et al., *Human Rights and Revolutions*, 21–44; Grandin, "Human Rights and Empire's Embrace"; and Ishay, *History of Human Rights*.

32. Van Isschot too found a process of rights-layering in Colombia in his *Social Origins of Human Rights*, 10.

33. For example, the Chilean Catholic Church's Vicariate of Solidarity assisted the politically persecuted through its Legal Department. Its larger Social Department supported a vast array of organizations that addressed the popular sector socioeconomic crisis. This reflects a concept of rights and "human development" broader than the Legal Department's focus on political persecution suggests. Steve J. Stern, *Memorias en construcción: Los retos del pasado presente en Chile, 1989–2011* (Santiago: Museo de la Memoria y los Derechos Humanos, 2013), 58–59.

34. Schneider makes a similar argument in *Shantytown Protest in Pinochet's Chile* as related to the Communist Party's influence on protest in poblaciones. But the continuities went well beyond the Communist Party to include other political parties, organizations, and local organizing traditions.

35. Rebecca J. Atencio, *Memory's Turn: Reckoning with Dictatorship in Brazil* (Madison: University of Wisconsin Press, 2014), 22–23; Arturo Escobar, *Territories of Difference: Place, Movement, Life, Redes* (Durham, NC: Duke University Press, 2008).

36. For an analysis of the importance of the UNCTAD building to Santiago's urban politics before the coup, see Camilo D. Trumper, *Ephemeral Histories: Public Art, Politics, and the Struggle for the Street in Chile* (Berkeley: University of California Press, 2016).

37. The report's exclusion of mass repression of pobladores and the difficulties pobladores had in gaining inclusion in the Comisión's investigations when they had not been imprisoned in officially recognized locations prompted the Colectivo Memoria Histórica José Domingo Cañas to research mass repression in poblaciones. This investigation resulted in the publication of a study: Laura Moya, Ricardo Balladares, Claudia Videla, Alison Bruey, Hervi Lara, Andrés Carvajal, Mario Aballay, and Marcelo Alvarado, *Tortura en poblaciones del Gran Santiago (1973–1990)* (Santiago: Corporación José Domingo Cañas, 2005/Biblioteca Nacional-Memoria Chilena, 2015). This opening elicited calls for reconsideration of cases excluded from previous truth commission reports. See "Presentación de CODEPU acerca de casos muertos por explosión no reconocidos por Comisiones de Verdad," Santiago de Chile, Nov. 22, 2004, http://www.memoriaviva.com/Ejecutados/presentacion_codepu_explosionados.htm.

38. Exceptions include Garcés and Leiva, *El golpe en La Legua*; and Moya et al., *Tortura en poblaciones.*

39. GI, Villa Francia, July 3, 2004.

40. Truth commission reports mention mass *allanamientos* (search raids), but the type of repression they track is limited to death, disappearance, political prison, and torture. Pobladores appear in the reports as victims of disappearance and execution, and survivors of political prison and torture. However, the statistics are not broken down by place of residence, eliding the effects of sustained repression in concentrated territories.

41. March 29, the Día del Joven Combatiente, marks the anniversary of the assassinations of young MIR militants and brothers Eduardo and Rafael Vergara Toledo, who grew up in Villa Francia's social organizations and comunidad cristiana.

42. Chilevisión, "La Legua: El ghetto de la muerte," June 18, 2007.

43. I borrow "regimes of historicity" from Bevernage and Aerts, "Haunting Pasts," 393–94.

44. I borrow the term "memory struggles" from Steve J. Stern, *Remembering Pinochet's Chile: On the Eve of London 1998* (Durham, NC: Duke University Press, 2006); Steve J. Stern, *Battling for Hearts and Minds: Memory Struggles in Pinochet's Chile* (Durham, NC: Duke University Press, 2006); and Steve J. Stern, *Reckoning with Pinochet.*

45. For plebiscite results by *comuna* (municipality), see Jorge Chateau and Sergio Rojas, "Antecedentes electorales, vols. 1–2; Información sobre población, electores y resultados del plebiscito de 1988," Documento de Trabajo 428, Programa de FLACSO-Chile, Sep. 1989. Iglesias Vásquez points out that with the exception of La Cisterna, the opposition (the "No Campaign" that urged voters to vote "no"—against Pinochet—

in the 1988 plebiscite) garnered over 60 percent of the vote in Santiago's comunas populares. In La Cisterna the "No" still won by a wide margin: 57.6 percent to 40.4 percent. Meanwhile, Pinochet won by an average 20.7 point margin in the city's wealthy districts (Providencia, Las Condes, and Vitacura). "These pobladores," Iglesias Vásquez argues, "whom some analysts—such as the theorists of SUR—characterized as conformists or vandals, in all senses apolitical . . . were the same ones who guaranteed the triumph of the transition to democracy in an election." Iglesas Vázquez, *Rompiendo el cerco*, 308; Chateau and Rojas, "Antecedentes electorales," 38, 42.

46. For studies of the conflation of democracy with neoliberal economics, see Tomás Moulián, *Chile actual: Anatomía de un mito* (Santiago: LOM, 2002); and Paley, *Marketing Democracy*.

Chapter 1. La Legua, Villa Francia, and the Movimiento de Pobladores

1. C.D./C.S.D., June 18, 2004.

2. GI, Villa Francia, June 5, 2004.

3. Víctor Jara, "Lo único que tengo," *La Población*, Santiago, DICAP, 1972.

4. Benjamín Vicuña Mackenna, *Transformación de Santiago* (Santiago: Imprenta El Mercurio, 1872), 24–25, 35.

5. Garcés, *Tomando su sitio*, 15. Vekeman's organization also funneled CIA funding to the Christian Democrats. Penny Lernoux, *Cry of the People: The Struggle for Human Rights in Latin America—The Catholic Church in Conflict with U.S. Policy* (New York: Penguin, 1982), 25–28.

6. See Manuel Castells, "Movimiento de pobladores y lucha de clases en Chile," in *Huellas de una metamorfosis metropolitana: Santiago en EURE 1970/2000*, ed. Carlos de Mattos, Oscar Figueroa, Pedro Bannen, and Diego Campos (Santiago: Instituto de Estudios Urbanos y Territoriales, Pontificia Universidad Católica de Chile, 2006); and Equipo de Estudios Poblacionales CIDU, "Reivindicación urbana y lucha política: los campamentos de pobladores en Santiago de Chile," in de Mattos et al., *Huellas*.

7. Garcés, *Tomando su sitio*, 16.

8. Murphy, *For a Proper Home*, 41.

9. Garcés and Leiva, *El golpe en La Legua*, 26.

10. Rodrigo Hidalgo Dattwyler, *La vivienda social en Chile y la construcción del espacio urbano en el Santiago del siglo XX* (Santiago: DIBAM, 2005), 25; Murphy, *For a Proper Home*, 47; Elizabeth Quay Hutchinson, *Labors Appropriate to Their Sex: Gender, Labor, and Politics in Urban Chile, 1900–1930* (Durham, NC: Duke University Press, 2001), 3, 17, 23–26.

11. Murphy, *For a Proper Home*, 41, 45–46.

12. Murphy, *For a Proper Home*, 41–48; Armando de Ramón, *Santiago de Chile: Historia de una sociedad urbana (1541–1991)* (Santiago: Catalonia, 2007), 193–96.

13. Hildago Dattwyler, *La vivienda social*, 46–47, 53, 154–55.

14. de Ramón, *Santiago de Chile*, 197, 241; Garcés, *Tomando su sitio*.

15. Los Guaracheros, "Cómo se organizó la toma de Zañartu," in *La Población La Legua: Desde la historia oral hacia la historia local*, Colección 30 Años No. 5, ed. ECO (Santiago: ECO, 2012), 23.

16. de Ramón, *Santiago de Chile*, 241–42.

17. Grupo de Trabajo La Victoria, *La Victoria: Rescatando su Historia* (Santiago: ARCIS, 2007), 13–14; Garcés, *Tomando su sitio*, 126–46.

18. de Ramón, *Santiago de Chile*, 246.

19. Grupo de Trabajo La Victoria, *La Victoria*, 21–33; de Ramón, *Santiago de Chile*, 246.

20. de Ramón, *Santiago de Chile*, 243; Mario Garcés, "Los pobladores durante la Unidad Popular: Mobilizaciones, oportunidades políticas y la organización de las nuevas poblaciones," *Tiempo Histórico* 3 (segundo semestre 2011): 41.

21. Garcés, "Los pobladores durante la Unidad Popular," 48; de Ramón, *Santiago de Chile*, 249.

22. Murphy, *For a Proper Home*, 33. See also James Holston, *Insurgent Citizenship: Disjunctions of Democracy and Modernity in Brazil* (Princeton, NJ: Princeton University Press, 2008); Brodwyn Fischer, *A Poverty of Rights: Citizenship and Inequality in Twentieth-Century Rio de Janeiro* (Stanford, CA: Stanford University Press, 2008); and Bryan McCann, *Hard Times in the Marvelous City: From Dictatorship to Democracy in the Favelas of Rio de Janeiro* (Durham, NC: Duke University Press, 2014).

23. Garcés, *Tomando su sitio*, 13.

24. Castells, "Movimiento de pobladores," 308. Others lived on their employers' property as domestic laborers.

25. This had long been the case in Santiago. See Hutchinson, *Labors Appropriate to Their Sex*; Teresa Valdés, *Venid, benditas de mi padre*; Valdés and Weinstein, *Mujeres que sueñan*; Edda Gaviola, Eliana Largo, and Sandra Palestro, *Una historia necesaria: Mujeres en Chile, 1973–1990* (Santiago: ASDI, 1994); and Karin Alejandra Rosemblatt, *Gendered Compromises: Political Cultures and the State in Chile, 1920–1950* (Chapel Hill: University of North Carolina Press, 2000).

26. C.D./C.S.D., June 18, 2004; GI, Red de Organizaciones Sociales de La Legua, May 24, 2005.

27. Jaime Álvarez (Coño), "Historia de la población Nueva La Legua," in ECO, *La Población La Legua*, 54; ECO, *La Población La Legua*, 7.

28. Mago, "Una vida en La Legua," in ECO, *La Población La Legua*, 15, 17.

29. Los Guaracheros, "Cómo se organizó la toma de Zañartu," 21–23.

30. Los Guaracheros, "Cómo se organizó la toma de Zañartu," 25–26.

31. Niña, "Nací en La Legua," in ECO, *La Población La Legua*, 43.

32. Maroto later became an outspoken opponent of the dictatorship and public spokesperson for the MIR. In 1984 Cardinal Juan Francisco Fresno suspended Maroto from the priesthood. Mario Garcés, "Introducción," in *Memorias de la dictadura en La Legua: Relatos, historias, cuentos, poesía y canciones de su gente*, ed. ECO and Red de Organizaciones Sociales de La Legua (Santiago: ECO, 2001), 5; Álvarez, "Historia de

la población," 54; "Rafael Maroto P.: Homenaje contra el olvido," *Punto Final*, no. 761 (6–19 July, 2012).

33. E.M., November 11, 2002, PAMG. Subsequent priests included Manuel Ordenes (1953–60), Fernando Ariztía (1960–64), Luis Borremans (1964–75), Guido Peeters (1975–86), Ramón Aguilera (1987–93), Mariano Puga (1993–2002), and Gerardo Quisse (2002–). "Párrocos de La Legua," list on San Cayetano chapel wall, 2006.

34. *La Cuarta*, June 27, 2004; A.G., July 5, 2005.

35. J.R., Nov. 18, 2000, PAMG.

36. J.R., June 21, 2005.

37. J.R., n.d., PAMG.

38. J.R., Nov. 18, 2000, PAMG.

39. J.R., n.d., PAMG.

40. ECO, *La Población La Legua*, 7.

41. J.R., n.d., PAMG.

42. Luis Morales, "Voces de Chuchunco," in *Historias para un fin de siglo: Primer concurso de historias locales y sus fuentes*, ed. ECO (Santiago: Pehuén Editores, 1994), 83.

43. Gabriela Raposo Quintana, "Muerte y lugar: territorios del olvido, memoria y resistencia: Villa Francia, huellas de la dictadura militar, 1973–2010" (PhD diss., Pontificia Universidad Católica de Chile, 2012), 138.

44. Quoted in Raposo, "Muerte y lugar," 137.

45. I.P./J.M., Nov. 26, 2004.

46. ARNAD/FOS, "Nuestro Testimonio, Historia de la Comunidad Cristiana Cristo Liberador—Villa Francia," *Fe y Solidaridad* 32 (September 1980), 2.

47. Raposo, "Muerte y lugar," 140–41.

48. ARNAD/FOS, "Nuestro Testimonio," 2; Raposo, "Muerte y lugar," 140.

49. Michael Fleet, "Christian Communities in Chile and Peru," University of Notre Dame Kellogg Institute, Working Paper 183 (November 1992), 16.

50. These CCPs were not Comunidades Eclesiales de Base (CEBs, Ecclesial Base Communities). In Chile, CEBs were a product of the Catholic Church's conservative turn under Pope John Paul II, instituted in the 1980s and early 1990s when church authorities sought to reign in liberation theology by tightening hierarchical control over comunidades cristianas de base in general and especially CCPs like Cristo Liberador. Many members of CCPs rejected the shift to CEBs because of the rightward, anti-liberationist turn it represented. David Fernández, *La "Iglesia" que resistió a Pinochet* (Madrid: IEPALA, 1996), 25–26, 236, 309n9; Carol Ann Drogus and Hannah Stewart-Gambino, *Activist Faith: Grassroots Women in Democratic Brazil and Chile* (University Park: Penn State University Press, 2005), 40–41; Fernando Castillo, "Comunidades Cristianas Populares: La iglesia que nace desde los pobres," in *La Iglesia de los pobres en América Latina*, ed. Fernando Castillo, Joaquín Silva, Juan Sepúlveda, and Claudio Ramsy (Santiago: Programa Ecuménico de Estudios del Cristianismo/ECO-SEPADE, 1983), 88.

51. Aldunate, *Un peregrino*, 110.

52. ARNAD/FOS, "Nuestro Testimonio," 3; P.R.B., May 10, 2004; Eugenio Cabrera Molina, "Historia y protagonismo popular en Villa Francia" (undergraduate thesis, Universidad ARCIS, 2007), 38–39.

53. ARNAD/FOS, "Nuestro Testimonio," 3–5; Roberto Farías, "El cura Puga y su nueva cruzada," *Revista Paula*, Jan. 12, 2012; Aldunate, *Un peregrino*, 112; Lanzamiento del libro [Presentation of the book] *Teología práctica de liberación en el Chile de Salvador Allende* (Santiago: Ceibo, 2014) by Yves Carrier, *Revista Reflexión y Liberación*, Santiago, Sep. 2014, https://www.youtube.com/watch?v=vhYwDDFpM3s.

54. I.P./J.M., Nov. 26, 2004.

55. Murphy, *For a Proper Home*, 127–29.

56. Cabrera, "Historia y protagonismo," 52–71.

57. ARNAD/FOS, "Nuestro Testimonio," 4.

58. Cabrera, "Historia y protagonismo," 55.

59. Quoted in Raposo, "Muerte y lugar," 142.

Chapter 2. The Coup and the Past That Is Present

1. GI, Santa Adriana, June 21, 2004.

2. R.S., Jan. 18, 2003, PAMG.

3. GI, Villa Francia, July 3, 2004.

4. L.D., Nov. 11, 2002, PAMG.

5. J.S., Jan. 15, 2003, PAMG.

6. The memory of the event and the way it is narrated can tell much about history, political culture, and the meaning people ascribe to historical events, regardless of the recollections' accuracy. This chapter owes an intellectual debt to the work of Alessandro Portelli, Mario Garcés, Steve J. Stern, Daniel James, Florencia Mallon, and Peter Winn. See Alessandro Portelli, *The Battle of Valle Giulia: Oral History and the Art of Dialogue* (Madison: University of Wisconsin Press, 1997); Alessandro Portelli, "The Death of Luigi Trastulli: Memory and the Event," in *The Death of Luigi Trastulli and Other Stories: Form and Meaning in Oral History* (Albany: State University of New York Press, 199), 1–26; Garcés and Leiva, *El golpe en La Legua*; Mario Garcés, *Recreando el pasado: Guía metodológica para la memoria y la historia local* (Santiago: ECO, 2002); Stern, *The Memory Box of Pinochet's Chile: A Trilogy*, Durham, NC: Duke University Press, 2004; Daniel James, *Doña María's Story: Life History, Memory, and Political Identity* (Durham, NC: Duke University Press, 2001); Mallon, *Courage Tastes of Blood*; Rosa Isolde Reuque Paillalef, *When a Flower Is Reborn: The Life and Times of a Mapuche Feminist*, trans. and ed. Florencia Mallon (Durham, NC: Duke University Press, 2002); Peter Winn, *Weavers of Revolution: The Yarur Workers and Chile's Road to Socialism* (New York: Oxford University Press, 1989); and Peter Winn, "Oral History and the Factory Study: New Approaches to Labor History," *LARR* 14, no.2 (1979): 130–40.

7. Stern, *Reckoning with Pinochet*, 3.

8. Exceptions are Moya et al., *Tortura en poblaciones*; Garcés and Leiva, *El golpe en La Legua*; and the closing scenes of the film *Machuca* (dir. Andrés Wood, 2004).

9. An exception is Manuel Paiva, *Rastros de mi pueblo* (Santiago: Quimantú, 2005).

10. See Pepe Burgos, dir., *Más fuerte que la metralla*, Edición Taller Audiovisual Llalliypacha, Santiago, Sep. 2011, http://vimeo.com/55157807.

11. E.S., n.d., PAMG.

12. M.D., Oct. 3, 2002, PAMG. Alessandro Portelli found that collective memories of a massacre at Civitella Val di Chiana represented "divided memory" or a "fragmented plurality of different memories" divided along lines of politics, generation, socioeconomic class, and location. Portelli, *Battle of Valle Giulia*, 158. The concept of divided memory is useful for thinking about community oral histories. Establishing which versions are "accurate" or "inaccurate" may sometimes offer less insight than tracking the interplay of multiple narratives.

13. Portelli, *Battle of Valle Giulia*, 42–43.

14. E.S., n.d., PAMG.

15. R.S., Jan. 18, 2003, PAMG.

16. GI, Villa Francia, July 3, 2004. This also occurred in Mapuche communities of southern Chile. Mallon, *Courage Tastes of Blood*. Nor was the September 11 coup attempt the first. The U.S. Senate's Staff Report of the Select Committee to Study Governmental Operations with respect to Intelligence Services reports that there was a (failed) coup attempt on October 22, 1970, in an effort to prevent Allende from assuming office. "Covert Action in Chile, 1963–1973" (Washington, DC: Government Printing Office, 1975), 23, 26.

17. Carlos Altamirano, "Discurso en el Estadio Chile," Santiago de Chile, Nov. 9, 1973, in Gabriel Salazar, *Conversaciones con Carlos Altamirano: Memorias críticas* (Santiago: Random House Mondadori, 2010), 367.

18. Garcés and Leiva, *El golpe en La Legua*, 45; R.Q., Jan. 23, 2003, PAMG; Carlos Altamirano, "Discurso en el Estadio Chile," Santiago de Chile, Sep. 9, 1973, in Salazar, *Conversaciones*, 365; Sandra Castillo Soto, *Cordones Industriales: Nuevas formas de sociabilidad obrera y organización política popular (Chile, 1970–1973)* (Concepción: Escaparate, 2009), 295–96; Coordinadora Provincial de Cordones Industriales, Comando Provincial de Abastecimiento Directo y Frente Único de Trabajadores en Conflicto: Carta al Presidente Salvador Allende, Sep. 5, 1973, in Castillo, *Cordones*, 321–30.

19. Castillo, *Cordones*, 295–97.

20. GI, Villa Francia, July 3, 2004.

21. Patricio Quiroga Zamora, *Compañeros: El GAP: La escolta de Allende* (Santiago: Aguilar, 2001), 147.

22. GIG3, La Legua, "El día del golpe y los días que vinieron," n.d., PAMG.

23. GI, Angela Davis 1/2, winter 2004; Garcés and Leiva, *El golpe en La Legua*, 85–88; Bando Militar #2, #7, #9, in Roberto, Manuel Antonio and Carmen Garretón Merino, *Por la fuerza sin la razón: Análisis y textos de los bandos de la dictadura militar* (Santiago: LOM, 1998), 57–58, 62–64.

24. I thank Geoffrey C. W. Johnson and Joshua Salestrom for assistance with military terminology. Eduardo Gutiérrez González, *Ciudades en las sombras (Una historia*

no oficial del Partido Socialista de Chile) (Santiago: n.p., 2003), 21; Quiroga, *Compañeros*, 150; CEME/AC, "Combates en la Zona Sur de Santiago, Chile 11 de septiembre de 1973," 2005, 1–2.

25. Garcés and Leiva, *El golpe en La Legua*, 40, 50; Quiroga, *Compañeros*, 151–53, 162; CEME/AC, "Combates," 1–3; Eva Palominos Rojas, *Vuelo de mariposa: Una historia de amor en el MIR* (Concepción: Escaparate, 2007), 180–81; Cristián Pérez, "Historia del MIR: 'Si quieren guerra, guerra tendrán . . . ,'" *Estudios Públicos* 91 (Winter 2003): 7–8.

26. *Fuerzas Armadas*, 29; Quiroga, *Compañeros*, 162; CEME/AC, "Combates," 3.

27. Garcés and Leiva, *El golpe en La Legua*, 50.

28. Burgos, *Más fuerte que la metralla*; J.S., Jan. 15, 2003, PAMG.

29. D., Oct. 30, 2000, PAMG.

30. M., Nov. 18, 2000, PAMG.

31. Peter Winn, "The Furies of the Andes: Violence and Terror in the Chilean Revolution and Counterrevolution," in Grandin and Joseph, *Century of Revolution*, 244–45; Luis Corvalán, *De lo vivido y lo peleado: Memorias* (Santiago: LOM, 1997), 157.

32. Corvalán, *De lo vivido*, 156–57.

33. During the UP, counterrevolutionary violence killed three times more people than revolutionary violence. Winn, "Furies," 245, 259.

34. Corvalán, *De lo vivido*, 157.

35. GIG1, La Legua, n.d., PAMG. The rumor about Prats was widespread. See Gutiérrez, *Ciudades en las sombras*, 17; Corvalán, *De lo vivido*, 157; Salazar, *Conversaciones*, 375–76.

36. L.S., Nov. 4, 2004.

37. M.I., Oct. 15, 2000, PAMG.

38. Garcés and Leiva, *El golpe en La Legua*, 116; M.D., Oct. 1, 2001, PAMG.

39. CEME/AC, Wladimir Salamanca, "La Resistencia de La Legua," 2.

40. Garcés and Leiva, *El golpe en La Legua*, 53–54.

41. Garcés and Leiva, *El golpe en La Legua*, 33–36, 52–54; Stern, *Remembering Pinochet's Chile*, 44; GIG1, La Legua, Nov. 25, 2000, PAMG; CEME/AC, "Combates," 3; M.D., Oct. 1, 2001, PAMG.

42. Corvalán, *De lo vivido*, 157; Gutiérrez, *Ciudades en las sombras*, 20–21; Garcés and Leiva, *El golpe en La Legua*, 40, 50n70; Salazar, *Conversaciones*, 375–81.

43. Garcés and Leiva, *El golpe en La Legua*, 53–58; CEME/AC, "Combates," 3. Most sources indicate that the helicopter went down between one o'clock and four o'clock in the afternoon.

44. M.D., Oct. 3, 2002, PAMG; Burgos, *Más fuerte que la metralla*; P.C.C., Nov. 18, 2000, PAMG.

45. *Fuerzas Armadas*, 32–33. Salazar reports a bus with two officials and twenty-five men plus a car with himself and three Carabineros, for a total of thirty-one men. According to *La Tercera*, there were thirty-eight. *La Tercera*, Sep. 11, 1974.

46. *Fuerzas Armadas*, 33, *La Tercera*, Sep. 11, 1974; *El Mercurio*, Oct. 8, 1973.

47. *La Tercera*, Sep. 11, 1974; L.D., Nov. 11, 2002, PAMG.

48. *El Mercurio*, Oct. 8, 1973.

49. L.D., Sep. 9, 2000, PAMG.

50. L.D., Nov. 11, 2002, PAMG.

51. Garcés and Leiva, *El golpe en La Legua*, 34, 61–62.

52. M.D., Oct. 3, 2002, PAMG.

53. Garcés and Leiva, *El golpe en La Legua*, 62; *ICNRR*, 453; Juan Lira Morales, http://www.memoriaviva.com/Ejecutados/Ejecutados_L/lira_morales_juan.htm.

54. R.S., Jan. 18, 2003, PAMG.

55. M.D., Oct. 3, 2002, PAMG; R.S., Jan. 18, 2003, PAMG.

56. L.B., Apr. 16, 2003, PAMG.

57. Corvalán, *De lo vivido*, 157, mentions armed resistance at Sumar, the Universidad Técnica del Estado, and La Legua. There were also skirmishes near población La Victoria. Quiroga, *Compañeros*, 227.

58. *La Prensa*, Sep. 27, 1973; INDH, "Estudio de caso: Violencias y derechos humanos en La Legua," Santiago, 2015.

59. GI, 5a Sesión La Legua, Sep. 2, 2000, PAMG. For a discussion of conflicting testimonies, see Garcés and Leiva, *El golpe en La Legua*, 88–91.

60. GIG1, La Legua, n.d., PAMG.

61. See, for example, Myriam Olguín and Andrea Gamboa, *Propuesta comunitaria de prevención para La Legua* (Santiago: ECO, 2003), 31–36, 59; INDH, "Estudio de caso," 13.

62. Chau Johnsen Kelly, personal communication to author, Mar. 9, 2014.

63. LACC-UF, NACLA Archive of Latin Americana, Roll 47, Mulato Taboada, "Décimas populares que narran de cómo los fascistas asesinaron al presidente Allende, masacraron al pueblo chileno y de la resistencia que éste inició." *Cuadernos de Política Mundial* #2 [n.d.], 11.

64. Burgos, *Más fuerte que la metralla*.

65. M.D., Oct. 3, 2002, PAMG.

66. GI, Villa Francia, July 3, 2004.

67. *Huevón* is Chilean slang derived from slang for "balls" (testicles) (f. *huevona*). It can mean anything from "man"—as in "hey, man" / "oye, huevón"—to "dummy," "dumbass," "idiot," "jerk," or "asshole."

68. GI, Villa Francia, July 3, 2004. *Vieja conchetumadre* translates roughly to "motherfucking old woman."

69. CEDOC-ECO, Taller de Desarrollo Personal Las Araucarias, "Fue como despertar a la vida" (Villa Francia: Centro de Prevención y Desarrollo de la Familia Obispo Alvear, n.d.), 2.

70. GI, Villa Francia, July 3, 2004.

71. Cabrera, "Historia y protagonismo," 82–83.

72. GI, Villa Francia, July 3, 2004.

73. Cabrera, "Historia y protagonismo," 82–84.

74. Franck Gaudichaud, *Poder popular y cordones industriales: Testimonios sobre el movimiento popular urbano chileno, 1970–1973* (Santiago: LOM, 2004), 363, 367; "El 11

de Septiembre en el Cordón Cerrillos: Guillermo Rodríguez Morales (Sep. 11, 2012)," Radio Popular Enrique Torres 100.6 FM, http://radioenriquetorres.blogspot.com/2012 /09/el-11-de-septiembre-en-el-cordon.html; Pepe Burgos, dir., ed., *La Resistencia del Cordón Cerrillos*, Taller Audiovisual Llalliypacha, July 2012, http://vimeo.com/73022405.

75. Marcelo D. Cornejo Vilches, interview with Guillermo Rodríguez, "La auto-defensa del Cordón Industrial Cerrillos (1972–1973)," *Rebelión*, June 29, 2012, http://www.rebelion.org/noticia.php?id=152172.

76. "La autodefensa del Cordón Industrial Cerrillos"; "El 11 de Septiembre en el Cordón Cerrillos"; *La Resistencia del Cordón Cerrillos*; GI, Villa Francia, July 3, 2004.

77. Cabrera, "Historia y protagonismo," 84–86, 88.

78. GI, Villa Francia, July 3, 2004.

79. "El 11 de Septiembre en el Cordón Cerrillos"; *La Resistencia del Cordón Cerrillos*.

80. CEDOC-ECO, Taller de Desarrollo Personal Las Araucarias, "Fue como despertar a la vida," 2.

81. From the Right's perspective, the constitutional reforms of the 1920s had inappropriately expanded and legalized political rights for the poor and working classes and the Left. The UP was merely the last straw, the climax of a conflict with much deeper roots in early-twentieth-century struggles over political pluralism, suffrage, and the separation of church and state. See BCNSC, ACE, 66a sesión, Mar. 21, 1979, 426; "Exposición del Consejero señor Enrique Ortúzar Escobar en el Consejo de Estado, relativa a los fundamentos y disposiciones del anteproyecto de nueva Constitución Política de Chile," realizada en sesión [de la Junta de Gobierno] no 54a, Nov. 14, 1978, 6; BCNSC, *Mensaje Presidencial*, Sep. 11, 1974, 261; and Admiral José Toribio Merino's inaugural address in BCNSC, ADJ, Acta 1/88, Mar. 16, 1988, Sesión Inaugural del Período Legislativo Ordinario 1988, 4–15.

82. Clara Han, *Life in Debt: Times of Care and Violence in Neoliberal Chile* (Berkeley: University of California Press, 2012), 4–5.

83. Bevernage and Aerts, "Haunting Pasts," 393–94; R. S. Rose, *The Unpast: Elite Violence and Social Control in Brazil, 1954–2000* (Athens: Ohio University Press, 2006), 1–2.

84. Stern, *Remembering Pinochet's Chile*, 121.

85. Garcés and Leiva, *El golpe en La Legua*, 81–107.

86. C., Aug. 16, 2000, PAMG; GIG4, La Legua, n.d., PAMG.

87. GIG2, Jornada, Nov. 25, 2000, PAMG.

88. GIGI, La Legua, n.d., PAMG.

89. GI, Primera Sesión, La Legua, Aug. 15, 2000, PAMG.

90. M.B., Aug. 26, 2000, PAMG.

91. GI, Jornada La Legua, Nov. 25, 2000, PAMG.

92. M.D., October 1, 2001, PAMG; Garcés and Leiva, *El golpe en La Legua*, 67.

93. GIGI, La Legua, Nov. 25, 2000, PAMG.

94. GI, Villa Francia, Dec. 3, 2004.

95. E.S., n.d., PAMG.

96. GI, Villa Francia, July 3, 2004.

97. GI, Primera Sesión, La Legua, Aug. 15, 2000, PAMG.

98. GI, Villa Francia, July 3, 2004.

99. GI, 4 Sesión La Legua, Aug. 26, 2000, PAMG.

100. GIG2, Nov. 25, 2000, PAMG.

101. GI, Santa Adriana, June 21, 2004.

102. Narratives about social justice tend to combine what Portelli calls personal, communal, and institutional narrative modes. In poblaciones, this is most pronounced among people with political education. The Communist Party, especially, emphasized the importance of historicism and macro-level processes' effects on individual and collective experience. Portelli, *Battle of Valle Giulia*, 27.

103. A.D., May 31, 2005.

104. M.T.D., Nov. 5, 2004.

105. GI, Primera Sesión, La Legua, Aug. 15, 2000, PAMG.

106. L., Sep. 5, 2000, PAMG.

107. GIG1, La Legua, Aug. 12, 2000, PAMG.

108. GI, José María Caro, Nov. 28, 2004.

109. Gina de Pudahuel, Mar. 10, 2005.

110. Pinochet, quoted in *La Tercera*, Sep. 17, 1973.

Chapter 3. The Economy of Terror, 1973–1978

1. Leonardo Sepúlveda Toro, "Algo se cuela por los resquicios," in *Algo se cuela por los resquicios* (Santiago: n.p., 1987), 220–21.

2. G.G., Sep. 28, 2000, PAMG.

3. Sepúlveda, "Algo se cuela," 222, 228–30.

4. Sepúlveda, "Algo se cuela," 214–15.

5. Sepúlveda, "Algo se cuela," 230. Small red carnations symbolize remembrance of the dictatorship's victims.

6. Pilar Vergara, "Auge y caída del neoliberalismo en Chile: Un estudio sobre la evolución ideológica del régimen militar," Documento de Trabajo 216, Programa FLACSO-Chile, Aug. 1984, 5.

7. Winn, "Pinochet Era," 28.

8. The regime applied some monetarist policies in 1974, but it was not until 1975 that the dictatorship made neoliberalism official economic policy. Winn, "Pinochet Era," 26.

9. J. T. Way, *The Mayan in the Mall: Globalization, Development, and the Making of Modern Guatemala* (Durham, NC: Duke University Press, 2012), 95.

10. Sonia Alvarez, Evelina Dagnino, and Arturo Escobar, "Introduction: The Cultural and Political in Latin American Social Movements," in *Cultures of Politics, Politics of Cultures: Re-Visioning Latin American Social Movements*, ed. Sonia Alvarez et al. (Boulder, CO: Westview Press, 1998), 12.

11. This terminology is a result of a series of conversations with J. T. Way in September 2014. Most helpful were Michel de Certeau, *The Practice of Everyday Life* (Berkeley: University of California Press, 1984); E. P. Thompson, *The Making of the*

English Working Class (New York: Vintage, 1966) and "Custom, Law and Common Right," "The Moral Economy of the English Crowd in the Eighteenth Century," and "The Moral Economy Reviewed," in *Customs in Common: Studies in Traditional Popular Culture* (New York: New Press, 1993); Henri Lefebvre, *The Production of Space*, trans. Donald Nicholson-Smith (Malden, MA: Blackwell, 1991); AbdouMaliq Simone, "People as Infrastructure: Intersecting Fragments in Johannesburg," in *Johannesburg: The Elusive Metropolis*, ed. Sarah Nuttell and Achille Mbembe (Durham, NC: Duke University Press, 2008); Yi-Fu Tuan, *Space and Place: The Perspective of Experience* (Minneapolis: University of Minnesota Press, 1977); and Jorge Chateau, Bernarda Gallardo, Eduardo Morales, Carlos Piña, Hernán Pozo, Sergio Rojas, Daniela Sánchez, and Teresa Valdés, *Espacio y poder: Los pobladores* (Santiago: FLACSO, 1987).

12. Michel de Certeau defines "space" as a "practiced place"—one that derives its meaning and significance, and is determined by, the use to which people put it. In this concept of place and space, place refers to the physical thing (a street, a house, a plaza), and space denotes a semi-tangible manifestation, a force field of social meaning connected to a particular place that combines the physical place with people's use of it. People then derive meaning and significance from the space that they re-ascribe to the place itself and the activities that occur there in an ongoing cycle of social production of meaning. "A movement," writes de Certeau, "always seems to condition the production of space and associate it with a history." de Certeau, *Practice of Everyday Life*, 117–29.

13. See Tuan, *Space and Place*, on space and sentiment, "symbolic identification" with physical locations, and the process of inchoate urban areas coming to be considered neighborhoods by outsiders and their own residents.

14. Sofía Salimovich, Elizabeth Lira, and Eugenia Weinstein's discussion of the social psychology of fear during the dictatorship briefly mentions allanamientos. They identify three categories of fear: of physical harm, of "threat to one's livelihood," and of "threat to one's values." Sofía Salimovich, Elizabeth Lira, and Eugenia Weinstein, "Victims of Fear: The Social Psychology of Repression," in *Fear at the Edge: State Terror and Resistance in Latin America*, ed. Juan E. Corradi, P. W. Fagan, and M. A. Garretón (Berkeley: University of California Press, 1992), 74.

15. L.N.R, Aug. 23, 2000, PAMG.

16. Quote from Vergara, "Auge y caída," 126. See Marcus Taylor, *From Pinochet to the "Third Way": Neoliberalism and Social Transformation in Chile* (Ann Arbor, MI: Pluto Press, 2006), 34–51, for a discussion of neoliberal social engineering in Chile. See also Juan Gabriel Valdés, *Pinochet's Economists: The Chicago School in Chile* (New York: Cambridge University Press, 1995), 31–32.

17. Valdés, *Pinochet's Economists*, 31–32; Vergara, "Auge y caída," 127–28; Alfredo Rodríguez, *Por una ciudad democrática* (Santiago: SUR, 1983), 29. On "the irrationality of neoliberalism," see Taylor, *From Pinochet*, 34–51.

18. David Harvey, *A Brief History of Neoliberalism* (New York: Oxford University Press, 2005).

19. Taylor, *From Pinochet*.

20. Winn, "Pinochet Era," 25–28; Patricio Meller, *Un siglo de economía política chilena (1890–1990)* (Santiago: Andrés Bello, 1996), 187, 190.

21. FAVS, IM-IC Aug. 1976, 103–4. The unemployment statistics include the PEM.

22. FAVS, IM-IC, Sep. 1978, 165.

23. FAVS, IM-IC, Aug. 1976, 104.

24. Winn, "Pinochet Era," 28.

25. FAVS, IM-IC, Aug. 1976, 108. The Vicaría also indicates that the consumer price index (IPC) was disconnected from the economic reality of "the vast majority of people." The IPC assumed that families allocated 53.48 percent of their income to food, 14.46 to housing, 14.64 to clothing, and 17.42 to miscellaneous items (e.g., health care, education, transportation, and utilities).

26. FAVS, IM-IC, Sep. 1977, 17.

27. For a study of structural causes of starvation, see Amartya Sen, *Poverty and Famines: An Essay on Entitlement and Deprivation* (New York: Oxford University Press, 1986), 154–66. Sen found that free-market mechanisms siphoned food away from famine-stricken areas rather than into them.

28. FAVS, IM-IC, Feb. 1978, 33, 36–40.

29. *Cauce* 15, June–July 1984, 44.

30. See Sen, *Poverty and Famine*. The dictatorship and its supporters made much of the decline of infant mortality rates between 1973 and 1990. Although infant mortality rates improved, mortality and illness rates rose among children aged one to four. Gwynn Thomas, *Contesting Legitimacy in Chile: Familial Ideals, Citizenship, and Political Struggle, 1970–1990* (University Park: Penn State University Press, 2011), 154n54.

31. Meller, *Un siglo de economía política*, 187, 199.

32. Sergio Wilson, *La otra ciudad: De la marginalidad a la participación social* (Santiago: Editorial Jurídica Ediar Conosur, 1988), 95.

33. Winn, "Pinochet Era," 48.

34. Between 1969 and 1988, wealth was redistributed from the lower 40 percent of Santiago's population to the upper 20 percent. The lower 40 percent's share dropped from 19.4 percent to 12.6 percent while the upper 20 percent's share increased from 44.5 to 55 percent. The middle 40 percent remained relatively stable, dropping from 36.2 to 32.6 percent. Patricio Meller, Pilar Romaguera, Andrea Butelmann, Rodrigo Baño, and Manuel Canales, *Chile: Evolución macroeconómica, financiación externa y cambio política en la década de los 80* (Madrid: CEDEAL, 1992), 48. For redistribution during the Allende years, see Winn, "Pinochet Era," 16–19.

35. The dictatorship only posted better numbers in the area of export growth. Macroeconomic growth indicators of 1978–81 and 1984–89 represented recovery of the economy to pre-recession levels (1975 recession and 1981–84 recession) rather than new growth and expansion. In terms of unemployment, under Alessandri (1958–64) unemployment averaged 7.5 percent and under Frei (1964–70) 5.5 percent. Under Allende (1970–73) unemployment was 3.9 percent. During the dictatorship (1973–89), unemployment averaged 17.3 percent, rising to more than 30 percent during the recession of the early 1980s. Meller, *Un siglo de economía política*, 319–20.

36. *ICNPPT*, 204; *ICNRR*, 576.

37. *ICNPPT*, 205.

38. Report by Colonel Jorge Espinoza Ulloa, Director of SENDET, to the junta, BCNSC, ADJ, Acta 154a, September 6, 1974, Sesión Secreta, 4–8. The CIA reported 1,600 people killed during the first month after the coup but said that the true number of fatalities would probably never be known. It also reported that during the month following the coup, at any one time an estimated 14,000 people were being held as political prisoners. DDRS, CIA, Cable, October 12, 1973.

39. The working class was broken down into 8,206 skilled workers (30.11 percent), 5,681 unskilled workers (20.84 percent), and 791 bus, taxi, and chauffeur drivers (2.90 percent). The poor and working class also included some portion of the 4,174 professionals and technicians (15.31 percent), 4,114 students (15.09 percent), 580 housewives (2.13 percent), and 439 people of the passive sector (retired, unemployed, minors neither in school nor employed) (1.61 percent) tortured by state agents during the dictatorship. *ICNPPT*, 471–73. The rural working class constitutes an additional 3.34 percent of political prison and torture victims.

40. That is, 1,108 people, or 34.7 percent. The poor and working class also included some of the 75 technicians (2.3 percent), 391 students (12.2 percent), 154 merchants (4.8 percent), 47 housewives (1.5 percent), 26 retired people (0.8 percent) and 45 unemployed or occasional workers (1.4 percent) killed or disappeared during the dictatorship. *ICNRR*, 590.

41. Author's conservative calculation, taking into account only skilled blue-collar workers (obreros), unskilled blue-collar workers (obreros), drivers, and *campesinos* (small farmers). *ICNPPT*, 471–73; *ICNRR*, 590. See also Bruey, "Neoliberalism and Repression," 20.

42. *ICNPPT*, 204–5, 207; *ICNRR*, 576–77, 581.

43. Moya et al., *Tortura en poblaciones*.

44. Bando no. 5, *La Tercera*, September 13, 1973.

45. "La Viruela," *La Tercera*, September 28, 1973.

46. *La Tercera*, May 21, 1975. Leigh was an anti-communist hard-liner but favored capitalist developmentalism over neoliberalism.

47. DWAICD, "Discurso pronunciado por el Señor Comandante en Jefe de la Fuerza Aérea de Chile y Miembro de la Honorable Junta de Gobierno, General del Aire D. Gustavo Leigh Guzmán, al conmemorarse el cuadragésimo séptimo aniversario de la FACH," Santiago, Mar. 21, 1977.

48. Meller, *Un siglo de economía política*, 195.

49. BCNSC, ACE, 16a Sesión, Apr. 26, 1977, 56–57.

50. OECD, *Society at a Glance 2011: OECD Social Indicators* (n.p.: OECD, 2011), 66–69, www.oecd.org/social/societyataglance2011.htm. Between 1990 and 2006, Chile reduced its poverty level from 40 percent to 13.7 percent through state poverty-reduction initiatives and programs. Dante Contreras, "Poverty, Equality and Welfare in a Rapid-Growth Economy: The Chilean Experience," 2020 Focus Brief series (Washington, DC: International Food Policy Research Institute, 2007), 1; GINI Index

(World Bank Estimate), http://data.worldbank.org/indicator/SI.POV.GINI; "Piketty y la desigualdad en Chile," *El Mostrador*, Jan. 14, 2015, http://www.elmostrador.cl /noticias/pais/2015/01/14/piketty-y-la-desigualdad-en-chile-el-1-mas-rico-tiene-cerca-del -35-de-la-riqueza-nacional-y-es-la-cifra-mas-alta-del-mundo/.

51. On the decoupling of economics and violence in post-1990 public discourse, see Carlos Huneeus, *Chile, un país dividido: La actualidad del pasado* (Santiago: Catalonia, 2003), 125.

52. Paley, *Marketing Democracy*.

53. Paley, *Marketing Democracy*; Moulián, *Chile actual*; Nelly Richard, "Cities/ Sites of Violence: Convulsions of Sense and Official Routines," in *Cultural Residues: Chile in Transition* (Minneapolis: University of Minnesota Press, 2004), 15–29.

54. Huneeus, *Chile*, 104.

55. These critiques formed a sort of "hidden transcript," hidden not so much for fear of reprisal but because the media and policymakers did not often listen to pobladores on matters of economy or repression. See James C. Scott, *Domination and the Arts of Resistance: Hidden Transcripts* (New Haven, CT: Yale University Press, 1990).

56. Francesc Relea, "La otra cara del 'jaguar' de América Latina," *El País* (Madrid), Mar. 23, 1998, http://elpais.com/diario/1998/03/23/internacional/890607627_850215 .html.

57. M.I, Oct. 15, 2000, PAMG.

58. Garcés and Leiva, *El golpe en La Legua*, 99–100.

59. GIG4, La Legua, Nov. 25, 2000, PAMG.

60. L.D., Nov. 11, 2002, PAMG.

61. GIG4, La Legua, Nov. 25, 2000, PAMG.

62. GIG4, La Legua, Nov. 25, 2000, PAMG; GIG1, La Legua, Nov. 25, 2000, PAMG.

63. GIG4, La Legua, Nov. 25, 2000, PAMG; GIG4, La Legua, n.d., PAMG.

64. M.I, Oct. 15, 2000, PAMG.

65. *La Tercera*, Sep. 17, 1973; M.I., Oct. 15, 2000, PAMG.

66. L.D., Nov. 27, 2000, PAMG.

67. L.D., May 18, 2005.

68. L.D., May 18, 2005.

69. L.D., Sep. 27, 2000, PAMG. Garcés and Leiva note that many coup narratives consist of what pobladores could see through their windows. *El golpe en La Legua*, 24.

70. L.D., Nov. 11, 2002, PAMG.

71. L.D., Sep. 27, 2000, PAMG; C., Sep. 29, 2000, PAMG.

72. Garcés and Leiva, *El golpe en La Legua*, 100–107.

73. A.G., July 5, 2005. Conflict emerged between Carabineros and the Armed Forces following the coup over Carabineros' falling real wages; the junta's plan to bring Carabineros under the Defense Ministry's jurisdiction; clashes between the police and military over soldiers' disrespect for Carabineros; and Carabineros' displeasure with the military's practice of summarily executing people despite declarations that summary executions had been banned. Carabineros predicted that this would generate

hatred against the police and "come back to haunt them." DDRS, CIA, Cable, Nov. 3, 1973.

74. GI, Plenario, 2a Sesión, La Legua, Aug. 12, 2000, PAMG.

75. L.D., Nov. 11, 2000, PAMG.

76. *La Tercera*, Sep. 20, 1973; C., Sep. 29, 2000, PAMG.

77. L.D., Nov. 11, 2002, PAMG.

78. C., Sep. 29, 2000, PAMG.

79. E.S., n.d., PAMG.

80. D., Oct. 30, 2000, PAMG.

81. Pablo Policzer, *The Rise and Fall of Repression in Chile* (South Bend, IN: University of Notre Dame Press, 2009), 69, 82–83. This is not the only study that makes this claim. It is a dominant narrative that is often uncritically reproduced.

82. Moya et. al, *Tortura en poblaciones*, 73, 75–76, 80.

83. BCNSC, ADJ, Acta 112, Apr. 15, 1974, Sesión Secreta, 1–8; *Mensaje*, No. 310, July 1982, 334.

84. Moya et al., *Tortura en poblaciones*. Mass allanamientos of the Torres San Borja, a middle-class public housing complex in downtown Santiago, is one exception.

85. GI, Santa Adriana, June 21, 2004; GI, Trabajo Grupo La Legua, Aug. 12, 2000, PAMG.

86. "Nadine Loubet (o mejor, Odile): Estar ahí, en la vida misma," *Pastoral Popular* 202 (September 1990): 28–29. Bodies continued appearing in Chile's waterways until at least late 1976, when the Vicaría noted a "profusion" of cadavers in rivers and on beaches, some belonging to "common delinquents" and others unidentifiable, without fingers, faces disfigured, and tied with wire. FAVS, IM-IC, Oct. 1976, 7.

87. GI, Angela Davis 1/2, winter 2004. Pobladores originally named their neighborhood Angela Davis, but the dictatorship changed the name to Remodelación Américo Vespucio (1973) and later to Villa Héroes de la Concepción (1979).

88. GI, Villa Francia, July 3, 2004.

89. G.G., Sep. 28, 2000, PAMG.

90. *La Tercera*, Mar. 13, 1975.

91. *La Tercera*, Jan. 17, 1974.

92. María Elena Valenzuela, *La mujer en el Chile militar: Todas íbamos a ser reinas* (Santiago: CESOC, 1987), 63–115.

93. Valenzuela, *La mujer en el Chile militar*, 74–84; Patricia M. Churchryk, "From Dictatorship to Democracy: The Women's Movement in Chile," in *The Women's Movement in Latin America: Participation and Democracy*, 2nd ed., ed. Jane S. Jaquette (Boulder, CO: Westview Press, 1994), 73–74; Francesca Miller, *Latin American Women and the Search for Social Justice* (Hanover, NH: University Press of New England, 1991), 211–12.

94. P.C.C., Nov. 18, 2000, PAMG.

95. D., Oct. 30, 2000, PAMG.

96. Bandos Militares 1 and 35, in Sofía Correa Sutil, Consuelo Figueroa Garavagno, Alfredo Jocelyn-Holt Letelier, Claudio Rolle Cruz, and Manuel Vicuña Urrutia, *Documentos del Siglo XX chileno* (Santiago: Editorial Sudamericana, 2001), 379, 398.

97. *La Tercera*, Oct. 15, 1973.

98. D., Oct. 30, 2000, PAMG.

99. GI, Trabajo Grupo La Legua, Aug. 12, 2000, PAMG.

100. GI, Trabajo Grupo La Legua, Aug. 12, 2000, PAMG.

101. GI, Primera Sesión La Legua, Aug. 15, 2000, PAMG.

102. In other contexts, a variation of "seeing but not seeing," taking action or associating with people "*sin-saber-sabiendo*" (without-knowing, knowing), gave cover to people providing support to the clandestine opposition.

103. GIG3, La Legua, n.d., PAMG.

104. Memorial in La Legua, Comisión DD.HH de San Joaquín, December 2006; PAMG, Víctimas de La Legua, list compiled by Mario Garcés; PAAJB, Program, Centro Cultural Recuperando Nuestra Historia, Segundo Aniversario, Oct. 2002–4, Villa Francia.

105. L.D., Nov. 11, 2002, PAMG.

106. *La Tercera*, Sep. 18–19, 1973. Luis Hernán Errázuriz, "Dictadura militar en Chile: Antecedentes del golpe estético-cultural," *LARR* 44, no. 2 (2009): 140.

107. Way, *Mayan in the Mall*, 95. In Santiago in the 1970s, although cocaine and marijuana appeared in the discourse, its central features were poverty, "antisocials," and the Left.

108. Bruey, "Neoliberalism and Repression."

109. Jean Franco, *The Decline and Fall of the Lettered City: Latin America in the Cold War* (Cambridge, MA: Harvard University Press, 2002), 13.

110. "Liquidar a los delincuentes," *Ercilla*, no. 1991 (Sep. 26–Oct. 2, 1973): 47. See also "59 delincuentes detenidos en población José María Caro," *El Mercurio*, Oct. 7, 1973; and "Liquidar a los delincuentes," *Ercilla*, no. 1991 (Sep. 26–Oct. 2, 1973): 47; "200 detenidos en allanamiento a Villa Lo Ferrer," *La Tercera*, Mar. 27, 1974; "Otros cien hampones trasladan al norte," *La Tercera*, June 4, 1974; "Continúan limpiando Santiago de maleantes," *La Tercera*, June 16, 1974; "Comenzó razzia de marihuaneros en poblaciones," *La Tercera*, July 21, 1974; "Allanadas poblaciones Pablo de Rokha y San Rafael: FFAA y policías continúan con la "Operación Limpieza," *La Tercera*, Aug. 26, 1974; "Revisados 12 campamentos en otro operativo de limpieza," *La Tercera*, Sep. 9, 1974; and "Allanamiento en busca de delincuentes," *La Tercera*, Dec. 13, 1974.

111. "Liquidar a los delincuentes," *Ercilla*, no. 1991 (Sep. 26—Oct. 2, 1973): 47; *La Tercera*, Sep. 11, 1973 in *La Tercera Especiales*, http://docs.tercera.cl/especiales/2003/11-septiembre/politica/2210-pinochetjurapresidente.htm; *La Tercera*, Sep. 18, 1973.

112. FAVS, COPACHI, Departamental Penal, "Informe en derecho sobre la situación de las personas arrestadas y trasladadas a los campos de detenidos de Pisagua y Chacabuco, en virtud de las normas sobre Estado de Sitio, y en razón de tener ficha policial en la oficina de la Asesoría Técnica de Investigaciones," 3; "Allanadas poblaciones Pablo de Rokha y San Rafael: FFAA y policías continúan con la 'Operación Limpieza,'" *La Tercera*, Aug. 26, 1974; "Última redada: 281 detenidos," *La Tercera*, Aug. 2, 1974.

113. BCNSC, ADJ, Acta 134a, July 17, 1974, Sesión Secreta and ADJ, June 26, 1974, Memorandum Confidencial.

114. *La Tercera*, July 21, 1974; *La Tercera*, Aug. 26, 1974.

115. *La Tercera*, Mar. 27, 1974; "Liquidar a los delincuentes," *Ercilla*, no. 1991 (Sep. 26–Oct. 2, 1973): 47. Police characterized anyone with a police record or file (*ficha*) as delinquent, regardless of whether the person was involved in illegal activity or had an outstanding arrest warrant. A ficha meant that police suspected that a person could or would commit a crime. FAVS, COPACHI, Departamental Penal, "Informe en derecho," 1; Garcés and Leiva, *El golpe en La Legua*, 26.

116. GI, 5a Sesión La Legua, Sep. 2, 2000, PAMG.

117. GI, Plenario La Legua, August 12, 2000, PAMG.

118. FAVS, COPACHI, "Resumen de la situación de las personas detenidas en el campamento militar de Chacabuco," Apr. 18, 1975, 2.

119. FAVS, COPACHI, "Resumen de la situación," 1.

120. *La Tercera*, June 4, 1974; *La Tercera*, June 16, 1974; BCNSC, *Mensaje Presidencial*, Sección Ministerio de Defensa, Sep. 11, 1975, 78–79; FAVS, COPACHI, "Recurso de Amparo," Apr. 1, 1975, 2.

121. FAVS, COPACHI, "Resumen de la situación," 1–4.

122. FAVS, COPACHI, "Recurso de Amparo," 2.

123. FAVS, IM-IC, Oct. 1977, 30.

124. Bonilla was a powerful Pinochet rival associated with the Partido Demócrata Cristiano (PDC, Christian Democrat Party). The PDC gained popularity in the 1960s for expanding public housing programs and legalizing community organizations. In 1975 Bonilla died in a suspicious helicopter crash.

125. *La Tercera*, Apr. 19, 1974.

126. *La Tercera*, Jan. 29, 1974; *La Tercera*, Jan. 20, 1974.

127. For example, *La Tercera*, Jan. 20, 1974; BCNSC, ADJ, Acta 143a, Aug. 1, 1974, Exposición del Ministro de MINVU, 2; BMINVU, MINVU, *Memoria 1979*, 10.

128. BCNSC, ADJ, Acta 112a, Apr. 15, 74, Sesión Secreta, 2–3.

129. DWAICD, Director de Inteligencia Nacional al Ministro de Relaciones Exteriores (SECREDER), Feb. 8, 1977, Ejemplar no. 1, Hoja no. 1, DINA (R) No. B.V. 3550/178/1371, Ref. Minis. RR.EE. (SECREDER) (R) no. 4 del Jan. 4, 1977.

130. "¿Otra forma de represión?," *Mensaje*, no. 310 (July 1982): 334.

131. BCNSC, ADJ, Acta 8, Sep. 14, 1973, Sesión Secreta, 1.

132. Verónica Valdivia, "Lecciones de una Revolución: Jaime Guzmán y los Gremialistas, 1973–1980," in *Su revolución contra nuestra revolución: Izquierdas y derechas en el Chile de Pinochet (1973–1981)*, vol. 1, by Verónica Valdivia, Rolando Álvarez, and Julio Pinto (Santiago: LOM, 2006), 83, 88.

133. Author's count based on fragmented archival records from the Archivo Nacional Histórico. ANH, Intendencia de Santiago, Decretos, 1974 and 1975.

134. Organizations were dissolved by the mayor and their reconstitution ratified by the Intendencia. See, for example, ANH, Intendencia de Santiago, Decreto #214, Santiago, Apr. 25, 1974; ANH, "Formulario para Reconocimiento de Juntas de Vecinos," Intendencia de Santiago, 1974.

135. BCNSC, ADJ, Acta 5, Sep. 19, 1973, Sesión Secreta, 2; BCNSC, ADJ, Acta 14, Oct. 3, 1973, Sesión Secreta, 2.

136. The junta worried about the lack of popular sector support and discussed purchasing the shuttered left-wing paper *Clarín* to "have at [our] disposition a newspaper of popular acceptance and attraction." BCNSC, ADJ, Acta 39, Nov. 21, 1973, and Nov. 22, 1973, Sesión Secreta, 1–2.

137. *La Tercera*, Sep. 13, 1973; *La Tercera*, Sep. 15, 1973.

138. *La Tercera*, July 7, 1974.

139. BCNSC, ADJ, Acta 143a, Aug. 1, 1974, Sesión Secreta, 4.

140. BCNSC, ADJ, Acta 219a, July 29, 1975, Sesión Secreta, 4.

Chapter 4. Solidarity and Resistance, 1973–1978

Parts of this chapter previously appeared in Alison J. Bruey, "Transnational Concepts, Local Contexts: Solidarity at the Grassroots in Pinochet's Chile," in *Human Rights and Transnational Solidarity in Cold War Latin America*, ed. Jessica Stites Mor (Madison: University of Wisconsin Press, 2013), 120–42.

1. A.S.M.J., Mar. 12, 2005.

2. BSI, "El ateísmo del capitalismo: Un tema de poco consumo doctrinal y de mucha actualidad práctica," *Cristo Dialogante*, no. 9 (Nov. 1978).

3. R.F., Mar. 17, 2005. The Church divided Santiago into four administrative zones: North, South, East, and West. The zonal vicariates supported human rights defense and social work within their jurisdictions, forging a link between residents and organizations such as the Comité Pro Paz and Vicaría.

4. H.M.D, May 8, 2004.

5. GI, Villa Francia, July 3, 2004.

6. M.G., Dec. 21, 2004.

7. GI, Villa Francia, July 3, 2004.

8. N.P., July 7, 2005.

9. Elizabeth Jelin, *State Repression and the Labors of Memory*, trans. Judy Rein and Marcial Godoy-Anativia (Minneapolis: University of Minnesota Press, 2003), xviii.

10. Rolando Álvarez, *Arriba los pobres del mundo: Cultura e identidad política del Partido Comunista de Chile entre democracia y dictadura 1965–1990* (Santiago: LOM, 2011), 106, 120–26; Rolando Álvarez, *Desde las sombras: Una historia de la clandestinidad comunista* (Santiago: LOM, 2003).

11. Julio Pinto, "¿Y la historia les dio la razón?," in *Su revolución contra nuestra revolución*, by Verónica Valdivia, Rolando Álvarez, and Julio Pinto (Santiago: LOM, 2006), 1:186.

12. J.C., Feb. 2, 2004.

13. L.D., May 18, 2005.

14. Cabrera, "Historia y Protagonismo," 94.

15. GI, Villa Francia, July 3, 2004.

16. GI, Villa Francia, July 3, 2004.

17. This parallels, at a different party-institutional level, Katherine Hite's thesis that leftist leaders' ideologies, approaches to political practice, and "cognitive understandings" of politics changed little between the 1960s and 1990s. Katherine Hite, *When the Romance Ended: Leaders of the Chilean Left, 1968–1998* (New York: Columbia University Press, 2000), xv.

18. GI, Villa Francia, July 3, 2004.

19. GI, Villa Francia, July 3, 2004.

20. A.S.M.J., Mar. 12, 2005.

21. R.S., Jan. 18, 2003, PAMG.

22. GIG3, La Legua, n.d., PAMG. Sports clubs had long been important vehicles of socialization and politicization. Brenda Elsey, *Citizens and Sportsmen: Fútbol and Politics in Twentieth-Century Chile* (Austin: University of Texas Press, 2011).

23. GIG1, La Legua, n.d., PAMG.

24. L.D., Nov. 11, 2002, PAMG.

25. L.D., Nov. 11, 2002, PAMG.

26. J.C., Feb. 2, 2004.

27. J.M., April 22, 2004.

28. A.S.M.J., Mar. 12, 2005.

29. J.M., Apr. 22, 2004.

30. BCNSC, ADJ, Acta 3, Sep. 16, 1973, Sesión Secreta, 2; *La Tercera*, Sep. 15, 1973; *La Tercera*, Sep. 13, 1973; *La Tercera*, Sep. 17, 1973. For the political "struggle for the streets," see Trumper, *Ephemeral Histories*.

31. *La Tercera*, Sep. 20, 1973.

32. *La Tercera*, Sep. 18, 1973; *La Tercera*, Sep. 19, 1973.

33. *La Tercera*, Jan. 9, 1974.

34. GI, 5a Sesión La Legua, Sep. 2, 2000, PAMG.

35. Ollas comunes were similar to comedores in that they were communal cooking arrangements. Participants stayed to eat at comedores, and participants in ollas comunes took food home. Some people use the terms "comedor" and "olla común" interchangeably.

36. GI, Angela Davis 1 and 2, winter 2004.

37. GI, Villa Francia, July 3, 2004.

38. L.D., Nov. 11, 2002, PAMG.

39. L., Sep. 5, 2000, PAMG.

40. GI, 4a Sesión La Legua, Aug. 24, 2000, PAMG.

41. LACC-UF, NACLA Archive of Latin Americana, Roll 48, "COFFLA News Summary," no. 29, Sep. 29, 1973, 1; LACC-UF, NACLA Archive of Latin Americana, Roll 48, Memo, American Jewish Congress, Commission on International Affairs, Sep. 23, 1973, and Memo, Congreso Judío Latinoamericano, Buenos Aires, Nov. 19, 1973.

42. Manuel Bastías Saavedra, *Sociedad civil en dictadura: Relaciones transnacionales, organizaciones y socialización política en Chile* (Santiago: Ediciones Universidad Alberto Hurtado, 2013), 64–65.

43. María Angélica Cruz, *Iglesia, represión y memoria: El caso chileno* (Madrid: Siglo XXI Editores, 2004), 1, 7–8.

44. The regime did selectively repress and kill religious personnel. See Ana María Hoyl, *Por la vida* (Santiago: CESOC, 2003); José Aldunate, "El signo del martirio," in *Crónicas de una Iglesia liberadora*, by José Aldunate Lyon et al. (Santiago: LOM, 2000), 227–35.

45. Helmut Frenz, *Mi vida chilena: Solidaridad con los oprimidos*, trans. Sonia Plaut (Santiago: LOM, 2006), 137, 152.

46. Bastías, *Sociedad civil*, 64–65.

47. Fernando Ariztía, "El Comité de Cooperación para la Paz en Chile," in *Seminario Iglesia y Derechos Humanos en Chile*, by Fernando Ariztía et al. (Santiago: Arzobispado de Santiago/Fundación de Documentación y Archivo de la Vicaría de la Solidaridad, 2002), 13; Frenz, *Mi vida chilena*, 159; Pamela Lowden, *Moral Opposition to Authoritarian Rule in Chile, 1973–1990* (Oxford: St. Anthony's Press, 1996), 32.

48. Bastías, *Sociedad civil*, 65–66.

49. Brian H. Smith, *The Church and Politics in Chile: Challenges to Modern Catholicism* (Princeton, NJ: Princeton University Press, 1982), 334; Lowden, *Moral Opposition*, 33; Patricio Orellana and Elizabeth Quay Hutchinson, *El movimiento de derechos humanos en Chile, 1973–1990* (Santiago: CEPLA, 1991), 90–115. Although Christian Democrat lawyers worked with the Comité's legal department, Christian Democrats avoided working in the Comité and Vicaría at first, as party leadership discouraged contact with the Left. Orellana and Hutchinson, *El movimiento*, 74. Christian Democrats participated in greater numbers after 1976, as their party moved into the opposition. Ascanio Cavallo, *Memorias Cardinal Raúl Silva Henríquez*, vol. 2 (Santiago: Ediciones Copygraph, 1991), 73.

50. Roberto Bolton, *Testigo soy: Memorias del Rvdo. Roberto Bolton García* (Santiago: Impresor IGD, 2010), 252.

51. Bolton, *Testigo soy*, 254; P.R.B., May 10, 2004.

52. A.S.M.J., Mar. 12, 2005.

53. ARNAD/FOS, "Nuestro testimonio," 5.

54. A.G., July 5, 2005.

55. Roberto Bolton García, "El asilo contra la represión," in Aldunate et al., *Crónicas*, 153; Cristián Precht Bañados, "Del Comité Pro Paz a la Vicaría de la Solidaridad," in Ariztía et al., *Seminario Iglesia y Derechos Humanos*, 19.

56. Stites Mor, "Situating Transnational Solidarity," in Stites Mor, *Human Rights and Transnational Solidarity*, 2.

57. Marx posited two types of what could be understood as solidarity: "unity" of the industrial proletariat under capitalism, and the "ideal solidarity" or "*Gemeinschaft*" that would only be achieved in a communist society. Steinar Stjernø, *Solidarity in Europe: The History of an Idea* (New York: Cambridge University Press, 2009), 43–46, 48.

58. Mikhail Bakunin, "Three Lectures to the Swiss Members of the International" (1871), quoted in Stjernø, *Solidarity*, 57.

59. Jorge Arrate and Eduardo Rojas, *Memoria de la izquierda chilena*, vol. 1, *1850–1970* (Santiago: Javier Vergara Editor, 2003), 55–108 (esp. 97, 108); Sergio Grez Toso, *Los anarquistas y el movimiento obrero: La alborada de "la Idea" en Chile, 1893–1915* (Santiago: LOM, 2007); Gabriel Salazar and Julio Pinto, *Historia contemporánea de Chile I: Estado, legitimidad, ciudadanía* (Santiago: LOM, 1999), 39–41; Gabriel Salazar and Julio Pinto, *Historia Contemporánea de Chile II: Actores, identidad y movimiento* (Santiago: LOM, 1999), 112–22.

60. Arrate and Rojas, *Memoria*, 1:55–56, 58, 60–62.

61. Arrate and Rojas, *Memoria*, 1:62–63; Pope Leo XIII, *Rerum novarum*, Encyclical on Capital and Labor, 1891, w2vatican.va/content/leo-xiii/encyclicals/documents /hf_l-xiii_enc_15051891_rerum-novarum.html.

62. Pope Leo XIII, *Rerum novarum*.

63. Stjernø, *Solidarity*, 43–44. It appeared again in Pope Paul VI's *Gaudium Et Spes*, in 1965. See http://www.vatican.va/archive/hist_councils/ii_vatican_council/docu ments/vat-ii_const_19651207_gaudium-et-spes_en.html.

64. Mónica Echeverría Yáñez, *Antihistoria de un luchador (Clotario Blest 1823–1990)* (Santiago: LOM, 2013), 98–99.

65. Echeverría, *Antihistoria*, 104, 106.

66. *Revista Germen*, 1933, quoted in Echeverría, *Antihistoria*, 104.

67. Echeverría, *Antihistoria*, 102.

68. Alberto Hurtado, quoted in Oscar Jiménez, SJ, "Alberto Hurtado, precursor de La Iglesia Liberadora," in Aldunate et al., *Crónicas*, 14–15.

69. Jiménez, "Alberto Hurtado," 15.

70. Tracey Lynn Jaffe, "In the Footsteps of *Cristo Obrero*: Chile's Young Catholic Workers Movement in the Neighborhood, Factory, and Family, 1946–1973" (PhD diss., University of Pittsburgh, 2009), 144.

71. Jaffe, "In the Footsteps of *Cristo Obrero*," 145; Reinaldo Sapag Chain, "El Cardenal Silva y los trabajadores," in *El Cardenal Raúl Silva Henríquez y los Trabajadores*, ed. Bárbara Figueroa Sandoval, Monseñor Alfonso Baeza Donoso, and Reinaldo Sapag Chain (Santiago: Ediciones Copygraph, 2013), 29.

72. Jaffe, "In the Footsteps of *Cristo Obrero*," 2, iv.

73. Medellín Documents, Latin American Bishops, "Justice" Article 2, Sep. 6, 1968.

74. Medellín Documents, Article 10, Sep. 6, 1968.

75. Gustavo Gutiérrez, "Theology of Liberation," in *Gustavo Gutiérrez: Essential Writings*, ed. James B. Nickoloff (New York: Orbis, 2000), 29.

76. I thank Elizabeth Hutchinson for this observation and the quote from Gutiérrez that follows it. Elizabeth Q. Hutchinson, email communication, Jan. 11, 2011.

77. Gustavo Gutiérrez, "Notes for a Theology of Liberation (1970)," in *Liberation Theology at the Crossroads: Democracy or Revolution?*, ed. Paul E. Sigmund (New York: Oxford University Press, 1992), 212–13.

78. Gustavo Gutiérrez, "Understanding the God of Life," in Nickoloff, *Gustavo Gutérrez*, 63. "Preferential" meant priority, not exclusivity, see introduction in *Gustavo Gutérrez*, 13.

79. Roger Lancaster, *Thanks to God and the Revolution: Popular Religion and Class Consciousness in the New Nicaragua* (New York: Columbia University Press, 1988), xx, 67, 69.

80. Grupo de Cristianos por el Socialismo, "Génesis y Constitución de los CPS," in "Cristianos por el socialismo e Iglesia Liberadora," in Aldunate et. al, *Crónicas*, 53–55.

81. Cristianos por el Socialismo, *El pueblo camina . . . ¿Y los cristianos?* (Santiago: Secretariado de Cristianos por el Socialismo, [1972]), 48.

82. Aldunate, *Un peregrino*, 106.

83. José Aldunate Lyon, "La experiencia Calama," in Aldunate et al., *Crónicas*, 90; José Aldunate Lyon, "EMO: Presencia y acción en 25 años," in Aldunate et al., *Crónicas*, 95.

84. Not all priests and religious sisters who lived and worked among the poor participated in the Grupo Calama, and not all proponents of liberation theology adopted these practices.

85. J.R., June 21, 2005; Jaffe, "In the Footsteps of *Cristo Obrero*," 154.

86. Jaffe, "In the Footsteps of *Cristo Obrero*," 154n34.

87. BSI, H. Guzmán, "Creencias y no creencia popular," *Cristo Dialogante* Año 7, no. 14 (Sep. 1981): 7–18.

88. J.R., n.d., PAMG.

89. L.M., May 9, 2004.

90. J.C., Feb. 2, 2004.

91. Cardinal Raúl Silva Henríquez, quoted in Sapag Chain, "El Cardenal Silva y los trabajadores," in Figueroa et al., *El Cardenal Raúl Silva Henríquez*, 20.

92. Fernando Ariztía, "Algunas reflexiones sobre la solidaridad," *Boletín Zona Oeste*, no. 52–53 (Nov.–Dec. 1974), reproduced in *Mensaje*, no. 236 (Jan.–Feb. 1975): 46–49.

93. Sandra Rojas, *Vicaría de la Solidaridad: Historia de su trabajo social* (Santiago: Ediciones Paulinas, 1991), 12.

94. Rojas, *Vicaría de la Solidaridad*, 66–67, 76, 78.

95. R.F., Mar. 17, 2005.

96. Teresa Valdés et al., "Centros de Madres 1973–1989 ¿Sólo disciplinamiento?," Documento de Trabajo 416, Programa de FLACSO-Chile (July 1989), 23–28.

97. Armand and Michelle Mattelart, *La mujer chilena en una nueva sociedad* (Santiago: Editorial del Pacífico, S.A., 1968), 32, 113.

98. LACC-UF, NACLA Archive of Latin Americana, Roll 45, Arzobispado de Santiago, Vicaría de Pastoral Obrera, "Situación de la mujer trabajadora," *Documento*, Año 2, no. 11 (1979): 26.

99. Rojas, *Vicaría de la Solidaridad*, 76–78.

100. J.R., June 21, 2005.

101. Lira, quoted in Hoyl, *Por la vida*, 150–51.

102. FAVS, COPACHI, "Criterios esenciales de las tareas del Copachi," Santiago, Dec. 1975.

103. Ishay, *History of Human Rights*, 119.

104. J.C., Feb. 2, 2004.

105. J.R., n.d., PAMG.

106. Oral history research for this project suggests that this was true of Communists, Socialists, and the MIR in Santiago during the pre-coup period. For an in-depth study of the MIR's social activism in Concepción, see Marian E. Schlotterbeck, *Beyond the Vanguard: Everyday Revolutionaries in Allende's Chile* (Berkeley: University of California Press, 2018). See also Álvarez, *Arriba los pobres*, 80–86.

107. ARNAD/FOS, "Nuestro testimonio," 5.

108. Quoted in ARNAD/FOS, Luis Morales Herrera, *Villa Francia Tres: Testimonios sobre sus detenidos-desaparecidos* (Santiago: [n.p.], n.d.), 32.

109. ARNAD/FOS, "Nuestro testimonio," 8.

110. Quoted in Cabrera, "Historia y protagonismo," 113–14.

111. Quoted in ARNAD/FOS, Morales Herrera, *Villa Francia Tres*, 48. See also Lucía Sepúlveda Ruiz, *119 de nosotros* (Santiago: LOM, 2005), 77–79, 85–95.

112. I.P./J.M., Nov. 26, 2004.

113. A.S.M.J., Mar. 12, 2005.

114. Raúl Gutiérrez V., "Afrontando juntos de cesantía: La experiencia de una bolsa de cesantes," *Mensaje*, no. 287 (Mar.–Apr. 1980): 119–21.

115. H.M.D., May 8, 2004.

116. Rodrigo de Arteagabeitia, "En Villa Francia: Desde lo más profundo de la herida," *Mensaje*, no. 285 (Dec. 1979): 806–8.

117. H.M.D., May 8, 2004.

118. A.S.M.J., Mar. 12, 2005.

119. J.R., n.d., PAMG.

120. J.R., n.d., PAMG.

121. J.C., Feb. 2, 2004.

122. Brian H. Smith, "Chile: Deepening the Allegiance of Working-Class Sectors to the Church in the 1970s," in *Religion and Political Conflict in Latin America*, ed. Daniel H. Levine (Chapel Hill: University of North Carolina Press, 1986), 167, 175.

123. M.T.D., Nov. 5, 2004.

124. J.R., June 21, 2005.

125. L.T./M.V., Apr. 27, 2004.

126. L.T./M.V., Apr. 27, 2004.

127. A.S.M.J., Mar. 12, 2005.

128. A.S.M.J., Mar. 12, 2005.

129. J.R., June 21, 2005.

130. J.M., Apr. 22, 2004.

131. FAVS, Arzobispado de Santiago-Vicaría de la Solidaridad, "Solidaridad: lea y comente la Pastoral de la Solidaridad," pamphlet, 1975. See also "La Iglesia hoy: Orientaciones pastorales para Chile," *Mensaje*, no. 240 (July 1975): 325–30.

132. FAVS, Arzobispado, "Solidaridad."

133. Juan Ignacio Gutiérrez de la Fuente, SJ, "De la emergencia a la solidaridad," *Mensaje*, no. 240 (July 1975): 310.

134. FAVS, Arzobispado, "Solidaridad."

135. FAVS, Arzobispado, "Solidaridad." This provided a framework for what Sally J. Scholz defines as "political solidarity": a "particular form of solidarity that carries self-imposed moral requirements" understood as "a unity of individuals who have made a commitment to struggle for liberation." Sally J. Scholz, *Political Solidarity* (University Park: Penn State University Press, 2008), 21, 36.

136. Hoyl, *Por la Vida*, 225–97.

137. FAVS, Arzobispado, "Solidaridad."

138. "Manifiesto del Movimiento de Resistencia Popular al Pueblo de Chile," Sep. 1974, in Mauricio Ahumada and Pedro Naranjo, *Miguel Enríquez y el proyecto revolucionario en Chile: Discursos y documentos del Movimiento de Izquierda Revolucionaria, MIR* (Santiago: LOM, 2004), 346.

139. FLACSO/FERT, "La Unidad Popular y las Tareas del Pueblo de Chile," Berlin, GDR, July 27, 1975.

140. FLACSO/FERT, *Pueblo Cristiano*, Año 3, no. 5 (Jan.–Feb. 1976).

141. Enrique Dussel, "From Fraternity to Solidarity: Toward a *Politics of Liberation*," trans. Michael Barber and Judd Smith Wright, *Journal of Social Philosophy* 38, no. 1 (2007): 80, 84.

142. BSI, *Cristo Dialogante*, no. 8 (Aug. 1978): 2–6.

143. BSI, J.H.P., "Juan Pablo II, 'Papa de las fronteras,'" *Cristo Dialogante*, Año 7, no. 9 (Nov. 1978).

144. FAVS, IM–IC, Oct. 1976, 11–1, and FAVS, IM–IC, July–Dec. 1976, 98–115.

145. M.G., Dec. 21, 2004.

146. L.T./M.V., Apr. 27, 2004.

147. R.M./J.C./A.M., Oct. 24, 2003.

Chapter 5. Miracles, Mirages, and Mobilization, 1978–1982

1. BCNSC, ADJ, Acta 354a, Sep. 14, 1978, Sesión Secreta Legislativa, 27–28.

2. "Comunidad cristiana 'Villa Francia': Cristo exige la verdad," *Solidaridad*, no. 77 (Sep. 1979): 9.

3. Cristianos por el Socialismo, *El pueblo camina*, 43.

4. José Aldunate, "Romería a Lonquén: Pasión del Señor," *Mensaje*, no. 277 (Mar.–Apr. 1979): 156–60.

5. H.M.D., May 8, 2004.

6. The multivalent positionality of actually existing social subjects belies artificial theoretical notions of class purity previously applied to analyses of Latin American societies. See Mario Garcés, *El despertar de la sociedad: Los movimientos sociales en América Latina y Chile* (Santiago: LOM, 2012), 56.

7. Alvarez et al., "Introduction," in *Cultures of Politics*, 6, 12, 14–16. The body of new social movement theory of which this set of ideas is a part has been criticized for failing to question its foundational assumption that "the historicity, social bases, and origins of Latin American social movements have fundamentally changed, beginning

no later than the 1980s." Wickham-Crowley and Eckstein, "Persisting Relevance," 4. As Eckstein and Wickham-Crowley point out, the idea of "webs" is not new, nor is much else about new social movement theory or its "new" actors. Yet, despite its sometimes ahistorical claims, new social movement theory helped scholars depart from traditional Marxist analysis to consider the ways in which conditions other than relationships to modes of production have played into the development of social and political movements. Chilean scholars, even when they take a new social movement approach, tend not to disregard the importance of political economy, socioeconomic class, and state power to those movements.

8. Wickham-Crowley and Eckstein, "Persisting Relevance," 4.

9. FLACO/FERT, Unidad Popular, "Llamamiento al pueblo de Chile a formar un frente antifascista para derrocar la dictadura," Santiago de Chile, May 1, 1974, in *Boletín Informativo Chile Democrático-Roma*, no. 22 (June 22, 1974): 25. The Communist Party and Christian Democrats cooperated within the labor movement. Álvarez, *Arriba los pobres*, 121.

10. The term "popular movement" refers to "the sum or confluence of diverse movements of popular origin that share an ethos of socialist transformation of Latin American societies." It also means a movement centered in the popular sectors "in which everyone can participate" and that combines "in its practice and self-perception" elements related to "culture, organized labor, and politics." Mario Albuquerque et al., *Reconstrucción del movimiento popular bajo dictadura militar, 1973–1983*, Colección Cuadernos de Historia Popular, no. 11, Serie Historia del Movimiento Obrero, vol. 4 (Santiago: ECO, CETRA/CEAL, 1990), 5; Garcés, *El despertar de la sociedad*, 31, 59–60.

11. The Chilean socialist renovation predated the Reagan/Thatcher years, the Catholic Church's turn to the Right, and the rise of Solidarity in Poland. Esteban Teo Valenzuela, *Dios, Marx . . . y el MAPU* (Santiago: LOM, 2014), 174, 178. Lautaro was officially established in late 1982, the fruit of conversations and political reflection that began as early as 1979 as youth organizations gained increasing autonomy from the Church. Many militants of the 1980s had their start in Church-affiliated social organizations and the student movement. The organization peaked in the early 1990s. Gabriel Salazar and Julio Pinto, *Historia Contemporánea de Chile V: Niñez y juventud* (Santiago: LOM, 2002), 254; Nicolás Acevedo Arriaza, "¡¡Fuera Pinochet, Chile Popular!! El mestizaje político del MAPU-Lautaro en las protestas populares (1978–1985)" (undergraduate thesis, Universidad ARCIS, 2006).

12. Álvarez, *Arriba los pobres*, 121; Luis Rojas Núñez, *De la rebelión popular a la sublevación imaginada: Antecedentes de la historia política y militar del Partido Comunista de Chile y del FPMR 1973–1990* (Santiago: LOM, 2011); Ricardo Palma Salamanca, *Una larga cola de acero: Historia del FPMR 1984–1988* (Santiago: LOM, 2001); Humberto Arcos Vera, *Autobiografía de un viejo comunista chileno: Una historia "no oficial" pero verdadera* (Santiago: LOM, 2013); Hernán Vidal, *FPMR: El tabú del conflicto armado en Chile* (Santiago: Mosquito Editores, 1995).

13. Boeninger, *Democracia en Chile*, 282.

14. Joan W. Scott, "'Experience,'" in *Feminists Theorize the Political*, ed. Judith Butler and Joan Scott (New York: Routledge, 1992), 34–35. Temma Kaplan highlights the importance of protest spectacle in *Taking Back the Streets: Women, Youth, and Direct Democracy* (Berkeley: University of California Press, 2004).

15. J.C., Feb. 2, 2004.

16. The first AFDD hunger strike was in 1977; the 1978 and 1979 strikes appeared most often in oral histories.

17. This is not a teleological argument about the origins of the national protests but a comment on the importance that the 1978–82 period holds in *memorias soterradas* among those whose experience does not align with the idea that poblador protest was a spontaneous eruption of discontent in reaction to the 1980s debt crisis.

18. M. Angélica Bulnes, "José Piñera: 'Dar un golpe de timón, crear esquemas nuevos,'" *¿Qué Pasa?*, no. 454 (Dec. 27, 1979–Jan. 2, 1980): 7. Piñera also refers to these changes as a "silent revolution," a phrase later popularized by Joaquín Lavín, *Chile: Revolución Silenciosa* (Santiago: Zig-Zag, 1987).

19. Bulnes, "José Piñera," 11.

20. Bulnes, "José Piñera," 7–9; M. Angélica Bulnes, "Miguel Kast," *¿Qué Pasa?*, no. 465 (Mar. 13–19, 1980): 8.

21. FAVS, IM-IC, Nov. 1978, 31–37.

22. FAVS, IM-IC, Nov. 1978, 31–37. Gran Santiago unemployment data from FAVS, IM-IC, Oct. 1978, 11.

23. At its pre-1980s peak, in December 1976, the PEM employed 187,702 people nationwide. FAVS, IM-IC, Oct. 1978, 5–9, 20. During the 1980s crisis, the regime created a second emergency make-work program, the Occupation Program for Heads of Household (Programa de Ocupación para Jefes de Hogar, POJH).

24. FAVS, IM-IC, Nov. 1978, 31–38.

25. Between October 1977 and July 1979 the price of bread rose 105 percent, and by September 1980, workers' real wages had rebounded to only 51 percent of their September 1973 levels. FAVS, IM-IC, July 1979, 149; José Aldunate, SJ, and Jaime Ruiz-Tagle P., "Los ingresos reales de los trabajadores más pobres: La casera y su economía de mercado," *Mensaje*, no. 294 (Nov. 1980): 646.

26. FAVS, IM-IC, "Estudio comparativo del aporte nutritivo de la dieta del comedor infantil," Aug. 1977, 42.

27. FAVS, IM-IC, Oct. 1978, 38–39.

28. FAVS, IM-IC, Apr. 1978, 10–11.

29. Heidi Tinsman, *Buying into the Regime: Grapes and Consumption in Cold War Chile and the United States* (Durham, NC: Duke University Press, 2014).

30. The census describes *mejoras* as "constructions of light material that are improvised to care for a site or materials on a construction project etc. and are generally inhabited by the caretaker and his family." *Emergencia* housing is "a construction with exterior walls of wood, roof of zinc, slate, or phonolite, floor of dirt, foundation block, or planks, water inside or outside the house, pit toilet, and a maximum of two rooms." Ranked list created by author based on census data. Homes categorized as *casas* in the

census do not disaggregate the houses by socioeconomic class or location; the corresponding data presumably includes houses in poblaciones and in middle- and upper-class neighborhoods, without distinction. "*Casas*" excludes *conventillos* (tenements). The survey categories were televisions (black/white and color), washing machine, radio/radio-cassette/record player, refrigerator, floor-waxer/vacuum, telephone, motorbike, bicycle, car/van/truck, sewing/weaving machine, none, and undeclared. Instituto Nacional de Estadísticas (INE), *Vivienda, hogar y familia: XV Censo Nacional de Población y IV de Vivienda-Chile*, Región Metropolitana de Santiago (Apr. 1982), vol. 2, 88–89, 90–91.

31. This was also the case in Aconcagua. Tinsman, *Buying into the Regime*, ch. 2.

32. GI, 5a Sesión La Legua, Sep. 2, 2000, PAMG.

33. FAVS, IM-IC, "Encuesta aplicada en el Area Metropolitana a integrantes de Bolsas de Cesantes," Apr. 1978, 84.

34. Winn, "Pinochet Era," 39.

35. FAVS, IM-IC, "Informe Económico 1970–1977," Aug. 1977, 10–11, 17–19, 21–22.

36. FAVS, IM-IC, Apr. 1978, 10; and FAVS, IM-IC, "Informe económico primer semestre 1978," Sep. 1978, 156, 168.

37. Patricio Meller, *The Unidad Popular and the Pinochet Dictatorship: A Political Economy Analysis* (New York: St. Martin's, 2000), 88, 90, 97; Winn, "Pinochet Era," 40–42.

38. FAVS, IM-IC, June 1981, 5.

39. Jorge Hourton P., auxiliary bishop of Santiago, letter to the CECH, Vicarios Episcopales de Santiago y otras instancias a quienes interesa, "'BASTA YA' a la Policía Política," Santiago, Oct. 9, 1978, in FAVS, IM-IC, Sep. 1978, "Informe Especial."

40. FAVS, IM-IC, July 1979, 149, and FAVS, IM-IC, June 1979, 39.

41. "Orientaciones políticas de la educación popular," in *ECO en el horizonte latinoamericano (I): La educación popular bajo la dictadura*, Colección 30 Años, by ECO, vol. 2 (Santiago: ECO, 2012), 81. See also FLACSO/FERT, "Manifiesto del Partido Comunista de Chile," Santiago, May 1979, 1. This document does not use the phrase "fin del reflujo," but it acknowledges the rising mobilization in 1978 and 1979 as a *despertar político* (political awakening).

42. Gabriel Salazar, *La historia desde abajo y desde dentro* (Santiago: Facultad de Artes, Universidad de Chile, 2003), 393, 425, 431.

43. "Prácticas educativas y organización popular," in ECO, *ECO en el horizonte latinoamericano (I)*, 57.

44. "Prácticas educativas y organización popular," 61.

45. Salazar, *La historia desde abajo*, 425–26. In Chile two "social citizen movements"—those of 1822–28 and 1918–25—escaped the control of traditional political actors and institutions to birth new, albeit liberal-capitalist, political orders. Gabriel Salazar, *En el nombre del poder popular constituyente (Chile, siglo XXI)* (Santiago: LOM, 2011), 31–32.

46. Los Guaracheros, "Cómo se organizó la toma de Zañartu," 26–27.

47. "Orientaciones políticas de la educación popular," 80–81.

48. Rojas, *Vicaría de la Solidaridad*, 88.

49. J.C., Feb. 2, 2004.

50. See Schlotterbeck, *Beyond the Vanguard*; and Álvarez, *Arriba los pobres*.

51. M.G., Dec. 21, 2004.

52. "Orientaciones políticas de la educación popular," 82.

53. J.M., Apr. 22, 2004.

54. A.S.M.J., Mar. 12, 2005.

55. M.G., Dec. 21, 2004.

56. M.G., Dec. 21, 2004.

57. Hernán Vidal, *Dar la vida por la vida: Agrupación Chilena de Familiares de Detenidos Desaparecidos (Ensayo de Antropología Simbólica)* (Santiago: Mosquito Editores, 1996), 104–5.

58. H.M.D., May 8, 2004; Mario Garcés and Nancy Nicholls, *Para una historia de los DD.HH. en Chile: Historia institucional de la Fundación de Ayuda Social de las Iglesias Cristianas FASIC 1975–1991* (Santiago: LOM, 2005), 74–78; "Participantes en la huelga de hambre de los F.D.D. en la Parroquia de 'Jesús Obrero' (22 y 24 de mayo al 7 de junio, 1978)," in Aldunate et al., *Crónicas*, 243–44.

59. P.R.B., May 10, 2004.

60. A.S.M.J., Mar. 12, 2005.

61. A.S.M.J., Mar. 12, 2005.

62. I.P./J.M., Nov. 26, 2004.

63. A.S.M.J., Mar. 12, 2005.

64. L.E., Nov. 2004.

65. List of parish priests, San Cayetano chapel wall, July 2006; Marjorie Agosín, *Tapestries of Hope, Threads of Love: The Arpillera Movement in Chile*, 2nd ed. (Lanham, MD: Rowman and Littlefield, 2007); Jacqueline Adams, *Art against Dictatorship: Making and Exporting Arpilleras under Pinochet* (Austin: University of Texas Press, 2013).

66. L.D., May 18, 2005; J.R., June 21, 2005; FAVS, IM-IC, Aug. 1978, 14; Blanca Saldías, "Aquí, en mi parroquía San Cayetano," in ECO and Red de Organizaciones Sociales de La Legua, *Memorias de la dictadura en La Legua*, 40.

67. FAVS, IM-IC, Mar.1979, 21; *La Tercera*, July 29, 1979.

68. "Laicos: Salir de la sacristía," *Solidaridad*, no. 111 (Mar. 1981): 13.

69. J.R., June 21, 2005; L.D., May 18, 2005.

70. L.D., May 18, 2005.

71. GIG1, La Legua, Nov. 25, 2000, PAMG.

72. L.D., Nov. 11,2002, PAMG.

73. M.I., Oct. 15, 2000, PAMG.

74. GIG1, La Legua, Nov. 25, 2000, PAMG.

75. GIG1, La Legua, Nov. 25, 2000, PAMG.

76. Stern, *Battling for Hearts and Minds*, 163.

77. J.R., June 21, 2005.

78. FAVS, IM-IC, Sep. 1979, 21–23; *La Tercera*, Sep. 9, 1979; *La Tercera*, Sep. 10, 1979.

79. Quoted in Acevedo Arriaza, "¡¡Fuera Pinochet!!," 63.

80. Irene Agurto, Manuel Canales, and Gonzalo de la Maza, eds., *Juventud chilena: Razones y subversiones* (Santiago: ECO/FOLICO/SEPADE, 1985), 88–89; Salazar and Pinto, *Historia Contemporánea de Chile V*, 238–41.

81. L.E., Nov. 2004.

82. CEDOC-ECO, "Horizonte," Boletín Informativo Comunidad Cristiana Cristo Liberador, Nov. 1981.

83. CEDOC-ECO, "Horizonte," Boletín Informativo Comunidad Cristiana Cristo Liberador, [1981], 6–7.

84. CEDOC-ECO, "Horizonte," [1980], 7–8.

85. J.R., Nov. 18, 2000, PAMG.

86. J.R., June 21, 2005.

87. M.T.D., Nov. 5, 2004.

88. M.T.D., Nov. 5, 2004.

89. M.G., Dec. 21, 2004.

90. M.T.D., Nov. 5, 2004.

91. M.V./L.T., Apr. 27, 2004.

92. M.T.D., Nov. 5, 2004.

93. M.V./L.T., Apr. 27, 2004.

94. J.R., Nov. 18, 2000, PAMG.

95. M.G., Dec. 21, 2004.

96. The FASIC quietly defended prisoners who met these criteria. CODEPU (est. 1980 and linked to the MIR) later took up the legal defense of people implicated in deaths. Garcés and Nicholls, *Para una historia de los DD.HH.*, 112.

97. M.V./L.T., Apr. 27, 2004.

98. GIG1, La Legua, Nov. 25, 2000, PAMG.

99. GI, Angela Davis 1/2, winter 2004.

100. Jokes from BSI, "Encuentro de las comunidades cristianas populares: Una Iglesia que nace del pueblo," *Policarpo*, Año 1, no. 6 (Dec. 1981): 9; and BSI, "Pinochet y los chistes," *Policarpo*, Año 2, no. 13 (Sep. 1982): 9.

101. I borrow the term "la ciudad escindida" from Clarisa Hardy and Victoria Legassa, *La ciudad escindida (Los problemas nacionales y la Región Metropolitana)* (Santiago: PET, 1989).

Chapter 6. National Protest and Possibility, 1983–1990

1. GI, Jornada La Legua, Nov. 25, 2000, PAMG.

2. A.D., May 31, 2005. Alejandra attributes the comment about the dead in the dispute of power to Andrés Pascal Allende.

3. Marcelo Puente, "Compañero." The song tends to be used in homages to the MIR.

4. Gabriela Raposo dates the consolidation of the armed left in the sector to 1982. Raposo, "Muerte y lugar," 180–82.

5. Robin D. G. Kelley, *Freedom Dreams: The Black Radical Imagination* (Boston: Beacon, 2002), ix.

6. Moulián, *Chile actual*, 277; Manuel Antonio Garretón, "El regimen militar chileno en la encrucijada" *Mensaje*, no. 326 (Jan.–Feb. 1984): 40; Lydia Chavez, "State of Siege Is Imposed in Chile," *New York Times*, Nov. 7, 1984.

7. "Paro Nacional: Una seria advertencia" and "El peligro de la eclosión social," *Cauce*, Año 1, no. 30 (Nov. 6–12, 1984): 14–15.

8. Cathy Schneider, "Mobilization at the Grassroots: Shantytowns and Resistance in Authoritarian Chile," *Latin American Perspectives* 18, no. 1 (1991): 92–112.

9. On opposition leaders' hopes for 1986, see "Este es el año decisivo," *Fortín Mapocho*, Dec. 30, 1985, 6–7.

10. Morris H. Morley and Chris McGillion, *Reagan and Pinochet: The Struggle over U.S. Policy toward Chile* (New York: Cambridge University Press, 2015), 81, 89; Victor Figueroa Clark, "The Forgotten History of the Chilean Transition: Armed Resistance against Pinochet and US Policy towards Chile in the 1980s," *JLAS* 47, no. 3 (2015): 23–24, 26.

11. Patricio Aylwin Azócar, "Protesta pacífica: Derecho y deber cívicos," *Hoy*, no. 306 (June 1–7, 1983): 9.

12. CEDOC-ECO, Eusebio Nájera, "Jóvenes: Del protagonismo a la exclusión," in ECO, *Los movimientos sociales frente al plebiscito*, Taller de Análisis Movimientos Sociales y Coyuntura No. 2, Aug. 1988, 15.

13. The CECH differentiated between the violence of the terrorist state and the violence of the armed resistance—as differentiated, too, from the violence of popular sector protest: "Both forms [of violence, by the state and by the armed left] are equally inhumane . . . but objectively state violence is more serious because the authorities, by definition, are called upon to repress crime with the weapons of truth and justice." CECH, "Iglesia servidora de la Vida," quoted in "Lo más grave es el terrorismo de Estado," *Fortín Mapocho*, Nov. 18, 1985, 7. See also Alexander Wilde, "The Institutional Church and Pastoral Ministry: Unity and Conflict in the Defense of Human Rights in Chile," in *Religious Responses to Violence: Human Rights in Latin America Past and Present*, ed. Alexander Wilde (South Bend, IN: University of Notre Dame Press, 2016), 171.

14. "Tienen algo que decir," *Hoy*, no. 381 (Nov. 5–11, 1984): 22.

15. "'Estamos aburridos de que nos maten,'" *Fortín Mapocho*, Oct. 7, 1985, 16.

16. The 1980s are the subject of a fragmented scholarly literature. Many analyses focus on political structures and institutions. See, for example, Carlos Huneeus, *El régimen de Pinochet*, 2nd ed. (Santiago: Editorial Sudamericana, 2002); Loveman and Lira, *Las ardientes cenizas del olvido*; Ascanio Cavallo et al., *La historia oculta del régimen militar: Memoria de una época 1973–1988* (Santiago: Grijalbo Mondadori, 1997); Paul W. Drake and Iván Jaksić, eds., *The Struggle for Democracy in Chile, 1982–1990* (Lincoln: University of Nebraska Press, 1995). Others assess pobladores' political consciousness,

describe pobladores' social organizations, and examine the rise of "new" social movement actors. See, for example, Oxhorn, *Organizing Civil Society*; Valdés and Weinstein, *Mujeres que sueñan*; and studies of popular sector organizations published by the Programa de Economía del Trabajo (PET), SUR-Profesionales, and FLACSO-Chile. A smaller subset of literature addresses the national protests in poblaciones. See, for example, Gonzalo de la Maza and Mario Garcés, *La explosión de las mayorías: Protesta Nacional 1983–1984* (Santiago: ECO, 1985); Schneider, *Shantytown Protest*; Antonia Garcés Sotomayor, "Los rostros de la protesta: Actores sociales y politicos de las jornadas de protesta contra la dictadura militar en Chile (1983–1986)" (undergraduate thesis, Universidad de Santiago de Chile, 2011).

17. Alfredo Riquelme Segovia, *Rojo atardecer: El comunismo chileno entre dictadura y democracia* (Santiago: DIBAM, 2009), 125; Álvarez, *Arriba los pobres*, 121.

18. Álvarez, *Arriba los pobres*, 131.

19. FLACSO/FERT, *AIR*, Apr. 1982.

20. FLACO/FERT, *AIR*, Apr. 1982; J.C., Feb. 2, 2004; Arrate and Rojas, *Memoria de la izquierda chilena*, 2:324; FLACSO/FERT, *El Rebelde*, no. 194 (Jan. 1982): 13; FLACSO/FERT, *El Rebelde*, no. 193 (Dec. 1982): 14.

21. CEDOC-CODEPU, "Marcha del Hambre en José María Caro" and "La marcha del 15 de diciembre," *CODEPU Boletín Mensual*, no. 17 (Dec. 1982); FLACO/FERT, *AIR*, Feb. 1983.

22. FLACSO/FERT, *AIR*, Feb. 1983.

23. Daniel Levine, "The Evolution of the Theory and Practice of Rights in Latin American Catholicism," in Wilde, *Religious Responses*, 28.

24. Levine, "Evolution of the Theory and Practice of Rights," 33; ARNAD/FOS, Boletín Juvenil Poblacional, *La Nuez*, Año 1, no. 2 (July 1983): 6.

25. CEDOC-ECO, *Horizonte*, no. 3 (Dec. 1981): 6.

26. CEDOC-ECO, *Horizonte*, no. 3 (Dec. 1981): 11.

27. Bruey, "Transnational Concepts, Local Contexts"; Wilde, "Institutional Church," 179.

28. M.T.D., Nov. 5, 2004. The protest Vía Crucis grew into a thousands-strong, citywide procession.

29. GI, Jornada La Legua, Nov. 25, 2000, PAMG.

30. ARNAD/FOS, Vicaría de Pastoral Obrera, *Dialogando* (June 1982), 1.

31. CEDOC-CODEPU, "1982: Tres versiones para un año crítico," *CODEPU Boletín Mensual*, no. 17 (Dec. 1982): 7.

32. ARNAD/FOS, *Páginas Sindicales*, Separata, Año 6, no. 55 (n.d.).

33. J.C., Feb. 2, 2004.

34. *Principios*, no. 27, Apr.–May–June 1983; GI, Red de Organizaciones Sociales de La Legua, May 24, 2005.

35. FAVS, IM-IC, May 1983, 13–14; *El Mercurio*, May 6, 1983.

36. de la Maza and Garcés, *La explosión de las mayorías*, 73–75; ARNAD/FOS, *Páginas Sindicales*, Separata, Año 6, no. 55 (n.d.).

37. ARNAD/FOS, Instructivo no. 2, in *Boletín Sindical*, "11 de mayo: Día de la Protesta Nacional," V Región, May 1983; Patricia Verdugo, "Protesta en vez de paro," *Hoy*, no. 303 (May 11–17, 1983): 7.

38. J.R., July 21, 2005.

39. J.C., Feb. 2, 2004.

40. A.S.M.J., Mar. 12, 2005.

41. M.G., Dec. 21, 2004.

42. M.T.D., Nov. 5, 2004.

43. J.M., Apr. 22, 2004.

44. "Una jornada larga y tensa," *Hoy*, no. 304 (May 18–24, 1983): 9.

45. M.G., Dec. 21, 2004.

46. Garcés Sotomayor, "Los rostros de la protesta," 99–100.

47. E.M., Nov. 11, 2002, PAMG.

48. *Principios*, no. 27 (Mar.–Apr.–May 1983).

49. GIG1, La Legua, n.d., PAMG.

50. *Principios*, no. 27 (Mar.–Apr.–May 1983).

51. E.M., Nov. 11, 2002, PAMG.

52. J.C., Feb. 2, 2004.

53. GI, 5a Sesión La Legua, Nov. 2, 2000, PAMG.

54. *Principios*, no. 27 (Mar.–Apr.–May 1983).

55. C.S., May 8, 2004.

56. L.E., Nov. 2004.

57. A.S.M.J., Mar. 12, 2005; A.D., May 31, 2005; M.T.D., Nov. 5, 2004.

58. "Una jornada larga y tensa," *Hoy*, no. 304 (May 18–24, 1983): 10.

59. Cabrera, "Historia y protagonismo," 162.

60. I.P./J.M., Nov. 26, 2004.

61. BSI, *Policarpo*, Año 2, no. 19 (May 1983).

62. M.T.D., Nov. 5, 2004.

63. J.C., Feb. 2, 2004.

64. Eric Hazan, *A History of the Barricade*, trans. David Fernbach (New York: Verso, 2015), ix.

65. J.S., Jan. 15, 2003, PAMG.

66. GIG1, La Legua, n.d., PAMG.

67. GI, Villa Francia, June 5, 2004.

68. M.T.D., Nov. 5, 2004.

69. GI, 4a Sesión La Legua, n.d., PAMG.

70. J.S., Jan. 15, 2003, PAMG.

71. Patricia Verdugo, "Después del cacerolazo," *Hoy*, no. 304 (May 18–24, 1983): 6; de la Maza and Garcés, *La explosión de las mayorías*, 29.

72. de la Maza and Garcés, *La explosión de las mayorías*, 29; "Una jornada larga y tensa," *Hoy*, no. 304 (May 18–24, 1983): 10; Jaime Ruiz-Tagle P., "Las protestas, la violencia y el retorno a la democracia" *Mensaje*, no. 333 (Oct. 1984): 457.

73. FAVS, IM-IC, V/1983, 15; BSI, *Policarpo*, Año 2, no. 20 (June 1983); *Solidaridad*, 2a Quincena, May 1983, 5–7; *Mensaje*, no. 320 (June 1983): 339; ARNAD/FOS, *Páginas Sindicales* 55 Separata, Año 6, "Experiencia de lucha: Primera Protesta Nacional," May 1983, 6.

74. GI, Santa Adriana, Nov. 21, 2004; GI, José María Caro, Nov. 27, 2004.

75. "Sector sur de Santiago en estado de alerta: Búsqueda de hampones y subversivos en tres poblaciones: Operación Peineta dejó 100 detenidos," *La Tercera*, May 15, 1983; "Amplio operativo policial," *El Mercurio*, May 15, 1983; ARNAD/FOS, *Páginas Sindicales* 56, Año 6 (June 1983): 4.

76. ARNAD/FOS, *Páginas Sindicales* 56, Año 6 (June 1983): 7.

77. Patricia Verdugo, "Depués del cacerolazo," *Hoy*, no. 304 (May 18–24, 1983): 6.

78. BCNSC, ADJ, Acta 14/83a, June 16, 1983, Sesión Legislativa, Secreta y Extraordinaria, 2.

79. BCNSC, ADJ, Acta 14/83a, June 16, 1983, Sesión Legislativa, Secreta y Extraordinaria, 8. At this point in the 1980s Carabineros and the CNI were the institutional face of repression. A state of siege also meant reactivating "wartime military tribunals" (*tribunales militares en tiempos de guerra*) under the military's purview.

80. Quoted in Patrick Guillaudat and Pierre Mouterde, *Los movimientos sociales en Chile: 1973–1993* (Santiago: LOM, 1998), 142.

81. Meller, *Unidad Popular and the Pinochet Dictatorship*, 88–89, 134; Jorge Leiva, economist for the Programa de Economía del Trabajo, in CEDOC-CODEPU, "1982: Tres versiones para un año crítico," *CODEPU Boletín Mensual*, no. 17 (Dec. 1982): 7; Meller et al., *Chile: Evolución macroeconómica*, 48; Rodríguez, *Por una ciudad democrática*, 57; María Elena Valenzuela, "The Evolving Roles of Women Under Military Rule," in Drake and Jaksić, *Struggle for Democracy*, 168; Felipe Larraín B., "The Economic Challenges of Democratic Development," in Drake and Jaksić, *Struggle for Democracy*, 284; Morley and McGillion, *Reagan and Pinochet*, 37.

82. BCNSC, ADJ, Acta 14/83a, June 16, 1983, Sesión Legislativa, Secreta y Extraordinaria, 4–5, 8, 14, 16, 21.

83. Benavides responded that "what's after that" is to create a new reserve, to which Merino replied, "with whom?" "So, it's complicated," concluded Benavides. BCNSC, ADJ, Acta 14/83a, June 16, 1983, Sesión Legislativa, Secreta y Extraordinaria, 9–10, 14.

84. BCNSC, ADJ, Acta 14/83a, June 16, 1983, Sesión Legislativa, Secreta y Extraordinaria, 12.

85. BCNSC, ADJ, Acta 14/83a, June 16, 1983, Sesión Legislativa, Secreta y Extraordinaria, 13.

86. A handful of dissenters broke from the party's position, including Bernardo Leighton Guzmán, who, with his wife, Ana María Fresno Ovalle, survived a subsequent regime-sponsored assassination attempt in Italy in 1975.

87. BCNSC, ADJ, Acta 19, Oct. 10, 1973, Sesión Secreta, 2. This meeting entered the record as minutes taken by the junta's secretary, which was the practice early in the

junta's tenure. Later minutes consist of transcribed audio recordings. The quotes in this segment are recorded as paraphrased in the meeting minutes.

88. BCNSC, ADJ, Acta 14/83a, June 16, 1983, Sesión Legislativa, Secreta y Extraordinaria, 13–14.

89. de la Maza and Garcés, *La explosión de las mayorías*, 39.

90. Garcés Sotomayor, "Los rostros de la protesta," 24–25, 44.

91. de la Maza and Garcés, *La explosión de las mayorías*, 43.

92. de la Maza and Garces, *La explosión de las mayorías*, 54.

93. BCNSC, ADJ, Acta 9/84e, June 16, 1984, Sesión Legislativa Extraordinaria, 16.

94. Pinochet wanted to declare a state of siege to stop the opposition media from ridiculing him. Members of the junta discouraged him from this idea, arguing that imposing a state of siege for that reason would damage the regime's international image. They spent much of the discussion seeking other justifications for authorizing the measure. BCNSC, ADJ, Acta 22/84e, Aug. 30, 1984, Sesión Legislativa Extraordinaria, 7, 12–13, 21.

95. Under Juan Francisco Fresno, the archbishop of Santiago, and with the Vatican's support, the institutional Church shifted from its previous position of dissent and denunciation into a "mediating role" between the centrist opposition and the regime. Wilde, "Institutional Church," 175.

96. "Acuerdo Nacional," *Cauce* 38, Año 2 (Sep. 3–9, 1985): 4; Garcés Sotomayor, "Los rostros de la protesta," 55. The Acuerdo did not include the "officialist" political parties—the Unión Democrática Independiente (UDI, Independent Democratic Union) and Avanzada Nacional—or the leftist MDP.

97. "Acuerdo Nacional," *Cauce* 38, Año 2 (Sep. 3–9, 1985): 4.

98. "'Estamos aburridos de que nos maten,'" *Fortín Mapocho*, Oct. 7, 1985, 16.

99. Patricia Richards, *Pobladoras, Indígenas, and the State: Conflicts Over Women's Rights in Chile* (New Brunswick, NJ: Rutgers University Press, 2004), 85.

100. CEDOC-ECO, "Pobladores y transición: Los caminos de la democratización local," in ECO, *La democratización en la base: Movimiento poblacional y gobierno local*, Taller de Análisis Movimientos Sociales y Coyuntura, no. 4 (July 1989): 15.

101. CEDOC-ECO, "De la protesta al plebiscito: el camino hacia una nueva coyuntura," in ECO, *Los movimientos sociales frente al plebiscito*," Taller de Análisis Movimientos Sociales y Coyuntura, no. 2 (Aug. 1988): 3–4.

102. Figueroa Clark, "Forgotten Transition"; Morley and McGillion, *Reagan and Pinochet*.

103. GI, Plenario La Legua, Nov. 25, 2000, PAMG.

104. For example, Iván Ortiz C., "Juventud popular urbana," *Mensaje*, no. 327 (Mar.–Apr. 1984): 106–8; "Más a fondo," *Solidaridad*, 2a Quincena, May 1983, 17; "Entre la esquina y la parroquia," *Solidaridad*, 2a Quincena, July 1982, 19; "Conociéndolos a fondo," *Solidaridad*, 2a Quincena, Apr. 1983, 17. ECO-Educación y Comunicaciones, the Centro de Investigación y Formación de la Zona Sur de Santiago (DECU), and the Equipo Juvenil SUR Profesionales did surveys and studies of poblador youth during the 1980s.

105. CEDOC-ECO, Irene Agurto, "Juventud popular: ¿Amenaza o promesa?" *Educación y Solidaridad*, no. 11 (Aug. 1985): 7n2.

106. CEDOC-ECO, Agurto, "Juventud popular," 6, 10–11; Ortiz, "Juventud popular urbana," 106.

107. CEDOC-ECO, Agurto, "Juventud popular," 5–6.

108. Garcés Sotomayor, "Los rostros de la protesta," 93–94, 98.

109. I borrow "freedom dreams" from Kelley's *Freedom Dreams*.

110. David Scott, *Omens of Adversity: Tragedy, Time, Memory, Justice* (Durham, NC: Duke University Press, 2014), 121. Scott borrows the term "postmemories" from Marianne Hirsch, *Family Frames: Photography, Narrative, and Postmemory* (Cambridge, MA: Harvard University Press, 1997).

111. GI, Jornada La Legua, Nov. 25, 2000, PAMG.

112. A.D., May 3, 2005.

113. GI, Primera Sesión La Legua, Aug. 5, 2000, PAMG.

114. GI, Jornada La Legua, Nov. 25, 2000, PAMG.

115. Daniel Levine, *Popular Voices in Latin American Catholicism* (Princeton, NJ: Princeton University Press, 1992), quoted in Drogus and Stewart-Gambino, *Activist Faith*, 38.

116. M.T.D., Nov. 5, 2004.

117. M.V./L.T., Apr. 27, 2004.

118. Alison J. Bruey, "Protesta Poblacional: Non-Violent Resistance and All Forms of Struggle at the Grassroots, Chile 1978–1986," International Congress of the Latin American Studies Association, San Francisco, California, May 2012. Marlene Martínez Ángel found that MIR militants interpreted joining the party as an extension of previous social and political values and practices rather than a break from them. Marlene Martínez Ángel, "La experiencia política de los militantes del MIR (1973–1989)," *Proposiciones* 36 (2007): 131.

119. J.R., June 21, 2005.

120. J.R., Nov. 18, 2000, PAMG.

121. M.V./L.T., Apr. 27, 2004.

122. A.S.M.J., Mar. 12, 2005.

123. L.D., Nov. 11, 2002, PAMG.

124. C.D./C.S.D., June 18, 2004.

125. J.M., Apr. 22, 2004.

126. Garcés Sotomayor, "Los rostros de la protesta,"108.

127. V.H., Aug. 7, 2005.

128. V.H., Aug. 7, 2005.

129. J.R., Nov. 18, 2000, PAMG.

130. V.H., Aug. 7, 2005; J.M., Apr. 22, 2004; Patricia Politzer, *La ira de Pedro y los otros* (Santiago: Planeta, 1988), 67–79, 81–85.

131. Wilde, "Institutional Church," 177.

132. A.S.M.J., Mar. 12, 2005.

133. A.D., May 31, 2005.

134. Cabrera, "Historia y protagonismo," 162–66.

135. L.E., Nov. 2004.

136. GI, Jornada La Legua, Nov. 25, 2000, PAMG.

137. GIG1, La Legua, Nov. 25, 2000, PAMG; Drogus and Stewart-Gambino, *Activist Faith*, 87.

138. Wilde, "Institutional Church," 175; Drogus and Stewart-Gambino, *Activist Faith*, 85–86; de la Maza and Garcés, *La explosión de las mayorías*, 110–12.

139. Salazar and Pinto, *Historia contemporánea de Chile II*, 126. For a more extensive study, see Gabriel Salazar, *La violencia política popular en las "Grandes Alamedas": La violencia en Chile 1947–1987 (Una perspectiva histórico popular)*, 2nd ed. (Santiago: LOM, 2006).

140. Garcés Sotomayor points out that workers and pobladores were relatively tolerant of political violence as a form of struggle against the dictatorship, which generated differences with party elites. It also generated distance from socioeconomic sectors more closely affiliated with the Center and the Right, scaring the middle class especially. Garcés Sotomayor, "Los rostros de la protesta," 70, 100.

141. V.H., Aug. 7, 2005.

142. J., Oct. 26, 2006.

143. FLACSO/FERT, *AIR*, no. 34 (Feb. 1982).

144. V.H., Aug. 7, 2005.

145. CEDOC-CODEPU, *Intransigente: Boletín CODEPU Regional*, [post-Mar. 29, 1985]; A.S.M.J., Mar. 12, 2005; Figueroa Clark, "Forgotten History," 20–21.

146. Salazar and Pinto, *Historia contemporánea de Chile II*, 126–27.

147. Francisco Estévez, "Juventud poblacional: Explicación y juicio sobre la violencia," in Agurto et al., *Juventud chilena*, 133–35.

148. See Paley's *Marketing Democracy* for a study of grassroots demobilization and Drogus and Stewart-Gambino, *Activist Faith*, on the Church post-1989.

149. Pablo Vergara Toledo and Aracely Romo died in 1988. Their bodies appeared on Cerro Ñielol in Temuco. The official story is that a bomb they were allegedly planting malfunctioned and killed them. The inconsistencies in the official story and the forensic record suggest that they were captured and assassinated. See CODEPU, "Presentación de CODEPU acerca de casos muertos por explosión," http://www.memo riaviva.com/Ejecutados/presentacion_codepu_explosionados.htm.

150. M.T.D., Nov. 5, 2004.

151. I.P./J.M., Nov. 26, 2004.

152. A.S.M.J., Mar. 12, 2005.

153. A.D., May 31, 2005.

154. The UDI, a party created in 1983 as a political vehicle for Pinochetistas and ultraconservative Catholics (e.g., integralists, Legionaries of Christ, Opus Dei), funneled militants into poblaciones during the 1980s via state structures—municipal governments, neighborhood councils, and the like—to build political clientele among the urban poor. This strategy paid off electorally during the 1990s, but during the 1980s it appears to have had little influence on anti-regime, pro-democracy pobladores. Verónica

Valdivia et al., *Su revolución contra nuestra revolución*, vol. 2, *La pugna marxista-gremialista en los ochenta* (Santiago: LOM, 2008), chaps. 3 and 4.

155. Juan Bustos Troncoso, *Cambios en la significación de la democracia en Chile 1977–1991: Del "imaginario democrático" a la "democracia de los acuerdos"* (Concepción: Escaparate, 2014), 103–5; Paley, *Marketing Democracy.*

156. Quoted in Garcés, *El despertar de la sociedad,* 23.

157. Ricardo Ffrench-Davis, *Entre el neoliberalismo y el crecimiento con equidad: Tres décadas de política económica en Chile,* 2nd ed. (Santiago: Dolmen, 2001), 258.

158. A.S.M.J., Mar. 12, 2005

159. Garcés, *El despertar de la sociedad,* 23.

Epilogue

1. *Diario U de Chile,* "Abogado Nelson Caucoto: 'Caso del niños del SENAME constituye terrorismo de Estado,'" Oct. 21, 2016, http://radio.uchile.cl/2016/10/21/abogado-nelson-caucoto-caso-de-ninos-del-sename-constituye-terrorismo-de-estado/.

2. The INDH's board of directors includes designees appointed by the president of the Republic, the senate, the chamber of deputies, the deans of the law schools of national universities, and human rights organizations. See http://www.indh.cl/resena-institucional.

3. Paulo Álvarez Bravo, "Pensando en los 15 años de la Intervención estatal en La Legua," in *Memoria Anual 2015,* by Comité de Defensa y Promoción de Derechos Humanos de La Legua (Santiago, 2016), 19–22, https://ddhhlalegua.files.wordpress.com/2013/05/memoria-annual-2015.pdf; INDH, "Estudio de Caso," 38, 42–43.

4. INDH, "Estudio de Caso," 3.

5. Alston, quoted in INDH, "Estudio de Caso," 3.

6. INDH, "Estudio de Caso," 45, 52–64.

7. Moyn, *Last Utopia,* 4.

8. Hunt, *Inventing Human Rights.*

9. Moyn, *Last Utopia,* 121.

10. Moyn, *Last Utopia,* 12.

11. With the exception of Álvarez's *Desde las sombras* and *Arriba los pobres,* the historiography of the Left tends to treat the coup as a near-total rupture and turns its focus to repression, reorientation of political strategy, and political marginalization. The literature is strongly marked by the defeats of the 1970s, 1980s, and 1990s, and histories of the Left during this period tend to concern themselves, explicitly or implicitly, with the defeats and their causes.

12. M.T.D., Nov. 5, 2004.

13. By "mass" I mean protests or concentrations of ten thousand people or more, or that constituted a national incident of note that appeared in the media or was mentioned in the junta's meetings.

14. INDH, "Estudio de Caso," 38.

Bibliography

Archives and Libraries

Archivo Nacional de la Administración (Archivo Siglo XX)
Archivo Nacional Histórico (Miraflores)
Biblioteca de la Pontificia Universidad Católica-Lo Contador
Biblioteca de la Universidad Alberto Hurtado
Biblioteca del Congreso Nacional-Sede Compañía
Biblioteca del Ministerio de Vivienda y Urbanismo
Biblioteca José Martí
Biblioteca Luis Montt
Biblioteca Nacional de Chile
Biblioteca San Ignacio
Centro de Documentación CODEPU
Centro de Documentación ECO
Centro de Documentación Isis Internacional
Centro de Documentación Museo de la Memoria y los Derechos Humanos
Centro de Estudios Miguel Enríquez-Archivo Chile (digital)
Facultad Latinoamericana de Ciencias Sociales-Chile
Fundación Documentación y Archivo de la Vicaría de la Solidaridad
Latin American and Caribbean Collection, University of Florida
Memorial Library, University of Wisconsin–Madison
Mudd Library, Yale University
Museo Histórico Nacional
National Security Archive, George Washington University (digital)
Personal Archive Alison J. Bruey (PAAJB)
Personal Archive Mario Garcés (PAMG)
Sterling Memorial Library, Yale University
Thomas G. Carpenter Library, University of North Florida
US Library of Congress

Newspapers, Periodicals, Pamphlets, Newsletters

Agencia Informativa de la Resistencia
Análisis
APSI
Apuntes para el Diálogo
Araucaria de Chile (Madrid)
Barricada
Boletín Informativo Chile Democrático-Roma
Boletín Sindical
Boletín Zona Oeste
Boletín Zona Sur
Cal y Canto
Cauce
CODEPU Boletín Mensual
Cristo Dialogante
Cuadernos de Política Mundial
Dialogando
Diario Oficial
Diario U de Chile
Documento
El Ciudadano
El Mercurio
El Mostrador
El País (Madrid)
El Rebelde
El Rebelde en la Clandestinidad
El Siglo
Ercilla
EURE
Fe y Solidaridad
Fortín Mapocho
Hechos Urbanos
Horizonte
Hoy
Intransigente: Boletín CODEPU Regional
La Cuarta
La Nuez
La Prensa
La Tercera (*de la Hora*)
Mapuexpress
Mensaje
New York Times

No Podemos Callar
Páginas Sindicales
Pastoral Popular
Policarpo
Principios
Pueblo Cristiano
Punto Final
¿Qué Pasa?
Revista Paula
Solidaridad
The Clinic

Television Programs, Films, and Audio Recordings

Calle Santa Fe, Dir. Carmen Castillo.
Chela, Dir. Lars Palmgren, Göran Gester, Lars Bildt.
Chile: Las imágenes prohibidas, Chilevisión, 2013.
"Cuando Chile Cambió de Golpe," *Informe Especial*, TVN, 2003.
El Botón de Nácar, Dir. Patricio Guzmán.
El Edificio de los Chilenos, Dir. Macarena Aguiló.
Estadio Nacional, Dir. Carmen Luz Parot.
"La Antesala del 11 de Septiembre de 1973," *Contacto*, Canal 13, 2003.
"La Legua: El Ghetto de la Muerte," Chilevisión, July 18, 2007.
La Batalla de Chile, Dir. Patricio Guzmán.
La Memoria Obstinada, Dir. Patricio Guzmán.
La Resistencia del Cordón Cerrillos, Dir. Pepe Burgos.
Los 80, Canal 13 (2008–14).
Los Archivos del Cardenal, TVN (2011–14).
Machuca, Dir. Andrés Wood.
Más Fuerte que la Metralla, Dir. Pepe Burgos.
Nostalgia de la Luz, Dir. Patricio Guzmán.
Salvador Allende, Dir. Patricio Guzmán.
Teleanálisis, 1984–89.
24 Horas, TVN, 2003–6.
Víctor Jara, *La Población*, Santiago, DICAP, 1972. Audio recording.

Government, Church, and Human Rights Organization Documents

Actas de las Sesiones de la Honorable Junta de Gobierno (1973–90).
Actas del Consejo de Estado (1976–88).
Acuerdos de la H. Junta de Gobierno (1981–89).
Colección Cien Entrevistas, Museo de la Memoria y los Derechos Humanos.
Comisión Chilena de Derechos Humanos, Informes and Informes Anuales.

Comisión Nacional de Verdad y Reconciliación, *Informe de la Comisión Nacional de Verdad y Reconciliación. Vols. I–III.* (Santiago: La Corporación, 1996).

Comisión Nacional sobre Prisión Política y Tortura, *Informe de la Comisión Nacional sobre Prisión Política y Tortura* (Santiago: Gobierno de Chile, Ministerio del Interior, 2005).

Comité de Defensa y Promoción de Derechos Humanos de La Legua, *Memoria Anual 2015* (Santiago, 2016).

Corporación Nacional de Reparación y Reconciliación, *Informe sobre calificación de víctimas de violaciones de derechos humanos y de violencia política* (Santiago: Ministerio del Interior, 1996).

Fundación Protección a la Infancia Dañada por los Estados de Emergencia (P.I.D.E.E.): Archivo.

INDH. "Estudio de caso: Violencias y derechos humanos en La Legua," Santiago, 2015.

INE, *Vivienda, hogar y familia: XV Censo Nacional de Población y IV de Vivienda-Chile*, Región Metropolitana de Santiago (April 4, 1982).

Intendencia de Santiago, *Decretos* and *Oficios* (1973–83).

"Los Archivos Secretos de la Dictadura," digital collection included with Dorat Guerra, Carlos and Mauricio Weibel Barahona. *Asociación ilícita. Los archivos secretos de la dictadura.* Santiago: Ceibo, 2012.

Medellín Documents, Latin American Bishops, Medellín, Colombia.

Memoria Viva, http://www.memoriaviva.com/.

Mensajes Presidenciales (1974–84).

MINVU *Memorias* (1974–84).

US Central Intelligence Agency (1973–90).

US Department of State (1973–90).

US Senate's Staff Report of the Select Committee to Study Governmental Operations with respect to Intelligence Services. "Covert Action in Chile, 1963–1973." Washington, DC: Government Printing Office, 1975.

Vicaría de la Solidaridad, Caja Campesinos y Pobladores (1979–85).

Vicaría de la Solidaridad, Informe Mensual-Informe Confidencial (1976–83).

General Bibliography

Adams, Jacqueline. *Art against Dictatorship: Making and Exporting Arpilleras under Pinochet.* Austin: University of Texas Press, 2013.

Acevedo Arriaza, Nicolás. "¡¡Fuera Pinochet, Chile Popular!! El mestizaje político del MAPU-Lautaro en las protestas populares (1978–1985)." Undergraduate thesis, Universidad ARCIS, 2006.

Agosín, Marjorie. *Tapestries of Hope, Threads of Love: The Arpillera Movement in Chile.* 2nd ed. Lanham, MD: Rowman and Littlefield, 2007.

Agurto, Irene, Manuel Canales, and Gonzalo de la Maza, eds. *Juventud chilena: Razones y subversiones.* Santiago: ECO/FOLICO/SEPADE, 1985.

Ahumada, Mauricio, and Pedro Naranjo. *Miguel Enríquez y el proyecto revolucionario en Chile: Discursos y documentos del Movimiento de Izquierda Revolucionaria, MIR.* Santiago: LOM, 2004.

Albuquerque, Mario, Mario Garcés, Pedro Milos, Víctor Hugo Miranda, and Marcela Segall. *Reconstrucción del movimiento popular bajo dictadura militar, 1973–1983*. Colección Cuadernos de Historia Popular 11, Serie Historia del Movimiento Obrero, vol. IV. Santiago: ECO, CETRA/CEAL, 1990.

Aldunate Lyon, José, SJ. *Un peregrino cuenta su historia*. Santiago: Ediciones Ignacianas, [2002?].

———. "El signo del martirio." In Aldunate Lyon et al., *Crónicas*, 227–35.

———. "EMO: Presencia y acción en 25 años." In Aldunate Lyon et al., *Crónicas*, 93–99.

———. "La experiencia Calama." In Aldunate Lyon et al., *Crónicas*, 89–92.

Aldunate Lyon, José, Roberto Bolton García, Juana Ramírez Gonveya, Humberto Guzmán Rubio, Mariano Puga Concha, Oscar Jiménez Lazo, Margarita Westwood Gil, and Rosa Parissi Morales. *Crónicas de una Iglesia liberadora*. Santiago: LOM, 2000.

Álvarez, Jaime (Coño). "Historia de la población Nueva La Legua." In ECO, *La Población La Legua*, 50–58.

Álvarez, Rolando. *Arriba los pobres del mundo: Cultura e identidad política del Partido Comunista de Chile entre democracia y dictadura 1965–1990*. Santiago: LOM, 2011.

———. *Desde las sombras: Una historia de la clandestinidad comunista*. Santiago: LOM, 2003.

Alvarez, Sonia E., Evelina Dagnino, and Arturo Escobar. "Introduction: The Cultural and the Political in Latin American Social Movements." In *Cultures of Politics, Politics of Cultures: Re-Visioning Latin American Social Movements*, edited by Sonia Alvarez, Evelina Dagnino, and Arturo Escobar, 1–29. Boulder, CO: Westview Press, 1998.

Arcos Vera, Humberto. *Autobiografía de un viejo comunista chileno: Una historia "no oficial" pero verdadera*. Santiago: LOM, 2013.

Ariztía, Fernando. "El Comité de Cooperación para la Paz en Chile." In Ariztía et al., *Seminario Iglesia y Derechos Humanos*, 11–18.

Ariztía, Fernando, Cristián Precht, Enrique Palet, José Zalaquett, Mariá Luisa Sepúlveda, Pedro Ossandón, Rodrigo Tupper, Claudio Orrego, and Elizabeth Lira. *Seminario Iglesia y Derechos Humanos en Chile*. Santiago: Arzobispado de Santiago/Fundación de Documentación y Archivo de la Vicaría de la Solidaridad, 2002.

Arrate, Jorge, and Eduardo Rojas. *Memoria de la izquierda chilena*. Vol. 1, *1850–1970*. Santiago: Javier Vergara Editor, 2003.

———. *Memoria de la izquierda chilena*. Vol. 2, *1970–2000*. Santiago: Javier Vergara Editor, 2003.

Atencio, Rebecca J. *Memory's Turn: Reckoning with Dictatorship in Brazil*. Madison: University of Wisconsin Press, 2014.

Ávalos, Juan. "Odas al pueblo humillado." In Grupo Amistad por un Mundo Mejor, *Poesía de Villa Francia*, 29–34.

Bastías Saavedra, Manuel. *Sociedad civil en dictadura: Relaciones transnacionales, organizaciones y socialización política en Chile*. Santiago: Ediciones Universidad Alberto Hurtado, 2013.

Bevernage, Berber, and Koen Aerts. "Haunting Pasts: Time and Historicity as Constructed by the Argentine *Madres de Plaza de Mayo* and Radical Flemish Nationalists." *Social History* 34, no. 4 (2009): 391–408.

Boeninger, Edgardo. *Democracia en Chile: Lecciones para la gobernabilidad.* Santiago: Andrés Bello, 1997.

Bolton, Roberto. *Testigo soy: Memorias del Rvdo. Roberto Bolton García.* Santiago: Impresor IGD, 2010.

Bolton García, Roberto. "El asilo contra la represión." In Aldunate Lyon et al., *Crónicas,* 151–54.

Bruey, Alison J. "Limitless Land and the Redefinition of Rights: Popular Mobilisation and the Limits of Neoliberalism in Chile, 1973–1985." *JLAS* 44, no. 3 (2012): 523–52.

———. "Neoliberalism and Repression in *Poblaciones* of Santiago de Chile." *Stockholm Review of Latin American Studies,* no. 5 (September 2009): 17–27.

———. "Transnational Concepts, Local Contexts: Solidarity at the Grassroots in Pinochet's Chile." In Stites Mor, *Human Rights and Transnational Solidarity,* 120–42.

Bustos Troncoso, Juan. *Cambios en la significación de la democracia en Chile 1977–1991: Del "imaginario democrático" a la "democracia de los acuerdos."* Concepción: Escaparate, 2014.

Cabrera Molina, Eugenio. "Historia y protagonismo popular en Villa Francia." Undergraduate thesis, Universidad ARCIS, 2007.

Castells, Manuel. "Movimiento de pobladores y lucha de clases en Chile." In de Mattos et al., *Huellas,* 299–340.

Castillo, Fernando. "Comunidades Cristianas Populares: La iglesia que nace desde los pobres." In *La Iglesia de los pobres en América Latina: Antología,* by Fernando Castillo, Joaquín Silva, Juan Sepúlveda, and Claudio Ramsy, 81–105. Santiago: Programa Ecuménico de Estudios del Cristianismo, ECO-SEPADE, 1983.

Castillo Soto, Sandra. *Cordones Industriales: nuevas formas de sociabilidad obrera y organización política popular (Chile, 1970–1973).* Concepción: Escaparate, 2009.

Cavallo, Ascanio. *Memorias Cardinal Raúl Silva Henríquez.* Vol. 2. Santiago: Ediciones Copygraph, 1991.

Cavallo, Ascanio, Manuel Salazar, and Oscar Sepúlveda. *La historia oculta del régimen militar: Memoria de una época 1973–1988.* Santiago: Grijalbo Mondadori, 1997.

Chateau, Jorge, Bernarda Gallardo, Eduardo Morales, Carlos Piña, Hernán Pozo, Sergio Rojas, Daniela Sánchez, and Teresa Valdés. *Espacio y poder: Los pobladores.* Santiago: FLACSO, 1987.

Chateau, Jorge, and Sergio Rojas. "Antecedentes electorales. Vols. 1–2. Información sobre población, electores y resultados del plebiscito de 1988." Documento de Trabajo 428, Programa FLACSO-Chile, September 1989.

Churchryk, Patricia M. "From Dictatorship to Democracy: The Women's Movement in Chile." In *The Women's Movement in Latin America: Participation and Democracy,* edited by Jane S. Jaquette, 65–107. 2nd ed. Boulder: Westview Press, 1994.

Constable, Pamela and Arturo Valenzuela. *A Nation of Enemies: Chile under Pinochet.* New York: W.W. Norton, 1991.

Contreras, Dante. "Poverty, Equality and Welfare in a Rapid-Growth Economy: The Chilean Experience." 2020 Focus Brief series. Washington, DC: International Food Policy Research Institute, 2007.

Corradi, Juan E., P. W. Fagan, and M. A. Garretón, eds. *Fear at the Edge: State Terror and Resistance in Latin America*. Berkeley: University of California Press, 1992.

Correa, Sofia, Consuelo Figueroa Garavagno, Alfredo Jocelyn-Holt Letelier, Claudio Rolle, and Manuel Vicuña Urrutia. *Documentos del Siglo XX chileno*. Santiago: Editorial Sudamericana, 2001.

Corvalán, Luis. *De lo vivido y lo peleado: Memorias*. Santiago: LOM, 1997.

Cristianos por el Socialismo. *El pueblo camina . . . ¿Y los cristianos?* Santiago: Secretariado de Cristianos por el Socialismo, [1972].

Cruz, María Angélica. *Iglesia, represión y memoria: El caso chileno*. Madrid: Siglo XXI Editores, 2004.

de Certeau, Michel. *The Practice of Everyday Life*. Berkeley: University of California Press, 1984.

de Mattos, Carlos, Oscar Figueroa, Pedro Bannen, and Diego Campos, eds. *Huellas de una metamorfosis metropolitana: Santiago en EURE 1970/2000*. Santiago: Instituto de Estudios Urbanos y Territoriales, Pontificia Universidad Católica de Chile, 2006.

de la Maza, Gonzalo, and Mario Garcés. *La explosión de las mayorías: Protesta Nacional 1983–1984*. Santiago: ECO, 1985.

de Ramón, Armando. *Santiago de Chile: Historia de una socieded urbana (1541–1991)*. Santiago: Catalonia, 2007.

Drake, Paul W., and Iván Jaksić, eds. *The Struggle for Democracy in Chile, 1982–1990*. Lincoln: University of Nebraska Press, 1991.

Drogus, Carol Ann, and Hannah Stewart-Gambino. *Activist Faith: Grassroots Women in Democratic Brazil and Chile*. University Park: Penn State University Press, 2005.

Dussel, Enrique. "From Fraternity to Solidarity: Toward a Politics of Liberation." Translated by Michael Barber and Judd Smith Wright. *Journal of Social Philosophy* 38, no. 1 (2007): 73–92.

Echeverría Yáñez, Mónica. *Antihistoria de un luchador (Clotario Blest 1823–1990)*. Santiago: LOM, 2013.

ECO, ed. *ECO en el horizonte latinoamericano (I): La educación popular bajo la dictadura*. Colección 30 Años no. 2. Santiago: ECO, 2012.

———. *La Población La Legua: Desde la historia oral hacia la historia local*. Colección 30 Años no. 5. Santiago: ECO, 2012.

ECO, and Red de Organizaciones Sociales de La Legua. *Memorias de la dictadura en La Legua: Relatos, historias, cuentos, poesía y canciones de su gente*. Santiago: ECO, 2001.

Elsey, Brenda. *Citizens and Sportsmen: Fútbol and Politics in Twentieth-Century Chile*. Austin: University of Texas Press, 2011.

Equipo de Estudios Poblacionales CIDU. "Reivindicación urbana y lucha política: Los campamentos de pobladores en Santiago de Chile." In de Mattos et al., *Huellas*, 341–73.

Errázuriz, Luis Hernán. "Dictadura militar en Chile: Antecedentes del golpe estético-cultural." *LARR* 44, no. 2 (2009): 136–57.

Escobar, Arturo. *Territories of Difference: Place, Movement, Life, Redes.* Durham, NC: Duke University Press, 2008.

Espinoza, Vicente. *Para una historia de los pobres de la ciudad.* Santiago: SUR, 1988.

Estévez, Francisco. "Juventud poblacional: explicación y juicio sobre la violencia." In Agurto, *Juventud chilena,* 128–35.

Fernández, David. *La "Iglesia" que resistió a Pinochet.* Madrid: IEPALA, 1996.

Ffrench-Davis, Ricardo. *Entre el neoliberalismo y el crecimiento con equidad: Tres décadas de política económica en Chile.* 2nd ed. Santiago: Dolmen, 2001.

Figueroa Clark, Victor. "The Forgotten History of the Chilean Transition: Armed Resistance against Pinochet and US Policy towards Chile in the 1980s." *JLAS* 47, no. 3 (2015): 491–520.

Figueroa Sandoval, Barbara, Monseñor Alfonso Baeza, and Reinaldo Sapag Chain. *El Cardenal Raúl Silva Henríquez y los Trabajadores.* Santiago: Ediciones Copygraph, 2013.

Fischer, Brodwyn. *A Poverty of Rights: Citizenship and Inequality in Twentieth-Century Rio de Janeiro.* Stanford, CA: Stanford University Press, 2008.

Fleet, Michael. "Christian Communities in Chile and Peru." Working Paper 183, University of Notre Dame Kellogg Institute, November 1992.

Franco, Jean. *The Decline and Fall of the Lettered City: Latin America in the Cold War.* Cambridge, MA: Harvard University Press, 2002.

Frazier, Lessie Jo. *Salt in the Sand: Memory, Violence, and the Nation-State in Chile, 1890 to the Present.* Durham, NC: Duke University Press, 2007.

Frenz, Helmut. *Mi vida chilena: Solidaridad con los oprimidos.* Translated by Sonia Plaut. Santiago: LOM, 2006.

Fuerzas Armadas y Carabineros: Septiembre de 1973: Los cien combates de una batalla. Santiago: Editorial Gabriela Mistral, [n.d.].

Garcés, Mario. *El despertar de la sociedad: Los movimientos sociales en América Latina y Chile.* Santiago: LOM, 2012.

———. "Introduction." In ECO and Red de Organizaciones Sociales de La Legua, *Memorias de la dictadura en La Legua,* 4–7.

———. "Los pobladores durante la Unidad Popular: Mobilizaciones, oportunidades políticas y la organización de las nuevas poblaciones." *Tiempo Histórico* 3 (segundo semestre 2011), 37–53.

———. *Recreando el pasado: Guía metodológica para la memoria y la historia local.* Santiago: ECO, 2002.

———. *Tomando su sitio: El movimiento de pobladores de Santiago, 1957–1970.* Santiago: LOM, 2002.

Garcés, Mario, and Sebastián Leiva. *El golpe en La Legua: Caminos de la historia y la memoria.* Santiago: LOM, 2005.

Garcés, Mario, and Nancy Nicholls. *Para una historia de los DD.HH. en Chile: Historia institucional de la Fundación de Ayuda Social de las Iglesias Cristianas FASIC 1975–1991.* Santiago: LOM, 2005.

Garcés Sotomayor, Antonia. "Los rostros de la protesta: Actores sociales y políticos de las jornadas de protesta contra la dictadura militar en Chile (1983–1986)." Undergraduate thesis, Universidad de Santiago de Chile, 2011.

Garretón Merino, Manuel Antonio, Roberto Garretón Merino, and Carmen Garretón Merino. *Por la fuerza sin la razón: Análisis y textos de los bandos de la dictadura militar*. Santiago: LOM, 1998.

Gaudichaud, Franck. *Poder popular y cordones industriales: Testimonios sobre el movimiento popular urbano, 1970–1973*. Santiago: LOM, 2004.

Gaviola, Edda, Eliana Largo, and Sandra Palestro. *Una historia necesaria: Mujeres en Chile, 1973–1990*. Santiago: ASDI, 1994.

Grandin, Greg. "Human Rights and Empire's Embrace: A Latin American Counterpoint." In Wasserstrom, *Human Rights and Revolutions*, 191–212.

———. *The Last Colonial Massacre: Latin America in the Cold War*. Chicago: University of Chicago Press, 2011.

Grandin, Greg, and Gilbert M. Joseph, eds. *A Century of Revolution: Insurgent and Counterinsurgent Violence during Latin America's Long Cold War*. Durham, NC: Duke University Press, 2010.

Green, James N. *We Cannot Remain Silent: Opposition to the Brazilian Military Dictatorship in the United States*. Durham, NC: Duke University Press, 2010.

Grez Toso, Sergio. *Los anarquistas y el movimiento obrero: La alborada de "la Idea" en Chile, 1893–1915*. Santiago: LOM, 2007.

Grupo Amistad por un Mundo Mejor, ed. *Poesía de Villa Francia: Andarás en el bosque de los aves que somos*. Santiago: Grupo Amistad por un Mundo Mejor, 2008.

Grupo de Cristianos por el Socialismo. "Génesis y Constitución de los CPS." In Aldunate Lyon et al., *Crónicas*, 53–55.

Grupo de Trabajo La Victoria. *La Victoria: Rescatando su Historia*. Santiago: ARCIS, 2007.

Guillaudat, Patrick, and Pierre Mouterde. *Los movimientos sociales en Chile: 1973–1993*. Santiago: LOM, 1998.

Gutiérrez, Gustavo. "Notes for a Theology of Liberation (1970)." In *Liberation Theology at the Crossroads: Democracy or Revolution?*, edited by Paul E. Sigmund, 199–213. New York: Oxford University Press, 1992.

———. "Theology of Liberation." In *Gustavo Gutiérrez: Essential Writings*, edited by James B. Nickoloff, 28–29. New York: Orbis, 2000.

———. "Understanding the God of Life." In Nickoloff, *Gustavo Gutiérrez*, 60–64.

Gutiérrez González, Eduardo. *Ciudades en las sombras (Una historia no oficial del Partido Socialista de Chile)*. Santiago: [n.p.], 2003.

Han, Clara. *Life in Debt: Times of Care and Violence in Neoliberal Chile*. Berkeley: University of California Press, 2012.

Hardy, Clarisa, and Victoria Legassa. *La ciudad escindida (Los problemas nacionales y la Región Metropolitana)*. Santiago: PET, 1989.

Harvey, David. *A Brief History of Neoliberalism*. New York: Oxford University Press, 2005.

Hazan, Eric. *A History of the Barricade*. Translated by David Fernbach. New York: Verso, 2015.

Hidalgo Dattwyler, Rodrigo. *La vivienda social en Chile y la construcción del espacio urbano en el Santiago del siglo XX*. Santiago: DIBAM, 2005.

Hirsch, Herbert. *Genocide and the Politics of Memory: Studying Death to Preserve Life*. Chapel Hill: University of North Carolina Press, 1995.

Hite, Katherine. *When the Romance Ended: Leaders of the Chilean Left, 1968–1998*. New York: Columbia University Press, 2000.

Holston, James. *Insurgent Citizenship: Disjunctions of Democracy and Modernity in Brazil*. Princeton, NJ: Princeton University Press, 2008.

Hoyl, Ana María. *Por la vida*. Santiago: CESOC, 2003.

Huneeus, Carlos. *Chile, un país dividido: La actualidad del pasado*. Santiago: Catalonia, 2003.

———. *El régimen de Pinochet*. 2nd ed. Santiago: Editorial Sudamericana, 2002.

Hunt, Lynn. *Inventing Human Rights: A History*. New York: Norton, 2007.

———. "The Paradoxical Origins of Human Rights." In Wasserstrom et al., *Human Rights and Revolutions*, 3–20.

Hutchinson, Elizabeth Quay. *Labors Appropriate to Their Sex: Gender, Labor, and Politics in Urban Chile, 1900–1930*. Durham, NC: Duke University Press, 2001.

Iglesias Vázquez, Mónica. *Rompiendo el cerco: El movimiento de pobladores contra la dictadura*. Santiago: Ediciones Radio Universidad de Chile, 2011.

Ishay, Micheline R. *The History of Human Rights: From Ancient Times to the Globalization Era*. Berkeley: University of California Press, 2008.

Jaffe, Tracey Lynn. "In the Footsteps of *Cristo Obrero*: Chile's Young Catholic Workers Movement in the Neighborhood, Factory, and Family, 1946–1973." PhD diss., University of Pittsburgh, 2009.

James, Daniel. *Doña María's Story: Life History, Memory, and Political Identity*. Durham, NC: Duke University Press, 2001.

Jelin, Elizabeth. *State Repression and the Labors of Memory*. Translated by Judy Rein and Marcial Godoy-Anativia. Minneapolis: University of Minnesota Press, 2003.

Jiménez, Oscar. "Alberto Hurtado, precursor de La Iglesia Liberadora." In Aldunate Lyon et al., *Crónicas*, 13–19.

Kaplan, Temma. *Taking Back the Streets: Women, Youth, and Direct Democracy*. Berkeley: University of California Press, 2004.

Kelley, Robin D. G. *Freedom Dreams: The Black Radical Imagination*. Boston: Beacon, 2002.

Klubock, Thomas Miller. "Ránquil: Violence and Peasant Politics on Chile's Southern Frontier." In Grandin and Joseph, *A Century of Revolution*, 121–59.

Lancaster, Roger. *Thanks to God and the Revolution: Popular Religion and Class Consciousness in the New Nicaragua*. New York: Columbia University Press, 1988.

Larraín B., Felipe. "The Economic Challenges of Democratic Development." In Drake and Jaksić, *Struggle for Democracy*, 279–304.

Lavín, Joaquín. *Chile: Revolución Silenciosa*. Santiago: Zig-Zag, 1987.

Lefebvre, Henri. *The Production of Space*. Translated by Donald Nicholson-Smith. Malden, MA: Blackwell, 1991.

Lernoux, Penny. *Cry of the People: The Struggle for Human Rights in Latin America—The Catholic Church in Conflict with U.S. Policy*. New York: Penguin, 1982.

Levine, Daniel. "The Evolution of the Theory and Practice of Rights in Latin American Catholicism." In Wilde, *Religious Responses to Violence*, 27–61. South Bend, IN: University of Notre Dame Press, 2016.

Levine, Daniel H., ed. *Religion and Political Conflict in Latin America*. Chapel Hill: University of North Carolina Press, 1986.

Los Guaracheros. "Cómo se organizó la toma de Zañartu." In ECO, *La Población La Legua*, 21–27.

Loveman, Brian, and Elizabeth Lira. *Las ardientes cenizas del olvido: Vía chilena de reconciliación política (1932–1994)*. Santiago: LOM, 2000.

———. *Políticas de reparación: Chile 1990–2004*. Santiago: LOM, 2005.

Lowden, Pamela. *Moral Opposition to Authoritarian Rule in Chile, 1973–1990*. Oxford: St. Anthony's Press, 1996.

Mago. "Una vida en La Legua." In ECO, *La Población La Legua*, 14–20.

Mallon, Florencia. *Courage Tastes of Blood: The Mapuche Community of Nicolás Ailío and the Chilean State, 1906–2001*. Durham, NC: Duke University Press, 2005.

Martínez Ángel, Marlene. "La experiencia política de los militantes del MIR (1973–1989)." *Proposiciones* 36 (2007): 126–153.

Mattelart, Armand, and Michelle Mattelart. *La mujer chilena en una nueva sociedad*. Santiago: Editorial del Pacífico, S.A., 1968.

McCann, Bryan. *Hard Times in the Marvelous City: From Dictatorship to Democracy in the Favelas of Rio de Janeiro*. Durham, NC: Duke University Press, 2014.

Meller, Patricio. *The Unidad Popular and the Pinochet Dictatorship: A Political Economy Analysis*. New York: St. Martin's, 2000.

———. *Un siglo de economía política chilena (1890–1990)*. Santiago: Andrés Bello, 1996.

Meller, Patricio, Pilar Romaguera, Andrea Butelmann, Rodrigo Baño, and Manuel Canales. *Chile: Evolución macroeconómica, financiación externa y cambio política en la década de los 80*. Madrid: CEDEAL, 1992.

Miller, Francesca. *Latin American Women and the Search for Social Justice*. Hanover, NH: University Press of New England, 1991.

Morales, Luis. "Voces de Chuchunco." In ECO, *Historias para un fin de siglo: Primer concurso de historias locales y sus fuentes*, 71–134. Santiago: Pehuén Editores, 1994.

Morley, Morris H., and Chris McGillion. *Reagan and Pinochet: The Struggle over U.S. Policy toward Chile*. New York: Cambridge University Press, 2015.

Moulián, Tomás. *Chile actual: Anatomía de un mito*. Santiago: LOM, 2002.

Moya, Laura, Ricardo Balladares, Claudia Videla, Alison Bruey, Hervi Lara, Andrés Carvajal, Mario Aballay, and Marcelo Alvarado. *Tortura en poblaciones del Gran Santiago (1973–1990)*. Santiago: Corporación José Domingo Cañas, 2005/Biblioteca Nacional de Chile Memoria Chilena, 2015.

Moyn, Samuel. *The Last Utopia: Human Rights in History*. Cambridge, MA: Harvard University Press, 2010.

Murphy, Edward. *For a Proper Home: Housing Rights in the Margins of Urban Chile, 1960–2010*. Pittsburgh: University of Pittsburgh Press, 2015.

Nickoloff, James B., ed. *Gustavo Gutiérrez: Essential Writings*. New York: Orbis, 2000.

———. "Introduction." In Nickoloff, *Gustavo Gutiérrez*, 1–22.

Niña. "Nací en La Legua." In ECO, *La Población La Legua: Desde la historia oral hacia la historia local*. Colección 30, Años no. 5, 42–47. Santiago: ECO, 2012.

Olguín, Myriam, and Andrea Gamboa. *Propuesta comunitaria de prevención para La Legua*. Santiago: ECO, 2003.

Orellana, Patricio, and Elizabeth Quay Hutchinson. *El movimiento de derechos humanos en Chile, 1973–1990*. Santiago: CEPLA, 1991.

Oxhorn, Philip D. *Organizing Civil Society: The Popular Sectors and the Struggle for Democracy in Chile*. University Park: Penn State University Press, 1995.

Paiva, Manuel. *Rastros de mi pueblo*. Santiago: Quimantú, 2005.

Paley, Julia. *Marketing Democracy: Power and Social Movements in Post-Dictatorship Chile*. Berkeley: University of California Press, 2001.

Palma Salamanca, Ricardo. *Una larga cola de acero: Historia del FPMR 1984–1988*. Santiago: LOM, 2001.

Palominos Rojas, Eva. *Vuelo de mariposa: Una historia de amor en el MIR*. Concepción: Escaparate, 2007.

Pérez, Cristián. "Historia del MIR: 'Si quieren guerra, guerra tendrán . . .'" *Estudios Públicos* 91 (invierno 2003): 5–44.

Pinto, Julio. "¿Y la historia les dio la razón?" In *Su revolución contra nuestra revolución: Izquierdas y derechas en el Chile de Pinochet (1973–1981)*, vol. 1, by Verónica Valdivia, Rolando Álvarez, and Julio Pinto, 153–205. Santiago: LOM, 2006.

Policzer, Pablo. *The Rise and Fall of Repression in Chile*. South Bend, IN: University of Notre Dame Press, 2009.

Politzer, Patricia. *La ira de Pedro y los otros*. Santiago: Planeta, 1988.

Portelli, Alessandro. *The Battle of Valle Giulia: Oral History and the Art of Dialogue*. Madison: University of Wisconsin Press, 1997.

———. "The Death of Luigi Trastulli: Memory and the Event." In *The Death of Luigi Trastulli and Other Stories: Form and Meaning in Oral History*, 1–26. Albany: State University of New York Press, 1991.

Power, Margaret. "The U.S. Movement in Solidarity with Chile in the 1970s." *Latin American Perspectives* 36, no. 6 (2009): 46–66.

Precht Bañados, Cristián. "Del Comité Pro Paz a la Vicaría de la Solidaridad." In Ariztía et al., *Seminario Iglesia y Derechos Humanos*, 19–32.

Quiroga Zamora, Patricio. *Compañeros: El GAP: La escolta de Allende*. Santiago: Aguilar, 2001.

Raposo Quintana, Gabriela. "Muerte y lugar: Territorios del olvido, memoria y resistencia: Villa Francia, huellas de la dictadura militar, 1973–2010." PhD diss., Pontificia Universidad Católica de Chile, 2012.

Reuque Paillalef, Rosa Isolde. *When a Flower Is Reborn: The Life and Times of a Mapuche Feminist*. Edited, translated, and with an introduction by Florencia Mallon. Durham, NC: Duke University Press, 2002.

Richard, Nelly. "Cities/Sites of Violence: Convulsions of Sense and Official Routines." In *Cultural Residues: Chile in Transition*, 15–29. Minneapolis: University of Minnesota Press, 2004.

Richards, Patricia. *Pobladoras, Indígenas, and the State: Conflicts over Women's Rights in Chile*. New Brunswick, NJ: Rutgers University Press, 2004.

Riquelme Segovia, Alfredo. *Rojo atardecer: El comunismo chileno entre dictadura y democracia*. Santiago: DIBAM, 2009.

Rodríguez, Alfredo. *Por una ciudad democrática*. Santiago: SUR, 1983.

Rojas, Sandra. *Vicaría de la Solidaridad: Historia de su trabajo social*. Santiago: Ediciones Paulinas, 1991.

Rojas Núñez, Luis. *De la rebelión popular a la sublevación imaginada: Antecedentes de la historia política y militar del Partido Comunista de Chile y del FPMR 1973–1990*. Santiago: LOM, 2011.

Rose, R. S. *The Unpast: Elite Violence and Social Control in Brazil, 1954–2000*. Athens: Ohio University Press, 2006.

Rosemblatt, Karin Alejandra. *Gendered Compromises: Political Cultures and the State in Chile, 1920–1950*. Chapel Hill: University of North Carolina Press, 2000.

Salazar, Gabriel. *Conversaciones con Carlos Altamirano: Memorias Críticas*. Santiago: Random House Mondadori, 2010.

———. *En el nombre del poder popular constituyente (Chile, siglo XXI)*. Santiago: LOM, 2011.

———. *La historia desde abajo y desde dentro*. Santiago: Facultad de Artes, Universidad de Chile, 2003.

———. *La violencia política popular en las "Grandes Alamedas": La violencia en Chile 1947–1987 (Una perspectiva histórico popular)*. 2nd ed. Santiago: LOM, 2006.

Salazar, Gabriel, and Julio Pinto. *Historia contemporánea de Chile I: Estado, legitimidad, ciudadanía*. Santiago: LOM, 1999.

———. *Historia Contemporánea de Chile II: Actores, identidad y movimiento*. Santiago: LOM, 1999.

———. *Historia contemporánea de Chile IV: Hombría y feminidad*. Santiago: LOM, 2002.

———. *Historia Contemporánea de Chile V: Niñez y juventud*. Santiago: LOM, 2002.

Saldías, Blanca. "Aquí, en mi parroquía San Cayetano." In ECO and Red de Orgranizaciones Sociales de La Legua, *Memorias de la dictadura en La Legua*, 39–41.

Salimovich, Sofia, Elizabeth Lira, and Eugenia Weinstein. "Victims of Fear: The Social Psychology of Repression." In *Fear at the Edge: State Terror and Resistance in Latin America*, edited by Juan E. Corradi, P. W. Fagan, and M. A. Garretón, 72–89. Berkeley: University of California Press, 1992.

Sapag Chain, Reinaldo. "El Cardenal Silva y los trabajadores." In *El Cardenal Raúl Silva Henríquez y los Trabajadores*, edited by Bárbara Figueroa Sandoval, Monseñor

Alfonso Baeza Donoso, and Reinaldo Sapag Chain, 15–35. Santiago: Ediciones Copygraph, 2013.

Schlotterbeck, Marian E. *Beyond the Vanguard: Everyday Revolutionaries in Allende's Chile.* Berkeley: University of California Press, 2018.

Schneider, Cathy Lisa. "Mobilization at the Grassroots: Shantytowns and Resistance in Authoritarian Chile." *Latin American Perspectives* 18, no. 1 (1991): 92–112.

———. *Shantytown Protest in Pinochet's Chile.* Philadelphia: Temple University Press, 1995.

Scholz, Sally J. *Political Solidarity.* University Park: Penn State University Press, 2008.

Scott, David. *Omens of Adversity: Tragedy, Time, Memory, Justice.* Durham, NC: Duke University Press, 2014.

Scott, James C. *Domination and the Arts of Resistance: Hidden Transcripts.* New Haven, CT: Yale University Press, 1990.

Scott, Joan W. "'Experience.'" In *Feminists Theorize the Political,* edited by Judith Butler and Joan Scott, 22–40. New York: Routledge, 1992.

Sen, Amartya. *Poverty and Famines: An Essay on Entitlement and Deprivation.* New York: Oxford University Press, 1986.

Sepúlveda Ruiz, Lucía. *119 de nosotros.* Santiago: LOM, 2005.

Sepúlveda Toro, Leonardo. "Algo se cuela por los resquicios." In *Algo se cuela por los resquicios,* 209–30. Santiago: n.p., 1987.

Simone, AbdouMaliq. "People as Infrastructure: Intersecting Fragments in Johannesburg." In *Johannesburg: The Elusive Metropolis,* edited by Sarah Nuttell and Achille Mbembe, 68–90. Durham, NC: Duke University Press, 2008.

Smith, Brian H. "Chile: Deepening the Allegiance of Working-Class Sectors to the Church in the 1970s." In *Religion and Political Conflict in Latin America,* edited by Daniel H. Levine, 156–86. Chapel Hill: University of North Carolina Press, 1986.

———. *The Church and Politics in Chile: Challenges to Modern Catholicism.* Princeton, NJ: Princeton University Press, 1982.

Stern, Steve J. *Battling for Hearts and Minds: Memory Struggles in Pinochet's Chile.* Book 2 of The Memory Box of Pinochet's Chile Trilogy. Durham, NC: Duke University Press, 2006.

———. *Memorias en construcción: Los retos del pasado presente en Chile, 1989–2011.* Santiago: Museo de la Memoria y los Derechos Humanos, 2013.

———. *Reckoning with Pinochet: The Memory Question in Democratic Chile.* Book 3 of The Memory Box of Pinochet's Chile Trilogy. Durham, NC: Duke University Press, 2010.

———. *Remembering Pinochet's Chile: On the Eve of London 1998.* Book 1 of The Memory Box of Pinochet's Chile Trilogy. Durham, NC: Duke University Press, 2006.

Stern, Steve J., and Scott Straus. "Embracing Paradox: Human Rights in the Global Age." In *The Human Rights Paradox: Universality and Its Discontents,* edited by Steve J. Stern and Scott Straus, 3–28. Madison: University of Wisconsin, 2014.

Stites Mor, Jessica, ed. *Human Rights and Transnational Solidarity in Cold War Latin America.* Madison: University of Wisconsin Press, 2013.

———. "Situating Transnational Solidarity within Critical Human Rights Studies of Cold War Latin America." In Stites Mor, *Human Rights and Transnational Solidarity*, 3–18.

Stjernø, Steinar. *Solidarity in Europe: The History of an Idea*. New York: Cambridge University Press, 2009.

Taylor, Marcus. *From Pinochet to the "Third Way": Neoliberalism and Social Transformation in Chile*. Ann Arbor, MI: Pluto Press, 2006.

Thomas, Gwynn. *Contesting Legitimacy in Chile: Familial Ideals, Citizenship, and Political Struggle, 1970–1990*. University Park: Penn State University Press, 2011.

Thompson, E. P. "Custom, Law and Common Right." In *Customs in Common: Studies in Traditional Popular Culture*, 97–184. New York: New Press, 1993.

———. *Customs in Common: Studies in Traditional Popular Culture*. New York: New Press, 1993.

———. *The Making of the English Working Class*. New York: Vintage, 1966.

———. "The Moral Economy of the English Crowd in the Eighteenth Century." In Thompson, *Customs in Common*, 185–258.

———. "The Moral Economy Reviewed." In Thompson, *Customs in Common*, 259–351.

Tinsman, Heidi. *Buying into the Regime: Grapes and Consumption in Cold War Chile and the United States*. Durham, NC: Duke University Press, 2014.

Tironi, Eugenio. *Autoritarismo, modernización y marginalidad: El caso de Chile, 1973–1989*. Santiago: SUR, 1990.

———. "El fantasma de los pobladores." *Estudios Sociológicos* 4, no. 12 (1986): 391–97.

———. "La revuelta de los pobladores. Integración social y democracia." *Nueva Sociedad* 83 (May–June 1986): 24–32.

———. "Marginalidad, Movimientos Sociales y Democracia." *Proposiciones* 14 (August 1987).

Trumper, Camilo D. *Ephemeral Histories: Public Art, Politics, and the Struggle for the Streets in Chile*. Berkeley: University of California Press, 2016.

Tuan, Yi-Fu. *Space and Place: The Perspective of Experience*. Minneapolis: University of Minnesota Press, 1977.

Valdés, Juan Gabriel. *Pinochet's Economists: The Chicago School in Chile*. New York: Cambridge University Press, 1995.

Valdés, Teresa. *Venid, benditas de mi padre: Las pobladores, sus rutinas y sus sueños*. Santiago: FLACSO, 1988.

Valdés, Teresa, and Marisa Weinstein. *Mujeres que sueñan: Las organizaciones de pobladoras en Chile: 1973–1989*. Santiago: FLACSO, 1993.

Valdés, Teresa, Marisa Weinstein, and María Toledo. "Centros de Madres 1973–1989 ¿Sólo disciplinamiento?" Documento de Trabajo 416, Programa FLACSO-Chile, July 1989.

Valdivia, Verónica. "Lecciones de una Revolución: Jaime Guzmán y los Gremialistas, 1973–1980." In *Su revolución contra nuestra revolución: Izquierdas y derechas en el Chile de Pinochet (1973–1981)*, by Verónica Valdivia, Rolando Álvarez, and Julio Pinto, 1:49–100. Santiago: LOM, 2006.

Valdivia, Verónica, Rolando Álvarez, and Julio Pinto. *Su revolución contra nuestra revolución*. Vol. 1, *Izquierdas y derechas en el Chile de Pinochet (1973–1981)*. Santiago: LOM, 2006.

Valdivia, Verónica, Rolando Álvarez, Julio Pinto, Karen Donoso, and Sebastián Leiva. *Su revolución contra nuestra revolución*. Vol. 2, *La pugna marxista-gremialista en los ochenta*. Santiago: LOM, 2008.

Valenzuela, Esteban Teo, *Dios, Marx . . . y el MAPU*. Santiago: LOM, 2014.

Valenzuela, María Elena. "The Evolving Roles of Women under Military Rule." In Drake and Jaksić, *Struggle for Democracy*, 161–87.

———. *La mujer en el Chile militar: Todas íbamos a ser reinas*. Santiago: CESOC, 1987.

Van Isschot, Luis. *The Social Origins of Human Rights: Protesting Political Violence in Colombia's Oil Capital, 1919–2010*. Madison: University of Wisconsin Press, 2015.

Vergara, Pilar. "Auge y caída del neoliberalismo en Chile: Un estudio sobre la evolución ideológica del régimen militar." Documento de Trabajo 216, Programa FLACSO-Chile, August 1984.

Vicuña Mackenna, Benjamín. *Transformación de Santiago*. Santiago: Imprenta El Mercurio, 1872.

Vidal, Hernán. *Dar la vida por la vida: Agrupación Chilena de Familiares de Detenidos Desaparecidos (Ensayo de Antropología Simbólica)*. Santiago: Mosquito Editores, 1996.

———. *FPMR: El tabú del conflicto armado en Chile*. Santiago: Mosquito Editores, 1995.

Wasserstrom, Jeffrey N. "The Chinese Revolution and Contemporary Paradoxes." In Wasserstrom et al., *Human Rights and Revolutions*, 21–44.

Wasserstrom, Jeffrey N., Greg Grandin, Lynn Hunt, and Marilyn B. Young, eds. *Human Rights and Revolutions*. 2nd ed. New York: Rowman and Littlefield, 2007.

Way, J. T. *The Mayan in the Mall: Globalization, Development, and the Making of Modern Guatemala*. Durham, NC: Duke University Press, 2012.

Wickham-Crowley, Timothy P., and Susan Eckstein. "The Persisting Relevance of Political Economy and Political Sociology in Latin American Social Movement Studies." *LARR* 50, no. 4 (2015): 3–25.

Wilde, Alexander, ed. *Religious Responses to Violence: Human Rights in Latin America Past and Present*. South Bend, IN: University of Notre Dame Press, 2016.

———. "The Institutional Church and Pastoral Ministry: Unity and Conflict in the Defense of Human Rights in Chile." In Wilde, *Religious Responses to Violence*, 150–90.

Wilson, Sergio. *La otra ciudad: De la marginalidad a la participación social*. Santiago: Editorial Jurídica Ediar Conosur, 1988.

Winn, Peter. "The Furies of the Andes: Violence and Terror in the Chilean Revolution and Counterrevolution." In Grandin and Joseph, *A Century of Revolution*, 239–75.

———. "Oral History and the Factory Study: New Approaches to Labor History." *LARR* 14, no. 2 (1979): 130–40.

———. "The Other 9/11: My Coup Diary." *ReVista: Harvard Review of Latin America* (Spring 2004).

————. "The Pinochet Era." In *Victims of the Chilean Miracle: Workers and Neoliberalism in the Pinochet Era, 1973–2002*, edited by Peter Winn, 4–70. Durham, NC: Duke University Press, 2004.

————. *Weavers of Revolution: The Yarur Workers and Chile's Road to Socialism*. New York: Oxford University Press, 1989.

Wright, Thomas C. *Impunity, Human Rights, and Democracy: Chile and Argentina, 1990–2005*. Austin: University of Texas Press, 2014.

Index

61–62, 227n102; dictatorship and, 9, 14–15, 214n6, 217n34; economy of terror and, 67, 78–79, 90; mobilization and, 136–39, 147–57, 161, 164, 242n9; national protest and, 168–71, 174–75, 179, 181–82, 187–90, 194, 196, 199, 202; *pobladores* movement and, 22, 24–33, 36–37; resistance and, 4, 96–115, 120–25, 130; *trabajo de masas* (mass work) and, 174

Communist Youth, 32, 42, 49–50, 78–79, 108, 130, 161, 164, 194, 196

comunas populares (poor and working-class municipalities), 19, 218n47

comunidad cristiana (Christian community): dictatorship and, 13, 15, 218n41; mobilization and, 131, 137, 139, 145, 151–56, 162–65; national protest and, 168, 170, 175, 182, 196–201, 204; *pobladores* movement and, 34–35, 221n50; resistance and, 107, 111, 114, 120–27, 130

Comunidad Cristiana Popular (Popular Christian Community) [CCP], 34–35, 131, 221n50

Comunidad Juvenil (Catholic Youth Community), 120

concentration camps, 80

Concertación: coup and, 4–5, 9, 17–19, 40, 61–62, 214n6; democracy and, 76–77; governability and, 76; national protest and, 171–73, 193, 206–7; neoliberalism and, 210–11; "No" campaign of, 171

Confederación de Trabajadores del Cobre (Copper Workers' Confederation) [CTC], 169–70, 177–79, 186

Conferencia Episcopal de Chile (Episcopal Conference of Chile) [CECH], 106, 113, 172, 244n39, 247n13

conquistar la casa propia (conquer home-ownership), 23–28, 37

conscripts, 85–87

Consejo Nacional de Menores (National Council on Minors), 92

conservatism: Catholicism and, 84, 109, 111–12, 125–26, 221n50, 242n11, 253n154; economy of terror and, 67, 74, 84, 230n41; mobilization and, 162, 168; national protest and, 201, 253n154; *pobladores* movement and, 24, 221n50; resistance and, 109, 111–12, 125–26. *See also* Right

consumerism, 35, 55, 71, 134, 142–44, 168, 229n25

continuity and rupture, 4, 11, 15, 147

Contreras Sepúlveda, Manuel, 92

conventillos (tenements), 22, 24–27, 243n30

Coordinadora de Agrupaciones Poblacionales (Coordinator of Poblador Associations) [COAPO], 148–49

Coordinadora de Organizaciones Políticas y Sociales de Las Rejas, 182–83

Coordinadora Metropolitana de Pobladores (Metropolitan Coordinator of Pobladores) [METRO], 148–49

Coordinadora Nacional Sindical (National Trade-Union Coordinator) [CNS], 177

Corporación de Mejoramiento Urbano (Urban Improvement Corporation) [CORMU], 46

Corporación Nacional del Cobre (National Copper Corporation) [CODELCO], 178

corruption, 5, 36, 39, 53, 211

Corvalán, Luis, 47, 115

coup: abyss of, 63–64; activists and, 39, 41–42, 48, 55, 58–59, 64; Allende and, 4, 16, 38–39, 45–47, 49, 55, 59, 223n16, 223n18, 225n63; "antisocial" categorization and, 88–90, 92, 233n107; authoritarianism and, 6, 18; bloody veil and, 66–70, 77, 81–88, 95, 137; cadavers and, 51, 56, 58, 232n86;

coup (*continued*)

rights and, 5–11, 207–11; justice and, 5; mobilization and, 132–33, 140, 150, 158, 161, 166; national protest and, 167–75, 183, 185, 191–94, 197, 199, 202, 204–6, 253n154; neoliberalism and, 4–9, 12–13, 19, 43, 76–77, 133, 140, 166, 168–69, 173–74, 192–93, 206–11, 219n46; *pobladores* movement and, 5–11, 24, 27, 31–32, 35, 37; resistance and, 98, 105, 108; Unidad Popular and, 4, 15

democratization, 7–8, 76, 154, 189, 191, 206, 217n29

depressions, 72, 205

deregulation, 71, 134, 144

detention, 54, 63, 78, 82–84

Día del Joven Combatiente (Day of the Young Combatant), 40, 205

Díaz, Víctor, 46

dictatorship: activists and, 5–6, 9–15, 18–19, 215n18, 217n31; "antisocial" categorization and, 88–90, 92, 233n107; arrests and, 84, 137, 185, 234n115; authoritarianism and, 6, 18; Catholicism and, 6, 10–13, 15, 19, 96; Cold War and, 7, 9–11; Communist Party and, 9, 14–15, 214n6, 217n34; *comunidad cristiana* (Christian community) and, 13, 15, 218n41; Concertación and, 4–5, 9, 17–19, 40, 61–62, 76–77, 171–73, 193, 206–7, 210–11, 214n6; conscripts and, 85–87; coup and, 39 (*see also* coup); democracy and, 4–20, 216n24, 219n46; downward moral displacement and, 67, 70, 77, 89–94, 118, 171; economic miracles and, 6, 13, 130, 214n9; education and, 4–5, 12, 19; elitism and, 5–9, 13, 19–20, 217n31; end of, 205–6; executions and, 11, 42, 65, 218n40, 231n73; export growth and, 229n35; food and, 3, 9, 18–20; grassroots organizations and, 5–15, 19–20, 215n18; housing and, 14, 19; justice

and, 6, 9, 16, 18; labor and, 5, 9–10, 12; Left and, 6, 8–9, 11–13, 16–18, 19, 214n7, 217n29; make-work and, 72, 243n23; Marxism and, 10, 12, 15; militants and, 218n41; military and, 13, 16–17, 19; mortality rates and, 229n30; narratives and, 6–7, 10, 17, 214n11, 215n17; national protest and, 7–9, 13–20, 167–75, 183–97, 201–6; neoliberalism and, 4–5, 7, 9, 12–13, 18–19, 206–11; Pinochet and, 4, 7, 15, 19, 39, 41, 61, 75, 77, 133, 171, 173, 185–87, 215n18; *pobladores* movement and, 5–19; police and, 3–4, 13, 17; poverty and, 6, 216n24; priests and, 15, 213n1; propaganda and, 16, 55, 66, 99–100, 103, 142, 152–53, 202; radicals and, 5, 7, 13, 18; raids and, 17, 44, 49, 56–58, 69, 75, 78–93, 97, 101–4, 107, 157, 159, 185, 207, 218n40, 228n14, 232n84; repression and, 4–6, 13, 15–19; resistance and, 97–98 (*see also* resistance); scholarship of 1980s on, 215n18; social division and, 85–86; socialism and, 4, 7, 9, 11, 15, 19; social rights and, 4, 9, 11–12, 19; solidarity and, 6, 10–12, 17, 217n33; Somoza and, 10, 170; state of siege and, 133, 137, 169, 186–91, 207, 250n79, 251n94; students and, 3, 10, 216n24; surveillance and, 44, 85, 87, 93; *tomas* and, 14; torture and, 5, 7, 11, 16, 218n40; unemployment and, 19, 216n24; Unidad Popular and, 4, 15–16; urban poor and, 4, 12; women and, 9, 13, 15

Dirección de Inteligencia Nacional (National Intelligence Directorate) [DINA], 74, 79, 81, 92, 96, 99, 102–8, 120, 123, 130, 133, 145

Dirección Nacional de Industria y Comercio (National Industry and Commerce Directorate) [DIRINCO], 94

88; violence and, 66–67, 70, 73–77, 81–85, 87–88, 93–95, 231n51; women and, 73, 79, 82, 84–87, 90; youth and, 78–79, 81, 84

Educación and Comunicaciones (ECO), 138, 146–47, 150, 191, 213

education: activists and, 10, 39, 41, 102, 150, 175, 177, 199–200, 211; Allende and, 4; class size and, 4; coup and, 40, 61–63, 227n102; dictatorship and, 4–5, 12, 19; economy of terror and, 67, 92, 95, 229n25; mobilization and, 131, 134, 138, 140–41, 146, 150, 153, 157–61, 164; national protest and, 172, 174, 176, 192–93, 195; neoliberalism and, 207–8; *pobladores* movement and, 32; resistance and, 107, 124–25, 129; student protests and, 39–40, 167, 175, 177, 180, 185, 200, 211, 242n11 (*see also* students); teachers and, 10, 23, 31, 44

Ejército de Liberación Nacional (National Liberation Army) [ELN], 47

El Bosque Air Force Base, 56

electricity, 31, 34, 51, 59, 141, 175, 184

elitism: class purity and, 241n6; coup and, 40, 57, 64; dictatorship and, 5–9, 13, 19–20, 217n31; economy of terror and, 71, 77; mobilization and, 135; national protest and, 168–71, 173, 180, 183, 190–91, 193, 204–6, 253n140; neoliberalism and, 211; *pobladores* movement and, 25; resistance and, 97, 111–12, 129

El Mercurio (newspaper), 40, 51

El País (newspaper), 77

El Pinar, 32, 90, 122, 182

El Salvador, 10

encyclicals, 109–11, 238n61

Enríquez, Miguel, 46

Escobar, Arturo, 134–35

Espinoza Ulloa, Jorge, 74

Espíritu Santo, 32, 122

evictions, 24, 27, 30

executions, 11, 42, 65, 218n40, 231n73

extremists, 13, 17, 54, 77, 84–85, 89, 92, 171

fascism, 24, 79, 133, 136, 201

Federación Obrera de Chile (Workers Federation of Chile) [FOCH], 109–10

Fernández Fernández, Sergio, 131, 133

Ferraris, Gustavo, 3

fin del reflujo (end of the ebb), 135, 139, 145–47, 244n41

floods, 21, 25–26, 103, 183

food: coup and, 55; dictatorship and, 3–4, 9, 18–20; economy of terror and, 72–73, 78, 80, 92, 229n25, 229n27; malnutrition and, 141–42, 159; mobilization and, 141–43, 156; national protest and, 174–76, 192, 197; *pobladores* movement and, 35–36; prices of, 35–36, 73, 229n25, 243n25; resistance and, 97, 104, 116–17, 120, 122, 129, 236n35; soup kitchens and, 12, 72–73, 103, 107, 115–17, 120–22, 125, 130, 147–48, 151, 156, 160, 176, 236n35

Food and Agriculture Organization (FAO), 142

Franco, Jean, 90

Freedom Dreams (Kelley), 169, 252n109

free market, 66, 71, 143, 229n27

Frei Montalva, Eduardo, 14, 22–23, 26, 174, 188

Frente de Estudiantes Revolucionarios (Revolutionary Students Front) [FER], 102

Frente Juvenil de Unidad Nacional (National Unity Youth Front), 133

Frente Patriótico Manuel Rodríguez (Manuel Rodríguez Patriotic Front) [FPMR], 15, 41, 136, 164, 168, 171, 196, 204

Frente Unitario de Mujeres Pobladoras (Unitary Front of Poblador Women), 174

Frenz, Helmut, 106
Friedman, Milton, 70
Fundación de Ayuda Social de las
    Iglesias Cristianas (Social Assistance
    Foundation of the Christian
    Churches) [FASIC], 159, 209,
    246n96

Gandhi, 10
Garcés, Mario, 24, 51, 57, 206, 213
gay men, 84, 90–91
gender, 67, 84, 89, 104, 109, 148
General Bonilla (neighborhood), 101
General Comments of the Committee
    on the Rights of the Child, 208
Germán Riesco, 32, 44, 182
God, 61, 96, 112, 114, 118, 124, 129, 132,
    176, 209
Good Samaritan, 127–28
Gospels, 96, 113, 126, 129, 164
Gossens, Anita, 31
graffiti, 102–3, 150, 202
Gran Santiago, 141, 243n22
grassroots organizations: activism and,
    5–15, 19–20; coup and, 5–15, 19–20, 41;
    dictatorship and, 5–15, 19–20, 215n18;
    economy of terror and, 67–68; Left
    and, 9–15, 25, 37, 41, 67, 98–99, 115,
    126, 130, 136, 138, 148, 174, 190–91,
    199–200, 209–10; mobilization and,
    135–38, 148–50, 165; national protest
    and, 174, 190–91, 199–201, 206,
    252n118, 253n148; neoliberalism and,
    208–11; resistance and, 98–99, 108, 115,
    126, 130; solidarity and, 6, 10, 12, 35,
    98, 115, 126, 135, 215n18
Great Depression, 72
Grenada, 194
Grupo Calama, 35, 113, 239n84
Grupo de Amigos Personals (Group of
    Personal Friends) [GAP], 47, 50
Grupo Social Cristiano Germen,
    110–12

Guerra Popular Prolongada (Prolonged
    Popular War), 136
Gutiérrez, Gustavo, 112

Han, Clara, 57
Harvey, David, 71
Hayek, Friedrich, 70
health care, 4, 19, 67, 92, 120, 131, 134,
    140, 229n25
Herminda de la Victoria, 21–22, 27–28
Héroes de la Concepción, 15, 103,
    232n87
hippies, 82, 84, 90
historical memory, 15–18
Hite, Katherine, 236n17
Ho Chi Minh, 150
Holy Week, 119, 166
homeless, 12, 21, 26, 28, 90, 137, 139, 149,
    166
homo economicus, 71
Hospital Barros Luco/Trudeau, 51
housing: affordable, 23, 37, 92, 132, 145,
    148–49, 190; *campamentos* and, 25–27,
    103, 141–42; *conventillos* and, 22,
    24–27, 243n30; dictatorship and, 14,
    19; economy of terror and, 65, 67,
    91–92, 95, 229n25, 232n84, 234n124;
    evictions and, 24, 27, 30; home own-
    ership and, 23–28, 30, 37, 81; low-
    income, 25; mobilization and, 132,
    134, 139, 141–42, 145, 148–49, 243n30;
    National Housing Program and, 26;
    national protest and, 174, 190, 192;
    neoliberalism and, 208; ollas com-
    munes and, 145, 148, 175, 183, 236n35;
    Operación Sitio and, 14, 23, 26, 28, 33;
    pobladores movement and, 21–30,
    34–35, 37; resistance and, 103, 117; san-
    itation and, 24–25, 73, 141; *tomas* and,
    14, 21–30, 36; Unidad Popular and, 34;
    Villa Francia and, 34
human rights: activists and, 5–6, 9–12,
    19, 39, 98, 105, 111, 115, 126, 135, 153,

157, 166, 175, 191, 198–99, 207, 215n15, 215n18, 217n31; American Convention on Human Rights and, 208; American Declaration of the Rights and Duties of Man and, 208; Catholicism and, 11; Chilean Penal Code and, 208; Comisión Chilena de Derechos Humanos and, 209; coup and, 3, 39, 60, 111, 209–10; democracy and, 5–11, 207–11; economy of terror and, 76, 83, 91; emergency of, 105–8; expansion of traditional focus on, 16; General Comments of the Committee on the Rights of the Child and, 208; Instituto Nacional de Derechos Humanos (INDH) and, 207–8, 211, 254n2; International Covenant on Civil and Political Rights and, 208; International Day of the Declaration of Human Rights and, 175; Left and, 210; mobilization and, 131–35, 145, 151, 153, 156–58, 161, 166; national protest and, 175–76, 191, 195, 198–99, 206; neoliberalism and, 4–9, 19, 39, 76, 98, 166, 206–11, 215n18; pluralism and, 19; *pobladores* movement and, 5–11, 24; resistance and, 15, 98, 105–18, 122, 126; social organizations and, 12; solidarity and, 105–8; United Nations and, 133; Universal Declaration of, 10–11, 208, 217n31; violation of, 4–11, 24, 60, 76, 91, 116, 131, 135, 145, 206, 208, 210; violence and, 6–7, 11, 20, 76, 145, 166, 176, 207–8, 215, 247n13
Human Rights Day, 132
Hunger Marches, 132, 138, 169, 174–78
hunger strikes, 128, 132, 138, 151, 153–59, 243n16
hunger wages, 5
Hurtado Cruchaga, Luis Alberto, 111
Hutchinson, Elizabeth, 238n76
hygiene, 24–25, 73, 141

Independence Day Te Deum, 188
India, 10
Indumet, 46–47, 49, 53
Industrial Workers of the World, 109
inflation, 72–73, 75, 133, 140, 143–44, 187
Instituto Nacional de Derechos Humanos (INDH), 207–8, 211, 254n2
International Covenant on Civil and Political Rights, 208
International Day of the Declaration of Human Rights, 175
International Women's Day, 132, 174
invisible hand, 70
Izquierda Cristiana (Christian Left), 15, 136

Jaffe, Tracey, 111, 113
Jakarta, 44–45
Jara, Víctor, 21, 28, 80, 161
Jelin, Elizabeth, 98
Jesus Christ, 112, 114, 127–29, 160–61
Jesús de Nazaret parish, 34
Jews, 105–6
José Cardijn (neighborhood), 34
José María Caro (neighborhood), 15, 117
Jota (Communist Youth), 32, 42, 49–50, 78–79, 108, 130, 161, 164, 194, 196
jóvenes, 170, 193–95, 198, 201–3, 205
junta: coup and, 45; dialogue with, 187–91; divide-and-rule tactics and, 171, 174, 187–91; economy of terror and, 71, 74–75, 85, 90, 92–94, 230n38, 231n73, 234n136; Matthei and, 186–90; mobilization and, 133; national protest and, 185–90, 250n87, 251n94; neoliberalism and, 254n13; *pobladores* movement and, 23, 35–36; public sector support and, 235n136; resistance and, 106, 126–27; state of siege and, 133, 137, 169, 186–91, 207, 250n79, 251n94; useful fools and, 186–91

Junta de Abastecimiento y Precios (Supply and Price Committee) [JAP], 35–36, 117

juntas de vecinos (neighborhood councils), 23, 31, 36, 78–79, 92–94, 97, 117, 253n154

justice: coup and, 39–40, 43, 52, 58, 60–62; democracy and, 5; dictatorship and, 6, 9, 16, 18; economy of terror and, 65–66, 76–77, 92, 94–95; mobilization and, 132–33, 153–58, 161, 166; national protest and, 168–69, 176, 194–95, 198, 206, 247n13; neoliberalism and, 211; *pobladores* movement and, 18–20, 24; resistance and, 110, 112–13, 118, 121, 124, 126, 128; social, 5–6, 40, 61–62, 66, 77, 94–95, 110, 113, 118, 121, 124, 126, 155, 168, 195, 227n102

Juventud Obrera Católica (Catholic Worker Youth) [JOC], 32, 79, 86, 111, 113

Kast, Miguel, 140
Kautsky, Karl, 109
Kelley, Robin D. G., 169, 252n109
kidnapping, 65, 108, 153, 158
King, Martin Luther, Jr., 10

La Bandera, 15
labor: anti-worker labor laws and, 67; *bolsa de cesantes* and, 115–17, 121, 143, 145, 147–48, 151, 160, 176, 178, 183; coup and, 41, 46, 48–51; dictatorship and, 5, 9–10, 12; economic growth and, 72–73, 76, 133, 138, 140, 143, 187, 206, 229n35, 230n50; economy of terror and, 67, 70–74, 82, 89, 94; inflation and, 72–73, 75, 133, 140, 143–44, 187; make-work and, 72, 243n23; Minimum Employment Program and, 72, 141, 145, 229n21, 243n23; MOAC and, 34, 111, 113, 124; mobilization and, 132, 134, 138–40, 144–45,

148, 150, 152, 156, 242n9, 242n10; national protest and, 170, 177–78, 180, 182, 185–86, 197; organized, 9, 13, 134, 148, 185–86, 242n10; *pobladores* movement and, 23, 25, 27–28, 32, 37; real wages and, 73, 187, 231n73, 243n25; recession and, 65, 72, 75, 229n35; resistance and, 98, 109–20; rights and, 5; shortage of, 140; strikes and, 109, 132, 138, 169, 177–78; *trabajo de hormiga* (ant's work) and, 13, 98, 139, 166, 176, 183; *trabajo de masas* (mass work) and, 174; unemployment and, 115–17, 121, 143, 145, 147–48, 151, 160, 176, 178, 183; unions and, 10, 25, 27, 32, 37, 41, 46, 50–51, 67, 70–71, 74, 82, 89, 109, 113–14, 117, 119, 134, 145, 177; working-class demographics and, 230n39

Labor Code, 67, 139
La Chimba, 22
La Faena, 15
La Granja, 141, 158, 175, 185
La Legua, 213; background of, 14; as combative, 41; as concentration camp, 80; coup and, 3–4, 24, 37, 38–64; economy of terror and, 65, 72, 77–92; Emergencia, 3–4, 26, 28–31, 46, 49, 78, 91, 107, 184, 207–8; as "Ghetto of Death," 17–18; mobilization and, 143, 147, 156–65; national protest and, 75, 167, 177–78, 180–84, 192, 194, 196–97, 199–200, 203; neoliberalism and, 207–8, 211; Nueva La Legua, 25–26, 28–31, 53, 78, 180, 184; *pobladores* movement and, 24, 35–37; protest culture of, 14–15, 17; resistance and, 41, 51–52, 97, 99, 101, 103–4, 107–8, 113, 117, 119, 122–24; San Cayetano and, 30–32, 51, 80, 107, 114, 119, 122–24, 156–61, 200, 221n33, 245n65; surveillance in, 85; *tres* Leguas of, 28–32; Vieja, 25–29; youth and, 164

La Moneda, 4, 16, 31, 39, 45–47, 69, 132, 165

Lancaster, Roger, 113

La Nuez (newsletter), 176

La Pincoya, 15

La Población (Jara), 21, 28

Lara Petrovich, Eduardo, 120–21, 153–54

La Tercera (newspaper), 40, 94

Latin American Bishops' Conference, 111–12

Lautaro. *See* Movimiento Juvenil Lautaro

Law for the Permanent Defense of Democracy, 15

Leal Díaz, Miguel, 168, 204–5

Left: Catholicism and, 10–13, 15, 19, 31–37, 41, 84, 98, 106–15, 117, 119–28, 148, 151, 158–59, 209, 237n49; Cold War and, 9; constitutional reforms and, 226n81; *construcción de izquierda* (building of), 210–11; coup and, 16, 44–45, 47, 49, 53–54, 57–58, 62, 226n81; dictatorship and, 6, 8–9, 11–13, 16–19, 214n7, 217n29; economy of terror and, 66–67, 71, 77, 81–82, 84, 89–90, 93, 233n107; grassroots organizations and, 9–15, 25, 37, 41, 67, 98–99, 115, 126, 130, 136, 138, 148, 174, 190–91, 199–200, 209–10; human rights and, 210; mobilization and, 134–38, 140, 145–46, 148, 151–54, 157–64; national protest and, 168–75, 177, 182, 185–91, 195–202, 205, 251n96; neoliberalism and, 209–10, 251n96, 254n11; *pobladores* movement and, 22, 24–25, 28, 31–37, 41; resistance and, 97–115, 118–29, 236n17, 237n49; second defeat of, 170–71; Unidad Popular and, 31–32

legends, 40

legitimacy, 18, 134, 136, 139–40, 191–92, 203

leguïnos, 42, 56, 78–80, 101, 158, 207–8

Leigh Guzmán, Gustavo, 75, 94

Leiva, Sebastián, 24, 51, 57

Leninism, 150, 154

Letelier, Orlando, 133

Levine, Daniel, 175–76

Ley de Habitaciones Obreras, 25

Ley de Seguridad del Estado (State Security Law), 159

Ley Maldita, 15

liberation theology, 9, 13, 35, 112–13, 124, 161, 170, 193, 221n50, 239n84

liberty: economy of terror and, 67, 70; national protest and, 169, 176, 179, 184, 197; neoliberalism and, 208, 211; *pobladores* movement and, 3, 9, 18–20; resistance and, 112, 118, 126, 129

Lira, Elizabeth, 228n14

Lonquén, 132, 158

looting, 57, 78

Los 119, 153

Loubet, Nadine "Odile," 83

Luke, Bible book of, 127

Lutherans, 106

machine guns, 42, 46, 50, 78–79

machista behavior, 160

Madariaga, Mónica, 133

Madeco, 15, 44, 50

Mademsa, 44

make-work programs, 72, 243n23

malnutrition, 141–42, 159

Mapocho River, 21, 83, 103

Mapuche communities, 211, 214n7, 223n16

March Against Hunger, 175

marginalization, 8–9, 23, 32, 40, 57, 80, 131, 134, 168, 191–92, 200, 206, 214n11, 215n17, 254n11

marijuana, 160, 233n107

Maroto, Rafael, 31, 35, 107, 220n32

Martí, Farabundo, 10

martyrs, 88, 166

Marxism: activists and, 12–13; Catholicism and, 10, 12, 15, 98, 107–17, 122, 125, 127–28, 242n11; Cold War and, 98; dictatorship and, 10, 12, 15; economy of terror and, 71, 75, 82, 92; mobilization and, 136, 139–40, 150, 154, 166, 241n7; national protest and, 177, 188; *pobladores* movement and, 22–31; resistance and, 98, 105, 107–28, 237n57; solidarity and, 12, 98, 108–17, 127–28, 136, 237n57; war on, 75

Marx, Karl, 109, 237n57

Mass, 114, 123–24, 155

mass protest, 7, 13, 98, 173–77, 186, 211

Mater et Magistra (encyclical), 110

Matthei, Fernando, 186–90

May Day, 132, 177

mejora-emergencia homes, 142, 243n30

memoirs, 40, 107

memorias soterradas (underground memories): coup and, 15–18, 39–43, 57–63; mobilization and, 138, 243n17; national protest and, 168

Mendoza, César, 186

Merino, José Toribio, 186–87, 189

Merino Molina, Pedro, 130

Methodists, 106

Metropolitan Cemetery, 83

middle class, 23, 40, 92, 97, 175, 180, 232n84, 253n40

militants: coup and, 41–42, 46, 49, 56; dictatorship and, 218n41; economy of terror and, 70; mobilization and, 136–37, 151–53, 161–64, 242n11; national protest and, 153n154, 168, 181, 196–97, 199–202, 205, 252n118; neoliberalism and, 210; *pobladores* movement and, 24; resistance and, 102, 106, 121, 127

military: coup and, 13, 16–17, 19, 39, 41, 44–62, 223n24; detentions and, 54, 63, 78, 82–84; dictatorship and, 13, 16–17, 19; economy of terror and, 69, 76, 78–87, 91, 93–94, 231n73; executions

and, 11, 42, 65, 218n40, 231n73; flirtation strategies on, 60–61; junta and, 85 (*see also* junta); machine guns and, 42, 46, 50, 78–79; mobilization and, 144, 158, 164; national protest and, 13, 173, 178, 186, 189, 202, 250n79; resistance and, 101, 103; tribunals and, 250n79

missionaries, 31, 80, 107

mobilization: activists and, 134–39, 145–58, 162–66; Allende and, 136, 140; annual protest demonstrations and, 132; authoritarianism and, 139–41, 144, 148, 154; capitalism and, 136, 140, 244n45; Catholicism and, 137, 148, 151, 154–55, 158–59, 165; Cold War and, 135; Communist Party and, 136–39, 147–57, 161, 164, 242n9; *comunidad cristiana* (Christian community) and, 131, 137, 139, 145, 151–56, 162–65; conservatism and, 162, 168; Cristo Liberador and, 131–32, 137, 139, 151–56, 159–64; debt and, 141, 143–44, 148, 160, 243n17; democracy and, 132–33, 140, 150, 158, 161, 166; economic miracles and, 133, 136, 140, 150, 166; economic mirages and, 134, 140, 144, 165; education and, 131, 134, 138, 140–41, 146, 150, 153, 157–61, 164; *terremotos* (earthquakes) and, 146; elitism and, 135; *fin del reflujo* (end of the web) and, 135, 139, 145–47, 244n41; food and, 141–43, 156; glory years and, 139–45; grassroots organizations and, 135–38, 148–50, 165; housing and, 132, 134, 139, 141–42, 145, 148–49, 243n30; human rights and, 131–35, 145, 151, 153, 156–58, 161, 166; Hunger Marches and, 132, 138, 169, 174–78; hunger strikes and, 132, 138, 151, 153–59, 243n16; junta and, 133; justice and, 132–33, 153–58, 161, 166; labor and, 132, 134, 138–40, 144–45, 148, 150, 152, 156,

Movimiento Obrero de Acción Católica (Catholic Action Worker Movement) [MOAC], 34, 111, 113, 124
Moyn, Samuel, 208–9, 217n31
murals, 63, 167–69, 205
murder, 60–61, 81, 158
Murphy, Edward, 23, 27
Mussa, 32
myths, 20, 40

narratives: coup and, 38–45, 52–56, 59–60, 64, 214n11, 215n17, 222n6, 223n12, 227n102; dictatorship and, 6–7, 10, 17, 214n11, 215n17; economy of terror and, 91, 99, 104, 231n69, 232n81; mobilization and, 134; national protest and, 168, 171; neoliberalism and, 210–11; oral histories and, 4, 14–16, 34, 41–42, 59–61, 79, 99–100, 170, 205, 210–11, 213, 240n106; *pobladores* movement and, 24, 28, 31, 34; propaganda and, 16, 55, 66, 99–103, 142, 150–53, 202; social justice and, 227n102
National Congress, 22
National Health Service, 34
National Housing Program, 26
National Liberation Front, 10
National Party, 32
national protest: activists and, 167–72, 175–79, 184, 187, 191–94, 197–200, 204–5; Allende and, 194, 201; authoritarianism and, 193, 200, 204, 206; barricades and, 13, 18, 56, 169–70, 175, 178, 180–85, 193, 195, 197, 200–203; *caceroleo* and, 174, 178–83; capitalism and, 193; Catholicism and, 176, 182–83; Communist Party and, 168–71, 174–75, 179, 181–82, 187–90, 194, 196, 199, 202; *comunidad cristiana* (Christian community) and, 168, 170, 175, 182, 196–201, 204; conservatism and, 201, 253n154; coup and, 39–40, 43, 63;

Cristo Liberador and, 176, 179, 182, 195–96, 200; death and, 167–74; debt and, 169, 174, 186–87; democracy and, 167–75, 183, 185, 191–94, 197, 199, 202, 204–6, 253n154; dictatorship and, 7–9, 13–20, 167–75, 183–97, 201–6; divide-and-rule tactics and, 171, 174, 187–91; economy of terror and, 70–71, 77, 81, 93; education and, 172, 174, 176, 192–93, 195; elitism and, 168–71, 173, 180, 183, 190–91, 193, 204–6, 253n140; fasts and, 132; food and, 174–76, 192, 197; future of country and, 192–204; grassroots organizations and, 174, 190–91, 199–201, 206, 252n118, 253n148; housing and, 174, 190, 192; human rights and, 175–76, 191, 195, 198–99, 206; Hunger Marches and, 132, 138, 169, 174–78; junta and, 185–90, 250n87, 251n94; justice and, 168–69, 176, 194–95, 198, 206, 247n13; labor and, 169–70, 177–78, 180, 182, 185–86, 197; La Legua and, 75, 167, 177–78, 180–84, 192, 194, 196–97, 199–200, 203; Left and, 168–75, 177, 182, 185–91, 195–96, 198, 200–202, 205, 251n96; liberty and, 169, 176, 179, 184, 197; making of, 177–80, 204; Marxism and, 177, 188; mass, 7, 13, 98, 173–77, 186, 211; *memorias soterradas* and, 168; militants and, 153–54, 168, 181, 196–97, 199–202, 205, 210, 252n118; military and, 13, 173, 178, 186, 189, 202, 250n79; mobilization and, 132–39, 145–47, 151–54, 157–64; Movimiento de Acción Popular Unitaria (MAPU) and, 170, 175, 202; Movimiento de Izquierda Revolucionaria (MIR) and, 168, 170–71, 174–75, 182, 190, 196, 198, 202, 204, 210, 246n3, 252n118; murals and, 63, 167–69, 205; narratives and, 168, 171; neoliberalism and, 168–71, 173–74, 186–87, 192–93, 204, 206, 210–11;

obtaining experience in, 169–70; peaceful, 7, 18, 158, 170–72, 178; petitions and, 132, 139, 202; Pinochet and, 167, 169, 171, 173, 185–87, 190, 251n94, 253n154; *pobladores* movement and, 7–8 (see also *pobladores* movement); police and, 168, 175, 180–85, 198–99, 203; poverty and, 193, 196, 206; priests and, 170, 195–96, 199–201; protest climate and, 170; radicals and, 169, 171, 201, 204; repression and, 168–73, 176–78, 181–86, 191, 193, 195, 198, 200, 202–4, 206, 250n79; resistance and, 106, 112, 119, 130; Right and, 172–74, 189, 253n140; rising tide of, 174–77; San Cayetano and, 200; Santiago and, 168–70, 173–75, 178, 180–85, 187, 190–91, 194, 196, 205, 251n95; social commons and, 176; socialism and, 171, 175, 182, 190–94, 196, 204; social justice and, 168, 195; social movement webs and, 170, 175–82, 190, 195, 200–202, 204; social rights and, 173, 193; solidarity and, 106, 112, 119, 130, 176, 197–99, 204; state of siege and, 133, 137, 169, 186–91, 207, 250n79, 251n94; students and, 167, 175, 177, 180, 185, 199–200, 206; tear gas and, 182, 185; terrorism and, 168–69, 171–72, 247n13; torture and, 177, 202; unemployment and, 169, 174, 176, 187, 193, 205–6; Unidad Popular (UP) and, 174, 177, 179, 188, 194; urban poor and, 187, 193, 253n154; useful fools and, 186–91; Villa Francia and, 167–68, 176, 182–84, 195–200, 203–5; violence and, 170–74, 176, 184–85, 190–91, 200–203, 253n140; women and, 174, 179–80, 185, 196–98; youth and, 168–82, 191–206, 251n104
national security, 7, 11, 84, 90, 145
National Stadium, 16, 56, 79–80, 101
Nazer, Sergio, 107

neoliberalism: activists and, 207, 210–11; authoritarianism and, 211; Catholicism and, 209; Chicago Boys and, 70; Cold War and, 70–71; coup and, 29–30, 43; democracy and, 4–9, 12–13, 19, 43, 76–77, 133, 140, 166, 168–69, 173–74, 192–93, 206–11, 207–11, 219n46; dictatorship and, 4–5, 7, 9, 12–13, 18–19, 206–11; economy of terror and, 66–67, 70–77, 94; education and, 207–8; elitism and, 211; Friedman and, 70; grassroots organizations and, 208–11; Hayek and, 70; housing and, 208, 215n18; human rights and, 4–9, 19, 39, 76, 98, 166, 206–11; junta and, 254n13; justice and, 211; La Legua and, 207–8, 211; Left and, 209–10, 254n11; liberty and, 208, 211; mobilization and, 133–35, 140–41, 143, 165–66; narratives and, 210–11; national protest and, 168–71, 173–74, 186–87, 192–93, 204, 206, 210–11; *poblaciones* and, 209, 211; police and, 207–8, 211; poverty and, 208; radicals and, 5, 7, 13, 67, 71, 134, 143, 171, 214n9; raids and, 207; repression and, 209–11, 215n18, 254n11; resistance and, 98, 116, 125, 128, 130; romance with, 76; Santiago and, 209, 213; self-interest and, 70–71; Smith and, 70; socialism and, 210; social rights and, 209–10; students and, 211; torture and, 207, 209; transition to, 70–73; unemployment and, 210; Unidad Popular (UP) and, 209–10; violence and, 7, 13, 40, 66–67, 70, 73–77, 94, 166, 173, 208; youth and, 192–93, 211
Neruda, Pablo, 31
newsletters, 128, 139, 160, 176, 213n1
newspapers, 31, 40, 77, 85, 235n136
New Testament, 10
Nicaragua, 10, 170, 202
Nixon, Richard, 4

nongovernmental organizations
(NGOs), 10, 15, 138, 146, 192, 210
Nuestra Señora de la Paz, 31
Nuestra Señora de los Parrales, 158
Nueva La Habana, 15
Nueva La Legua, 25–26, 28–31, 53, 78,
180, 184
Nueva Lo Espejo, 15
Nuevo Amanecer, 15
nuns, 15, 18, 83, 137, 154–55, 158, 199

"Odas al pueblo humillado" (Ávalos), 3, 5
Old Testament, 10, 129
ollas comunes, 145, 148, 175, 183, 236n35
Operación Retorno, 136
Operación Sitio, 14, 23, 26–28, 33
oral histories, 4, 14–16, 34, 41–42, 59–61,
79, 99–100, 170, 205, 210–11, 213,
240n106
Organization for Economic Cooperation
and Development (OECD), 76,
230n50
Ortúzar, Ignacio, 158–59
Oscar Balboa (neighborhood), 15
Oyarce, José, 46

Paloma (magazine), 62
Panal strike, 138
Paro Patronal (Bosses' Strike), 35
patriotism, 15, 85, 127, 136, 168
Peeters, Guido, 31, 107, 123–24, 156–58,
161, 200–201, 221n33
Pentecostals, 106
petitions, 132, 139, 202
Pinochet, Augusto: Alessandri and, 75;
Bonilla and, 234n124; Chacarillas
speech and, 133; Christian Democrat
Party and, 234n124; coup of, 39, 41,
60–61, 214n6, 216n24, 218n45; dictatorship of, 4, 7, 15, 19, 39, 41, 61, 75,
77, 133, 171, 173, 185–87, 215n18; economy of terror and, 71, 75, 77, 84; end
of, 205–6; as hero of murderers, 61;

mobilization and, 131–33, 137, 139, 144,
165; national protest and, 167, 169,
171, 173, 185–87, 190, 251n94, 253n154;
plebiscite defeat of, 171; resistance
and, 106; State Council of, 75; state of
siege and, 133, 137, 169, 186–91, 207,
250n79, 251n94; strikes and, 169
Pinochet, Lucía Hiriart de, 131–32, 137,
139
Piñera, José, 139
Plan pastoral del Episcopado chileno, 113
Plaza de la Constitución, 16
plebiscites, 19, 171, 173, 214n6, 216n24,
218n45
poblaciones: coup and, 39–45, 48, 50, 64;
dictatorship and, 4–19; economy of
terror and, 67–77, 81–86, 89–95;
mobilization and, 134–42, 145, 148–53,
158–59, 162, 165–66; national protest
and, 169 (*see also* national protest);
neoliberalism and, 209, 211; *pobladores*
movement and, 23, 26–28, 32–37;
resistance and, 97–105, 108, 111, 113–
19, 122, 125–30; solidarity and, 97–105,
108, 111, 113–19, 122, 125–30
pobladores movement: activists and, 27,
36–37; Allende and, 32, 35–36; authoritarianism and, 24; capitalism and,
22–23; Catholicism and, 29–37, 41;
Communist Party and, 22, 24–33,
36–37; *comunidad cristiana* (Christian
community) and, 34–35, 221n50; conservatism and, 24, 221n50; *conventillos*
and, 22, 24–27, 243n30; Cristo Liberador and, 34–36, 221n50; democracy
and, 5–11, 24, 27, 31–32, 35, 37; dictatorship and, 5–19; downward moral
displacement and, 67, 70, 77, 89–94,
118, 171; education and, 32; elitism
and, 25; food and, 35–36; grassroots
organizations and, 25, 35 (*see also*
grassroots organizations); homeless
and, 12, 21, 26, 28, 90, 137, 139, 149,

priests (*continued*)

Calama and, 35, 113, 239n84; liberation theology and, 9, 13, 35, 112–13, 124, 161, 170, 193, 221n50, 239n84; mobilization and, 137, 154–58, 163, 245n65; national protest and, 170, 195–96, 199–201; *pobladores* movement and, 31, 34–35, 220n32, 221n33; resistance and, 107, 109, 111, 113–14, 117, 119–28

Programa de Empleo Mínimo (Minimum Employment Program) [PEM], 72

Programa de Ocupación para Jefes de Hogar (Occupation Program for Heads of Household) [POJH], 243n23

Promoción Popular (social policy), 22

propaganda, 16, 55, 66, 99–103, 142, 150–53, 202

psychological issues, 73, 80, 82, 84–85, 91, 192, 208, 214n11, 228n14

Pudahuel Sector 18, 15

Pueblo Cristiano (newsletter), 127

Puente, Marcelo, 168, 246n3

Puga, Mariano, 34–35, 107, 120–24, 154–56, 200, 221n33

Quadragesimo Anno (encyclical), 111

¿Que Pasa? (magazine), 139, 165, 166

Quinta Normal, 101

radicals: coup and, 5, 7, 13, 18, 63; dictatorship and, 5, 7, 13, 18; economy of terror and, 67, 71; mobilization and, 134, 143, 156, 160–64; national protest and, 169, 171, 201, 204; neoliberalism and, 5, 7, 13, 67, 71, 134, 143, 171, 214n9; *pobladores* movement and, 35; resistance and, 110, 112–13, 123, 125; youth and, 4, 13, 134, 156, 160, 162, 201, 204

Radio Moscow, 78, 100

raids: cleansing, 91–92; coup and, 17, 44, 49, 56, 58, 69, 78–87, 90–93, 97,

101–4, 157, 159, 207, 218n40; dictatorship and, 17, 44, 56–57, 69, 75, 78–90, 93, 97, 107, 185, 218n40, 228n14, 232n84; economy of terror and, 69, 75, 78–93, 228n14, 232n84; mobilization and, 157; neoliberalism and, 207; resistance and, 97, 104; search, 17, 44, 56–57, 69, 75, 78–90, 93, 97, 107, 185, 218n40, 228n14, 232n84

Reagan, Ronald, 133, 242n11

real wages, 73, 187, 231n73, 243n25

Rebelión Popular de Masas (Popular Rebellion of the Masses), 136

recession, 65, 72, 75, 229n35

Red de Organizaciones Sociales de La Legua, 213

refugees, 78, 106, 159

rehabilitation, 16, 91, 121, 151

Rengifo, Blanca, 83

reporters, 40, 77, 92, 166, 180

repression: "antisocial" categorization and, 88–90, 92, 233n107; arrests and, 84, 137, 185, 234n115; coup and, 4–6, 13, 15–19, 42, 49, 52, 57–64, 215n18, 217n31, 218n37, 218n40; delinquents and, 82, 89–92, 193, 195, 199, 232n86, 234n115; dictatorship and, 4–6, 13, 15–19; economy of terror and, 67–95, 231n55; hidden transcript of, 231n55; mobilization and, 132, 136–41, 144, 147–48, 154, 156–59, 163; national protest and, 168–73, 176–78, 181–86, 191, 193, 195, 198, 200, 202–4, 206, 250n79; neoliberalism and, 209–11, 215n18, 254n11; *pobladores* movement and, 24, 26; Pope's neutral stance on, 105–6; raids and, 17, 44, 49, 56, 58, 69, 78–87, 90–93, 97, 101–4, 157, 159, 207, 218n40; resistance and, 96–101, 104–8, 117–18, 121, 123, 125–30; selective, 67, 69, 81, 87, 89, 97, 172; surveillance and, 44, 85, 87, 93; union leaders and, 97; of women, 84

Rerum Novarum (Leo XIII), 109–11

resistance: activists and, 97–102, 105, 110–11, 113, 115–16, 119–21, 125–26, 130, 240n106; Allende and, 103, 106, 113; cadavers and, 51, 56, 58, 232n86; capitalism and, 96, 110–12, 128–29, 237n57; Catholicism and, 96, 98, 102–3, 106–30; Communist Party and, 4, 96–115, 120–25, 130; *comunidad cristiana* (Christian community) and, 107, 111, 114, 120–27, 130; conservatism and, 109, 111–12, 125–26; coup and, 41–43, 48–49, 52–55, 58–59, 64; Cristo Liberador and, 107, 119–24, 129; democracy and, 98, 105, 108; education and, 107, 124–25, 129; elitism and, 97, 111–12, 129; food and, 97, 116–17, 120, 122, 129, 236n35; free market and, 66, 71; grassroots organizations and, 98–99, 108, 115, 126, 130; housing and, 103, 117; human rights and, 15, 98, 105–11, 115–16, 118, 122, 126; junta and, 106, 126–27; justice and, 110, 112–13, 118, 121, 124, 126, 128; labor and, 98, 109–20; La Legua and, 41, 51–52, 97, 99, 101, 103–4, 107–8, 113, 117, 119, 122–24; Left and, 97–115, 118–27, 236n17, 237n49; liberty and, 104, 112, 118, 126, 129; martyrs and, 88, 166; Marxism and, 98, 105, 107–28, 237n57; militants and, 102, 106, 121, 127; military and, 101, 103; monetarist policies and, 66, 227n8; Movimiento de Acción Popular Unitaria (MAPU) and, 99, 102, 106, 114; Movimiento de Izquierda Revolucionaria (MIR) and, 99, 102, 110, 114, 120, 125, 127, 130, 240n106; national protest and, 106, 112, 119, 130; neoliberalism and, 98, 116, 125, 128, 130; networks for, 12–13, 15, 37, 53, 55, 64, 83, 93, 99, 105, 107, 130, 134, 183, 195, 198; Pinochet and, 106; *poblaciones* and, 97–105, 108, 111,

113–19, 122, 125–30; police and, 103–5, 119, 123; poverty and, 98–99, 112, 118; priests and, 107, 109, 111, 113–14, 117, 119–28; radicals and, 110, 112–13, 123, 125; raids and, 97, 104; repression and, 96–101, 104–8, 117–18, 121, 123, 125–30; researching rebellion and, 14–15; San Cayetano and, 107, 114, 119, 122–24; Santiago and, 96–99, 105, 107, 111, 113–15, 119, 125, 235n3, 240n106; social commons and, 97–98, 105, 108, 115, 122, 125, 130; social injustice and, 66, 77, 94; socialism and, 97, 99, 101–2, 106, 109–10, 113–14, 118, 125, 240n106; social justice and, 110–13, 118, 121, 124, 126; social rights and, 116; solidarity and, 97–98, 105–22, 125–30, 237n57, 241n135; student protests and, 39–40, 167, 175, 177, 180, 185, 200, 211, 242n11; students and, 102–3, 119; subterfuge and, 104; tattoos and, 90–91; torture and, 105, 107–8; *trabajo de hormiga* (ant's work) and, 13, 98, 139, 166, 176, 183; unemployment and, 115–17, 120–23, 127, 130; Unidad Popular (UP) and, 99, 107, 113, 120, 127; urban poor and, 97; Villa Francia and, 41, 54–57, 96–101, 104–5, 107, 113–14, 119, 122–24, 129; violence and, 97, 125–26; women and, 103–4, 116–18, 121–22, 126; youth and, 108, 111, 117, 120, 130

Richards, Pablo, 34–35

Richards, Patricia, 191

Right: Catholicism and, 242n11; constitutional reforms and, 226n81; coup and, 44, 226n81; economy of terror and, 93; mobilization and, 242n11; national protest and, 172–74, 189, 253n140

Rojas, Sandra, 116–18

Romero, Óscar, 10, 166

Rubilar Morales, Gerardo, 108

Socialist Party, 15, 32, 44–50, 99, 102, 114, 136, 182, 190

social justice: coup and, 6, 40, 61–62, 227n102; economy of terror and, 66, 77, 94–95; mobilization and, 155; narratives on, 227n102; national protest and, 168, 195; resistance and, 110–13, 118, 121, 124, 126

social movement webs: mobilization and, 134–35, 138–39, 145, 151–53, 155, 158, 166; national protest and, 170, 175–82, 190, 195, 200–202, 204

social rights: coup and, 40; dictatorship and, 4, 9, 11–12, 19; mobilization and, 131–32, 158, 165; national protest and, 173, 193; neoliberalism and, 209–10; resistance and, 116

social security, 5, 67, 131, 134, 139–40

Solidaridad (magazine), 132, 137, 165–66

solidarity: attack on, 85; betrayal and, 43, 54, 60, 206, 211; Catholicism and, 6, 11–12, 35, 98, 108–19, 125–28, 130, 155, 158, 217n33, 242n11; Cold War and, 129; coup and, 43, 52–54, 58–59; dictatorship and, 6, 10–12, 17, 217n33; economy of terror and, 80, 85; grassroots organizations and, 6, 10, 12, 35, 98, 115–22, 126, 135, 215n18; human rights and, 105–8; looting and, 57, 78; Marxism and, 12, 98, 108–17, 127–28, 136, 237n57; mobilization and, 132, 135–37, 151, 153–59, 164, 242n11; national protest and, 106, 112, 119, 130, 176, 197–99, 204; networks for, 12–13, 15, 37, 53, 55, 64, 83, 93, 99, 105, 107, 130, 134, 183, 195, 198; *poblaciones* and, 97–105, 108, 111, 113–19, 122, 125–30; *pobladores* movement and, 21, 28, 35; *Rerum Novarum* and, 109–10; resistance and, 97–98, 105–22, 125–30, 237n57, 241n135; seeds of, 105–8; social division and, 85–86; two types of, 237n57; Vicariate of Solidarity and,

217n33; youth and, 130, 158–59, 164, 197–99, 204, 242n11

Somoza dictatorship, 10, 170

soup kitchens, 12, 72, 103, 107, 115, 176

Southern Cone, 89–90

Southern Prefecture, 46

Soviet Union, 10, 41, 171

state of siege, 133, 137, 169, 186–91, 207, 250n79, 251n94

Stern, Steve, 6, 39, 57

Stites Mor, Jessica, 10, 108

Stjernø, Steinar, 108–9

Straus, Scott, 6

students: coup and, 3, 10, 39–41, 44, 216n24; demographics for, 141, 230n39, 230n40; dictatorship and, 3, 10, 216n24; mobilization and, 141, 145, 150, 153, 242n11; neoliberalism and, 211; persecution of, 145; protests by, 39–40, 167, 175, 177, 180, 185, 199–200, 206, 211, 242n11; resistance and, 102–3, 119

subterfuge, 104

suicide, 85, 91, 154

Sumar-Nylon, 44, 49

Sumar-Polyester, 46–47

SUR Profesionales, 8, 218n45, 247n16, 251n104

surveillance, 44, 85, 87, 93

tattoos, 90–91

teachers, 10, 23, 31, 44

tear gas, 182, 185

Teitelboim, Volodia, 115

terrorism: international, 66; national protest and, 168–69, 171–72, 247n13; poverty and, 98; state, 98 (*see also* economy of terror)

Thatcher, Margaret, 242n11

theft, 202

theory of marginality, 22–23

Tinsman, Heidi, 142

Vicuña Mackenna industrial corridor, 46, 78, 103

Vidal, Hernán, 153–54

Villa Canadá, 34

Villa Francia, 213; assassinations in, 218n41; Ávalos and, 5; background of, 33–34; as combative, 41; coup and, 5, 36–39, 41, 43–44, 54–57, 59–60, 63; economy of terror and, 72, 77, 83, 88; housing and, 34; junta and, 35–36; mobilization and, 131–33, 137, 151–56, 159, 161–64; national protest and, 167–68, 176, 182–84, 195–200, 203–5; *pobladores* movement and, 21, 33–37; protest culture of, 14–15, 17; resistance and, 41, 54–57, 96–101, 104–5, 107, 113–14, 119, 122–24, 129; youth and, 164

Villagra Astudillo, José, 120–21, 153–54

Villa René Schneider, 15

violence: assassinations and, 60, 99, 102, 133, 164, 166, 174, 202, 204, 214n7, 250n86, 253n149; beatings and, 86, 137, 158, 185; bloody veil and, 66–70, 77, 81–88, 95, 137; bombs and, 4, 45, 47, 57–58, 69, 97, 170, 253n149; cadavers and, 51, 56, 58, 82–83, 232n86; counterrevolutionary vs. revolutionary, 224n33; coup and, 40–44, 47, 51, 57–58, 61–62, 64; criminals and, 13, 17–18, 40, 80, 84, 88–93, 111, 169, 185, 189; Day of the Carabinero and, 81; detentions and, 54, 63, 78, 82–84; drugs and, 207; economy of terror and, 66–67, 70, 73–77, 81–85, 87–88, 93–95, 231n51; executions and, 11, 42, 65, 218n40, 231n73; extremists and, 13, 17, 54, 77, 84–85, 89, 92, 171; human rights and, 6–7, 11, 20, 76, 145, 166, 176, 207–8, 215, 247n13; kidnapping and, 65, 108, 153, 158; latent, 8; *Los 119* and, 153; machine guns and, 42, 46, 50, 78–79; mobilization and, 137–38,

145, 159, 164, 166, 247n13; murder and, 60–61, 81, 158; national protest and, 170–74, 176, 184–85, 190–91, 200–203, 253n140; neoliberalism and, 7, 13, 40, 66–67, 70, 73–77, 94, 166, 173, 208; Peeters and, 158–59; *pobladores* movement and, 224n45, 225n57; police, 84–85, 158–59, 168, 184–85; political, 6, 8, 11, 13, 40, 57, 66–67, 70, 75–77, 85, 88, 94–95, 97, 138, 145, 164, 170, 172–74, 190–91, 200–203, 208, 215n17, 216n24, 253n140; political manipulation of, 8; raids and, 17, 44, 49, 56, 58, 69, 78–87, 90–93, 97, 101–4, 157, 159, 207, 218n40; resistance and, 97, 125–26; San Cayetano and, 51, 80, 107; social, 6–8, 11, 13, 40, 42, 51, 57–58, 64, 66–67, 70, 75–77, 81, 84–88, 94–95, 97, 125–26, 137, 145, 166, 171–73, 190, 201–3, 207–11; state of siege and, 133, 137, 169, 186–91, 207, 250n79, 251n94; state-perpetrated, 11, 57, 67, 73–88, 94–97, 174, 208, 247n13; student protest and, 211; torture and, 42 (*see also* torture); use of spectacle and, 68–69, 85, 87; vandalism and, 7, 18, 171, 219; youth and, 42, 81, 84, 159, 166, 168–69, 171–73, 176, 191, 201–5

vivienda social (low-income housing), 25

Wasserstrom, Jeffrey N., 10

water, 21, 25, 28, 30–31, 34, 46, 52, 73, 141, 232n86, 243n30

Way, J. T., 67, 89

Wealth of Nations (Smith), 70

Weapons Control Law, 44

Weinstein, Eugenia, 228n14

Winn, Peter, 67

women: Catholic ideologies on, 84; Comité de Defensa de los Derechos de la Mujer and, 174; coup and, 45, 58, 60, 63; dictatorship and, 9, 13, 15;

women (*continued*)
economy of terror and, 73, 79, 82, 84–87, 90; flirtation strategies of, 60–61; Frente Unitario de Mujeres Pobladoras and, 174; International Women's Day and, 132, 174; mobilization and, 132–33, 136, 148–51, 154, 156, 158, 165; national protest and, 174, 179–80, 185, 196–98; *pobladores* movement and, 22, 24, 27–28, 36, 117, 150, 174; poverty and, 21; repression of, 84; resistance and, 103–4, 116–18, 121–22, 126

work camps, 91

World Council of Churches (WCC), 105–6

World Health Organization (WHO), 142

World Jewish Congress, 105–6

youth: Church recruitment of, 159–64; counselors and, 159–60; coup and, 9, 13, 15, 42, 48–50, 214n7; Cristo Liberador and, 159–64; drugs and, 159–60; economy of terror and, 78–79, 81, 84; education and, 10 (*see also* education); General Comments of the Committee on the Rights of the Child and, 208; *jóvenes* and, 170, 193–95, 198, 201–3, 205; lack of fear of, 158–60; La Legua and, 164; machista behavior and, 160; mobilization and, 133–34, 136–37, 139, 141, 148–52, 156, 158–66, 242n11; national protest and, 168–82, 191–206, 251n104; neoliberalism and, 192–93, 211; newsletter of, 160; *pobladores* movement and, 31–32, 35–36; radicals and, 13, 134, 156, 160, 162, 201, 204; resistance and, 108, 111, 117, 120, 130; rise of, 159–65; San Cayetano and, 161–62; solidarity and, 130, 158–59, 164, 197–99, 204, 242n11; Villa Francia and, 164; violence and, 42, 81, 84, 159, 166, 168–69, 171–73, 176, 191, 201–3, 204–5

Yungay, 15

Zanjón de la Aguada, 26
Zañartu, 25–26, 28, 30

Critical Human Rights

Memory's Turn: Reckoning with Dictatorship in Brazil
REBECCA J. ATENCIO

Prisoner of Pinochet: My Year in a Chilean Concentration Camp
SERGIO BITAR; translated by ERIN GOODMAN; foreword and
notes by PETER WINN

*Bread, Justice, and Liberty: Grassroots Activism and Human Rights in Pinochet's
Chile* ALISON J. BRUEY

*Archiving the Unspeakable: Silence, Memory, and the Photographic Record in
Cambodia* MICHELLE CASWELL

Court of Remorse: Inside the International Criminal Tribunal for Rwanda
THIERRY CRUVELLIER; translated by CHARI VOSS

How Difficult It Is to Be God: Shining Path's Politics of War in Peru, 1980–1999
CARLOS IVÁN DEGREGORI; edited and with an introduction by
STEVE J. STERN

*Trauma, Taboo, and Truth-Telling: Listening to Silences in Postdictatorship
Argentina* NANCY J. GATES-MADSEN

From War to Genocide: Criminal Politics in Rwanda, 1990–1994
ANDRÉ GUICHAOUA; translated by DON E. WEBSTER

*Innocence and Victimhood: Gender, Nation, and Women's Activism in Postwar
Bosnia-Herzegovina* ELISSA HELMS

www.ingramcontent.com/pod-product-compliance
Lightning Source LLC
Chambersburg PA
CBHW071014280326

41935CB00011B/1354